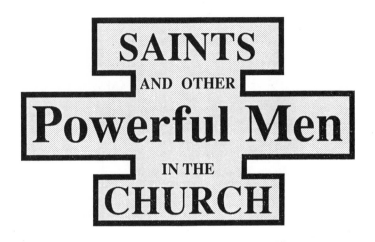

SAINTS
AND OTHER
Powerful Men
IN THE
CHURCH

Bob and Penny Lord

Journeys of Faith
1-800-633-2484

Other Books by Bob and Penny Lord

THIS IS MY BODY, THIS IS MY BLOOD - Book I
Miracles of the Eucharist
THIS IS MY BODY, THIS IS MY BLOOD - Book II
Miracles of the Eucharist
THE MANY FACES OF MARY
a Love Story
WE CAME BACK TO JESUS
SAINTS AND OTHER POWERFUL WOMEN
IN THE CHURCH
HEAVENLY ARMY OF ANGELS
SCANDAL OF THE CROSS AND ITS TRIUMPH
MARTYRS - THEY DIED FOR CHRIST
THE ROSARY - THE LIFE OF JESUS AND MARY
ESTE ES MI CUERPO, ESTA ES MI SANGRE
Milagros de la Eucaristía
LOS MUCHOS ROSTROS DE MARIA
una historia de amor

Excerpts and photos from TREASURE IN CLAY by Fulton J. Sheen
copyright ©1980 by the Society for the Propagation of the Faith
Used by permission of Doubleday, a division of Bantam Doubleday Dell
Publishing Group, Inc.
Excerpts and photos of DON BOSCO used by permission from
Don Bosco Publications
Excerpts and photos of PADRE PIO used by permission from
Voice of Padre Pio
Excerpts and photos of ST. MAXMILIAN KOLBE used by permission of
Franciscan Marytown Friars
Photos of ST. AUGUSTINE used by permission from Augustinian Recollects

ISBN 0-926143-09-3

Cover Art by Diane St. Germain

Dedication

We want to begin by specially dedicating this book to a most powerful man in our Church, *Karol Wojtyla*, our *Pope John Paul II*. We believe the courage and confidence we've been given, to take on the work of writing books, doing television programs, and speaking before large assemblies of people, has come from the inspiration we've received from *this* man. He is so like the people, we write about in this book.

He has the daring of Paul the Apostle, the intellect of Augustine, the humility of Francis, the charisma of Anthony, the poetry of John of the Cross, Peregrine's trust in the Healing Power of the Lord, the love of the priesthood of John Vianney, the love of children of Don Bosco, the humor of Miguel Pro, the love of Mary of Maxmilian Kolbe, the image of the Crucified Christ of Padre Pio, and the overpowering presence of Fulton J. Sheen, all wrapped up in one person.

He is the essence of what we're trying to bring across in the *Powerful Men in the Church*. As his brothers before him, he is *touchable*! We love all our Popes. But, the Lord has given us a special gift in John Paul II, in that he touches the *common man*. We feel that he is speaking directly to *us*. And while he is brilliant, we *understand* what he tells us. His message is *simple*; he gives us the courage to say simple things to the people of God, and be understood. We say that in times of crisis, the Lord sends us Saints and Other

Powerful Men in the Church. *We are in times of crisis!*
Thank you, Jesus, for sending us John Paul II, our Pope.

It's so exciting to see the Lord in action. In working on
this book, we have reached out to brothers and sisters all
over the world, for help. The response has been awe-
inspiring. All have gone out of their way to give us as much,
no, *more* than we could possibly use in our book. We could
hear, through the responses, *"Yes, this saint is important."*
"Yes, I want to help bring this example to the people of God."
Jesus put us together with just the people He wanted, so that
this book would truly represent the power He has given to
those who, before us, said *"Yes!"*

We dedicate this book to you, who saw the need so
much, you went beyond the realm of courtesy, to help us
make it happen. Whether it be by helping us with research,
finding a book for us, hard-to-get photographs, or just by
your support and your prayers, we thank you. Know that
you are in our prayers, and that your Powerful Man in the
Church is looking down on you, smiling.

Diane St. Germain - who painted our cover - a talented
artist, sister in Christ and friend, who tirelessly prayed and
painted, placing herself on the Cross, very often dying to her
needs and those of her family, believing in this work and her
part in it. And to her family, who, with her, said *yes!*

Fr. Giustino, an Augustinian priest from the Shrine of
St. Rita in Cascia, Italy. While he has given us many insights
on St. Augustine, we believe that by who he is, we have been
gifted to know St. Augustine in a more personal way.

Fr. Oldfield and Fr. Huse, Augustinian Recollects of
Oxnard, California, for allowing us to photograph the
beautiful stained-glass windows, depicting the life of St.
Augustine, and explaining the story of the windows.

Fr. Max Mizzi OFM, St. Francis Basilica, Assisi, for his
insights on the way St. Francis is being accepted by non-
Catholics in Protestant strongholds in Europe.

Fr. George Kennedy, OCD, for continuing to instruct us about the Carmelite Order, and in particular, for finding an out-of-print book on the life of St. John of the Cross, which has been enormously helpful in the chapter on St. John.

Fr. James Hurley, Don Bosco Publications, for pointing us in the right direction, in choosing the reference books to use, as well as the photographs of Don Dosco.

Fr. Harold Cohen, S.J., for introducing Miguel Pro to us, and making us fall in love with him. It was Fr. Cohen's devotion to Blessed Pro that caused us to investigate his life.

Padre Alejandro Burciaga M.Sp.S., Guadalajara, Mexico, our Spiritual Director, brother and friend, who most epitomizes Blessed Pro, with his joy and love of Jesus, in his everyday message of the Good News.

Dr. Kavanaugh S.J., Loyola Marymount, Los Angeles, for digging through the library there to find an out-of-print book, which details the life of Miguel Pro.

Brother Francis OFM, Conv. Marytown, IL, for providing us with photographs of St. Maxmilian Kolbe, and his sensitivity on the saint. Also, special thanks to Ave Maria Press, Notre Dame, IN, for putting us in touch with Brother Francis.

Fr. Joseph Pio, Our Lady of Grace Monastery, San Giovanni Rotondo, Italy, for his ongoing support, over the years; but in particular for the help he gave us, putting together the research books, reading over and correcting the manuscript, and helping us with the photographs we needed for the life of Padre Pio.

Society for the Propagation of the Faith, for providing us with the photographs of Archbishop Fulton J. Sheen.

Luz Elena Sandoval and Brother Joseph, without whom nothing ever gets done. When we made the decision to bring out such a large book, over 500 pages, on *twelve* powerful men in the Church, they gulped a bit, because they have to do much of the research, proof-reading and editing.

They handle these loving tasks in addition to running the book and video ministry, the pilgrimage ministry, scheduling our talks, and putting out our Good Newsletter four times a year. Brother Joseph was given a word of knowledge. Because we don't have enough people to do the work, we have to *Work Smart!*

We want to ask the Lord and our Lady to specially bless two very special and powerful people in our lives, our daughter Sr. Clare, who has been such a source of insights and wisdom over the years, and our grandson Robert Ziminsky, who has been the inspiration of so much we have written. We thank them for their love and support.

The teamwork of the Lord's people gave us such a feeling of togetherness with the Body of Christ. We believe this is just a small indicator of how Jesus wants all of us to work together, to bring the Good News to His people.

There are many brothers and sisters who support our Ministry, because they believe the work we're doing is of the Lord. These are the ones who arrange our talks, distribute flyers, promote our book and video ministry, arrange housing and transportation, and just about anything else that is needed to get the job done. We praise Our Lord Jesus that there are so many of you, it is impossible to list all your names in this dedication. We know who you are; more importantly, *Jesus knows who you are.* We thank you for your support; we love you. And Jesus loves you.

†

We'd like to mention a very special lady, *Margaret Michelette*, from San Antonio, who went to the *Father* this past Spring. Margaret had been a constant supporter, arranging talks and housing, whenever we went to San Antonio. We will miss her very much, but we know she's still working for us in Heaven.

†

Table of Contents

This book is also lovingly dedicated:
to the Powerful Men in my life - who have brought Jesus to me.

My father: I always thought Jesus had blue eyes and red hair, because my father did. Jesus was sensitive, gentle, patient but firm, loving, giving, always with a surprise, a gift. I remember running down the steps, after answering the door bell, to my father's open arms. I would try to find the surprise, I knew he had somewhere on him. I respected my father; he was my *primary* teacher. I liked and loved my father. My father always made me feel *rich*, although we lived in a cold-water flat in Brooklyn. He made me feel safe, secure. I knew we would never be hungry, as long as we had our father. He taught us to love people as they *were*, not as we wanted them to be. He was my first glimpse of Jesus.

My husband: When my father died, Bob asked, if he could ever be the man my father was. "Never!" I cried, "There was only one of him." My husband became for me all my father was and so much more. *Now, Jesus had a great sense of humor.* When Bob met me, I didn't trust people. Sheltered, when I started to meet people, they were not always loving and sincere the way my family was. *"Why don't you allow others to see how very beautiful you are inside?"* I thought, *Thank God you are so blind, Bob!* I believed, my father and mother called me beautiful because they were my family. And so, now Jesus gave me confidence to be who *I* really was, to like and love myself through *now*, a dark haired, freckled faced Irishman, who became my Jesus on earth. I learned of Jesus' *fidelity* through joys and sorrow. Jesus became *Spring-time*, because that's Bob's favorite *time* of the year. Each morning brought new promise, Bob with new hope and expectations of a better life. Through my Jesus, my Bob, I see people as they *could* be.

Penny Lord

Introduction

We knew we were going to write this book. During our talks this last year, we *jokingly* told people we had to give men equal time, after having written our book on Saints and Other Powerful *Women* in the Church, first. But we were not aware how important it would be!

We have to share that we were really excited about getting into this book. Naturally, we had the same problem, we had when we began our tribute to the *Women* in our Church: *whom to choose*. We can't really even say we used a formula, in picking out the men we wanted to share with you. We pray, we left all of that to the Holy Spirit. True, there were certain ones we knew up front, we *had* to write about, Penny's Anthony, my Francis. These are people, we've grown up with, in the Church. We've loved them for a long time. We knew we wanted to share *them* with you.

But then there were others, brothers we had heard about and studied a little, during our Pilgrimages to the Shrines. But we didn't know as much about them as we believed we should, in order to write about them. We wanted to know more about them; so we began to delve more deeply into their lives. Still, we left the final decision up to the Holy Spirit.

While we were still in the beginning stages of the book, as we were working on our first chapters on those we *knew*, and then going on to those who, of the many hundreds of Saints and men, the *Lord* would choose, we received a phone call from *Sister Briege McKenna*.

She had just returned from a thirty day *silent retreat* in Dublin. For anyone who knows Sister Briege, you know that for her to be silent for thirty days, is a miracle in itself. She told us the only reading material she brought with her, was our book, *Saints and Other Powerful Women in the Church.* She said it affirmed her vocation. We felt extremely complimented by this, although our intent had not been to focus on the religious life.

Then she hit us with her next line, which bowled both of us over! She told us the Lord had spoken to her, in her heart, the way He does with Sister Briege. She said the message she received was, *"Tell Bob and Penny to write a book, affirming my priests."*

We felt challenged by her statement, a little inadequate, and very nervous. Who were we to affirm priests? What qualifications did we have, what insights could we share, which would bring that message across to our Royal Order of the Priesthood? We prayed a lot on this. What should we do differently than we had done before? What great perceptions could we give them, that would touch them, and lift them up?

We thought about how the flavor of our talks had changed in the last year. In traveling all over the country, we had become startlingly aware of the crisis in vocations to the priesthood, but more than that, the *struggle* of our priests to remain loyal to their vocations. We found ourselves *pleading* with our audiences to lift our priests up, not knock them down, to love and pray for them, to show them how much they were needed. Our Lord promised us the gates of Hell would not prevail against His Church. *But without priests, we don't have a church!*

The first two chapters we wrote, strangely enough, or was it God's plan, turned out to be the first and the last chapter, Paul the Apostle, and Archbishop Fulton J. Sheen. We shared notes on what the Lord had given us to write. It seemed the answer to our questions were right there in what we had written. Paul, the blustering, fiery champion of Jesus, wrote, *"In the end, there are three things that matter,*

Faith, Hope, and Love. And the greatest of these is Love." And Fulton J. Sheen, the prophet of the Twentieth Century, wrote, *"No introduction is necessary to another priest; nothing to live up to, nothing to live down. No introduction is necessary; Christ has already introduced them to one another."*

We pray that you will find something in what we've written that will make you want to go to your priest, and thank him for being a priest. Luz Elena tells us that in Mexico, they used to kiss the priest's hands, out of respect for their being consecrated. You may not feel comfortable doing it. But do go up and tell them how much you appreciated their homily; mention something they said, which touched you. Let them know you weren't sleeping during the Mass. Thank them for their *"fiat."*

We believe there's much to be learned, from reading about those who have preceded us. These are men who said *"yes"* to Jesus, knowing in advance that their lives would never be the same. They fell in love with Jesus, and through *Him*, their brothers and sisters. You and I are that family of Christ, these saints fought for. The battle for the Church over the centuries, has always been for the *people of God.* All the wars that have ever been waged, including those of the Twentieth century, have been for the people of God. There were those who wanted to protect and save the people of God; then there have been those who have wanted to *destroy* the people of God, hoping thereby, to destroy God Himself. We know that will never happen!

By reading this book, you'll be revisiting some old friends, Saints you have known from your childhood. But we think you will be pleased to meet some new friends, brothers you may have only *heard* of before now, or about whom you knew very little. You will get to love them as we love them, and as they love you. We invite you now, to join us, as we pay tribute to the *Powerful Men in our Church.*

Left:
A brilliant flash of light streaked across the sky. Saul was thrown to the ground. He heard a voice: *"Saul, Saul, why do you persecute me?"*

Right:
When we went to the Church of St. Paul Outside the Walls, in Rome, a formidable statue of St. Paul loomed high above us. He wielded a huge double-edged sword; he stared deep into our souls.

St. Paul the Apostle

*"May I never boast of anything
but the Cross of our Lord Jesus Christ!"*
Gal 6:14

In the history of our Church, no man stands out more clearly as a zealot and role model, than does St. Paul, the Apostle. The Church as we know it today, the Church of the Gentiles, would not exist were it not for the unceasing pursuit of Paul to bring the Gospel to the four corners of the earth. He took to heart, Jesus' command, *"Go into the whole world, and proclaim the good news to all creation.*[1]*"*

Paul has always impressed us by his singleness of purpose, his unflinching courage, his relentless drive, and his ability to stir men's hearts, whether by his public speaking, or by his writings. Luke has chronicled the experiences of Paul in the Acts of the Apostles. They read like tales of high adventure. Paul's letters have inspired the greatest minds of our Church, including, but not limited to St. Augustine, St. Thomas Aquinas, St. Francis of Assisi, St. Anthony, St. John of the Cross, and St. Teresa of Avila. Read about *any* of the great Saints; you'll find the teachings of Paul. Of all the Apostles, for us, he is the most *touchable*, the most *approachable*, the most *identifiable*. From this, you can gather that we are great fans of St. Paul.

We feel very close to Paul. Although we are born Catholics, we consider ourselves converts, or rather, *we are converting*. It's a never-ending process. When we first came back to the Church, we were overwhelmed by all the exciting

---

[1]Mk 16:15

13

people and things she had to offer. We were like kids in a candy store. There was so much *more* than we could absorb; so we didn't key into Paul, and his powerful role in the Church, right away. It wasn't until our first pilgrimage to Rome that we met Paul in a very personal way.

I think it's important for all of us, just once in our lives, to go to the places of the Saints, so that we can soak up their spirit, which never leaves these areas. There is such a strong sense of the Saints at their shrines. It permeates your skin, and goes deep into your soul.

That's what happened when we went to the Church of St. Paul Outside the Walls, in Rome. Paul was *martyred* in this area. After the Church was legitimized by Constantine, his bones were brought back to this *spot*, to be his final *resting place*. When we walked through the gates of the courtyard, a formidable statue of St. Paul loomed high above us. He wielded a huge sword[2]; he stared deep into our souls. He was so strong! We asked our guide why he was buried outside the city walls. The guide raised himself to his full five feet, two inches, and proclaimed, "*It was his right as a Roman citizen, Signor. The Christians were fed to the lions in the Colosseum during the persecution. But Paul was allowed to die outside the city walls with dignity, as was his birthright.*" That didn't make any sense. He was a Pharisee from the Holy Land, as best we knew. He was converted in Damascus, knocked down off his high horse, so to speak. How did he get to be a Roman citizen?

Then we went to the Mamertine Prison in Rome. This was Paul's home prior to his death. We walked down, deep into the dark, damp hole of the cave, There was a dim light from a bare 30 watt bulb, dangling from the ceiling. An exhaust fan made a feeble attempt to suck out the foul-

---

[2]There are two reasons for the sword - (1) He was decapitated with a sword - (2) He spoke of a two-edged sword (Heb 4:12)

smelling, humid air, which permeated the prison. It was damp and gloomy, a very depressing scene. *And that was now, in the twentieth century!* We could not begin to imagine how it had been when Paul was imprisoned here. Our priest was well-versed in Scripture, and the historical background of the Gospel. He shared with us the ending of Paul's letter to the Philippians. He shared Paul's last testimony to Timothy. They are the most touching, uplifting, beautiful letters Paul wrote. And they were written here, in the stinking bowels of the earth. We had never known much about this pioneer and martyr for our Faith, but here in this cell, we came to love him very much.

That's how they get you, these Saints. You ask a little question; you discover something that doesn't quite fit in, and the next thing you know, you're deeply engrossed in the life of the Saint. This is how we began to learn about Paul. We didn't do it to share with anyone. We were in love with Church. *This man was our Church!* We had to know more about him. Who was he? What made him turn so completely towards Jesus and the Gospel message, at the height of his persecution of the Church? We know now, why the Lord gave us the gift of being able to search out and study this man. Jesus wants us to know about those who struggled and died for us; He wants us to be proud of our ancestors, *and never forget them!* He wants us to follow in their footsteps. On that note, we invite you to join us as we share the life of one of the most powerful men our Church has ever known, St. Paul the Apostle.

†

Paul was born in Tarsus, a port city in the southeastern part of Turkey. He was from a Jewish family, who traced their roots back to the tribe of Benjamin. This Jewish community had been sent to Tarsus during the Diaspora[3]. Pompey had made Tarsus the capital of the province of Cilicia. Mark Anthony gave the people of Tarsus freedom, immunity, and the right to become Roman citizens, which accounts for Paul's reference to, and pride in, his Roman citizenship. He invoked his rights as a Roman citizen many times during his ministry to get out of some serious scrapes with the Jews.

Paul was originally named Saul, after the first king of the Jews. But the Jews in Tarsus had assimilated so greatly with the Romans that he was probably given the *Roman* equivalent of Saul, which is *Paul*, at birth. He was called Paul in public, and Saul among Jewish gatherings. It was not unusual for Jews who had integrated into foreign cultures to take on a Hebrew name, and an ethnic name. He grew up under two cultures, that of his Hebrew ancestors, and the Greco-Roman customs of his adopted country. He was greatly influenced by the Greek background; Greek was a second language to him; he studied Greek philosophers.

Nothing is certain as to *when* he came to Jerusalem. His whole family moved there when he was a young man. The year 30 A.D. is as good a barometer as it gets. Scripture scholars claim there was little possibility that he ever saw Jesus during His lifetime. There are others who believe that, while he may never have spoken to the Lord, he may have seen Him before His death. Remember, they really frequented the same circles. They were at different ends of the spectrum, but they were both religious men.

---

[3]Diaspora - The dispersion of Jewish communities to various parts of Asia, during the eighth and sixth centuries, B.C. This was done by their conquerors. These communities assimilated into the countries they lived in, but maintained their Hebrew faith.

Paul was a Pharisee. He studied under Gamaliel[4] for three or four years. This would have been during the time of Jesus' ministry, 30 to 33 AD. Jesus became very *prominent* after the arrest and murder of John the Baptist, probably about a year or so into His ministry. The temple area of Jerusalem was always abuzz with rumors about this new Prophet. The personality of Paul was that of a zealot, a *nosy body*, who had to know everything that was going on, all the time. Also, he was a defender of the Jewish law, which he believed Jesus was breaking. Paul would have agreed with those who considered Jesus a blasphemer and lawbreaker, who should be dealt with accordingly.

We don't mean to imply for a minute that Paul was ever a vindictive person. He was a *passionate* person. The Lord can work with people like Paul. His passion was for *God*. He had committed himself to the service of God. He truly believed he was doing the Lord's will in stamping out these blasphemers (Christians)[5]. The same firebrand fervor he employed in defending God against the Christians, was put to use in proclaiming our Lord Jesus Christ, after Paul's conversion. *It's so exciting to see God in action!* He chooses His people so carefully. We believe, Paul was part of the Divine Plan from before the beginning of time[6]. He was groomed so well for his part in Salvation history. The area of the world in which he was born, his knowledge of the

---

[4]Gamaliel - A teacher of the Hebrew law. He was considered one of the great teachers of the law, and was given the title of Rabban. He is credited as having said to the Sanhedrin, about the Apostles Peter and John, "*Let them alone. If their purpose or activity is human in its origins, it will destroy itself. If, on the other hand, it comes from God, you will not be able to destroy them without fighting God Himself.*"

[5]We begin to use the term *Christian* here to identify followers of Jesus. The expression, *Christian* did not actually come into use until Paul and Barnabas evangelized in Antioch in Syria, almost ten years later.

[6]Romans 8:28

Greek and Roman languages and cultures, his schooling in Jerusalem, all of this was necessary for his role in proclaiming the Gospel throughout the Roman Empire. We can't help but see the Lord's Hand in Paul's development.

All of the above is just to give us a feeling for this man specially chosen by God. We have to see him as a very human, very touchable *role model.* He had all the shortcomings of man: ambition, impulsiveness, pride, anger, bullheadedness and a sharp tongue. However, when used for the glory of God, they were turned into selflessness, determination, durability, suffering, poverty, fearlessness, humiliation and persecution besides. He could get extremely hot in defense of his converts, and the next moment, he could be as tender as a lamb. He ran the gamut of emotions, and offered all to his God. You have to know who this *"Great Lion of God"*[7] was, and what made him tick.

The first mention of Paul in the Gospel is as the young man who piled coats of those who stoned St. Stephen to death[8]. After the stoning of Stephen, the Christians scattered all over the area. Saul became the dread of the Christians as he received permission to hunt them down and *crush* the movement. He began in Jerusalem, tracking down Christians, going into house after house, dragging men and women out and throwing them into jail[9]. His reputation spread throughout Judea and Syria, very quickly. His very *name* brought fear to Christians.

Saul was not a vindictive or vengeful person, but he had a mission. He contended, he was ridding the Hebrew community of a plague that threatened its very existence. And as we mentioned before, he was very *ambitious.* Once given a job, he went at it tooth and nail. He believed, the

---

[7]St. Augustine - *"For he was a veritable lion, a red lion, the great lion of God."*

[8]Acts of the Apostles 7:58-59

[9]Acts of the Apostles 8:3

Lord had called him to do this. It was towards this end that Paul went to Damascus. He was on a roll! He had begun a momentum, which could not stop until all these offenders who had adopted this "*new way*," had been stamped out. It was about this time Jesus decided that He and Saul should have a talk. This confrontation took place on the road to Damascus.

Saul and his cohorts were traveling at breakneck speed to get to Damascus. A brilliant flash of light streaked across the sky. Saul was thrown to the ground. He tried to see what had happened, but the strong beam blinded him. He heard a voice; his head turned quickly in the direction of the sound. He could make out a figure, but it was hazy. "*Saul, Saul, why do you persecute me?*" Who could this be, he wondered. "*Who are you, sir?*" The voice responded, "*I am Jesus, the one you are persecuting.*" Jesus? How could this be Jesus? He was dead! Then Saul could see more clearly through the haze. The figure of a man became visible to him. *It was Jesus!* Saul could actually make out the figure of Jesus. The voice continued, "*Get up and go into the city, where you will be told what to do.*" The figure of Jesus faded slowly, and then all went black. Saul could see nothing. He got up, groped around, completely blind, though his eyes were wide open.

The Long Hard Road to Acceptance

Saul was led by the hand, to the house of Judas in Damascus. His companions were shocked and confused by what had happened to him. Saul's mind was reeling. He asked to be alone. He refused food or drink. He had to think; he had to sort it out. Accepting the possibility that he had ever been wrong about anything was not in Saul's makeup. Now, he had to consider the likelihood that everything he had said, or thought, or done against these Christians had been a big mistake.

Jesus was alive! It was as they had all said. He had risen from the dead! Saul had seen Him! Saul's logical mind kicked in. Oh my God, he thought, that means that all He had preached was correct. He *was* the Messiah. He *is* the Messiah! It was not at all the image the Jews had accepted as the Messiah[10]. If that was so, then everything that Saul had done was anti-Christ. The words that kept coming back at him, lashing at his soul were, "*Why have you persecuted Me?*" Had he persecuted Jesus? He thought He was dead. But He had risen; He was truly God. That meant that Saul was fighting God Himself. That was not his intention at all. He meant to defend God, to glorify God.

For three days, Saul stayed by himself in a dark room, not eating or drinking, just agonizing over what he had done. But Saul was a very positive person. Though he had committed the unspeakable crime, he knew there was a way to make it right. *Hope* came into his soul. He would go back to all those who didn't believe, and explain the *truth* to them. He would shout it from the rooftops if he had to. They'd have to believe, once they saw his conversion. It made a lot of sense, but that's not what happened.

The first seeds of mistrust were felt in the heart of Ananias. The Lord appeared to him, and told him to go to the house of Judas, where he would find Saul of Tarsus. Ananias was a man of great faith, filled with the Holy Spirit. He never doubted the *Lord*; he thought, however, he had heard the wrong name. He proceeded to tell Jesus how this Saul was persecuting all the Christians, that he was in Damascus to search out Christians and imprison them. Was this the same Saul that Jesus was speaking of? Jesus

---

[10]Messiah - the Anointed One - in Greek, *Christos - the Christ -* A King David returned - they believed the Messiah to be a king, as strong as David, who would free the Jews from their enemies, and would restore the kingdom of Israel. They didn't want the Messiah that Jesus portrayed. They were looking for a military man.

convinced Ananias that He would use Saul in a mighty way to convert the Gentiles. Ananias went off to find Saul. We're not sure he was happy; but he did as Jesus commanded. At about the same time Ananias was having a conversation with Jesus, Saul was having a vision of Ananias coming to the house of Judas.

Ananias found Saul at the house, as Jesus had told him. He looked at the blind Saul. It was difficult to conceive that this helpless, docile man was the same one who had put such fear in the hearts of Christians. He went up to Saul, gingerly laid his hands on the blind man's head, and spoke very softly, *"Saul, my brother, I have been sent by the Lord Jesus who appeared to you on the way here, to help you recover your sight and be filled with the Holy Spirit."*

Something like scales fell off Saul's eyes, and he could see. Ananias prayed over him, then took him down to the river. He submerged Saul, baptizing him. Saul took food for the first time since his encounter with Jesus. He felt his strength come back to him slowly.

He had made a commitment to the Lord, to tell the whole world how he had been wrong in persecuting the Christians. He couldn't *wait* to go to the synagogue and share the good news with his Jewish brothers and sisters. They warmly welcomed him as the famous Rabbi from Jerusalem. But that was before he told them about his conversion. The mood changed quickly. Their expressions turned from baited anticipation to outraged anger. Accusations like *turncoat* and *traitor* were leveled at him. As he attempted to bare his heart to his brothers, a fury raged in the synagogue. He had to get out, and fast.

Paul in the Desert

This was the beginning of a long, lonely journey for Saul, now Paul. His own people, the Jews, wanted to kill him. They hated him for having turned away from them.

His new brothers, the Christians, didn't *trust* him. They weren't quite sure if he had really converted, or if he was employing a scheme to imprison all the Christians in Damascus. Those who had been involved in his conversion, Judas and Ananias, *believed* that the Lord had changed Saul. But they couldn't convince the others.

Paul went off by himself into the desert. Whether it was a conscious effort to follow in the footsteps of the Master, and John the Baptist, is not known for sure. But he took that time to empty himself of all that he had been, and allow the Lord to fill him with love and wisdom. He prayed; he fasted; he studied Sacred Scripture. He went deep within himself, to pull out all that was of the world, and replace it with the love of Jesus. Was it here that Jesus taught him about love, how nothing had any value without love? Did Jesus give him the insights here, which would touch the whole world for thousands of years to come?

Paul returned to Damascus. He began preaching to the Jews. His time in the desert paid off, because he spoke so brilliantly, and with such conviction that he began to sway Damascene Jews over to Christianity. He gathered around him his own small group of disciples. But he also amassed a good deal of hate from the Pharisees in the town. He had certainly affected the people there, because a scheme was concocted to *kill* Paul. He had to be lowered over the city wall by night in a basket to escape the threat on his life.

Paul returned to Jerusalem. It had been four years since he had been there. When he had left, it was to track *down* Christians. He was coming back a *disciple* of Jesus, intent on spreading the Gospel message. But while word had found its way to Jerusalem, of Paul's conversion, he was not trusted by the Christians. Naturally, he was hated by the Jews. He found himself alone again, without friends. But he had the Lord, and the Lord was in charge.

Jesus sent *Barnabas* to Paul. They had been friends in school many years before. He was the only Christian to befriend Paul. He believed the account of his conversion on the road to Damascus. The Lord worked through Barnabas. He insisted Paul meet Peter. Paul had wanted to meet with the Apostles, but feared he would not be able to, because of the hostility shown him by the Christians of Jerusalem. Barnabas walked him right through to Peter and James. Paul shared his conversion and the past three years. They accepted him openly. *He was home at last.*

Paul spent some time in Jerusalem. He followed the footsteps of Jesus, from the Upper Room to Gethsemane, to the house of Caiphas, to the Via Dolorosa, to Calvary. We can only speculate on what went through Paul's mind as he stood at the very spot where his Master had been slain. Did he feel guilt for not believing in Jesus? Did he believe that he might have been able to stop them, if he had only realized how Jesus had fulfilled Scripture? Whatever might have been, wasn't meant to be. This was the role the Lord gave Paul. He embraced it with all his heart. Did he meet Mary on the Via Dolorosa? It is said she walked the Way of the Cross every day for the rest of her life, except when she was with John in Ephesus. Did they talk? Did she look into his eyes, and through to his soul? She would have believed him without reservation. Did she give him strength for his mission, which was about to begin? We can only dream.

The persecution in Jerusalem had died down. The anger had subsided, but not towards Paul. The Jews would never forgive him for what he had done. And now, he was adding fuel to the fire. He went into the synagogues, and proclaimed the Gospel. Anger rose up in the Greek Jews to whom he spoke. His Christian brothers pleaded with him to take it easy, not step on touchy subjects, like the Mosaic law. Paul ignored them. He spoke of Moses' law as having been replaced by the *new covenant* of Jesus. This was blasphemy!

The old feelings of anger against the Christians in Jerusalem began to resurface. The Christians could see all their years of work, trying to live peacefully with the Jews, being destroyed by Paul's overzealous nature. When the Jews plotted to have Paul killed, the Christians took this as an opportunity to get him out of Israel. They took him by night to Caesarea. He wanted to visit the Christian communities on the way, but they wouldn't stop. They felt no peace until he was on a ship for Tarsus, "*to wait for instructions.*"

Paul's Great Mission

Paul was always a strong man. Even though he wanted the approval of the Christian brothers in Jerusalem, he would not have sacrificed the Gospel for this acceptance. Nor would he have left because of their insistence, even if his life was being threatened. He was quite willing to die a martyr's death, as had Stephen. So while he would have had no problem resisting the attempts to rush him out of town, it was something that happened in the Temple in Jerusalem that prompted him to leave.

He went into ecstasy during prayer at the Temple. Our Lord Jesus spoke to him, and gave him his mission. He told him, "*You must make haste. Leave Jerusalem at once because they will not accept your testimony about Me.*" When Paul questioned Jesus, blaming the lack of acceptance on his participation in the stoning of Stephen, Jesus told him, "*Be on your way. I mean to send you far from here, among the Gentiles.*" Paul knew it was the Lord's wishes that he leave Jerusalem, and so he sailed for Tarsus, where he waited for instructions.

He waited, and waited in Tarsus for word from the Church of Jerusalem. Each day, he expected it to come, but the days turned into months, and the months turned into years. Four years, he waited. This was completely contrary to Paul's nature. He was an activist, a mover and shaker.

What was the Lord doing in Paul's life in Tarsus, those four years? How did Paul keep from going berserk, as he *obediently* waited on the word of the Lord? We believe the key word here is obedience. Jesus can see the whole picture, not just one part. He knew what He would be asking of Paul in the years to come. He knew how Paul would have to relinquish his fiery personality in favor of blind obedience.

Nothing is known for sure about what Paul did for those four years in Tarsus, other than resume his trade as tentmaker. He probably went into synagogues around Tarsus, to preach the Good News of Jesus to the Jews. But we're sure he was very restless, because he knew his mission was to be more than whatever he was doing in Tarsus.

During this time, the Lord was truly working in Antioch. Even though Antioch was filled with pagan rituals, debauchery and the lot, many Christian Jews had fled to this city, as a result of Saul's persecution of them in Jerusalem. Included in this group was Simon of Cyrene, and his family. These believers went around Antioch, preaching about Jesus, and claiming converts everywhere they spoke. Word got back to Jerusalem about the great fervor for the Lord in Antioch. Barnabas was sent to see what was happening, and help in any way he could. When he arrived at Antioch, he found a small, but *thriving* church. The Antiocheans had become a group within the city, respected by all, even by many of the pagans.

Barnabas found *fertile souls* here. He knew there was great potential in Antioch. But he needed help! A charismatic figure was required if mass conversion was to come about. Jesus whispered in Barnabas' ear. *"Go to Tarsus. Paul has been waiting. He is ready."* Barnabas was overwhelmed by the excitement in Antioch. What work for the Lord could be accomplished with Paul at his side. Barnabas went to Tarsus to fetch Paul.

We know that Paul and Barnabas had a good relationship. Barnabas was the one who introduced Paul to Peter and James. But we don't know what Paul's initial reaction was to Barnabas. In some writings, we are told Paul was extremely joyous at the reunion with his old friend, and the prospect of going to Antioch. Yet, we also read that Paul's immediate reaction was to let loose of all the anger and disappointment which had stored up those four *long* years. He might have said something like, *"Where have you been? I've been waiting here for four years!"*

Be that as it may, Paul joined Barnabas in Antioch. His enthusiasm was so great, you would think he had just experienced his conversion on the road to Damascus. He was on fire! He was *eloquent*. He embraced the people of Antioch, and they in turn, accepted him for who he was. Gone was the coldness and mistrust he had felt in Jerusalem. These people loved him, and listened intently as he shared about Jesus. He and Barnabas worked together for a year building the church of Antioch.

Antioch was actually faring much better than Jerusalem. A plague had been predicted; it took place in Israel during the year Paul and Barnabas were working in Antioch. The brothers decided to put aside food and money to help their community in Jerusalem. When they had enough of an offering, they sent Paul and Barnabas to Jerusalem, to give it to the community there.

At about this time, the third generation of Herods had cast his scourge on the Christians of Israel. He wanted to get in the good favor of the Jews, so he arrested James, the brother of John, and had him beheaded. This was so well accepted by the people, he decided to do Peter next. He imprisoned him just prior to Passover, with the intention of beheading him right after the feast. The Christian community met in the house of Mary, mother of John Mark[11]. All prayed feverishly for Peter's deliverance.

During their prayer, a loud knocking at the door was heard. Fear struck the heart of the little band of disciples. One of the women went nervously to the door. When she asked who was there, she recognized the voice of Peter. She became so excited, she ran into the room where they were praying, to tell them the good news. *She forgot to open the door!* Peter banged on the door until the woman regained her composure. She opened it, and all embraced him.

Peter shared how he had been fast asleep in the prison, chained hands and feet. He felt someone tugging at his cloak. He opened his eyes; a brilliant light pierced the darkness of the cell. There was a beautiful young man standing over him. It had to be an Angel of the Lord. He told Peter to get up. Peter raised his hands to show the Angel the double chains. But they slipped off his wrists, as if they had never been locked. Peter and the young man walked past the guards, who looked through them, but didn't see them. They came to an iron gate; it opened as they approached. The Angel walked a short distance with Peter, and then disappeared. Peter explained that he was in a trance, the entire time. He only vaguely recalled the events. The Lord told him to go to the house where they were all praying; that's how he came to knock on the door.

There was not only great joy at the miraculous release of Peter, but a sense of needed *affirmation* from the Lord. His people had to know that He was watching over them, protecting them, guiding them. It gave them the strength to continue on. However, as a precaution, Peter was sent out of the city for a few weeks. He had just left when Paul and Barnabas arrived.

---

[11]John Mark was Barnabas' cousin. He is also the author of the Mark's Gospel.

Paul and Barnabas were elated over the events of their trip to Jerusalem. They were welcomed warmly, not only for the contribution, they had brought from Antioch, but because of the progress they were making in Antioch. Although they didn't spend much time in Jerusalem, Paul could feel that he was much more accepted than he had been five years before. He was one of them.

Paul and Barnabas returned to Antioch, bringing John Mark with them. But there was an urgency about them to move on. They shared their belief that the Lord was calling them beyond Antioch, to the pagan world of the Gentiles. The Church in Antioch didn't want to lose them, and as they correctly pointed out, there was enough to do in Antioch for ten Pauls and Barnabas'. This is where the four years of living in the desert of Tarsus worked for Paul. He was obedient to the elders of the Church of Antioch. The old Paul would have been off in a shot, booking passage to wherever he felt he was being called. But the new Paul, the converted Paul didn't. Even though he and Barnabas knew in their hearts that their desires were the Lord's also, they worked and waited.

Jesus came to their rescue during a prayer meeting. One of the brothers was inspired to let the Holy Spirit speak through him. The words he spoke were, "*Set aside Barnabas and Saul for me to do the work for which I have called them.*" Paul and Barnabas, as well as the elders of the community, prayed and fasted. The brothers laid hands on them, and they departed. They brought John Mark with them, and set sail for Cyprus.

Paul's First Journey of Faith

Paul and Barnabas were so excited about their mission. They had to know they were making history in this first journey, to go where no Christian had ever preached the word of Jesus before. They were straining at the bit. After such a successful year in Antioch, plus the encouragement they received in Jerusalem, they knew that the whole world was ready for the message of Jesus. Right? *Wrong!* In baseball terms, we would have to say they struck out fifteen times. They went from town to town, first appealing to the Jews in the synagogues, and then, not having been successful with them, the Gentiles. There was little or no interest. The seed had been sewn, but the fruits did not become evident until Barnabas went back to Cyprus without Paul, some time later. At this time, their spirits were low; but they were not ready to give up.

They went from one end of the island to the other. No one seemed interested in the message of Jesus. Before they shook the dust from their heels, they made their very last stop in Cyprus, Paphos. There was a Roman governor there, Sergius Paulus, who had heard of their travels throughout the island and was interested to hear their message. They were invited to speak before him. The Lord chose this time and this place, speaking before a Roman, to have Paul take the lead. It all made sense! He was a Roman citizen! Even though Barnabas was a *native* of Cyprus, it was more important to a Roman to hear from a fellow Roman. After all, Paul knew the mentality of the Romans. He knew how to appeal to this man. He was also a better speaker. Barnabas had no problem with any of this. But we begin to see a little resentment surfacing in John Mark.

Paul spoke brilliantly. Everything he said appealed to the Roman governor. He highlighted points which were crucial, such as his (Paul's) previous disbelief in the Resurrection of Jesus from the dead. This was a very touchy point. He bolstered his argument by expounding on his conversion on the road to Damascus. It looked like the governor was won over. Then Satan snuck in, in the form of a Jewish magician, Bar-Jesus. He began ridiculing everything Paul said. He made loud noises, which even perturbed the *governor*. Finally, he resorted to crude insults and caustic remarks. Paul, who was equal to anyone when it came to blowing steam, was not about to let everything be lost. The Holy Spirit took over. He got up, pointed his finger at the man and said,

> *"You are an impostor and a thoroughgoing fraud, you son of Satan and enemy of all that is right! Will you never stop trying to make crooked the straight paths of the Lord? The Lord's hand is upon you even now! For a time you shall be blind, unable so much as to see the sun."*

The magician immediately went blind. Paul was shocked at what happened, but he never blinked an eyelash. Under his breath, he praised the Holy Spirit for coming to his aid at this most important time. The governor was completely won over by the power of Paul. He believed! The Word of God was finally accepted in Cyprus.

Paul and Barnabas were not aware until *after* the incident, Bar-Jesus had been very powerful in the governor's eyes. He wielded great influence on Sergius Paulus. Bar-Jesus feared that the governor would be won over by Paul's words, and his hold over him would be lost. He was willing to do anything to discredit Paul and Barnabas. But the Lord had His way!

Soon after, the three disciples left Cyprus and sailed for Perga in Pamphylia, back in Asia, but quite a distance from where they had begun. Winter was settling in; the weather turned brutal. Paul was anxious to continue on to the cities of Galatia. He warned his companions about the hardships they would endure, as they journeyed through the malaria-infested plains of Pamphylia, and up the bitter cold mountains, before they reached their first stop. John Mark used this excuse to leave Paul and Barnabas. He couldn't see the sense in taking such risks, exposing themselves to the elements. This was partly true. In addition, however, his resentment for *Paul* had become full-blown. He was convinced Paul was trying to make himself the important one at the expense of his cousin, Barnabas. We're not sure what forced the final decision for John Mark, the dangers ahead, or his feelings for Paul. Whatever the case, he told them he would not continue.

This made for a very uncomfortable situation for Barnabas. It's never good when there are three; two is *easier.* When there's a third person in any situation, it can lead to arguments. Paul and Barnabas were clear in their aims. They had a job to do. The mandate had been given them by the Lord Himself. Nothing could get in the way of it. But John Mark was Barnabas' cousin. He loved the young man; but he also loved Paul. Whatever he did, whichever road he traveled, there would be hurt feelings by *one.* But he knew the path, the Lord had chosen for him. It was a difficult decision for Barnabas. He'd prayed to Jesus for guidance, and the Lord told him to go on. He went on with Paul.

Both men were hurt and disappointed that John Mark abandoned them in Perga. But Paul was offended as well. We don't know what words flew between him and John Mark. We must remember that Paul was very sensitive, all his life, about his position as an Apostle and his former persecution of the Christians. He believed that every attack made on him was partially due to who he *had been.* He always felt he had to prove himself; that he was suspect. The incident with John Mark didn't help build his self esteem. But, following the instructions of Jesus, Paul and Barnabas shook the dust, and began their treacherously dangerous journey.

Their first stop was Antioch in Pisidia, not to be confused with Antioch in Syria, where they had begun. They went into the synagogue on the Sabbath. They wore their shawls, which distinguished them as Scribe and Levite. The leaders were happy to have foreigners come into their midst to speak to them. They welcomed Paul and Barnabas, motioning them to speak. They were brilliant. They began at the beginning, with the exodus from Egypt. They talked about the prophets, then on to King David, and down the line to John the Baptist and Jesus. They astonished their listeners with their knowledge of Scripture, how this Jesus of Nazareth fulfilled all the prophecies of the Old Testament. When they finished, the leaders asked them to return the following week on the Sabbath, to speak again on the same subject. People began to follow them and stayed with them all week. It was exciting! The Lord was working powerfully.

The following week, the synagogue was packed, so much so, there were people standing outside, listening. Jews and Gentiles as well, were present. The Acts of the Apostles tells us *"almost the entire city gathered to hear the Word of God."* The satan of *jealousy* crept into the assembly. The Jews, the very same ones who had invited them to return, became *envious* when they saw such a large crowd of Gentiles as well as Jews. The Jewish leaders began to taunt Barnabas and Paul; they criticized and contradicted everything they said. But Paul and Barnabas continued. They weren't about to stop. Finally, however, Paul had had enough. He turned to them, pointed his finger at them, and cried out,

> *"The Word of God has to be declared to you first of all;*
> *but since you reject it and thus convict yourselves as*
> *unworthy of everlasting life, we now turn to the Gentiles.*
> *For thus were we instructed by the Lord: 'I have made*
> *you a light to the nations, a means of salvation to the*
> *ends of the earth.'"*

The Gentiles were excited, upon hearing this. They began to shout praises to the Lord. Paul and Barnabas turned their attention to this more receptive group. They preached the Word of God. It was embraced, and spread to the entire area. Paul and Barnabas were ecstatic with the acceptance they received from the Gentiles; but we have to believe there was a touch of sorrow that their own people, their fellow Jews, had rejected them. And to make it worse, they had to know it was all because they had drawn such a large crowd. The Jews *had been* receptive, even excited to hear them speak the week before. They had asked them to come back! Then they let their jealousy get the best of them, and they lost out to the Gentiles.

Unfortunately for Paul and Barnabas, the ill feelings which had germinated that Sabbath day, didn't end when they left with the Gentiles. The Jews were furious. They agitated some key people in the town against Paul and Barnabas. Pretty soon, things became very uncomfortable. But they didn't run at the first sign of adversity. They tried to turn it around, get on the good side of those who were against them. Even when their lives were so seriously threatened that the disciples they had converted, urged them to leave, they refused. Finally, a plot was hatched by their enemies. Paul and Barnabas were arrested, and scourged with thirty-nine lashes each, the same as Our Lord Jesus. Then they were dragged to the gates of the city, and thrown out. They were in physical pain, but exhilarated. Might Paul have wondered if Stephen had experienced this same spiritual joy as he was being stoned to death? He could now understand the look of rapture on Stephen's face as he died.

Paul and Barnabas were not ones to lick their wounds. They took a short time to heal from the beating. Disciples from the town came out to them and ministered to them. *And then they were on the road again.*

On their way from Antioch in Pisidia to Iconium, they praised the Lord for the conversions that had taken place there. They shared excitedly with each other the abundant blessings which had been bestowed on them and the community. They knew that the Spirit would continue to grow in that area. They were so on fire, they couldn't wait to get to the next place. The Lord does that. Just watching the Spirit at work through them, made all the danger, all the abuse, verbal and physical, count for nothing. They were so full of the Lord, they would have walked through fire to be able to spread the Gospel.

The next town, Iconium, proved to be more dangerous than Antioch. It had been pretty much taken over by the Romans. They had brought with them, all their pagan practices. The rest of the city consisted of Greeks and Jews. The climate of Iconium was anything but spiritual. Paul and Barnabas worked at jobs during the day; then at night, and on the Sabbath, they preached the Word of God.

They went to the synagogue first, to present the Good News to the Jews. Their words won many over to the "*new way*" of Jesus. But there were as many Jews who were not converted. Paul and Barnabas were also able to persuade many of the *Gentiles* to embrace Jesus. What happened in effect was, they split the town. Half the Jews and Gentiles converted. But the other half did not. The devil entered into those who were against Jesus. They brooded and plotted the entire time, Paul and Barnabas were in Iconium, which was many months. Finally, their enemies were able to enlist the aid of the Gentiles who had not gone over to Paul and Barnabas. This time, they planned to scourge Paul and Barnabas, and then *stone them* to death.

Their newly converted disciples got wind of the conspiracy; they warned Paul and Barnabas. Again, the two didn't want to leave. They felt they were just making a major *breakthrough*. They feared all their work would have been ineffective if they left now. But common sense prevailed. What would they accomplish if they were dead? There were still other areas to evangelize. So, once more, they left a budding community, to go to yet another town, and begin all over again. The next town was Lystra. A major miracle was to take place here.

They began in Lystra, by evangelizing the Jewish family with whom they were staying. Then they branched out, to other Jews, then the Gentiles. One day, they were at the city gate, near the temple of Jupiter. There was a big crowd! Paul couldn't resist the potential of preaching to this many people at one time. Once again, Paul's knowledge of Greek and Roman mythology proved to be of great assistance in speaking to this crowd. Using their culture as a door-opener, he spoke flowingly of the God, Jesus, His love, and care for the suffering. A cripple sat at the steps, listening with such faith and hope! Paul kept looking at him. The Holy Spirit inspired Paul. He knew that Jesus would give him the miracle he needed to sway the people. He went over to the cripple, and commanded him to get up, in the name of Jesus. When the man rose to his feet and walked, the crowd went wild!

But the response was not one that Paul and Barnabas expected. The pagan upbringing of the crowd took over; they thought Paul and Barnabas were *gods!* Word spread quickly throughout the town. Paul and Barnabas weren't aware this was what they were thinking. But when the priest from the temple of Zeus, way outside of town, came in with offerings to these two gods, Paul and Barnabas knew the miracle had gone the wrong way. The people were calling Barnabas *Zeus*, and Paul *Hermes*. They rushed out into the crowd. They had to stop this! They tore their garments, yelling as they did so, "*No, we're not gods! We're humans, just like you!*" Finally, after much effort, the people calmed down, and Paul was able to instruct them that it was Jesus, not he or Barnabas, who had cured the lame man, the same Jesus who had died for them, and been raised from the dead.

It was in Lystra that Paul converted Timothy, who would become a disciple. Real progress was being made in

Lystra, converting the Jews and Gentiles to the ways of Jesus. But at the same time, the Jews who had tried to kill Paul and Barnabas in Antioch in Pisidia, and Iconium, joined forces, and came to Lystra to poison the minds of the people.

We don't know if Paul and Barnabas were aware of their enemies' presence in Lystra. They felt free to go about the city, preaching. So much so that one day, Barnabas and Timothy were evangelizing in one location, while Paul was in the *town*, preaching to a large crowd. He was so caught up in his discourse that he didn't notice his enemies walking through the crowd, whispering to the people. All of a sudden, the mob began closing in on him. Too late he realized he was surrounded. Just then, a large stone went flying through the air, and struck him on the head. He staggered from the blow. He felt his head; blood was flowing from it. Another stone whizzed by and hit him again. He went down. The last thing he remembered was a mass of people grabbing at his clothes. They were out to kill him!

He was dragged out of the city, and thrown into a ditch, left to die. However, the Lord was not nearly finished with Paul, not yet. Word got back to his disciples. Barnabas and Timothy rushed to the ditch with others, and rescued Paul. When they saw the limp, bloody body, laying in the ditch, they thought for sure Paul was dead. But he was strong stock. The Lord knew this when He chose him. Paul moaned, then opened his eyes. All the disciples let out a sigh of relief, followed by praises of God. They took Paul away. But they knew they had to leave Lystra, *for now*.

The next day, Paul and Barnabas left; they went to the last town on their first mission, Derbe. There's not a whole lot known about their time in Derbe, other than they stayed there about a year, and converted many to the Faith. The reason we mention this place is, if you look at the map of Paul's first mission, Derbe is located fairly close to Antioch in Syria, where they *began* their journey, and where they would be *returning*, a distance of perhaps a hundred miles. Also, the town they would have to pass if they went directly to Antioch in Syria would have been his home town, Tarsus. And yet, they *backtracked*, retraced their steps through all the towns they had already visited. *Why did they do that?*

We know *what* they did in these towns. They reaffirmed and strengthened the little churches they had built, by ordaining priests, and setting up *community*. By their presence, they witnessed to the safekeeping the Lord had provided them. Paul and Barnabas gave assurance to their new disciples that the Lord would take care of them. But *why* did they return? Their lives were in great danger, going back through these towns. The same people who wanted to kill them before, still wanted to see them dead. We're sure they didn't walk the streets freely as they had done previously. Still, they took a great risk going into the towns.

We believe, the reason they did it was to instill courage in the new communities. Paul was so bruised and beaten, he looked like a Crucified Christ. But he was a *living sign* that God takes care of those who love Him. Paul and Barnabas gave their spiritual children the strength they would need to prevail. A quote in the Acts of the Apostles that verified this was an instruction they left with the people, *"We must undergo many trials if we are to enter into the reign of God."*

Paul's Struggle with the Church of Jerusalem

Paul and Barnabas had spent four years on this first missionary journey. The Lord had accomplished much through their *fiat*. Great strides had been made in developing the Church of the Gentiles. We believe they thought they would return *triumphant* to Antioch in Syria. Maybe they even expected a little pat on the back, for a job well-done. What they didn't expect was what was in store for them shortly after they arrived home.

Judaizers[12] came to Antioch from Jerusalem. They insisted that all Gentile Christians had to be circumcised, there could only be one Christian community, the Jewish converts who observed the *Jewish law* to the letter. They criticized Paul and Barnabas. They actually used the struggles, Paul and Barnabas had endured during their missionary journey, against them. They claimed that the division in these towns would not have happened if the Gentiles would have gone over to the Jewish laws, immediately. This dispute took place at a large assembly in Antioch. Nearly everyone there was a pagan convert. The Judaizers shouted out, "*Unless you are circumcised according to Mosaic practice, you cannot be saved.*"

Paul and Barnabas went through the ceiling! It was inconceivable, after four years of evangelizing *hard*, barely escaping death on many occasions, bearing the wounds of his suffering on his body for all to see, that it was all in vain. There was so much involved in this dispute. These *converts* were not just *numbers*, a scoreboard. *They were people!* They had hearts and souls; they had faces. They were not second-class citizens in the Church! To Paul and Barnabas, it went much farther than Hebrew rituals. There was a big question which had to be answered. Was salvation dependent on faith in Jesus Christ, and all that implied, His death and Resurrection, or was salvation contingent on following the laws of Moses? Did Jesus give us a *new Covenant*, or was it an extension of the old Covenant?

When Paul and Barnabas were rejected by the Jews, and embraced by the Gentiles, for whatever reason, they never thought it necessary to impose Jewish laws on these converts. They were not converting to a form of *Judaism*, but to *Christianity*. Circumcision would have been a painful,

---

[12]Judaizers - Jewish Pharisees who had converted to Christianity. They maintained that Gentile Christians had to follow the Mosaic Laws.

humiliating ordeal, and for what? Paul pointed to the conversion of Cornelius, at the hands of Peter. Was he circumcised? They pointed out the workings of the Holy Spirit during their missionary journey. Were they dreaming this happened? The Jews would not budge! The tension mounted.

The poor people of the Church of Antioch were in the middle. They looked to James and the heads of the Church of Jerusalem as their spiritual leaders. They looked to Paul and Barnabas as their own, as if they had been raised by the Spirit from their own ranks. They were so proud of the work these two had done in the name of Jesus. They couldn't go against them. It was determined that Paul and Barnabas go to Jerusalem, to present this problem to James and Peter. They brought Titus with them as an example of a pagan, who had converted to the Lord.

It was a touchy situation, going in. We don't know how Paul felt about having to go to Jerusalem, as if he were on trial. It had been five years since he had been there last. His accomplishments had been the talk of the Christian world. But now they were in question. Had he been orthodox in his teaching? Would he have to go back to these beautiful converts, and tell them he had been wrong about their not having to adhere to Jewish law? To Paul's logical way of thinking, it didn't make sense. It was not according to the teachings of Jesus, or the concept of the New Covenant. These and many other things went through Paul's mind as he went back to stand before the council in Jerusalem.

At the council meeting, Barnabas stood up and recounted their four year missionary journey. He introduced Titus as an example of the fiber of the pagan converts. That's when the riot began. What actually happened depends on which account you read. In the Acts of the Apostles, it goes like this. "*Some of the converted Pharisees then got up and demanded that such Gentiles be circumcised* and told to keep the Mosaic law."[13]   But if you read Paul's letter to the Galatians, it reads like this.   *"Certain false claimants to the title of brother were smuggled in; they wormed their way into the group to spy on the freedom we enjoy in Christ Jesus and thereby to make slaves of us, but we did not submit to them for a moment."*[14]

Whatever the case, Paul jumped to his feet and lashed out at the assembly.   He defended his converts, and his understanding of the New Covenant. To his way of thinking, they were denying the merits of Jesus' Crucifixion.   The situation became hot. Peter, James and John stepped in and called for quiet. They took Paul and Barnabas into a private meeting. Paul explained his conviction that salvation came from faith in Jesus, and His death and Resurrection, not on circumcision and adherence to Mosaic laws.   Paul and Barnabas shared their last four years on the road, how the Holy Spirit had worked so powerfully, in converting pagans to the new way of Jesus.

They spoke with such certainty, the apostles could do nothing other than agree with them, congratulate them, and lay hands on them.   The next day, James made the announcement to the council that the Gentiles did not have to undergo circumcision. The battle had been won, but there was still a great war to be fought.

Paul and Barnabas returned to Antioch, victorious, *so they thought.* But shortly after, Peter came to visit the church of Antioch. At first, everything was beautiful. Peter sat with the gentile converts, and broke bread with them.   But a contingent of Judaizers had followed, to spy on Peter and Paul. They used a great deal of peer pressure on Peter. He gave in to it; he removed himself from the Gentile Christians. He turned down invitations to be with them, so as to satisfy

---

[13]Acts of the Apostles 15:5
[14]Galatians 2:4-5

the Judaizers. Even when he would go to a gentile community, he sat at a table separate from them. Pretty soon, all the Jewish converts did the same. The gentiles could see what was happening, and were hurt by Peter's actions. They felt he was alienating himself from them. Paul was aware of it. Anger began to build inside him. *When Barnabas followed Peter's lead,* and separated himself from his own people, to sit with the Jews, Paul knew he had to act.

He could see everything he had worked for, all that had been accomplished in those five years of evangelizing the gentiles and his recent victory at Jerusalem, crumbling into dust. He knew the jeopardy, he placed himself into, suggesting that the prince of the apostles, Peter, was behaving contrary to the teaching of Jesus. Who was he, Paul, to dare chastise the man whom Jesus had made head of the Church? But he had to do it. He got up in the middle of the assembly, and corrected Peter and the others who were putting the law before *Jesus.* He ended his statement on a powerful note *"For if justice is by the law, then Jesus died in vain!"*

Not a word was spoken. But everybody understood. A piercing silence blanketed the assembly. All eyes converged on Peter. He and Barnabas ran over to Paul, and embraced him. And while the problem of Jewish dietary laws continued to plague the gentile converts, the lines were clearly established. Faith in Jesus overshadowed adherence to the Mosaic laws.

Paul and Barnabas separate

Paul felt the call to go back on the road. He wanted to start out by visiting the towns, he and Barnabas had evangelized the last four years. Barnabas was ready to go. They wanted to share the good news of the progress that had been made, regarding circumcision and the dietary laws. Then Barnabas asked for *John Mark* to join them. *Paul said no!* He had a stubbornness about him! To give him credit, he never quite knew who were his *friends* and who were his *enemies*. John Mark had abandoned Paul and Barnabas on their first mission. Paul never forgot this. He wasn't quite sure if Mark still harbored resentment towards him because he took the lead from Barnabas. And to be honest, on such an intense trip as they were planning, they knew they would have enough trouble with those who were *against* them. They certainly did not need problems with their own.

Barnabas judged that Paul was being pig-headed about John Mark, which he was. But Paul wouldn't budge. We don't know how hot it got between the two friends. Barnabas knew that John Mark had great contributions to make to the Church. Rejection of this kind, at this time, could have discouraged the young man from doing the important work God had planned for him. Barnabas couldn't let this happen, so he made a difficult decision. He and *John Mark* went together on a missionary journey. Paul chose Silas to accompany him on his voyage.

We have to take a minute out here to put the spotlight on Barnabas. True, this chapter is about Paul, but it's also about the early Church, our Church. Barnabas is a very strong part of that movement. The Holy Spirit used Barnabas, throughout his life, as a tool to bring Paul to the forefront. It was Barnabas who befriended Paul in Jerusalem when everybody else distrusted him. Barnabas brought him to Peter and James. The Holy Spirit inspired Barnabas to go to Tarsus and recruit Paul to work with him in Antioch. Nobody asked Barnabas to go Tarsus and get Paul, if he felt he needed him in Antioch. This was all done by Barnabas, as he said "*Yes*" to the Holy Spirit.

Barnabas was a better judge of character than Paul. In the same way that he saw in Paul what no one else could see, he had to have been able to see the same traits in his cousin, John Mark. History has proven him right in this. John

Mark, now called Mark the Evangelist, made extremely valuable contributions to the Church. He became Peter's secretary; he wrote a good deal of his Gospel from what Peter dictated to him. Also, if we read Paul's letter to the Colossians, 4:10, we realize that John Mark worked for Paul at a *later* date, so obviously, they reconciled.

Barnabas was actually an *unsung hero* of the infant Church. As we owe the development of the gentile Church to a great degree to Paul, we owe the same debt of gratitude to Barnabas, without whom we might not have had Paul, without whom we might not have had our Church today.

Paul brings the Gospel to Europe

With Silas as his new partner, Paul set out for his second missionary journey. This time, he began where he had ended his first voyage, in Derbe. His focus in visiting these churches was to build on what he had done before, add new converts, and designate heads of the communities. In Lystra, he kept the promise he had made to Timothy[15], to come back for him, and have him join Paul and Silas on their missionary journey.

Paul planned to go to Ephesus, but he was blocked *"by the Holy Spirit."* They tried another direction, but the Spirit blocked them again. No one could figure out what the Lord was doing. They went down to Troas, where Paul renewed the acquaintance of Luke, the physician. As Paul shared about what had been happening in his evangelization, Luke's heart burned. He wanted to be part of it. Luke told Paul about the untapped possibilities in Macedonia, to the northwest. Paul was excited about this.

---

[15]Timothy - Paul's beloved disciple - traveled with Paul, sometimes as advance man for Paul, or at Paul's request, to various cities in Greece and Turkey. He was ordained bishop of Ephesus by Paul. He is the Timothy named in Paul's letters to Timothy, and also in 1 Corinthians 16:10 - He died a martyr's death in 97 a.d.

One night, Paul had a dream. In it, a man pleaded with him, "*Come over to Macedonia and help us.*" He immediately made plans to go to Macedonia. As soon as Luke heard this, he was determined to join them. This was the beginning of Luke's partnership in the Lord with Paul. It was also the first giant step for Jesus, into Europe.

In 1985, we led a pilgrimage "*In the Footsteps of St. Paul*", which we should have named, "*In Search of St. Paul.*" There were almost no shrines in Greece or Turkey attributed to Paul. In Athens, at the Aeropagus, where he spoke, there was a little plaque. At the Agora, in Corinth, there was just a small mention. But we did manage to find the brook where Lydia was baptized in Philippi. She was the first European converted to the Faith by Paul and his little band. We celebrated Mass on this spot. Our priest, who had a good working knowledge of St. Paul, explained to us that it was probably not as big a deal for Paul and his followers, as it was for us, that this was where he made his first imprint on Europe. At that time, there was the Asian province, and the Macedonian province. But they were all part of the Roman Empire. For Paul, it was like going from California to Arizona. But for us, it was a very special place!

No matter what Paul and his men did, they got into trouble. In Philippi, they had decided to keep a low profile. They went around *quietly* doing their work. They had been there a few months and were making moderate progress in converting the gentiles over to Jesus. A girl began following them, who was possessed by an evil spirit. She was a fortune teller for money. She taunted Paul and Silas. She screamed obscenities at them, and sarcastically yelled to the people, "*These men are servants of the Most High; they will make known to you a way of salvation.*"

Paul tried to ignore her. He didn't want any trouble, or to draw too much attention to what they were doing. But after two days, he'd had it. He turned to the girl and

Left:
St. Paul, the Apostle, took Jesus' command to heart, *"Go into the whole world, and proclaim the good news to all creation."*

Below:
They dragged him into the center of Philippi, and had him thrown into prison, chained: hands, feet and neck, to the wall of the cell.

commanded a spirit leave her body. When her bosses saw the spirit leave her, they realized their source of income was gone; they attacked Paul and Silas, and began beating them. They dragged them into the center of town, and had them thrown into prison. They were chained, hands, feet and neck, to the wall of the cell. That night there was a violent earthquake. All the chains of the prisoners came loose. The Roman guard thought they had escaped, and was about to commit suicide, when Paul yelled out that they were still there. The guard realized these men were from the Lord, and asked how he could be saved. Paul baptized him and his whole household. The next day, they were freed. But they had to leave the city! However, he left Luke to continue the work, they had begun.

In Thessalonica, their situation was very similar to what had happened on their first missionary journey. They went into the synagogue and spoke to the Jews. Many converted over to Jesus. The Jews who did *not* convert, became violent; they wanted to kill Paul and his followers. They went to Boroea, where the same thing happened. The Jews from Thessalonica riled up those from Boroea, and Paul was a hunted man again. He left Silas and Timothy to continue working in Boroea, and *he* took a boat to Athens.

Greeks in general, and Athenians in particular, were always interested in *new things*. Their pet phrase was, "What is the newest development?" When Paul started preaching in the public squares, they became mildly interested in what he was saying. They invited him to the Aeropagus, to speak to a larger contingency of Athenians. The first thing he noticed was a statue of a "god unknown." He jumped on that immediately to introduce Jesus to them. He was creating an interest. He could feel them going with him. Then he spoke of Jesus' Resurrection. He saw a cloud form over their eyes. Most just sneered and walked away. A few said politely, "We must hear you on this topic some other time." He knew he was finished there. He shook the dust from his feet, and went on. There was still a whole world out there.

He went to Corinth. It was possibly the most morally bankrupt city he had ever visited. But he found, as he evangelized this city, they lacked one fault the Athenians had in excess, *pride*; this made it possible to reach them, whereas it was *impossible* to reach the Athenians. He met a Jewish couple, Aquila and Priscilla, who had been banished from Rome, because they were *Jews*. They were tentmakers, as was Paul. He stayed with them and worked in their common trade. On the sabbaths, he went into the synagogues to preach to the Jews.

By the time Timothy and Silas came from Macedonia, Paul was in the thick of debate with the Jews. He was making some progress, but not a whole lot. His anger flared up again; he turned them off. He shouted at them, "*Your blood be on your own heads. I am not to blame! From now on, I will turn to the Gentiles.*"

Fortunately, he converted a man who had a house next door to the synagogue. He allowed Paul to set it up as his church, to teach and preach to the gentiles. Slowly but surely, the Church of Corinth began to grow. Paul spent over a year in this town, reaching out to every corner of the city possible, speaking to whomever he could. But his heart was in Thessalonica. Silas and Timothy had brought him news of great strides which had been made there, despite the persecution by the Jews. They longed to see Paul again, and listen to his words. But he and they knew it would be a death sentence for him to return there. In addition, he was needed in Corinth to continue the work, he had begun there. He prayed for a way to reach out to his brothers in Thessalonica. The Spirit answered. "Paul, Silvanus and Timothy, to the church of the Thessalonians who belong to God the Father, and the Lord Jesus Christ. Grace and peace be yours." *Paul composed his first letter!*

The Epistles of St. Paul

The Acts of the Apostles do not give us the heart and spirit of Paul as much as the extraordinary gift he left us with his *letters*. We get to know Paul, the *man*, the *apostle*. We are able to dig deep into his soul. We are privileged to feel his joys and sorrows, his frustrations, his hurts, his anger, his tenderness, and probably more important than anything, the direct line he had from the Holy Spirit. The Lord worked powerfully, through the epistles of St. Paul.

As we have mentioned in many of our books, the Lord uses everything we have, all the gifts we've been given, for *His Glory*. Again, we must highlight the teachings of Paul, in light of his Greco-Roman background. The Lord used all of this, in the teachings Paul sent to the infant churches all over Greece and Turkey. The term *Epistle* is given to Paul's works, as opposed to *letter*. An epistle is the highest generation of a letter. Actually, the only common denominator between a letter and an epistle is its form. But an epistle is so much more than a letter and that's what the Lord gave us through Paul. His epistles were of an artistic literary form, much like an essay or drama. They aimed at a larger audience, as opposed to a one-on-one communication.

Through his epistles, Paul was able to touch the *hearts* of his people. Usually, his writings were broken up into two parts, *doctrine*, in which he taught the truths of the Church to his people, and *instructional*, how to live their lives according to the message of Jesus. Through his epistles, Paul was almost able to be there. In addition, his message remained after he was gone, for the *next* generation of believers. His writings were so inspired, most of the 32 Doctors of the Church have used them as a basis for their own writings. And none of them ever considered their writings to be on an equal par with Paul's.

Paul used what was available in his time, *to the maximum*. He was a leader in communications, an

innovator. He had his own brand of genius, which no one in
the Church has ever disputed. But we have our own
geniuses today. Where are our St. Paul's? We seem to be
overwhelmed by the advances Satan has made in the field of
communications. We're so far behind, we don't think we
stand a chance. But it's not true. It's no different today,
than it was in St. Paul's time. Greed, permissiveness,
promiscuity, idolatry, lust for power, all these evils jammed
the communications lines of Paul's days. He was not nearly
as popular in his time, as the writers of the day. And yet,
how much do we know of the writings of anyone else of the
first century, A.D.? How do *they* stack up with the fame of
St. Paul? We have an extremely strong role model in Paul.
He fought the odds, not only outside the church, but *inside*
as well. History has proven that he was victorious. We can
follow in the footsteps of St. Paul. All we have to do is die to
ourselves and be reborn in Christ. It's *incredibly* logical.

Paul used his letters to be in two places at once. While
he continued on his missionary journeys, he wrote to
churches in other parts of the world, often before he was
going to be there, or right after he had left. He also used his
letters to do problem-solving in some of the churches where
false doctrine, or the ever-present obstacle of Gentile
Christians adhering to the Mosaic Law, cropped up. Most of
the time, his letters were effective. Other times, he had to
follow them up by visiting a particular church, or sending one
of his disciples, Timothy, Titus or Luke.

The Journey Continues

Paul had always wanted to go to Ephesus. He felt it to
be fertile territory to spread the word of Jesus. But he was
always blocked, for one reason or another. The more
difficult it became to go there, the more he knew he had to.
On his way back from Corinth, he had to wait for a short
time to change boats at Ephesus. He hurried to the local

synagogue to feel out the waters. While he didn't make any converts, he did detect interest, so he promised to return the following Spring. He continued on his journey back to Antioch, where he spent the winter.

Finally, he got to Ephesus! His conjecture about how open it was to conversion, turned out to be correct. But it didn't come from where he expected. He spent three months in the synagogue, trying to convince the Jews there, Jesus was the Messiah. They wouldn't budge! Eventually, he just picked up and left. He went to the Gentiles. That was an *uphill fight* all the way. He was bucking the religion of Diana, which had survived over 1,000 years. It was a religion of sensuality and materialism. In addition, merchants manufactured and sold images of Diana by the thousands. It was *big business!* How Paul was going to replace that with the Gospel, could only be through the miraculous.

But the Lord worked through Paul, and his followers. He was able to speak in a huge hall, owned by one of his converts, Tyrannus, where Gentiles came from all over Asia. The tide turned quickly, and the Church of Ephesus was created. He spent two years there. Miracles were attributed to Paul's intervention in Ephesus. To many, these miracles became the turning point for their conversion. The Lord uses whatever He has to, in order to bring the sheep into the fold.

Paul and his ever-growing number of disciples worked at a feverish pace for those two years. It was almost as if Paul knew he had so much to accomplish, and so little time in which to do it. He evangelized Ephesus and the seven churches, mentioned in the Book of Revelations, during this time in Ephesus.

But we don't want to give you the impression that all was roses with Paul and the churches he founded. Just the opposite, Paul suffered all his life at the hands of those he evangelized. His writings, for the most part, were in defense of his authority, and his struggles throughout his ministry.

The Years of Imprisonment

Paul wanted to go back to Jerusalem. He had traveled this area of Macedonia and Asia many times, in his second and third journeys. At Troas, it seemed like his whole world was falling apart. He became physically and emotionally ill. The situation in Corinth was bad; Ephesus was even worse. It was probably the fever, but for the first time since he began, he felt like a failure. He wanted to go home! He felt the need to be back where it all began. He could feel the Lord calling him to Jerusalem. After he sent Titus and Luke to deliver his epistle to the Church of Corinth, he visited that town a last time, to settle the differences in the Church there.

It was during the winter in Corinth, when he could not travel, he began to look towards new horizons. He truly believed his work was finished in Asia. He also knew the Lord was calling him to go to Rome. That would be the greatest triumph in his life, if he could convert the pagans of Rome. During this winter, he carefully wrote his famous letter to the Romans. He wanted to encourage the little church that had developed there, and also set the stage, if the Lord allowed him, to evangelize in that great metropolis. Once the plan was in his heart, he moved with great haste towards Jerusalem. He would spend Pentecost there, and then set out for Rome.

He knew he should stop in Ephesus, to handle the many problems that existed in the Church there, but he didn't want to take the time. When their ship landed at Miletus, about thirty miles from Ephesus, he sent for the leaders from Ephesus to meet him in Miletus.

He gave an inspired, emotional talk to the leaders. He had to know more than he let on. At certain times in his address, he referred to his approaching persecution and even death. Statements like "*I am on my way to Jerusalem, compelled by the Spirit and not knowing what will happen to me there - except that the Holy Spirit has been warning me from city to city that chains and hardships await me. I put no value on my life if only I can finish my race...*" and "*I know as I speak these words that none of you....will ever see my face again.*" gave his followers a strong indicator that he was walking toward his destruction. As he bid them farewell, they broke down and wept over him. It was possibly the hardest goodbye he had ever had to make.

From the time they set foot in Syria, warnings came for Paul not to go to Jerusalem. The ship docked at Tyre for a short time, to unload cargo. Paul and his disciples found brothers there, with whom they stayed for a week. Nothing but warnings came to them that Paul should *stay away* from Jerusalem. Then, when the boat docked at Caesarea, they spent time in the home of a man whose four daughters had the gift of prophecy. A prophecy was given Paul that he would be in chains in Jerusalem. Still, he would not listen! After pleading with him as much as they could, they knew it was no use. He was determined to go to Jerusalem, no matter what.

Paul arrived in Jerusalem for Pentecost. He was greeted with that same guarded *reserve* he had always experienced from the leaders there. They praised the Lord for what accomplishments had been made through Paul in Asia and Europe. But the problem of the Jews, who believed he was playing down the importance of the Mosaic law among the Jewish Christians, cropped up again. Would he never be free of this? Wouldn't they ever understand that Jesus gave us a New Covenant, which superseded the old law? James told him that not only were the *Jews* in Jerusalem angry with him, but the *Jewish Christians* as well, wanted to kill him.

James thought it extremely important that Paul take part in the purification ceremony in the temple at Jerusalem, to show the Jews how much he respected the Mosaic laws. This was a major *problem* for Paul. He had preached over and over again that it was not necessary to adhere to the Mosaic Law to be a Christian! He had gentile disciples with him, here in Jerusalem. Would they think he was betraying them? Yet, on the other hand, he knew how important the law was to the Jews. He didn't want to alienate the Jewish Christians, either! After much prayer, Paul agreed to do as James asked. It was a very humiliating experience. He had to shave his head, as did four others of his group. But in the back of his mind, his own words came to him,

"For free though I was to all, unto all have I made myself a slave that I might gain the more converts. And I have to become to the Jews a Jew that I might gain the Jews." (1 Cor 9:20)

All was going well. It was almost the end of the seven-day period of purification. Paul had adhered to all the laws of the feast. Then, some Jews from Asia spotted him in the temple area. They incited the other Jews there, by falsely accusing Paul of bringing a gentile into the Inner Court[16]. Before long, they had all converged on him, trying to kill him. A Roman centurion saw the riot and broke it up. Paul really wasn't trying to *escape* from the mob. *He wanted to convert them!* He asked the centurion (in his best Greek) if he could speak to the people. He began by witnessing to his own conversion. About mid-point, the crowd became furious! They tried to kill him. The centurion had to rescue him again. He decided to scourge Paul.

This was where Paul became very dramatic. He knew just the right time to say just the right thing. He waited until

---

[16]Inner Court of the temple - a very holy place, which would be blasphemed if a pagan (gentile) entered into it.

the Roman guard had tied him to the post. The whipping was about to begin. Paul called the centurion over and asked him, matter-of-factly, *"Is it legal to flog a Roman citizen without a trial?"* A Roman citizen? Panic set in. It was one of the worst crimes possible for a Roman citizen to be denied his rights by other Romans. The centurion didn't want to have any part of this. Paul was released immediately and kept in the fortress. His young nephew came to the fortress, to warn Paul about a plot by the Jews against his life. This was a perfect excuse for the commander to get rid of Paul. Under heavy guard, he was transferred during the night to Caesarea, to be tried by the governor.

Paul stayed a prisoner in Caesarea for two years, through two governors. The first didn't want to release him, but could not turn him over to the Jews because he was a Roman citizen. He kept Paul imprisoned for his entire term as governor. His successor *had no problem* turning him over to the Jews. He asked Paul if he would submit to a trial in Jerusalem. Paul knew this was instant death. So, once again, he prevailed on his standing as a citizen of Rome and demanded he be heard by the Emperor. To his way of thinking, it would get him out of the hotbed of Israel. He would much rather take his chances in Rome.

Everything that could have happened did happen, on that fateful journey to Rome. They were shipwrecked! Paul was bitten by a poisonous snake. But the Lord was in charge. He protected Paul, Luke, and the others. He not only cared for them, but used them to bring converts to Christianity everywhere they stopped. Healings took place; conversions abounded. By the time Paul set foot in Italy, he was like a conquering hero, attacking the last great enemy. In Puetoli, the port from which they disembarked, brothers who recognized Paul, asked him to stay with them for awhile and share the Good News of Jesus. This was no problem with the centurion, who had been their companion, and guard throughout the trip. He had seen the miracles brought about through Paul. He was more friend than captor.

Paul didn't know it, but the brothers sent word to Rome that he was coming. So when he arrived, actually before he got into the city, groups of believers, not one, but two, came out to greet him. We can just envision Paul's excitement as he met with such enthusiasm. Here he was, walking with other prisoners, and he was being greeted like royalty in the greatest city in the world, Rome. The Lord was putting Paul back into high gear, after his long trip.

Probably because the situation in Israel had been so touchy, the governor of Judea had ordered a minimum-security house arrest for Paul. While he couldn't go running all over Rome, he was allowed to have people come to him. And he did! And they did! Paul was as active preaching the word of God from *this* place, as he had been in all his journeys throughout the world of that time. But his heart must have broken when his Jewish brothers rejected his teachings. We know that he never stopped, until the day he died, urging his Jewish brothers to come over to the New Covenant of Jesus. Towards the end of the Acts of the Apostles, when he was rejected by the Jewish community in Rome, he quoted from Isaiah to them. This passage may have summed up his life of frustration with his brother Jews.

"Go to this people and say:
You may listen carefully yet you will never understand;
You may look intently yet you will never see.
The heart of this people has grown sluggish.
They have scarcely used their ears to listen;
their eyes they have closed,
Lest they should see with their eyes,
hear with their ears,
understand with their minds,
And repent; and I should have to heal them."

Paul spent two years in his plush house arrest. His trial finally came up. He was heard in the Imperial court, which was very important to him. They could have killed him, as long as he could preach the Gospel in the Imperial Court of Rome. As it turned out, however, he was exonerated and freed. He went back on the road again. Information is sketchy as to exactly where he went, and what he did. He may have gone to Spain. It's pretty certain he went back to Philippi. But he was truly getting tired now. The years and the punishment, physical as well as spiritual and emotional, were getting to him.

"I have fought the good fight."

He picked the wrong time to come back to Rome, or was it the *Divine* Plan? Nero, in his insanity, had burned down the city of Rome. He needed a scapegoat to take the blame, so he chose the Christians. He spread false rumors throughout the city that the Christians had caused the fire. The great persecution began. Paul was well known as a leader of the Christians. So he was arrested, soon after his return to Rome in 67 A.D. Only this time it was not a cushy prison like the first time. He was put into the Mamertine prison, where he suffered out the last days of his life. It was not fair to put Paul into this kind of dingy hole. It would have been better to kill him off, immediately. He was too alive, too on fire for the Lord. He could only vegetate here. But the Lord is kind.

Paul knew this was the end of his journey. From here he would catapult into Heaven. He wrote his last will and testament, in his second letter to Timothy. In it, he shared how he was ready to meet his Lord, face to face. He shared,

"I am already being poured out in sacrifice, and the time
of my deliverance is at hand. I have fought the good fight;
I have finished the course; I have kept the faith. For the
rest, there is laid up for me a crown of justice, which the

St. Paul wrote some of the most touching, uplifting, beautiful letters here in the Mamertine Prison (below).

Lord, the just Judge, will give me in that day; yet not to me only, but also to those who love His coming."

One day, Paul heard the footsteps of the soldiers in the street above him. They came down into the hole which was his home. *It was time!* They brought him outside the city, which was his right as a Roman citizen. There they executed him, by chopping off his head.

We're sure they thought that this would silence Paul, just as they thought a crucifixion would silence Jesus. But it didn't silence Jesus, and it didn't silence His best friend, Paul. The roar of this great lion of God, has resounded throughout the entire world, and the echo of that sound has come down through the ages, filling the hearts of strong, powerful men and women, for almost two thousand years. Paul is a mighty comet that thunders past us, a bright light leading us out of the darkness.

We would like to leave you with one of his thoughts, *"All things are passing away. In the end there are three things that count, Faith, Hope and Love, and the greatest of these is Love."* We love you, St. Paul.

Augustine, Saint, Sinner & Son

"Our heart is restless until it rests in You."

When we speak of Saints, not meaning to be disrespectful, we sometimes say, they were *sinners*[1] who became *Saints*. If there is one, the world knows most for that distinction, it would have to be Saint Augustine. But he is so much more.

We talk of *touchability* and we think of this Saint. If we're not careful, we ignore his *strength*, and become comfortable in his *weakness*. We speak of conversion, and he comes right to the forefront of our minds. It's so *reassuring*; St. Augustine had 30 years to *reform* his life. We like that idea; convert me, Lord, but can You wait 'till *tomorrow*!

But as we travel deeper into his life, we discover not only the son Augustine, we encounter the *Saint of Prayer*, that relentless petitioner, his mother Monica. *He* led her to *her* sanctification, as *she* led *him* to his. This is a story of a priest and his mother. It's a story of *love*, powerful, unconditional, untiring love. It's not too popular a story, in our present age, because: number one, it's *true*; number two, it's about *hope*; number three it's about *faithfulness*; number four, it's about *conversion*; number five, it's about *love* and a mother's love, at that. This all adds up to that very unpopular message of the Gospel. But I think, it's *time* for

---

[1]"If we say, 'We are free of the guilt of sin,' we deceive ourselves; the truth is not to be found in us." (1John 1:8)

Left:
*Saint Augustine
is the
Saint of Prayer,
the prayer
of a relentless
petitioner, his
mother Monica.
This is a story of
love,
powerful,
unconditional,
untiring love,
between a priest
and his mother.*

Right:
*Monica started
Augustine's education
even before he was born,
consecrating him to God
and to His service.
Monica tells her son,
"Tolle Lege,"
which translates,
"Take and read."*

the Gospel. It's time for Miracles. It's time for sinners to turn into Saints. It's time for you and me.

"Our heart is restless until it rests in you." This, probably the most quoted statement of St. Augustine's Confessions, speaks clearly of man's struggle on earth and his search for God. We are told, by *Jesus*, the road is narrow; yet, not listening, we insist on taking that *wide* road which is so broad, we do not notice when we veer off.

God wastes nothing. As He is creating us, He is already formulating a plan, *His Dream* for us. Everything He places in us, every precious ingredient, including that most precious of all, *free will*, is a preparation for our complete life with Him in Heaven. Those of us who are parents remember our joy, as we planned, before our babies were born, the hopes and the dreams we had of what they would be like; what course they would take; what kind of life they would lead. We hold our breath until they are born, *praying*. When we see these little ones, for the first time, we just know they have to be the most perfect (outside of Jesus and Mary), ever born.

We hear the words, *"He delighted in His creation. He was well pleased. It was good."* Do we ever think how *He*, our God, feels, when we throw the gift of ourselves, He so carefully fashioned, back to Him, discarding His creation for the *plastic* substitute the world offers? Thank God, He has *generously* given us a Heavenly Mother, and an earthly mother like St. Monica, who *beg* Him for mercy for us, for just a little more time.

When we wrote of Mother Mary and *her many faces*[2], we called it a love story, a story of a Mother of unconditional love, who, over the centuries, has been intermediary between us and Her Son, and Her Son and us. *Parents*, as you read this chapter, bring your children, as St. Monica did before

---

[2]The Many Faces of Mary, a Love Story - Bob and Penny Lord 1987

you, to the foot of the Altar. *Children*, read this chapter as your very own. You may find yourself within the pages of this Saint, sinner, and son, Augustine.

†

Augustine and his childhood

On the 13th of November, 354 A.D., a child was born to a *pagan* father, Patricius, and a *Christian* mother, Monica, in Tagaste, North Africa. He was not very strong; most books, including his *Confessions* describe him as *puny*. He needed the additional milk of the slave women, never having enough. He grew up in the women's quarters, and at an early age, learned how to get what he wanted; and what he *wanted* was usually that which pleased his senses. As an infant, he soon discovered when to *smile* and when to cry. The infant grew into the boy and then the man later using *anger* to barrel his way through life and the stormy society into which he had been born.

Monica tried to rear her son, carefully. He was plainly the favorite, of her three children, even though he had inherited much of the self-will and violent temper of his father. From his earliest years, he had a haunting, gnawing, seeking of something or someone, that was to lead him into pain and questioning for most of his life. He wanted to *understand* everything, no matter what the cost.

His mother was born of generations of Christians. Although her husband was much older than Monica, she was *stronger*, especially in her Christian beliefs and practices. She looked upon their union as *Holy* and Sacramental, which very often became a thorn in her husband's side. As she was extremely beautiful; her *Holiness* and her husband's lustful desire of her were not compatible. How she tried to convert him, but to no avail! All her fasting, abstinence and religious observances did not help to draw him to the Church, either. Rather, it annoyed him; he wanted her all for himself! Out of love for her, he did, however, allow all their children's names to be inscribed among the *catechumens*.

St. Augustine's education started before he was born, St. Monica consecrating him to God and to His service. He wrote, *"he tasted the salt of God within his mother's womb."*

When Augustine was eight or nine years old, he became gravely ill, close to death. He asked to be baptized; but he soon recovered, and he set it aside. It was the accepted custom of the time, to wait until the *threat* of death before baptizing. They believed there were so many temptations for a child to succumb to, it would be *better* if he were an ignorant *catechumen* sinning, rather than a Baptized Christian whose sins would be more serious. St. Augustine, in company with other Fathers of the Church of his time, would help to eradicate this error from the Church.

School was a painful experience for Augustine

Augustine never forgot the cruel and unrelenting *dehumanization* to which he and the other children were subjected, at school. He received no sympathy, not even from his parents, as he complained of the constant, brutal beatings he received from his teachers, when he refused to read, write or study his lessons. His mother, who almost *idolized* him, laughed along with his father, accepting this treatment as normal. As a little boy, he preferred to play and talk idly in class. He was later to criticize those who had punished him, those *"men who did the same things themselves."* In his books, he *condemned* Roman Education; it had hit an even greater *low*, as it adopted the harsher customs of Africa. He wrote in his book, *City of God*:

"Who would not shrink back in horror and choose death, if he were given the choice between death and his childhood all over again."

Carrying the scars of humiliation, the rest of his life, he feared the disapproval of others. Augustine excelled in school, but because of his even greater fear of *ignorance*, he was never quite satisfied with himself. He absorbed Latin like a sponge. Having a good memory, he needed only to *hear* something, to retain what he heard. He became drawn to the theater, and developed the art of speaking eloquently. *This, God would use later for His Service.* Instead of using these gifts, he was *inattentive* in class, displayed a surly attitude and engaged in, often leading others in, the most horrendous escapades. In spite of this, when Augustine reached fourteen, his teacher recognized his superior intelligence and recommended he go on with his studies in the *humanities*.

His parents were overjoyed and proud. The only problem was money! Although very successful, his father Patricius, was having a bad year. His *false* god, of politics and money, was letting him, and others of his class, down. He could be called by many names, but above all, he was a good father. So, making huge sacrifices, he sent Augustine to a school in Madaura, where he could continue his studies.

Having reached the age of fifteen, he turned his appetite, from childish game-playing, to the *serious* business of reading the works of Homer, Virgil, Cicero and Ovid. He was not aware *why* he preferred Virgil, at first. Augustine later discovered, what had most attracted him, was the stormy, turbulent side of human love, this poet aroused in him. He wept, as he read the writings again and again, becoming intoxicated by the passionate scenes so vividly painted by the pagan poets. He wrote,

"My one desire in those days was to love and be loved."

Although outwardly very proper, inside Augustine, there was a war being waged. *Feelings* aroused by the pagan poets, filled his mind and soul with lustful desires. This slipped by Monica and Patricius, as Augustine, more and more, stood out amongst his fellow students, lunging way ahead of them scholastically. His father and mother were so pleased with him, they decided it was time to send him to Carthage, to attend schools where he could *further* his studies, in keeping with his abilities.

But, instead, because of money again, they would have to call him back home from Madaura. Augustine idled away a year at home, until they could *afford* to send him to Carthage. Skillfully hiding the torment inside him, even from his mother, he followed the path of *fulfillment through sin*. It not only did *not* provide the satisfaction or love he sought, but *added* to the depression that bound him into knots.

Even though she was not aware, what was going on inside her son, Monica would be responsible for his salvation. Was it the early training, she had imparted to him of the Faith? Was it that *longing* that burns in our hearts and minds and never lets go of us. Was it that *Truth* that always brings us back to our Mother Church? Or was it, Monica, true mother, possibly *without* realizing the danger her son was in, nevertheless prayed unceasingly for him and for his future? He *did* start to go back to church with his mother. He cried out for help, even asking *God* for the strength to lead a more virtuous life. His prayer went,

"...*Grant me chastity and continence (abstinence), but not yet!*"

Augustine sunk lower and lower, sin not only infecting him, but permeating his entire being. Monica began to discern the evil that was taking over in her son's life. She prayed! His *father*, now a catechumen on the way to becoming baptized, recognized the signs. These were the carnal desires he, too, had known. He thought of the perfect solution: marry him off!

Monica, not content to cry and worry, reached out to her son and asked him, outright, what his problem was. She spoke calmly, but compassionately, trying to get Augustine to confide in her. She warned him of the danger he was putting himself into, but all to no avail. *What did she know? She was a woman; what did she know of men's concerns, no less needs. Besides, he was so advanced intellectually, so beyond her understanding.* Later he spoke of this *woman* talk:

"*You were speaking to me through her, my God, and in ignoring her, I was ignoring You!*"

Are you ever tempted to say *nothing* to your children, judging they're not listening? If you do not speak, as Monica before you *did*, where will that voice come from, that wisdom, for them to remember? As with Augustine, will they, in time, hear and say "*yes*?" It couldn't have been easy for Monica, as her advice created a rift, a heart-break only a mother, estranged from her son, knows.

Augustine leaves for Carthage, city of pleasure and pride

Having saved the necessary funds to send him to Carthage, to further his education, his father was as pleased as any father could be. His *mother*, knowing she could do nothing to stop him, *redoubled* her prayers for her son. Augustine was sixteen years old.

Here, from a small town, we have a young man filled with young man desires, embarking to a large city of lustful men, with *grown men* cravings. Quite lost and unsure of himself, not as violent and vulgar as his new-found friends, he became more and more timid. The only thing that saved him was his desire to excel in his studies, and excel he did. He became a leader in the School of Rhetoric, and so the evil of *pride* forestalled, to a degree, the needs of the *flesh*.

He said: "*I was not yet in love, but I was in love with love, and from the depth of my need...I sought some object to love, since I was in love with loving.*"

The *mature man* could later see, it was *He*, for Whom Augustine was searching, the Living God, the Eternal Lover. But the *young* man sought and found the carnal love he craved. He had an affair! He was barely eighteen years old, when he became a *father*. So, here is Augustine, torn between his love for the woman and his baby, and the education he desired.

Augustine and Heresy

After her husband's death, through the generosity of a benefactor, St. Monica was able to join Augustine in Carthage. She came to encourage him with his studies. From his *Confessions*, we learn how she felt about education. St. Augustine relates, his father pushed him to study out of worldly ambition, but his mother looked to his studies to bring him back to God. She knew, although "*a little knowledge leads one away from God, much knowledge brings one back to God.*"

A book was to open his heart and mind to God. That book was *Cicero's Hortensius*. It changed the direction he had been taking; turning his prayers to God, it gave him a new purpose in life. He said, "*I was looking for an author and I found a man.*" Little did he know, at the time, the man he was on the road to discovering was the God-Man Jesus. It is heartwarming, when we read that even the learned Doctors and early Fathers of the Church did not know, half the time, what God had planned for them.

How did Hortensius touch Augustine? I dare say, differently than others who had read Cicero. You see, Augustine read with a soul that had been nurtured, as a child, by the Christian teaching of his mother. Although he found this book more exciting than anything he had ever read, something was lacking! His mother's words had not fallen on deaf ears; he longed for something more..."*the Name of Christ was not there!*"

Monica was elated. If a man's book could so transform him, what could the Word of God do! Augustine began to read Holy Scripture. But contrary to Monica's hopes and prayers, it did not lead him back to the Church. He found them too simple for his great mind:

"*...they seemed to me unworthy to be compared with
the majesty of Cicero. My conceit was repelled by their
simplicity, and I had not the mind to penetrate into their
depths. They were indeed of a nature to grow in your
little ones. But I could not bear to be a little one; I was
only swollen with pride, but to myself I seemed a great
man.*"

Later, another explanation he had was, as he was in sin,
his sinful life closed his mind to what the Sacred Scriptures
were saying, "*Since my heart was not pure, I could not
penetrate their meaning.*"

Monica continued to pray for her son to accept the gift
of faith, but she was to continue this prayer for twelve more
years, before she would realize her dream.

Augustine was born into a time of schism and heresy

His pride not allowing him to walk in the simple Truth,
Augustine was to grope through the darkness for answers to
questions he did not know. In his chase, he embraced one of
the more deadly heresies, that of the *Manichaeans*[3]. He was
not to find his way out of that *black hole* for *nine years*.

Monica prayed and cried while her son tried to sway her
in *his* direction. Although, Augustine says his mother never
weakened, I wonder if he ever knew her *pain*; she so wanted
to be in agreement with her beloved, precious son. What did
she feel as Christ's words came crashing in on her?

"*Whoever loves father or mother, son or daughter, more
than Me is not worthy of Me!*" (Matthew 10:37)

---

[3]The Manichaean doctrine, named after Manes, a heretic born in
Babylon around 276 A.D., would be revived in 13th century France
under a new name, Albigensianism. It was based on only two
principles, Good and Evil, that Satan is no less eternal than God, and
he is God's rival. Proposing His imitator was almost His *equal*! Our
world is divided between good and evil, and our very nature is the
battlefield between good and evil, between God and Satan. We are not
responsible for this conflict within us and we are powerless to control it.

St. Monica had a dream! St. Augustine writes,

"In her dream she saw herself standing on a wooden rule and a youth all radiant coming to her cheerful and smiling upon her, whereas she was grieving and heavy with her grief. He asked her - not to learn from her but, as is the way of visions, to teach her - the causes of her sorrow and the tears she daily shed. She replied she was mourning for the loss of my soul. He commanded her to be at peace and told her to observe carefully and she would see that where she was, there was I also. She looked and saw me standing alongside her on the same rule."[4]

Monica went directly to Augustine. She had *new* hope and determination. She interpreted her dream for him, confident he would understand, it meant he was called to return to the Catholic Church. He countered with: it *clearly* meant she would join him as a *Manichaean*. Standing toe to toe with this brilliant son of hers, she answered, never wavering for a minute,

"No. For it was not said to me where he is, you are, but where you are, he is."

It was obvious that Augustine was deeply moved by his mother's dream, but he wasn't ready to surrender, especially to this *simple* Faith, this *woman's* Faith.

How heavy was Monica's cross as she saw her son, now, not even attending church with her. She stood by, helplessly, for the next nine years, as he became swallowed up by the false teachings and promises of that dangerous sect of the Manichaeans. I am sure it took all the faith she had, to *believe* he would come back, and more to *live* that belief. And so, she prayed!

When she faltered, judging she needed more than prayer, she went to a Bishop. He told her, her son was too

---

[4]*Confessions*, Book Three, XI, p.55

blinded and deafened, by the attention he was receiving from the heretics, to listen to him or anyone else. But, trying to console her, he advised her not to dismay, as St. Augustine's questions were already stumping some of the heads of the heresy. Did that satisfy Augustine's mother? Here we have the persistent woman of the Bible, only now her name is Monica, crying, pleading for the Bishop to do *something*! Trying to remain patient, he insisted,

"Go your way; as sure as you live, it is impossible that the son of these tears should perish."

His mother accepted the Bishop's words as those from Heaven, itself, and she had peace, *momentarily*. Augustine's pride kept blocking him from admitting his mother was right. With the Manichaean sect, he could have his cake and eat it, too. They assured him he could lead a life of sin, yet still be saved through the merits of those *elect*, who lived a life of abstinence and total chastity.

From ages nineteen to twenty-eight, Augustine was to walk farther and farther away from the Truth. But he would not walk alone! With his gift of persuasion, he would lead many others away, as well. But, the Lord always sends another messenger. He would not listen to his mother, well how about his dear and trusted friend and disciple, whose name Augustine never gives us!

This young man had been deceived, along with Augustine, into believing the lies of Manichaeanism. He had, like many of his class, been fooled by their outward appearances of piety and virtue. As Augustine made long and faithful friendships, one of the difficulties he had, rejecting Manichaeanism, was facing the many friends he had enlisted to join. One of these was this young man, who never left his side.

When Augustine returned to Tagaste from Carthage, his friend accompanied him. The young friend suddenly came down with a high fever which had him more dead than alive. Augustine never left his friend. Now, like Augustine, he   had been enrolled in the register of catechumens, since infancy, but never baptized. It was understood he would be baptized upon the threat of death. That threat was here, and his friend was being baptized! Augustine looked on with skepticism bordering on contempt, as he saw, what he judged, *meaningless* drops of water being poured on his friend's feverish head. Surely, if he recovered, his friend would not believe this *old wives' tale.* But, he was wrong!

His friend recovered. As soon as Augustine had an opportunity to talk to his friend, he began to ridicule the *Baptism.* He stopped as quickly as he had begun. To his amazement, his friend looked at him with the disdain he would have for a mortal enemy, as if he no longer knew him. To quote Augustine,

"...in a burst of independence that startled me, (he) warned me that if I wished to continue our friendship I must cease that kind of talk."

Augustine was silent for possibly the *first* time in his life. He would *wait* until his friend was completely well; then, he would talk some sense into him. The only problem, his friend suddenly took a turn for the worse and *died.* Augustine was beyond consolation. He had lost a dear friend. No one and nothing could take his place. There was no consolation that could erase the pain; and so he grieved. Every one he saw reminded him his friend was dead. Why were *they* alive? Why was *he* alive and his friend dead? Augustine later wrote, he and his friend had "*one soul in two bodies.*" *Now*, how could he live half a person? He hated all living things; he *despised* the very light which made his darkness so much darker.

With no one *on earth* he could turn to, with no one *Above*, he would turn to, he was on the edge of despair. Although his mother knew Carthage was a city of sin and wholesale vice, she knew he could not remain in Tagaste with all his memories. So, she sent him off to Carthage. This she did, praying his opening a school of Rhetoric would take his mind and heart off the loss of his friend.

Augustine thirsts for the truth

In addition to the power of his mother's thirty years of prayers, an instrument God used to save Augustine's soul, was his *thirst for the truth*. What the Manichaeans taught him, no longer satisfied him. He was having a problem with their evasiveness as he dug deeper, searching for answers. Augustine had been so in love with the *beauty* of the word, he had not gone beyond to the *meaning* behind the word.

Here He goes again; our Faithful God comes to the rescue of His unfaithful, stubborn son. Enter Helpidius, a respected speaker, who just *happened* to be lecturing publicly, *in* Carthage, *when* Augustine was there. Always hungering to hear more Rhetoric so he could pass it on to his students, Augustine hung on to Helpidius' every word. Augustine knew very little about the Bible, having judged it too simple for his *great mind.* But suddenly, with his new awareness, of the emptiness and danger of beautiful words without meaning, he began to wonder if *Scripture* might have the key to the truth he was so desperately seeking. A light appeared to be breaking through. Scripture was coming alive! Although he was not aware of it, through this man, Helpidius, Augustine was being taught *Catholic doctrine.*

As Helpidius showed how Manichaeanism was in direct *conflict* with the New and Old Testaments, Augustine became less and less sure of the beliefs he had so vigorously proselytized. The lecturer was punching holes into Manichaeanism, exposing all its *contradictory* teachings. Having zealously embraced and spread *Manichaeanism,* Augustine was reluctant to publicly denounce it. Was the old monster of *pride* possibly telling him, he would most certainly lose much of the authority he held amongst *his* followers? In any event, the Manichaean bishop Faustus, whom they had *promised* would answer all Augustine's questions, would soon be arriving. And, since he knew all answers to all questions, he would surely put Augustine's mind to rest.

At first, Augustine was excited by Faustus. He was a fine man. He was modest. He behaved in a dignified manner. He was an eloquent orator. Years later, when comparing him with St. Ambrose, Augustine said,

"I was delighted with the sweetness of Ambrose's discourses. But even though they were sounder and more learned, they did not have the charm or power of those given by Faustus."

After having waited *nine years*, Augustine found that although Faustus spoke more eloquently than his predecessors, he was saying nothing new! Augustine became impatient as his hero lectured. He wanted to interrupt him. He needed answers to his many *unanswered* questions of the last nine years. But, as this was not the custom when the *great one* preached, Augustine requested a private audience with him.

Augustine was granted his audience. Monica had returned to Carthage to be near her son. Sensing the immense power this man had, and the danger he posed to Augustine's soul, she *prayed*. The big day came; Augustine arrived with his eager friends and followers. Now, they would have all their doubts answered! Augustine discovered very quickly, Faustus was not even a philosopher. Although he had an aptitude for *Rhetoric*, practicing it all the time, his words had no substance behind them. But still, Augustine would not give up. He was a little upset at the outcome of his first meeting, but there was always *the next time*. The next time and the next time came and went. Finally, Augustine had to admit, Faustus knew no more than his followers; and if he, who was so exalted among his followers, could not tell him anything, no one else could.   Later, Augustine spoke of this time:

> *"For Your Hand, O my God, in the secret of Your providence did not desert my soul; from the blood of my mother's heart, sacrifice for me was offered You day and night by her tears, and You did act with me in marvelous ways. For it was You, my God, who did it."*

Augustine goes to Rome

Disillusioned by Faustus and the heresy he had embraced, and upset by his students, whom he found more and more unreceptive and disruptive, Augustine planned to leave for Rome. The reason *he* was setting out for Rome, *he thought*, was, he would be more successful there, but God had other plans.

At first, Monica was very unhappy that her son was leaving for Rome; but then, when she saw she could not dissuade him, she decided she would go with him. Loving his mother, but unequivocally opposed to her accompanying him, Augustine lied to her; he told her the boat would leave the following day. When his mother arrived at the shore, and saw the boat had left, without her, she was beside herself. She had prayed to God, pleading with Him to keep her son from leaving. He let her down; was she upset! It was in *Italy* that Augustine would be converted, and her prayers answered. But Monica, like Martha (John 11:21), could not, at that moment in time, see her son rising from the death of his former life, and so she was angry with God.

Augustine spent a year completely oblivious of *Catholic* Rome. He spent most his time with his Manichaean friends. He discovered they were as dishonorable and deceitful as they claimed to be virtuous and honest. Rather than turn to St. Jerome, who could have answered and dispelled his many doubts, he held on to his deep-seated prejudice against the Catholic Church and turned to the Academics.   These

Academics or Agnostics were dissidents, decadent disciples of an Academy founded by Plato seven hundred years earlier. Their philosophy was that *truth* was *beyond* human intellect; nothing can be known with absolute certainty. Therefore, permanent doubt was the wisest course to take.

Hard as he tried to bury himself, teaching his students, his persistent *doubts* were eating at him. Man has a *need* for truth. Without this, the emptiness becomes unbearable and if not satisfied, leads to *death*. Augustine became so depressed, he lost all desire to live. But, not even this would lead him to be baptized! Here he was, in Rome, all alone, at the point of death, and he was dying without a priest, without Christ, without God. There was Monica, back in Africa, praying passionately, sensing, with her *motherly* instinct, the new and maybe, *final* danger her son was in.

Augustine, having doubted God, now doubted man. His friends, the Manichaeans and his new-found friends, the Academics had betrayed him; their *talking in circles* tired him. Their worldly attempts to explain the unexplainable, did not satisfy the gnawing questioning inside of him. The peace and acceptance he had expected from his students, in Rome, was not forthcoming; rather they proved more disappointing than those he had left in Africa.

Augustine learned of a chair of Rhetoric open in Milan. The prefect of Rome, who had final word over his acceptance or rejection, was a *pagan*. Augustine would need the *Manichaeans* to recommend him. And they did! *God*, with *His* incomparable sense of humor, used a *pagan* cult through a *pagan* authority to bring Augustine to the *Holy* Catholic Church. Why not? After all, God created all of us, Saints and sinners. Maybe this was *His* Merciful Way to forgive them, in part, for all the *innocent*, they had led astray through their errors.

St. Augustine meets St. Ambrose and all Heaven rejoices

St. Ambrose was the Bishop that would lead the stubborn, prideful Augustine to the Church. Why did God allow St. Augustine the luxury of so much pain and near death to body and soul? We believe, in our Ministry, that God works most powerfully and authoritatively, through our mistakes and our pain. There is something, like with St. Augustine, that speaks louder than even the words, when we speak from our own falling and rising and falling again, the *living* words being, *"Well, here I am, by the Grace of God."*

St. Ambrose was born a Roman in 334 A.D. and died April 4, 397. When Augustine met St. Ambrose, he was about fifty years old and had been a Bishop over ten years. They had more than a little in common. Although born of a Christian family, St. Ambrose, too, had not been baptized at birth. Having lost his father, young, he, like Augustine, was most influenced by his mother.

At thirty-five years of age, St. Ambrose was asked to become Bishop. He declined, at first, objecting he had not, as yet, been *baptized*. Within one week's time, he received the Sacraments of Baptism, Penance, First Holy Communion, Confirmation *and* Ordination.

This is the man who was to bring the treasure of Augustine into Christ's Church. It appears, *Augustine is always in the midst of turmoil*, either by his will, life's circumstance, or God's design. And so, here he was in Milan. It was being torn apart by dissensions between Catholics and *Arians*. Surprise you? Arianism[5] had been

---

[5]Arianism-a schism unleashed by Arius, a priest from Alexander, maintained that Christ was not equal "*in substance*" to God, but was the "*creature*" of the Father. Arius was asked by his Bishop to retract this heretical statement; he refused and was excommunicated. The first Ecumenical Council that met at Nicea, on June 19, 325, proclaimed that Christ was *consubstantial* (being of one and the same substance, as

gaining a foothold in the East and had spread to Milan. *Bishop* Ambrose had the difficult and unpopular mission of maintaining unity within the Church and peace in the city, and all this, without *compromising* the Faith.

Augustine first went to hear St. Ambrose preach because he thought he could absorb some of the renowned man's gifts of Rhetoric. St. Augustine writes,

"Yet along with the words, which I admired, there also came into my mind the subject-matter, to which I attached no importance. I could not separate them. And while I was opening my heart to learn how eloquently he spoke, I came to feel, though only gradually, how truly he spoke."[6]

A glimmer of *hope* cut through the clouds in Augustine's mind, as Ambrose's preaching began to dispel some of the doubts that had plagued him. He began to find the Catholic Faith *understandable*, plausible, simple for the ordinary man, yet not *too* simple for the *intelligent* man. This was an important step in his walk toward the Father. Others would follow, but like a baby taking his first steps, it would not be *easy* for Augustine. Wanting to do it his own way, he would continue to lose his balance and fall, until he accepted the guiding hand of his *Mother* Church.

The word *Mother* was not just a word to Augustine. He loved his mother with the fervor with which he loved life. So, when he finally gave his heart to this *Mother* Church, it was with this same ardor. Unlike the picture we may have of him, Augustine could *never* be considered a cold, intellectual, *way above our heads*, Saint. Augustine passionately loved and sought the truth, even before he recognized the truth he longed for, was *the Truth*, was God.

---

the three Divine Persons of the Trinity are of one substance) with God the Father. Thus Arianism was condemned.

[6]*Confessions*, Book Five

Augustine decided he would return to Church, only as a catechumen (as he had been as a child), until he was *enlightened* to do otherwise. As a catechumen, he was required to leave after the Liturgy of the Word. It didn't seem to bother him. Not knowing *Who* he was missing, he did not hunger for more. *Or* did he know, in his heart of hearts, that once he knew the Lord in the Eucharist, he would be helplessly in love! As he departed from the church, he could not wait to return the next day, to hear Scripture and the Bishop's homily. He found himself more and more excited by what he was learning. This would have to suffice, for now. God would use this to draw him to Him. If this is what would color Augustine's decision to continue attending Mass, well, God was not past wooing him that way.

Monica joins Augustine in Milan

It is most likely that *St. Augustine* called his mother to join him in Milan. Whatever the case, we know she left Tagaste, probably departing from Carthage in the year 385 A.D. Did all the fallen angels, in their fury, attack the ship, knowing the part Monica was playing in Augustine's life? Didn't they know the power was in her *prayers*, more than in her *physical* presence? Nevertheless, as they crossed the ocean, the sea became violent; the ship tossed and pitched from side to side. Even the most seasoned sailors *knew* they were going to perish. Monica never gave up hope, trusting in the word the Bishop had given her, *she would see her son a Catholic before she died.* That was enough for her!

The storm over, Monica stepped on Italian soil, and into her beloved son's open arms. Did Augustine try to hide the delight and need he had for his mother? We believe they hugged and cried, their special love surpassing language. As they walked away from the shore, Augustine excitedly shared what he knew Monica wanted to hear most:

he was a *practicing* catechumen and no longer part of the *Manichaeans*.

To his bewilderment, that did not surprise *or* satisfy her. Monica wanted him to be a *part* of the Church, Baptized and Confirmed; nothing but him being a professed member of the Mystical Body of Christ would satisfy her. Her hopes and expectations, the extent of her prayers for him were, he would marry within the Church. Little did she envision or suspect, for one moment, he would, one day, be consecrated to the Lord as a *Priest*.

Monica did not stop with the bone her son handed her; she went to see Bishop Ambrose. He listened kindly and attentively to this holy mother. He could see how very much she loved her son. Strengthened by his kindness, she expressed concern that the Bishop was doing little, *personally*, to encourage Augustine to be baptized. We wouldn't be surprised if she told him, *respectfully*, that when Augustine came to see him, eager to unburden his soul, Ambrose appeared to be indifferent. Was he ignoring him, never once looking up from what he was reading? Both Monica and Augustine recognized Ambrose's Holiness. She was not really questioning his actions. Monica was trying to move mountains! But, she was also trying to be obedient to the Will of God. So, she prayed!

Ambrose probably told the mother, it was not enough for Augustine to accept the Faith *intellectually*, with his head; he must *live* the Faith, with his heart. As Augustine was *living* with a companion, outside the Sacrament of Matrimony, this did not appear feasible. You never discover, from Augustine's writings, the *earthly* reason he could not take this girl, he loved and lived with for many years, as his wife. But he could not!

Augustine and the girl loved one another. They had been faithful to one another for fifteen years; but without the blessing of Almighty God, it was hopeless from the beginning. Their happiness was *overcast* by torment, the agony of trying to build a house without a foundation. Christ, the Cornerstone was *missing* in their relationship. Instead, their bedfellows were the fallen angels of jealousy, suspicion, fear, anger, and dissension. They were not bad people, only victims of the world and its lies.

The young woman had given Augustine a son. Years later, as he grieved over the death of this son, he called him, *"the son of my sin;"* but the young father, puffed up with pride, called his son *Adeodatus, "God-given."*

The young mother left Augustine and their son, after he converted, although she loved them very deeply. Following her lover's example, she, too, had *convert*ed. She joined a convent and spent the rest of her life loving and being loved by her one and only True God. Had *He* been looking after her, brushing off her knees, as He had Mary Magdalene, telling her she was beautiful and needed to sin no more?

Putting two and two together, reasoning *that* had been why Ambrose had hesitated to talk to her son, Monica prayed to God, only now, in thanksgiving, and *planned*. Knowing Augustine was not disposed to the life of a *celibate*, Monica set out to find a *suitable* wife for him. The young wife-to-be, chosen, was too young, and they had to wait two years to marry. Augustine missed his former companion. As he had in no way renounced his desires of the flesh, he took to himself *another* mistress. There was no mutual love between the two, and so they quickly tired of one another. He sent her packing.

(Author's note: After much pain in his life, brother Joseph said that he only found peace, after he accepted the Lord's plan for him, as a celibate! He shared, *"When God wants you, you will never have the gift of the right woman to be your mate, for He has chosen you for Himself."*)

Augustine was in the midst of self-made hell, again. He lived as if all that mattered in life was pleasure, and outside of pleasure there was nothing. But there was that rumbling inside of him, that war being waged between all he had learned as a child, and the Sodom and Gomorrah of his adult life.

Plato leads Augustine to the Catholic Faith

No matter where he goes, or what he does, the road to Jesus looms up in front of Augustine; and although he keeps walking the other way, he finds himself right back where he began. Augustine sees signs on the path, those leading directly to the Father, but that's too simple. It can't be right for him. So he follows other signs. Imagine the frustration when he discovers that although he's followed a road that was leading him away, he's *back*, at the door of his mother's Church, *again*.

Again, God is dealing with his son Augustine as He knows he will respond, from a *book*. *Again*, a book from a *pagan* will point Augustine to the *Truth*. Or is it that the Truth *cannot* be hidden, that *all* must reveal *It* even if they try to hide it? For us, the Lord has always been the Revealer, opening our eyes that we might see *good* and detest *evil*. The devil, on the other hand, the concealer, tries to *hide* wrong and *block* good. But, as with St. Augustine, God never gives up, never lets us stray far from His Saving Reach.

Augustine came across the books of Plato, translated by a recent convert to Christianity, Victorinus. What fascinated Augustine about Plato was how he reached beyond the materialism of the world, soaring toward concepts only explainable in the Light of God. Although this philosopher wrote before the days Christ walked the earth, his works pointed Augustine to the doctrine of the *Word*.

When Augustine was nineteen, *Cicero* set his mind and heart on fire. Now, at thirty-two, God was using another philosopher, Plato to call him to Himself. Augustine's problem was the same, always, the war between the spirit and the flesh. As he read Plato, he found he was really presenting the *Word*, in the light of St. John the Evangelist. He was confirming the teachings of the Catholic Church! Are you beginning to suspect that possibly the Faith was so much a part of Augustine, so ingrained, that when he read, he read with the *light* of this Church of his childhood?

He soon fell out of love with Plato, realizing he had been merely the bridge, for him to walk over, to John's Gospel. Nowhere, in Plato's works, did he find the words which burned in Augustine's heart,

"The Word became Flesh and made His dwelling among us." (John 1:14)

Plato, born before the time of the Spotless Lamb Who would save the world, knew and wrote nothing of the fall of man through the sin of Adam and Eve. Missing was God's Plan for our salvation. Nowhere was there, the Incarnation of the Word, God becoming Man, and That Man, our Lord, dying on the Cross, that we might live.

Though Augustine did not understand all these truths, he heard a voice persisting, crying out in the desert of his soul,

"Courage! I am the Food of the strong. And you will eat Me. But it is not I Who shall be changed into you, for you will be changed into Me!"

These words that spoke not to his mind, were received within the deep recesses of his heart. He wrote,

"There was from that moment no ground of doubt in me: I would have doubted my own life than have doubted that truth."

St. Augustine meets himself in St. Paul

St. John spoke to Augustine's heart, calling him to a higher *Love*. He was now ready to turn to the *city boy*, St. Paul. In Paul's letters, Augustine saw how St. Paul laid bare man's inner struggles, that ongoing war being waged inside of everyone of us, that battle between, as St. Paul says,

"What happens is that I do, not the good I will to do, but the evil I do not intend...This means that even though I want to do what is right, a law that leads to wrongdoing is always at hand..."

St. Paul's writings became a fountain from which Augustine would continue to drink the water of Salvation. Through them, he would quench the dryness of his soul. He would, as well, meet *himself* in St. Paul's tears of confession, later writing his own. Nowhere, was St. Augustine to relate, so personally, to his own struggles, discouragements, hopes and failures, that of running the race and seeing no victory, as in St. Paul's writings. He knew, through Paul, he, too, was on the road to Damascus and Jesus was pleading,

"Why do you persecute Me, Augustine?"

Now, the real battle would begin. He knew the Lover and he would never be satisfied with any less. He knew the price he was being asked to pay. Maybe, he wanted to say yes; but did it have to be today? He wrote,

"Come, Lord, work upon us, call us back, set us on fire and clasp us close, be fragrant to us, draw us to Your loveliness: let us love, let us run to You."

But his new self had not beaten his old self and so, as he cried,

"Lord, heal me, but not yet! Soon, but give me just a little while."

St. Ambrose, not only a man of his word but of his life

St. Augustine, in case you have not discovered this, as yet, was a *romanticist*. The Church was in danger. The forces of hell were being waged against her, and she was calling upon our Lord for a Saint. That Saint was, at this time and in this place, St. Ambrose.

Our precious Church was being split in two by schism, and was bleeding. Empress Justine, who once belonged to the Arian sect, demanded that Bishop Ambrose turn the church, attended by Catholics (believed to be the Cathedral of Milan), over to the *Arians*. St. Ambrose *refused*! The Empress sent in *troops* to forcibly take over the Cathedral. She and they were not ready for what they encountered; St. Ambrose was preaching to a church full of worshipers. As some would leave to go home to their families, they were quickly replaced by others.

Tribunes came with a summons for the Bishop to *relinquish* the Church to them. His important reply was a lesson to Augustine and to us,

"If the emperor demanded what belonged to me, even though everything I own belongs to the poor, I would not refuse. But the things of God are not mine. If anyone wants my patrimony (legacy), let him take it! If anyone wants my body, let him seize it! Do you want to put me in chains and lead me to death? I shall obey, and shall not allow my people to defend me. I shall not kiss the altar, begging for life. I prefer to be immolated on the altar."

Nothing shook Ambrose. He sang the Psalms with his people and order was maintained. As Ambrose fought so gallantly for the Church, God was doing battle, as usual, for Augustine.

This profession of faith, by Ambrose, only set Augustine more on fire. He admired and wanted to emulate him in every way, except one, he couldn't handle *celibacy*. His words, "*...only his celibacy seemed to me a heavy burden.*"

Let it be now! Let it be now!

One of Augustine's friends from Africa, Ponticianus, came to visit him, and God called Augustine, one more time. His friend saw a copy of St. Paul's Epistles on Augustine's desk. Surprised but *encouraged*, Ponticianus began to tell Augustine what he had seen in his travels, especially in Egypt. Whereas, Augustine had abandoned the Church of his childhood, Ponticianus had remained faithful to his religious roots.

As a high-ranking officer in the emperor's army, Ponticianus did much travelling, to countries like Gaul (France), Spain, Africa, Egypt and Italy. He shared with Augustine, one of the high points of his journeying was meeting *hermits* in Egypt, who had left the world and its successes, for lives in the desert. These men lived in bare cells, *individually*, separated from all the other hermits. They came together to pray once a week, on Saturdays. So removed from the world and all its comforts, they in spite, or was it because of it, swelled in number from *seven* thousand when their founder died, to *fifty* thousand. Augustine held onto every word his friend spoke, with bated breath. Everything he had read, whether it was Cicero or Plato, was like nothing compared to what his friend was describing.

Augustine wondered why he had never heard of these men before. (Author's note: It reminds of us how many people, after reading our book, "*This is My Body, This is My Blood*," have asked us the same question, over and over again, "Why did we never hear about these Miracles of the Eucharist, before now?") Ponticianus, encouraged by the rapt attention of not only Augustine, but of his friends who had joined them, was not *fully* prepared for the passionate outburst from St. Augustine,

"*What are we aiming at? Have we no higher hopes than to be friends of the Emperor? And what good will that do us? Why not become the friends of God?*"

Was Augustine not asking the age-old questions, "*What have I done with my life? What's it all about? Why are we on this earth?*"

As his friend continued speaking, it was as if Jesus was standing in front of him. Augustine was ashamed; he looked at everything he had thought and done in his life, as petty, selfish and vile. He felt dirty. He was repulsed by the image he saw of himself and his life. He felt naked and he did not like what he saw.

He was so overcome with emotion, he couldn't walk Ponticianus to the gate. Instead Augustine's friend Alypius went with him. As Alypius returned to Augustine, he could hear him crying out,

"The unlearned arise and take Heaven by force, and here we are with all our learning, stuck fast in flesh and blood!"

What Alypius could not hear was the voice, inside Augustine, crying, *"Let it be now! Let it be now!"*

Although Alypius was one of his closest friends and companions, Augustine needed to walk away even from *him*, into the garden, to be by himself. All the voices and temptations from the past, began raging! But then, through God's Mercy, they dimmed into a murmuring, almost a distant humming in his ears. A procession of Powerful Men and Women of our Church passed before his soul, as he suffered in the garden. Unlike the Savior, Who was calling him, he was not alone in the garden. As Jesus had the Angel of the Lord, so now He sent the Saints to console Augustine. They challenged and *encouraged* him to walk the path they had travelled before him. The joy and peace he saw in them, began to flood through him, and he felt long awaited tears cleansing him, washing him, purifying him.

Augustine could not stop crying. His crippling guilt was fighting the Lord's open Arms of forgiveness. He could not believe the Lord would forgive his many sins. His words, echoed over the centuries by other sinners adored by the Lord,

"'And You, Lord, how long? How long, Lord; will You be angry forever? Remember not our iniquities[7].' For I felt that I was still bound by them. And I continued my miserable complaining: 'How long, how long shall I go on saying tomorrow and again tomorrow? Why not now, why not have an end to my uncleanness this very hour?'"(Confessions, Book Eight)

As he was praying, a sweet voice, coming as if from a house nearby, repeated over and over again, "*Take and read! Take and read!*"

At first, suspecting some child had seen his misery and was poking fun at him, Augustine stood angrily riveted to the spot, but then he had a thought: *Possibly the Lord wanted him to read Scripture.* Running into the house, he picked up the Epistles of St. Paul and opened it randomly. The words that jumped out at him were:

"Let us live honorably as in daylight, not in carousing and drunkenness, not in sexual excess and lust, not in quarreling and jealousy. Rather, put on the Lord Jesus Christ and make no provision for the desires of the flesh."(Romans 13:13-14)

Good Show, Paul! Augustine didn't read any more. He had no need to; a peace rushed through him, filling him with a warm confidence he had never known before. It was as if he were receiving a Baptism of the Holy Spirit. He felt as new as a baby. He couldn't remember any of his past sins. He ran to the faithful woman in his life, his mother.

Monica, who has become known as the Saint of Persistence, the Saint of Hope, prayed *knowing* her Lord would come through. *Right!* And the Eleventh Hour God did come through, again. Or are we saying the Eleventh Hour God has been, and will continue coming through, for His children, now and forever. Did the expression, *He will*

---

[7]sins

not be outdone in generosity, come from Augustine and Monica? Because when Monica had prayed, little could she have ever realized the *gift* that the Lord would give her. (Author's Note: When I have meditated on my life with Bob, how wonderful it has been all these years, I thank God, He never allowed me to see this before we married. I would have desired life with Bob, so passionately, I would not have allowed the Lord to work; *I* would have tried to make it happen. Or seeing the joy that I would receive some day, my heart would have burst.)

Not one to do things in half measure, Augustine wanted nothing, but I mean *nothing*, but to serve God. Not even the honorable marriage arranged by Monica (and probably Bishop Ambrose), did he desire; this, the man who could not live without a woman! He wanted to live out his life as a hermit! He told his mother,

"It's all decided! I don't want to wait any more! I want only God: O Lord! I am Your servant, the son of your handmaid!"

It was not as easy as all that. In the days of Monica and Augustine, there were several steps that had to be taken before you could be baptized. Baptism or *regeneration*, or second birth, was calling Augustine to take a new course, that he might live a *new life* through the Grace of God and His Sacrament of Baptism.

All that had pleased him before, even his position as teacher of Rhetoric, was like so much nonsense to him in the light of the Lord, his God and the life he knew He had planned for him.

It is believed his conversion took place around August 28th. Forty-four years later, in 430, on August 28th, God would call this valiant warrior home to Him. Augustine no longer lived his life as if he had forever, no less forty-four years, but as if each moment was precious, and *painful* until he was united with his Lord through the Sacraments of His

Church. As catechumens were not baptized before Holy Saturday, he had eight, long months to wait!

Augustine lived the next few months trying to undo much of the harm he had done, the years before his conversion. As he had skillfully led so many of his friends away from the true Church of their childhood, he was now leading them *toward* her. He was given a villa where he and these young men could live a *shared-life* of prayer and contemplation. Monica joined them, not only as Augustine's mother, but as Spiritual mother of all the men, including her own grandson, Adeodatus (son of Augustine).

There were seven in all at Augustine's villa, at Cassicacum. He brought the Scriptures with him, again fashioning his little Community after the hermits of Egypt. The more he read the inspired Word of God, the more he grieved for the past and wanted to do something to help the future. God had prepared him for his vocation as a Spiritual guide and teacher. As he said in his *Confessions*,

> *"All these things I read and was on fire; nor could I find what could be done with those deaf and dead, of whom indeed I had myself been one for I had been a scourge, a blind raging snarler against the Scriptures, which are all honeyed with the honey of Heaven and all luminous with Your Light: and now I was fretting my heart out over the enemies of these same Scriptures. When shall I recall and set down all that belongs to those days in the country?"*

Some of the wisdom he taught the little band of disciples was:

> *"Let us think of God, let us seek Him, let us thirst for Him. He is the interior sun that shines within us...We shall be so* (wise or happy) *only when we know fully with both our minds and hearts: the Father who gives Truth; the Son Who is this Truth; and the Holy Spirit,*

through Whom we are joined to the Truth. These Three are seen as One by enlightened souls."

The Baptism of Augustine and his followers

The prayers of *mourning* that groaned out from within his heart, that exploded, throbbing, shaking the very foundation of his soul, were,

> *"Late have I loved You, O Beauty so ancient and so new; late have I loved You!...You were within me, and I outside and in my unloveliness fell upon those lovely things You have made. You were with me and I was not with You. I was kept from You by those things, yet had they not been in You, they would not have been at all. You did call and cry to me and break open my deafness; and You did send forth Your beams and shine upon me and chase away my blindness...I tasted You, and now hunger and thirst for You; You did touch me, and I have burned for Your Peace."*

This was the Augustine who received the healing waters of Baptism. On Holy Saturday, 387, Augustine and his loyal friends bowed before Ambrose. Entering the Baptismal area three times[8], they repeated these ancient words, a *Profession of Faith* that resounds in Heaven every time a new catechumen pledges to live and die by this, the Faith of Jesus Christ. When they entered the first time, they proclaimed: "*I believe in God!*" Upon the second entry, they went on to the Father's Son and declared: "*I believe in Jesus Christ!*" On the third entry, they professed: "*I believe in the Holy Spirit!*"

A weeping Augustine threw himself into the arms of his waiting Mother Church, as his earthly mother, that faithful mother of prayer, looked on. Now, she could die in peace.

Augustine gave up all ties with the world. He no longer desired to teach or pursue any of his former loves. Now,

---

[8]this was the Rite of Baptism, at that time, according to St. Ambrose's treatise *On the Sacraments.*

Left:
On Holy Saturday, 387, Augustine was baptized by St. Ambrose. Entering the Baptismal area, three times, he repeated a Profession of Faith; the first time saying "I believe in God!"; the second time, "I believe in Jesus Christ!"; the third time, "I believe in the Holy Spirit!"

Below:
The death of St. Augustine, surrounded by his followers

where would he and his little band of disciples settle down? It was already agreed they would have Monica for their Spiritual mother, but where? They left Milan for Ostia, a port outside of Rome, to await a ship to Africa. They would go back home, bring *their* newly found Faith to their African brothers and sisters.

God and Monica had a different plan. She was tired; besides, Augustine would no longer need her on earth. Now, she would serve not only him, in the *now*, but sons like him and their mothers, for all time.

In his *Confessions*, possibly the most poignant and revealing entries of Augustine are the following:

"When the day was approaching which she was to depart this life - a day that You knew though we did not - it came about, as I believe by Your secret arrangement, that she and I stood alone leaning in a window, which looked inwards to the garden within the house where I was staying, at Ostia on the Tiber; for there we were away from everybody, resting for the sea voyage from the weariness of our long journey by land. There we talked together, she and I alone, in deep joy; and forgetting the things that were behind and looking forward to those that were before, we were discussing in the Truth, which You are, what the eternal life of the Saints could be like, 'which eye has not seen nor ear heard, nor has it entered into the heart of man. '"

They finished contemplating on the Grace, which comes to us from *Above*, counting all else, worthless. She gently began speaking to her son of her departure, *without* him. She said,

"Son, for my own part I no longer find joy in anything in this world. What I am still to do here and why I am here I know not, now that I no longer hope for anything from this world. One thing there was, for which I desired to remain a little longer in this life, that I should

see you a Catholic Christian before I died. This God has granted me in superabundance, in that I now see you His servant to the contempt of all worldly happiness."

Her job on earth done, Monica was free to go to the Lord and Savior she had longed for, all her life. Her body, they said, just gave out, as she commended her spirit to Jesus. Monica died, a few days after her talk with her son. She was fifty-six years old and Augustine thirty-three. Everyone was in a state of shock, especially Augustine. As his holy mother went on to eternal life, new life was beginning for her son. But at the moment of separation, we are not thinking of what the Lord has *ahead*, but of *what* has happened, and *who* has passed on. Was Augustine thinking of all the suffering Monica had endured; and now that he was converted, she would not be there to enjoy it?

When we were *finally* healed from the death of our son, we realized that our *love*, that love that parents have for a child and a child has for them, will never die. It transcends all time and space.

At this time, in his dark night of the soul, all Augustine could feel was *his* loss. He and his son grieved, separately. Before they took her away, Adeodatus flung himself on his grandmother's lifeless body. If he could only keep her *here*. He kissed her for the last time. Little did the grieving boy, *and* his father, know, he would soon *follow* his grandmother and together they would *live* eternally joyful, with Jesus in the Kingdom.

Augustine fought back the tears, as they lowered his mother's body into the ground. He had to be strong for his son, and the others, to whom she had become a mother. But when he returned to the emptiness of the house without her, he broke down and wept uncontrollably.

Although surrounded by loved ones to console him, Augustine was quite alone. It was his turn to weep for the mother who had wept for *him* thirty of her fifty-six years. At first, the *enemy* of guilt and recrimination attacked him, playing mercilessly with his head and heart; but *the serpent* was no match for Monica's love which would *not* be buried. That mother's love and prayers, that had moved the Lord's Heart so many times to forgive her son, would not allow Augustine, with so much to do, to linger and bathe in a pool of tears.

But that would not be the end of the dark night for Augustine. Adeodatus had been baptized with his father. Augustine was so proud of him. He could see the unique wisdom his son already had, of God and His Plan, a knowledge far beyond his years. Augustine *knew* his son would be an instrument to bring many to the Kingdom; what he didn't know was, it was not to be on *earth*. Shortly after his baptism, Adeodatus died. He was about sixteen years old. When Augustine wrote later, of his son, he said,

"You took him early from this earth, and I think of him utterly without anxiety, for there is nothing in his boyhood or youth or anywhere in him to cause me fear."

It is true, Augustine received extraordinary Grace from God. But do not, for one moment, judge he did not grieve. Augustine had lost his mother, his son and his dearest friends; he would miss them the rest of his life. But God had no more time for Augustine to indulge in self-pity and self-recrimination! Augustine had punished himself enough for all the foolish mistakes he had made. *Now*, it was time for God to use him and his repentance to lead sinners, like himself, to the Church. Then, like *now*, in our days, the times were so urgent, the *now* had to be what was important. No time to look back, no time to look forward, only *time to live the now*.

St. Augustine went on to Africa to become Bishop of Hippo. He would write books out of a hunger to right the wrongs of the heresies and lies he had once advocated.

These books written with the love and the passion of a repentant and mourning sinner, would be quoted over the centuries, by most not even knowing from where they had come. These books, *which had to be written*, would someday help other chosen in their response to the Father. They would be used by the Mother who had called and waited so patiently for him, Mother Church. And because of them she would raise him to the honor of Doctor of the Church.

This great man, who is most quoted, most respected, most followed, never stopped being a son, speaking and writing of his mother, even thirty years after she had gone to join her husband and her Jesus in Heaven. We tried to share, in this chapter, some of the *touchable* parts of St. Augustine's life. Little did we expect it would be so very much the telling over and over again, of the undying, unconditional, hope-filled love of a mother for her son, and a son for his mother.

In this world, of little hope and less help, mothers cry and worry over their children. Children grow up too soon and are *lied* away from their mother's love, or so they think! Our grandson once said, *"Jesus cannot resist a mother's prayers."* And then, for us grandmothers, one day, he said, *"Even stronger than the pull a mother has with Jesus, is that of a grandmother."* Mothers and grandmothers, we have power. And that power is in prayer!

Bring your sons and daughters, maybe your husbands or brothers, up to the foot of the altar as Monica did. All she asked of her son, as she was dying, was that he *remember* her at the foot of the altar. Little did she suspect, Augustine would remember her, as he celebrated Mass *on the Altar*. As he raised the Consecrated Host, in sacrifice for sins, he raised all the love and sacrifice his mother had made for the salvation of his soul. That love stood with him, as victim-priest, he brought to the faithful, our Lord Jesus in His Body and Blood. And so, a mother never gave up and we have a

Saint whom we look to and remember, saying, *There's a place for us. There is a promised land. And that land is with You, Lord.*

†

Epilogue

We pray that reading this, our humble attempt to bring you a little of St. Augustine and his relationship with God, his mother and all the forces of Heaven and hell, you will now dig into that most beautiful and forceful of all autobiographies, *The Confessions of St. Augustine.* He called us to "*read, mark, learn, and inwardly digest.*" As we close this small chapter on this great man: Saint, sinner and son, we add to his words, "*and love.*"

†

Dedication

We first met you, St. Augustine, through an Augustinian Priest in far off Cascia. He was plainly in love with his Priesthood, the Eucharist and St. Rita, Saint of the Impossible. He spoke so simply as he shared the Miracle of the Eucharist, present there, in his church. He was so humble and loving as he recounted the life of St. Rita, we failed to see *(who we thought was)* St. Augustine in him. He did not appear lofty, above our heads, superior. He was one of us. P.S. St. Augustine was one of us. St. Augustine, like the rest of our family of Saints, *is* one of us. This chapter is dedicated to you, Padre Giustino, and to all our Priests and their mothers.

Photo Credits Augustinian Recollects, Oxnard, California
Excerpts and quotations from *The Confessions of St. Augustine*

Left:
The Blessed Virgin Mary appears to Monica as our Lady of Consolation, and gives her the leather belt our Lady wore at the time of the Crucifixion. She assured Monica that a mother with so many tears would eventually receive an answer to her prayers.

Right:
St. Augustine sees a little boy taking water in a shell from the sea, trying to empty it. He asks the boy what he is trying to do. The little boy responds that he is going to empty the sea with the seashell. St. Augustine tells him that is impossible. The little boy tells him, "It is easier for me to empty the sea with this seashell than for you to understand the Holy Trinity."

Left:
Francis is the brilliant, multi-faceted diamond of Jesus. He appeals to every aspect of humanity possible. He is Gospel!

Right:
The Cross of San Damiano came alive. Jesus spoke to Francis, *"Go and rebuild my Church, which as you can see, is in ruins."*

St. Francis of Assisi

"Lord, make me an instrument of Your peace."

When a pilgrim goes to the Basilica of St. Francis in Assisi, he is given a pamphlet which reads, *"An Encounter with St. Francis in Assisi."* This is what we will attempt to do in this chapter, introduce you to, and pray you experience such an encounter with the Poverello[1] of Jesus, your heart will burn to learn more about him. There is so much to know about St. Francis that it's impossible in this short chapter to tell it all. In addition, Francis touches everyone in a different way, as does Jesus. We believe that Francis was the closest human being on earth to mirror Jesus.

Francis draws you like a magnet. That's how he got to us. On our first pilgrimage to Europe and the Holy Land, a side trip was included to Assisi from Rome. It was our first time in Rome, we had only one day to spend there. We didn't want to leave Rome; there was too much we hadn't seen. So when our guide told us that the next morning, we would leave bright and early for Assisi, Penny and I thought to ourselves, *in your dreams*; we weren't going. We would explore Rome on our own. But the morning came, and we found ourselves boarding a bus for the three and a half hour drive to Assisi.

We only spent four hours in Assisi, and an hour and a half of that was lunch. So for all intents, we had two and a half hours in Assisi. There's no way you can even *begin* to experience Assisi in that period of time. When the bus was ready to go back to Rome, we begged for more time. *We*

---

[1]Poverello - Little One

didn't want to leave! But we had to leave. On our way back to Rome, we vowed that if we ever got back to Assisi, we'd spend a day and a half there. As it turned out, we returned the following year. Our planned day and a half extended to a week, and *still we didn't want to leave.* From that time, 1977, to this, we have visited Italy at least once a year, but for the most part, three or four times a year. We have never gone there and not spent at least two nights in Assisi, to bask in the illumination of St. Francis.

We've been asked many times, and even began asking ourselves, *"Why do you keep going back to Assisi?"* Is it because of the beauty of the town, and its surrounding area, including Santa Maria degli Angeli, the home of the Portiuncola²? There's no question that it is truly God's country, but there are many little towns in Europe that are beautiful. We believed then, and we do now, there is an air of Francis about Assisi, which has never left. His presence blankets the town. You can feel him everywhere you go, in the streets, in the churches, among the people, everywhere. And for a few years, we were content with that explanation, because *it is true.* But it's only part of the reason. About ten years ago, while we were doing research on this unique Saint, we came across the reason we keep going back to Assisi. Francis instructed the brothers, *"Come back to the Portiuncola at least once a year. The Spirit of Jesus and Mary are very strong here."* Yes, then we understood. The same Spirit and power that made Francis the exceptional Saint he is, has never left Assisi. That's what we felt in the air, the blanket that covers this holy ground. It is the Spirit, Jesus and Mary. Praise the Lord.

---

²Portiuncola - The little portion of land - the first church of St. Francis and his followers. It was given to them by the Benedictines, under the condition that it be made the center of his Fraternity. Francis, refusing to claim ownership of anything, paid the Benedictines a basket of fish per year for the use of the Portiuncola.

Francis of Assisi, God's Heavenly Contradiction

Francis is God's heavenly contradiction. Psychologists, psychiatrists, and analysts of human behavior have a field day, trying to determine *what it is* about this man that makes him beloved of the whole world. It's a fact that Francis is embraced by Catholics, Christians, non-Christians, atheists, and dictators. Lenin, the major molding force of the Bolshevik revolution, which plunged Russia into more than 70 years of Communism, had an extraordinary admiration for Francis of Assisi. On his deathbed, he said, *"If only we had 100 Francis' of Assisi, the revolution would have been a success."*

Eastern religious leaders go to the Hermitage of St. Francis, on Mount Subasio, high above Assisi, to have retreats, to learn about this man of God.

In Sweden, which has been officially Lutheran for over 450 years, a Franciscan Friar from Assisi, Fr. Max Mizzi, was asked to go there to instruct the people, not in the Catholic Faith, but in the ways of St. Francis. Each of his visits there has been successful; the churches were packed with eager, hungry listeners. A Third Order of St. Francis was established. Conversions to the Catholic Faith resulted. In our last meeting with Fr. Max, he told us his apostolate has extended into Denmark, and all the Scandinavian countries.

During the Reagan administration, while Brezhnev was still alive, relationships between the Communists and Americans were at a boiling point. The then Superior of the Basilica of St. Francis, Padre Michele, issued an open invitation to the two world leaders to come to Assisi, and talk about peace.

In 1986, Pope John Paul II gathered religious leaders from all over the world to Assisi, for a Day of Prayer for Peace. *And they all came!*

Protestant denominations have named churches after St. Francis of Assisi, and set up Religious Orders, based on the Rule of St. Francis.

These are just random examples that we've heard, over the years. There must be thousands of other, more dramatic instances where the name of Francis and his charism, were employed by people or groups outside the Catholic Church.

Who is Francis?

Francis is *everyman.* He is the brilliant, multi-faceted diamond of Jesus. He appeals to every aspect of humanity possible. *He is Gospel!* Francis encompasses every charism that Jesus taught us. He appeals to the rich and the poor, the mighty and the humble, the brilliant and the simple. Everyone can relate to Francis. *He is hope!* We find ourselves sinking and drowning in our world of today, which has buried its people in the quicksand of self love, consumerism, materialism and permissiveness. *The television commercials are lies!* We have finally come to terms with that. All the things we were told we *had to possess* to live the American dream, are killing us. There's nowhere to turn. Where is there a voice of sanity in an insane world? We look to Francis. He is proof that we can walk away from all of this, and be extremely happy. It can work. *He did it!* We turn to him in desperation, and he gives us hope in our hopelessness.

We have a very personal relationship with Francis. This is what gave us the courage to attempt to put the Francis we know, down on paper. As we delved into research on him, more for dates and facts than anything else, we became intimidated. There are so many brilliant people, who have written such intellectual studies on him, anything we would write could only be categorized, in the kindest sense, as simple.

But then the Lord gave us a word. Francis was all things to all people. He was extremely intellectual to those who needed that from him, but he was basically, like us, a very simple man. The only book he considered worthwhile to read, to study, and to fashion his life on, was the *Gospel*. And we know that the teachings of Jesus are simple; not always easy, but simple. With that encouragement to strengthen us, we invite you to meet, and fall in love with, a very powerful man in our Church, St. Francis of Assisi.

✝

Francis is so *touchable*. These days, when we see young men dressing in the latest fashions, driving the newest sports car, playing guitars, partying all the time, and chasing girls, we have a tendency to shake our heads, and mumble under our breath, admonitions like, "They'll turn out bad." That may be so; but that was also Francis.

Francis came from money. His father, Pietro di Bernardone, was in the garment business. The common term for it today would be the *rag business*. He imported most of his fabric from France. He loved France, because he made so much money there. For that reason, he named his son Francesco, in honor of France. Pietro's god was money, and he embraced that god with a passion. His wife, Pica, on the other hand, was a very spiritual lady. She was Francesco's spiritual influence during his youth. The Lord used the strength of his mother to create a balance in his life, and to bring Francis to Him when the time was right.

Pietro had great hopes for his oldest son, Francesco, even though he was a frail and sickly boy. In those days, merchants were not nobility, nor were nobility merchants. Pietro could probably have bought and sold many of the elite in Assisi, but that still did not make him aristocratic. He counted on this son to bring him into that exalted circle of the town. Francis was groomed all his life to be a *knight*. He wore the finest clothes. He learned to play five musical instruments. He was the life of the party. There were many parties. That was part of the training. Young Francesco di Bernardone was the party-planner of his time, and the most sought-after party guest of his clique. *And he loved it!* He enjoyed learning the role he was to play.

Signor, che cosa vuole? *(Lord, what do you want?)*

Although there was not much to wage war over in the little village of Assisi, shiny coats of armor were the fashion statement of the time, and naturally, the son of Pietro di Bernardone had to have the best coat of armor available. He had a handsome horse. He did everything that was required of an up-and-coming member of a noble society. The proper course of action for a young man of Francis' station was to go off to war, somewhere, anywhere.

He looked for a battle to fight, a cause to champion. A controversy arose between Assisi and Perugia, a nearby town. Francis *leapt* to the challenge. He went off to war. But the Lord's plan was not for Francis to be a warrior, by the *world's* standards. He was destined to be a warrior for the Gospel. So Francis was captured early in the game. He avoided being killed, but was imprisoned, until such time as a ransom could be paid. It took almost a year before he was released. He went back to Assisi, sick, but not deterred. He was going to find a war, if it was the last thing he did.

The Lord began chipping away at his heart during his recuperation period. He had a dream, in which he saw his father's house as a palace, with luxurious furnishings, and a beautiful wife. The dream was to become a prophecy, only the palace was the House of God, and the wife was Lady Poverty. One day, he traded clothes with a beggar, in the tradition of St. Martin of Tours. Values were changing for young Francesco. But he was still determined to find a war.

His opportunity came when Assisi joined with the Papal forces to do battle in Apulia, near the boot of Italy. Francis, and a group of young men from Assisi, set out for the war zone. He got as far as Spoleto, fifty miles away, where he stayed overnight. The Lord spoke to his heart. *"Francis, whom do you choose, the Master or the servant?"* Francis answered, *"The Master - Lord, what do you want me to do?"*

"Return to your own place," he was instructed. *"You will be told what to do. Your dream has to be interpreted differently; the palace and arms you saw are for other knights than those you had in mind; and your principality will be of another order."*

Francis did not go to war. He returned to Assisi, a changed young man. He was not the *party lover* he had been in the past. He spent time off by himself, listening, waiting for the Lord to tell him what He wanted of him. The Lord made Francis' senses very keen. After He had cleared out all the garbage in Francis' head, his eyes became very clear; his ears sharp; his nose could smell odors, rather than just the sweet fragrances he had been used to all his life. He began to see the poor, hear their cries, and smell the squalor they lived in. He could not reconcile that his family had so much, and these people so little. It didn't make any sense. He felt the need to balance things. So, in his simplicity, he took valuables from his home and cloth from his father, converted them into money, and gave it to the poor.

One time his mother saw him putting many, many loaves of bread in a sack. When she asked what this was for, he replied he wanted to share the bread with the poor. He had made a commitment to give alms to the poor. His mother attributed this strange behavior to the illness he had come down with during his imprisonment. His father was not as kind. He labeled Francis as "pazzo" (crazy).

This was the beginning of Francis' conversion, his response to the pull, away from the world and toward the Lord. He went to Rome on pilgrimage. He saw beggars on the steps of St. Peter's Basilica. He asked one to change clothes with him. He spent hours on those steps, begging for alms, in French[3]. He enjoyed the feeling of being dependent on the kindness of others. After a time, he changed back into his own clothes, and returned to Assisi.

The Lord placed on Francis' heart, *he was to hate the things he had formerly loved, and love the things he had formerly hated.* This instruction stayed with Francis all his life. He knew how he had been a prisoner to things of the world, possessions which possessed him. He had to make a conscious decision, every moment of his life, to denounce those things which had owned him. He also had to use the same determination to accept, no, *embrace* those things which repulsed him. High on this list were lepers. The sight and smell of them had always nauseated Francis. He couldn't bear the thought of looking at them, being near them, no less touching them. So he knew that he had to do just that, touch them.

He met a leper on the road, who was begging. The same fear and repugnance that Francis had always felt, began to surge up into his consciousness. As the beggar came closer, Francis fought the sick feeling that was overtaking him. At their moment of contact, Francis gave him a coin. As if that was not enough, he kissed his mangled hand. The leper, in return, gave Francis the kiss of peace. As the man embraced him, Francis cringed as he anticipated the smell of rotting flesh invading his nostrils. Instead, he sensed the most beautiful aroma. He could feel the fear peeling off his body. He was overcome by a strong sensation of joy and lightness. He felt as if he could fly. He was light as a feather. Soon after, he went to a leper hospital, and handed out coins to all the lepers, kissing their hands as he did. *He calculated the score as one for the Lord, and 9,000 to*

---

[3]Francis loved to speak in French, although he did not speak it well.

go. He felt compelled to seek out Lady Poverty, and take her for his bride.

He found himself in the broken-down church of San Damiano, a mile or so from the city. It was falling apart. But there was a beautiful crucifix there. Francis prayed seriously to the Lord. The question was always the same. "Lord, what do you want of me?" The Cross of San Damiano came alive. Jesus spoke to Francis, *"Go and rebuild my Church, which as you can see, is in ruins."*

Francis was always a simple man. He took the Lord literally. He began to rebuild the church of San Damiano. He believed this was his calling. He is so beautiful, so simple. This is why we have the courage to write about him. There was nothing confusing about the statement. The Lord asked him to rebuild his churches, so he got mortar and stone, and rebuilt. Was it simplicity, or humility? Did Francis know what the Lord *really meant* by those words, but thought He could not be asking the likes of Francis to be a major force in reforming the Church? Don't we all think that way very often? The Lord speaks to us, and we don't think it's possible that He wants *us* to be instrumental in bringing about change in His Church. We go back to Gideon[4] in the Old Testament. We're not sure if, in his case, it was humility or fear that made him hesitate. In any event, the Lord used Gideon for His glory. He was asking the same of Francis.

Antagonism built between Francis and his father. It came to a head when his father took him to court, for having stolen so many valuables from his warehouse and his home. Francis considered himself a *Religious* by this time, and therefore, not subject to civil authorities. He refused to

---

[4]Gideon was a young farmer. The Lord sent an Angel to tell him he was to save Israel from their enemies. Gideon asked, "How can I do this?" (Judges 6:11-16) But the Lord used Gideon mightily, and Israel was saved.

appear before a civil court. His father appealed to the Bishop, who convinced Francis that he had better appear before his father. Francis made a prophetic statement at that meeting, which took place in the center of town. He took off all his clothes, gave them to his father, and renounced his heritage. He said, "*From this moment forth, I am no longer Francis, son of Pietro di Bernardone, but Francis, child of God.*" It was a very dramatic moment, Francis standing in the middle of the square, stark naked. His father became enraged; he tried to punch Francis, but his younger son held his arm back. The Bishop, who had been presiding over the quarrel, took off his cloak and put it around Francis. God was telling the whole world, through this gesture of the Bishop that Francis was truly under the protection of *the* Father. Although we believe the Bishop was fully aware of Francis' spirituality, we believe the conscious reasoning for giving Francis his cloak was, he didn't want him walking around town without any clothes on.

As Francis was stripped of material possessions, he became happier. He took to wearing a coarse hermit's tunic, tied with a leather strap. He strolled through the town, so joyful, so light and airy, without a care in the world. He begged crusts of bread from the local people. They thought he was crazy. Very often, his begging was returned with insults. He praised God, blessed his attackers, and continued on his way.

Francis roamed the fields, looking for stones he could use in his building project. He was shocked to find these stones, laying in the fields, *were not free.* It was illogical. But when the local people chased him away, he knew he had to devise another plan. *He begged for stones!* Children of Assisi laughed and made fun of this crazy man, dressed like a beggar, carrying his bag of stones through the streets. But it didn't bother him. He had become so carefree that none of the world's problems bothered him.

Left:
Francis' father took him to court. Francis made a prophetic statement. Francis took off all his clothes, gave them to his father, and said, *"From this moment forth, I am no longer Francis, son of Pietro di Bernardone, but Francis, child of God."*

Right:
His Holiness had a dream. He saw a young man in pilgrim's garb, holding up the Church of St. John Lateran, the Cathedral of Rome. *That man was Francis.*

He grieved for the poor. It was such an imbalance for the rich to have so much more than they could ever use, while the poor could not even feed themselves. But although Francis was considered a radical in his day, he was not about social justice, as we know it today. He didn't encourage civil disobedience, or strikes. He didn't make demands that workers be treated more humanely, that salaries and benefits be increased. Francis was about the *Gospel*. He shared the Kingdom of *God* with the poor. He talked about the Beatitudes. They didn't want to hear this, while their stomachs were empty, their clothes were rags, and they lived in hovels. He didn't have any more money to give them. He followed the lead of St. Peter, who said, "*I have neither silver nor gold, but what I have, I give you!*" (Acts 3:6) Francis gave them the love of Jesus.

The priest in charge of the church of San Damiano, couldn't figure Francis out. When he first came to him with his plan of rebuilding the church, the priest thought he was pulling one of the pranks, he and his comrades were famous for. But after Francis insisted that he wanted to do this, the priest allowed him, although he was still very cautious. He wouldn't take any of the money Francis offered him, for fear of reprisals from Francis' father. But after the confrontation between Francis and Pietro di Bernardone, the priest was convinced of Francis' sincerity. He watched as the young man single-handedly worked feverishly to rebuild the church. He let Francis live there at the Church. He even fed him.

Now this is where it gets really interesting. The priest knew Francis came from a wealthy family, and was used to the best food. Francis himself had admitted that he could never eat anything he didn't like. The priest had special food brought in, which would be more to Francis' liking. Francis was not aware of this at the time, but soon realized what the priest had done. *This was not the way of the Gospel!* Francis decided it was time to beg for food. And so he did.

He took a bowl, following the example of the poor, and went from house to house, begging for *whatever*. And that's exactly what he got, *whatever*. At the end of his first day of begging, he looked at the bowl before him. It was a potpourri of leftovers, and near throw-aways. His stomach began to do flip-flops. He held his breath, and swallowed the food. It tasted like the most delicious gourmet food he had ever eaten. The Lord had taken yet another crutch away from him. He told the priest not to give him special food anymore . The Lord had cured him of that need.

During this construction period of Francis' life, one of the broken-down churches he worked on, was the little Benedictine chapel at Santa Maria degli Angeli. It was called the *Portiuncola*. It had been abandoned, and was in ruins. Francis rebuilt this church in honor of Our Lady, and leased it from the Benedictines for one barrel of fish per year. This became the first church of the *Franciscan Order*.

The church of San Damiano became the first church of the *Poor Clares*, in fulfillment of a prediction made by Francis. It was also during this time, after listening to a priest preaching the Gospel account of Jesus' sending out the disciples, two-by-two, without staff or bread or shoes, or any second garment that Francis changed his leather strap for a cord of rope. He was coming closer and closer to union with Lady Poverty.

Francis really had no grand ideas. There may have been a time when he fantasized how the palace he had dreamed about, would be filled with brothers and sisters, who had turned their lives over to God, as he had. But he *never* thought in terms of a *huge Fraternity*, which would then become a *major order*. He *never* considered that the Lord would use him to be the driving force behind the reform of the Church of the Middle Ages. He *never* thought his mission was to change the world. He was a simple man in love with Jesus, and His teachings in the Gospel. But we never stand still; we either go forward or backward. Francis was not one to go backward.

An extraordinary event took place. The young men of nobility of Assisi began to follow Francis. They saw something in this little man, call it joy or abandonment, but they wanted it. All of a sudden, their fine clothes and horses, their coats of armor, and trappings of the day that they'd considered so important, became so unimportant. They took on a dull, shabby color. Meanwhile, Francis, in rags, had a sheen and lustre that was *blinding*. The parents of these young people were completely dumbfounded. They could not possibly understand the attraction this demented young man could have on their children. Francis di Bernardone became a *dirty word* in Assisi.

Within a short period of time, he had six followers. One followed quickly on the heels of another, and then it was twelve. Now, they were like the apostles. Only the twelve included Francis. So, for all intents and purposes, they eliminated Judas Iscariot from the count. They went out, two by two, throughout the countryside, striving to refocus people on the Gospel, penance, and the Kingdom of God.

The world of Francis was not much different from our world today. No one was running around the countryside preaching repentance, or the values of the Gospel. These beliefs were not being *practiced* either. As a matter of fact, they were so out of mode that the people thought Francis and his followers were either drunks, or crazy. Ethics had gone topsy-turvy. Everything that was illegal and immoral was embraced as being the proper behavior, as if it were their God-given right.

Author's Note: Doesn't that sound like our world today? Famous actresses bring their children to abortion rallies, stating that they support abortion because of their children. That doesn't even make sense. Others claim abortion to be their sacred rights. Today, people practice open-sex, male with male,

male with female, female with female; they shoot up with drugs, using infected needles. Then they blame God if they are contaminated with venereal disease or AIDS. Mother Angelica made a very simple statement not too long ago. She said, "If you drink a quart of bourbon every day for twenty years, there's a good chance you'll get Cirrhosis of the Liver. Don't blame God."

But pretty soon, Francis and his followers became accepted by the local people. Their words began to strike home. Conversions came about, on a very minor scale. Little by little, people came back to Jesus and His Church. But, oh, so *slowly*. While we look at the growth of the radical teachings of St. Francis as being rapid, it still took *years* of high visibility for change to come about.

They were most effective, not by what they said, but by how they behaved. This was the prime cause of conversion. In the early days, when they entered a town, no one knew who they were. They experienced much difficulty getting anyone to house or feed them. They wound up sleeping in the cold and rain, with no protection from the weather, but the warmth of the Love of God. Then people would see them in Church, praying fervently. Moved with pity, some would go up to them and offer them money, which they refused. This made absolutely no sense. But soon, sympathy was replaced by trust, and then wholehearted interest. The Lord was converting His people through these simple Friars.

The Brothers become legitimate

The Lord put on Francis' heart that it was time to place the Fraternity, and his Rule, at the feet of His Holiness, Pope Innocent III. After that first big *"Yes"* to Jesus, everything came easier to Francis. There was such joy and anticipation in the twelve, as they walked merrily towards Rome and the Vatican. They shared their dreams, their prayers, their expectations. They were excited.

They met the Bishop of Assisi in Rome. When Francis explained what their mission was, he helped them to meet the Pope. Pope Innocent III was a very wise Pope. But his thinking was of the *world*. When Francis presented his dream to form a Fraternity, based on the Gospel, His Holiness thought it was virtually inconceivable for men of that time to live the way of the Gospel.

There's a moment in Zefferelli's film, **"Brother Sun, Sister Moon,"** about Francis and Clare, which deals with this apprehension of the Pope. In the film, when the Pope questioned the feasibility of anyone living the Gospel life, a Cardinal next to him, whispered in his ear, "Sire, you're suggesting that the Gospel is ancient history." Is the Gospel ancient history? Can a man live his life as prescribed by Jesus? Francis was convinced it could be done. The Pope was not so sure. He asked Francis to go and pray, and come back again in a few days.

That night, as His Holiness slept, he had a dream. In it, he saw a young man in pilgrim's garb, holding up the Church of St. John Lateran, the Cathedral of Rome. *That man was Francis.* The Pope pondered on the meaning of the dream. Was the Lord trying to tell His Pope that this raggedy young man and his motley group, somehow, were going to be instrumental in holding up the Church? When Francis and his followers returned, some days later, His Holiness regarded them with renewed interest. Even though his humanity could not equate Francis with the salvation of the Church, he allowed the Lord to decide for him. He embraced Francis, and gave him verbal permission to follow the unpretentious Rule he had written, using mostly passages from Scripture.

As Francis and his band of disciples headed joyfully back to Assisi, they were amazed that their request had been granted so quickly. In his simplicity, or humility, he didn't realize that *there was so much work to do, and so little time to do it.* The command the Lord had given him in the dilapidated church of San Damiano was truly taking shape, *"Go and rebuild My church, which, as you can see, is in ruins."* It all made so much sense now.

But there was a problem. Francis and his followers had been given authorization from a Church in Rome, which was burdened down with materialism. The basic premise of the new Fraternity was to renounce wealth and possessions. Many of the brothers had given up massive wealth to follow Francis and the Gospel life. How could they reconcile with a *rich Church?* Would they become embittered with the traditional Church, because of its non-compliance to the commands of the Gospel? Would they go around the countryside, pointing accusing fingers at the established hierarchy, thus causing dissension?

That's *not* what Francis wanted. That's not what he wanted from *his brothers.* He didn't want to separate himself from the Church, or from the rich. He wanted to minister to them. The Lord gave Francis a word, the smallest. He wanted him and his companions to consider themselves as the least of the brethren, the lesser brothers, the Friars Minor. He wrote in his Rule, *"and let them be lesser brothers,"* and in another place, *"I wish that this Fraternity be called the Order of the Friars Minor."*

The brothers took up residence in a hovel at Rivo Torto, about a mile from the Portiuncola. But the Lord didn't want them there. One night, while they were praying, a farmer brought a mule into the hut. While Francis' temper flared momentarily, he knew the Lord was calling them to another place. That place was the Portiuncola, around the Church of St. Mary, which he had rebuilt. They constructed little huts, which looked like Indian wigwams. It became the official headquarters of this new movement. It is still the headquarters of the Friars Minor, while the great Basilica of

St. Francis, on top of the hill at Assisi, is the home of the Conventuals[5].

Clare the Fairest in the Land

St. Bonaventure, in his Major Life of St. Francis, refers to Clare as *"the first flower in Francis' garden, and she shone like a radiant star, fragrant as a flower blossoming white and pure in springtime."*

Thomas Celano describes Clare as follows, *"...the most precious and the firmest stone of the whole structure (the Poor Clares)...She was of noble parentage, but she was more noble by grace; she was a virgin in body, most chaste in mind; a youth in age, but mature in spirit ...Clare by name, brighter in life, and brightest in character."*

Both men knew Clare, but St. Bonaventure didn't know her when she was a young girl. He was born four years before Francis died. But you can see from the flowing references to her, and from all we've ever read about her, she was a breathtakingly beautiful girl and woman. She was also exceptionally strong-willed. Francis knew this about her, but we doubt if he realized during his lifetime, how that uncompromising persistence would be his voice after his death, trying to hold onto the Rule he envisioned for the Fraternity.

The love story of Francis and Clare was as tender as that of Romeo and Juliet, except theirs was a spiritual love, which went far beyond the conjugal. Also, theirs had a very happy ending, because it was Christ-centered. Assisi is a small town. At the time of Francis and Clare, it was even

---

[5]There are different communities within the Franciscan order. The Friars Minor were closer to the Rule of St. Francis, while the Conventuals embraced the reforms of Brother Elias. Actually, today neither live the Rule of St. Francis, as he wrote it. Those who try hardest to maintain that Rule are the Capuchins, but even they have what is called Reform Capuchins. None of this existed during the early days of the movement.

smaller. As Clare was growing up, Francis had attained a certain notoriety in the town. But he was exciting! He spoke words she had never heard before. Her heart raced as she listened, and pondered on them. The Lord had placed Clare in that place, at that time, to be a spiritual partner to Francis. She said yes, and embraced the ideals that Francis espoused, possibly even more than he. When it came to Poverty, she outdid all the brothers.

When Francis had rebuilt the church of San Damiano, he had made a prediction that it would house holy religious women. He didn't know at that time, Clare would be the first, and the leader in this movement. But the Lord had given Francis many insights. Was his prediction part of the dream, or had he always considered that women would be a natural part of the evolution of the Fraternity? When Clare first came to him, to hear about his teachings, did a spark light in his heart? Did the Lord tell him that she was the one? We can only muse.

But from that first moment, their lives were eternally meshed, in the service of the Lord. Clare became the first woman to join his Community, followed in short order by her sister, St. Agnes of Assisi. He kept his distance from her the rest of his life, very often to her displeasure. His reasoning was that he would not allow the slightest hint of scandal to invade the fraternity of men, and most especially that of the "Poor Ladies". He found a strong ally in this child-woman. When Celano uses flowery terms like "*the firmest stone*" and "*mature in spirit,*" he's really talking about a tough lady. Clare upheld the vision of Francis all her life, to the extent of bucking heads with Bishops, Cardinals and Popes, and she got her way. There were times during Francis' lifetime, and especially after his death that Clare stood out as a very sore thumb to the Friars who were trying to reform the Rule.

The closest words we can find to define the relationship between Francis and Clare, would be those given us by Sirach 6: 15-17.

> *"A faithful friend is a sturdy shelter;*
> *he who finds one finds a treasure.*
> *A faithful friend is beyond price,*
> *no sum can balance his worth.*
> *A faithful friend is a life-saving remedy,*
> *such as he who fears God finds;*
> *For he who fears God behaves accordingly,*
> *and his friend will be like himself."*

That was Francis and Clare, only more. Clare was a friend in the truest sense of the word, most likely the best friend Francis ever had.

Francis' Focus

Francis was always very focused. He insisted on being focused. We believe he feared that if he veered even a micro-millimeter from his focal point, he was lost. He never considered himself very intelligent, or an eloquent speaker. But when you have a direct pipeline to the Holy Spirit, how smart do you have to be? You just let God's Words flow through you, and you will be considered the most brilliant of all men, and perhaps the most despised.

An excellent example of Francis' focus was his definition of *Perfect Joy*. It's an outlook that, if adopted, is almost a guarantee that you'll never be disappointed. Francis and Brother Leo were returning to Santa Maria degli Angeli. Francis said to Brother Leo,

> *"Brother Leo, even if a Friar Minor gives sight to the blind, heals the paralyzed, drives out devils, gives hearing back to the deaf, makes the lame walk, and restores speech to the dumb, and what is still more, brings back to life a man who has been dead four days, write that perfect joy is not in that."*

They walked along silently for a short distance. Francis was becoming emotional. He cried out loudly,

"Brother Leo, if a Friar Minor knew all languages and all sciences and Scripture, if he also knew how to prophesy and to reveal not only the future but also the secrets of the consciences and minds of others, write down and note carefully that perfect joy is not in that."

Then once again, a little farther on, Francis cried out to Brother Leo,

"Brother Leo, little lamb of God, even if a Friar Minor could speak with the voice of an Angel, and knew the courses of the stars and the powers of herbs, and knew all about the treasures in the earth, and if he knew the qualities of birds and fishes, animals, humans, roots, trees, rocks, and waters, write down and note carefully that true joy is not in that."

Brother Leo knew that Francis was on a roll. He also knew if he didn't finally ask the question, this would continue on until they reached Assisi. But he remained silent. Then Father Francis called out again,

"Brother Leo, even if a Friar Minor could preach so well that he should convert all infidels to the faith of Christ, write that perfect joy is not there."

By this time, the discourse had been going on for two miles. Leo decided it was time. He cried out to Francis, whom he loved more than life. *"Father, I beg you in God's name to tell me where perfect joy is!"* That was all Francis needed. He cried out with such delight,

"When we come to St. Mary of the Angels, soaked by the rain and frozen by the cold, all soiled with mud and suffering from hunger, and we ring at the gate of the Place and the brother porter comes and says angrily, 'Who are you?' And we say, 'We are two of your brothers', and he contradicts us, saying, 'You are not telling the truth. Rather you are two rascals who go

around deceiving people and stealing what they give to the poor. Go away!' And he does not open for us, but makes us stand outside in the snow and rain, cold and hungry, until night falls - then if we endure all those insults and cruel rebuffs patiently, without being troubled and without complaining, and if we reflect humbly and charitably that that porter really knows us and that God makes him speak against us, oh, Brother Leo, write that perfect joy is there!

"And if we continue to knock, and the porter comes out in anger, and drives us away with curses and hard blows like bothersome scoundrels, saying, 'Get away from here, you dirty thieves - go to the hospital! Who do you think you are? You certainly won't eat or sleep here!' - and if we bear it patiently and take the insults with joy and love in our hearts, oh, Brother Leo, write that that is perfect joy!

"And if later, suffering intensely from hunger and the painful cold, with night falling, we still knock and call, and crying loudly beg them to open for us and let us come in for the love of God, and he grows still more angry and says, 'Those fellows are bold and shameless ruffians. I'll give them what they deserve!' And he comes out with a knotty club, and grasping us by the cowl throws us onto the mud and snow, and beats us with that club so much that he covers our bodies with wounds - if we endure all those evils and insults and blows with joy and patience, reflecting that we must for love of Him, oh, Brother Leo, write, that is perfect joy!

"And now hear the conclusion, Brother Leo. Above all the graces and gifts of the Holy Spirit which Christ gives to His friends is that of conquering oneself and willingly enduring sufferings, insults, humiliations, and hardships for the love of Christ. For we cannot glory in all those other marvelous gifts of God, as they are not

ours but God's, as the Apostles say, 'What have you that
you have not received?'

"But we can glory in the cross of tribulations and
afflictions, because that is ours, and so the Apostles say,
'I will not glory save in the Cross of Our Lord Jesus
Christ!"'[6]

Francis' philosophy was simple. He wanted to live the
Gospel life. True, he wanted to *go out to teach all nations,*
and there must have been a certain amount of joy at the
beginning, when the fraternity grew so rapidly. Brothers
were going all over Europe, preaching the Gospel. But he
knew why he had to be a ramrod in his persistence. He
knew he could not go to the right or to the left; he had to
remain in the center of his vision, or he would lose it.

Francis considered anything other than the basic,
ground-zero commitment to poverty and the Gospel, as
distraction. He feared that distraction would lead to
division. Too many books would clutter the mind; the
Gospel would become vague. He didn't want his Friars to
read too much. There was nothing that could top the
Gospel, was there? And that's what their calling was, wasn't
it? He was happy with the little huts they had begun with,
nestled all around the Portiuncola. He and the brothers
could go off preaching for months at a time, and come back,
to find that nothing had been disturbed, because there was
nothing of any value to steal.

A perfect example of Francis' philosophy took place
when he was invited to have dinner at a Bishop's home.
Francis asked for the discarded bread[7]. The Bishop asked
Francis to at least eat the fresh bread. Francis' reply was, *"If*
I eat the fresh bread, I will want to eat the gravy. And if I eat

---

[6]The Little Flowers of St. Francis - Chapter VIII

[7]In those days, we didn't use knives and forks as eating utensils;
bread was used. When it was soaked and soggy, it was thrown on the
floor. It didn't matter if it was stale bread, because it was seldom eaten.

the gravy, I will want to eat the meat." Francis knew exactly who he was. He knew who his Friars were. Theirs was such a rigid, difficult road to walk, the slightest breach of a rule could make the entire structure crumble. Francis knew that. Unfortunately, others of his Fraternity did not.

Francis was not a great organizer. He wasn't meant to be. He was a leader, a father figure. But there were others who joined the Fraternity, who were good at organization. Francis was happy to have these devoted Friars take over the job of setting up provinces[8], and actually running them. The Fraternity had grown rapidly; there were too many Friars to be supervised, there was no way that Francis would have been able to handle it by himself. The original twelve were not prone to administration. That was too much like the world they had given up for the Gospel life. When eager new faces were willing to take on these loving tasks, and the Fraternity agreed that they were capable, the supervisory jobs were gladly given over to them.

But with such an influx of new people, at such a rapid pace, came different personalities. Many of the brothers brought new ideas with them, of how the Fraternity should *"interpret"* the Gospel life. They may have been good ideas, but they were not what Francis had envisioned. Many disagreed with the idea of the brothers *not learning* too much. They sincerely believed that without knowledge, they could not really understand the Gospel, nor could they defend the Faith against its persecutors. Francis did not trust books. He believed that, too often, good people put too much time and effort into the search for knowledge, and lose their desire for prayer and the holy life. Then, when they have been praised for their eloquence, pride takes over, and they go off on a bad track. Sometimes, even the quest

---

[8]The Franciscan Fraternity was broken up into geographical areas, called provinces. Leaders were appointed for each province.

for proficiency in Scripture, will leave a person more concerned with the study, than the Author. In our own time, we are told that some theologians have lost their focus, and even become atheists.

Others felt the Rule, as written by Francis, was too severe. Who could live in huts, on a starvation diet? No one could live this way. But, Francis pointed out, *they had been happy living this way, thank you very much!* The brothers pointed out to their Father in Faith, how other communities lived, such as the Benedictines. Father Francis praised St. Benedict, and the brother Benedictines. But he was *not* a Benedictine. He was a Friar Minor.

One area of contention which was sure to send Francis into orbit, was the mention of money or property. People wanted to give donations to the Friars. They were exhilarated by the work that was being done. Some Friars believed the money and property could be used to house the ever-growing Fraternity, and help the poor. Francis was adamant about not owning any possessions. As for money, it was dirty.

We have to remember that Francis came from money. Most of the early followers had plenty of money. Poor Bernard, his first companion, had to go into the center of Assisi, with all his money and possessions, and physically give it all away. That money could have been used to build Friaries, and feed the poor. But Francis had an instinct about ownership in the early days. It had not changed. *Money corrupts!* Was it right for the early disciples to give up everything, but not these newcomers?

Francis went through this struggle with the brothers for the rest of his life. But he could not deal with this problem on a daily basis. Francis had to be who he was, and do what the Lord had called him to do. He went off preaching, proclaiming the Good News of Jesus, converting sinners, turning the hearts of men back to the Lord. It was only when he got back to Assisi, or traveled into one of the provinces, and saw the way the new breed of Friars Minor were living the Gospel life that he went into a rage, followed by a deep depression. But he couldn't spend his life fighting that battle. There were too many other conflicts that the Lord had for him to handle.

He never lost his focus; he never changed his values. And although he was a brilliant speaker, he was unpretentious. We believe he spoke pure Holy Spirit. He was not commanding, except in his Holiness. What attracted so many to him, even those who would change his dream, was *who* he was, not *what* he did. They became enraptured with his consistency. He was never anything other than what he projected, and he only projected what the Lord had given him.

He received Heavenly insights. He was so open to Jesus, he could absorb all the instructions the Lord poured into him, and share them with the people on such a basic level. Everyone could understand him. He was simple for the simple-hearted, and educated for the astute-minded. A doctor of Theology from Siena once asked him to explain some difficult theological issues. Francis spoke the Holy Spirit so profoundly that the theologian blurted out, "*His theology soars aloft on the wings of purity and contemplation, like an eagle in full flight, while our learning crawls along the ground.*"

Francis goes to the Holy Land

The Crusades had become a way of life in Europe. No sooner had one ended than preparations were made for another. This had been going on for over 100 years when Francis decided the Lord was calling him to die a martyr's death in the land of our Savior's birth. He set out three times to get to the Holy Land, but was blocked twice, once by conditions, and the other by his own bad health.

Nevertheless, he was resolved to try again. Finally, in 1220, after the bodies of the first five Franciscan martyrs of the Holy Land were sent back to Europe, he forged ahead. He was determined to suffer a martyr's death for Jesus.

However, the Lord had different plans for Francis. It may have been for Francis' benefit; it may have been for the Saracens of that time; it may have been for the Crusaders, who had long since forgotten *why* they were in the Holy Land. In any event, the Lord guided Francis and a companion, Brother Illuminata, through the battle lines, to the Sultan of the Saracens. There are two very exciting stories of Francis' time with the Sultan, one of which is documented in the history of St. Francis, the other is told at the Church of the Holy Sepulchre, in Jerusalem.

Francis and his comrade were caught by the Arabs, beaten, and put in chains. Then they were brought before the Sultan. When asked why they had come, Francis shared his love of the Gospel and Our Lord Jesus. He was so simple, so sincere, so understandable, the Sultan was captivated by him. Francis was going after mass conversion. He offered to walk through burning coals with the Sultan's priests, if the Sultan agreed that he and his people would convert. The Sultan's priests were not too happy with the idea of walking on hot coals; in fact, they disappeared as Francis made the suggestion. The Sultan is said to have told Francis that if he were to convert, both he and Francis would be killed. But he offered Francis treasures, which had no interest to the Poverello.

The legend at the Church of the Holy Sepulchre is that Francis asked the Sultan to come into the Church with him, to pray at the tomb of Jesus. The Sultan replied that if he were to enter that church, the Moslems would make it into a mosque. Instead, the two prayed outside the Church of the Holy Sepulchre. Today, right at the edge of the Church of the Holy Sepulchre, stands a very small mosque, erected in honor of the Sultan, who had prayed there. The Sultan was so impressed with Francis, he would have converted, had not the threat of death hung over both their heads.

We have to stop here for a moment. Christians were being slaughtered in the Holy Land. Franciscans had been martyred there. Yet, Francis was able to go into the jaws of hell, and not only come out unscratched, but having successfully spread the Word of God to the Moslems. Why is that? We know for sure that he was protected by the Angels. But there's more. What did the Moslems see in Francis that they did not see in the Crusaders, or in the other Franciscans who went to the Holy Land to convert them?

We believe Francis had the ability to empty himself almost completely, and let Jesus reflect through him. It was no longer Francis who spoke to the Moslems; it was Jesus, *through* Francis. Very possibly, in this place and time, Francis put into practice his simple prayer.

Lord, make me an instrument of your peace.
Where there is hatred, let me sow love.
Where there is injury, pardon.
Where there is discord, unity.
Where there is doubt, faith.
Where there is error, truth.
Where there is despair, hope.
Where there is sadness, joy.
Where there is darkness, light.

O Divine Master, grant that I may not so much seek
To be consoled, as to console.
To be understood, as to understand.
To be loved, as to love.
For
It is in giving, that we receive.
It is in pardoning, that we are pardoned.
It is in dying, that we are born to eternal life.

Francis gives up his last possession

It's hard for us to picture Francis going through the roof. But that's exactly what happened. Before he returned to Italy, word came to him in the Holy Land that during his absence, brothers were changing the Rule without permission, buildings were going up, property being donated and accepted. It was almost as if his time in the Holy Land had been a *vacation*. Now, the real world of his Fraternity came crashing down on him, long distance.

His initial reaction was to fight. He was good and mad; he did fight. But there were too many, and they were all singing the same song, using different tunes. He was holding on. Whether he realized it at the time or not, he, who had despised possessions of any kind, had become possessive of the Friars Minor.

In the eyes of the world, he was justified. After all, *he* had started the fraternity. It was *Francis* whom everyone followed. *He* had the charisma. Would these thousands of men and women have flocked to live the Gospel life if *he* had not set the example before them? But Francis soon realized that there were too many *him's*, and *he's*, and *Francis'*. This was not the gift the Lord had given him years ago, when they began. The gift was total detachment, self-abandonment. His own cries of protest rang in his ears, *"Look at the birds in the sky. They do not sow or reap, they gather nothing into barns; yet your Heavenly Father feeds them. Are you not more important than they?"* Had Francis been tricked by the evil one, after his years of adamant rejection of ownership of any kind? Did he now covet his own Rule? The Lord gave Francis peace of mind with regard to this. He told him,

"Why are you disturbed, little man? Did I not place you over My Order as its shepherd, and now you do not know that I am its chief protector? I chose you, a simple man, for this task, that what I would do in you, to be (would be) *imitated by the rest, they might follow*

*who wish to follow. I have called; I will preserve and
feed; and I will choose others to repair the falling away
of others, so that if a substitute is not born, I will make
him to be born."*[9]

Francis resigned as head of the Friars Minor in 1220, six
years before his death. He appointed his second follower,
Peter of Catani, his successor. We can only speculate as to
why he did this. Nothing is certain, but we can read in
between the lines. The Fraternity had become *very* large.
Francis was not an administrator. Plus, and very up front, he
disagreed with many of the innovations they were making.
Francis was not beyond coming back from a trip, and upon
finding out that someone had built a house for the Friars,
going to the top of the house, and proceeding to tear it
apart. He disagreed with all the *niceties* that were finding
their way into the houses of the *lesser brothers*. Granted,
what *he* considered *niceties* were *basics of life* that even the
poorest, well not the poorest, but *almost* the poorest,
possessed. Nonetheless, that's not what they were about.

We can't really make a judgment about those who
wanted the Rule relaxed. We don't know what was in their
hearts. Did they really believe they could follow the Rule of
Francis, *without* following the Rule of Francis? Did they
think the Friars Minor would be better served if everyone
had a roof over their heads, a few square meals a day, and
the like? On the other hand, could 5,000 Friars be living in
mud huts all over Europe? Were all the opponents of the
Gospel Life concept right, and Francis wrong? Was that first
Pope, Innocent III, right? Was it too hard a life? That's a
debate that will most likely never be resolved. St. Francis of
Assisi, one of the most important Saints in the history of the
Church, believed his understanding of the Gospel life was
possible! St. Clare of Assisi, who was right up there with

---

[9]Celano Second Life Chapter CXVII, No. 158

Francis, *insisted* it could be done. St. Agnes of Assisi, Clare's sister, and second member of the Poor Clares, *believed* it, because she *lived* it all her life. But there were many others who disagreed with him. We probably won't know who was right or wrong until we are in the Kingdom, and then it won't matter all that much.

Bishop Hugolino of Ostia, protector of the Friars Minor, and later Pope Gregory IX, may have actually leaned towards poverty as a preference. On a historic occasion, Sts. Francis and Dominic[10] were together with him in Rome. The Bishop posed the question to both of them. *"In the primitive church, the pastors were poor and were men of chastity, not men of greed. Why do we not in the future make Bishops and prelates from among your brothers (Franciscans and Dominicans), who excel all others by their learning and example?"*

It was an interesting concept, but both Francis and Dominic rejected such an idea. Dominic's reasoning was *"My brothers have been raised to a high station, if they only knew it; and even if I wanted to, I could not permit them to acquire any other dignity."* Francis' explanation was similar in content, but it reflected who he insisted they should be. He said, *"Lord, my brothers are called minors so that they will not presume to become greater. Their vocation teaches them to remain in a lowly station and to follow the footsteps of the humble Christ, so that in the end they may be exalted above the rest in the sight of the Saints."*

Bishop Hugolino's speculation won out after the deaths of Sts. Francis and Dominic. Both Franciscans and Dominicans have served Mother Church as Bishops, and do to this day. An interesting aside is that Bishop Hugolino,

---

[10]St. Dominic was founder of the Dominicans (Domini Cani, God's Watchdogs), Order of Preachers. He and St. Francis were credited with being the major forces behind the reformation of the Church of the Middle Ages.

after he became Pope Gregory IX, canonized both St. Francis and St. Dominic, during his pontificate.

Francis rewrites the Rule

The year was 1221. The Friars Minor had outgrown Francis, and his simple little Rule of 1209. There was more sophistication in the Fraternity than there had been in the early days. Learned men had become attracted to the Friars Minor, but they needed more intellectual meat than Francis' simple Rule provided. He found that he had to explain so many aspects of the Rule to the Brothers, which had been taken for granted for years. Therefore, it was determined that in order to clarify the Rule, especially in the light of new changes that had taken place, a *new* Rule had to be written.

Francis insisted that he would do it. He had written the first Rule, and he would incorporate whatever changes were going to be made in it. He believed until his dying day, the original Rule was dictated to him directly by the Lord. In his Testament, written just prior to his death, he stated,

> *"When God gave me some Friars, there was no one to tell me what I should do; but the Most High Himself made it clear to me that I must live the life of the Gospel. I had this written down briefly and simply and His Holiness, the Pope, confirmed it for me. Those who embraced this life gave everything they had to the poor. They were satisfied with one habit, which was patched inside and outside, and a cord, and trousers. We refused to have anything more."*

From this, we can gather he didn't feel the need to expand on what he had written in 1209, because it had come directly from God. But as he demanded obedience from his Friars, he was obedient to his Fraternity. In addition, he had to agree that the circumstances of the Friars Minor, with thousands of members spread all over Europe, was quite different from the little band of twelve, for whom the original Rule had been written.

So Francis set out to rewrite the Rule. He expanded and elaborated somewhat on his original Rule, but by and large, he came up with a slightly updated version of the *same thing*. He had one of the Friars camouflage it with Scripture passages, but it didn't help. It was unacceptable. It had to be done all over again.

It was not all in vain, however. Francis was able to *slip in* as part of the Rule, an admonition. *"They (the Friars) should let it be seen that they are happy in God, cheerful and courteous, as is expected of them, and be careful not to appear gloomy or depressed like hypocrites."*[11]

Again, we're reading in-between the lines, but it has become common knowledge that people had entered into the Fraternity who were not cheerful and courteous, and indeed walked around with a gloomy exterior, and what could have been considered false piety. In the early days, when Francis discerned on each potential Friar himself, he had a test he gave to all, but especially those who seemed somber and introverted. He had them follow him into the fields, where he jumped around, laughing and singing, generally acting silly, and ordered them to do the same. If they couldn't become comfortable with this type of conduct, Francis sent them away, because they did not have the freedom to be a Friar.

At any rate, Francis had to rewrite the Rule. We have to point out here that *not everybody disagreed* with Francis, as to how the Rule should be. This is what created the split in the movement, which, in one form or another, exists to this day. There were many Friars who believed the original Rule was fine; it didn't need any adjustment. As far as they were concerned, just give them that Rule and a Bible, and point

---

[11]However, this was taken out of the Rule of 1223.

them in a direction. They were not necessarily in the minority; they were just not in headship.

Francis, accompanied by Brother Leo and one other, went off by themselves, up on a mountain, and worked on the new Rule. At one point, Francis rewrote the Rule, came down off the mountain, and gave it to a Friar[12]. It was either lost, or possibly, the Friar, having read it, considering it the same as the previous one, threw it away. No one knows for sure. However, Francis had to go back at it again. For some reason, the Friars who were looking for some laxity in the poverty part of the Rule, approached Brother Elias[13], and shared their fears that the new Rule would be as stern as the first. They urged him to go to the mountain and speak to Francis. He agreed, on condition that they accompany him.

When Brother Elias and the ministers arrived at the place where Francis was staying, he shared the fear of the ministers that Francis was writing a Rule too hard for them to follow. Francis looked to the heavens, and spoke to Jesus, *"Lord, did I not tell You they would not have confidence in You?"* The Friars all fell to their knees and covered their faces, because the Lord answered Francis instantly. He said,

"Francis, nothing in the Rule comes from you; everything in it comes from Me. I wish this Rule to be observed to the letter, to the letter, without gloss, without gloss, without gloss. I am aware of human weakness, but I also know the help I wish to give it. Let those who do not want to observe the Rule leave the Order!"

Francis turned to the brothers. *"Did you hear? Do you want me to have it repeated?"* Brother Elias and the others ran for their lives down the mountain, striking their breasts.

---

[12]According to St. Bonaventure's Life of St. Francis, it was Brother Elias to whom Francis gave the copy of the Rule.

[13]Brother Elias had a great influence on Francis. He became the Vicar in 1221, after the death of Peter Catani. This new Rule was written during his vicariate.

What a marvelous relationship Francis had with Jesus. He was not only able to get Him to talk to the Friars on command, but he had the confidence that, if need be, Jesus would repeat the statement. *And he was probably right!*

But in spite of this, the new Rule was pushed through. This time, the powers that be, took no chances that it would not be acceptable by the majority of the Brothers. Canon lawyers were called in. They made changes, and organized it according to *legal terms*. Then it was brought to Cardinal Hugolino[14], who lent his expertise to the Rule. It was shortened. Much of the flavor of Francis was taken out; it was legalistic, but it was still clear. Francis did not want anyone interpreting the Rule[15]. He didn't want anyone finding loopholes in the Rule.

We don't believe that Francis was really happy with what had been done, but he was too drained, physically and spiritually, to fight. In addition, he could feel the dissension and in-fighting among his brothers. One of his heartfelt sorrows was to see brothers mouthing Scripture without meaning, using the Gospel as a sword. In the final analysis, unity was more important than maintaining the Rule, no matter how much he believed it had been dictated to him by Jesus, Himself.

The new Rule was presented to the Brothers at a Chapter meeting in June of that year. It went to Rome, where further studies were done on it. Finally, in November, 1223, it was given to the brothers as the new Rule.

The Beginning of the End

Francis removed himself from the everyday workings of the Fraternity. It had gotten away from him. He didn't want

---

[14]Protector of the Friars Minor. Later became Pope Gregory IX.

[15]In his Testament, written shortly before his death, he states emphatically in two different places, *"I strictly forbid any of my Friars.....to interpret the Rule or these words, saying, 'This is what they really mean.'"*

to be part of decision-making, and yet, he couldn't keep his nose out of the everyday happenings.   He had to put distance between himself and his beloved Assisi.   He spent a great deal of time in seclusion, with just Brother Leo, Brother Masseo and Brother Angelo[16].   It was important to Francis to surround himself with old friends, to be reminded of the way it had been in simpler times.   He covered himself with a blanket of joy.   Even in his sufferings, his illnesses which kept him in constant pain, he exuded joy.   *This was a decision!*   He instructed his Friars to go to the privacy of their rooms, if they wanted to bemoan their outcast state. But when they were in the presence of people, they must reflect the joy of Jesus.   And so he practiced what he preached.   He went off by himself.   His companions stayed a safe distance, available to minister to Francis when he needed them, but always allowing him the space he needed, to let it all out with the Lord.

He had extraordinary discussions with Jesus, His Mother Mary, the Saints before him, and his special friends, the Angels.   We have to believe they counselled and consoled Francis.   They gave him a hint of the Kingdom, so that he wouldn't take the disappointments of the earth too seriously.   His brothers and sisters, the Saints, shared some of the struggles *they* had to endure while on earth, and how insignificant these struggles became in Heaven.   We have to believe, Francis told them that he didn't care for himself; his concerns were for his Friars, and for our Lord Jesus, who gave him the Fraternity in the first place.   We pray that Francis was given peace in the knowledge that Jesus could take care of Himself, and He would always take care of the brothers who followed in Francis' footsteps.

---

[16]These three brothers, Leo, Masseo and Angelo, are the three Friars, who compiled a book of narratives on the life of Francis, called *The Three Companions.*

Francis and his faithful company of three, went to the mountain of Alverna (La Verna) to pray, from the Feast of the Assumption (August 15) to the Feast of St. Michael (September 29). He called this period the Lent of St. Michael. Francis had a special rapport with Mary and Michael from the early days of his conversion. He went to them often, for comfort and consolation, when things got rough. He was going there now to *give,* by fasting in honor of their feasts; but he knew he would be *receiving* from them as well.

He always had an exalted devotion to St. Michael. He felt that Michael should be honored because he had the office of presenting souls to God. He also said *"Everyone should offer to God, to honor so great a prince (Michael), some praise or some special gift."* He loved Mary reverently. As he loved Jesus, he could not do otherwise than love *"the womb that bore Him."* He sang to her, offered special prayers to her, shared his joys and sorrows with her. She was his very best friend, the Mother of his God. While he was honoring Michael, he was also honoring Mary on the Feast of her Assumption into Heaven, August 15, and her birthday, September 8.

There was a crag on that mountain, a deep crevice which separated one part of that high place from the other. Tradition has it that at the very moment Our Dear Lord Jesus died, this mountain split in two, as the whole earth shook in protest over the demonic act of murdering our Savior. Francis loved to sit on that jagged rock, and meditate on the Passion of Jesus. The brothers brought him some bread and water from time to time, but for the most part, he was alone with his Lord and Savior.

According to the Divine Plan, another special Feast fell during the Lent of St. Michael. It took place on September 14, and was called The Exaltation of the Cross. Today, we celebrate it on the same day, but we call it the Triumph of the Cross. On that day, in 1224, the Lord gave Francis a distinctive gift, as reward for a lifetime of service. Might not our Lord also have been telling Francis that he was right, he had shepherded his flock the way Jesus wanted, but that it didn't matter anymore? For on this day, Jesus gave His brother Francis, the gift of His wounds, His Stigmata.

Francis had been meditating deeply on the Passion of our Lord. He had asked his best Friend, Jesus, for two gifts. The first was that somehow, before he died, he might feel the wounds of Jesus in his own body and soul; and secondly, he might experience Jesus' love for those who inflicted the wounds on His Body, and killed Him. Francis went through *a dark night of the soul*. His mind kept interfering with his spirit. He thought of what he had given up, his Fraternity, his Rule. He tried desperately to put these things in the back of his consciousness, and just zero in on the pains of His Redeemer. His humanity fought him all through the night, but with the dawn, a stillness, a heavy blanket of peace came over the mountain. Everything was quiet; not a sound from any of the creatures. It was as if they knew what was to come, and were preparing themselves for the entrance of a Heavenly Being.

Light began to emerge from the darkness. Francis thought it was Brother Sun greeting him. But the light was too intense, much stronger than the sun. The curtain separating Heaven from earth split open. A figure came forth, slowly, and carried the brilliant light with it. Francis couldn't look at it; the light was too strong. Then the Lord allowed Francis' eyes to open. Before him, suspended in the air, was a huge Angel, who appeared to be made of fire, he was so bright; but there were no flames coming from him. *He had six wings, two extended over his head, two extended as if for flight, and two covering his body.*[17] The angel was nailed to

---

[17]Celano First Life no. 94

a cross; the wounds of Jesus flared up, and shivered against the light. They were of a deep crimson, sprinkled with gold.

Francis stood up joyfully, to greet the Seraph[18]. At that moment, beams of heated illumination shot out of the Angel's wounds, and penetrated Francis' body, hands, feet and side. He fell from the force of the thrust; his body experienced devastating pain, mixed with inconceivable joy. His blood raced throughout his body; he was sure he would die. Then the sensation calmed down to a constant throb of joy and pain. He looked up at the Heavenly creature. The eyes of the Angel were studying Francis. The stare was compelling. There was at once fear and bliss, mixed together. He didn't know what was happening to him. The eyes of the Angel were the most beautiful he had ever seen. He could not look away from them.

The Heavenly vision spoke gently to Francis' heart. He told him things he had to hear, which were for him alone; he would not in his lifetime, reveal them to anyone. He stayed with Francis for the better part of an hour. This is according to the testimony of the farmers, and mule keepers at the foot of the mountain. They mistook the brilliant light for the sun coming up, and began their day. Then, when it disappeared, and the natural sun came out, it was colorless by comparison.

Many insights were revealed to Francis on top of Mount Alverna. His whole life was put into perspective. He finally understood his journey, and while his humanity would tend to kick in over the next two years, he could always fall back on this time, and the revelations he received, and a peace would come over him.

---

[18]Seraph is the name of the Angels of the Angelic choir of Seraphim, which is one of the choirs who adore before God. The word comes from the Hebrew "fiery" (Is 6: 1-4).

A Saint for all time

Francis had been considered a Saint from the early days of the movement. But now, as he bore the wounds of Christ on his body, the people proclaimed his Sainthood from the mountaintops. They clamored over him more than they had ever done before. They wanted to touch his tunic, his wounds, anything. They were convinced healings would take place just by being in his shadow. *And they did!* Throughout his trip from Mount Alverna back to Assisi, notable miracles and cures took place. He spoke brilliantly wherever he went. As if he were not famous enough before, his reputation as the Crucified Christ spread like wildfire. He was truly a Saint on earth.

As he drew nearer to his beloved Assisi, however, he could hear and sense the inner turmoil which had been going on since the new Rule had been established. There was so much infighting, so many egos, so much distrust. Everything that Francis had wanted his brothers to die to, was surfacing strongly. For him, one of the worst aspects of this discord was how out of character the brothers looked. They shouldn't be wearing tunics, and acting the way they were. They made a mockery out of their calling. They were supposed to be the good guys; only the bad guys acted like that.

Francis felt the anxieties returning. But he couldn't give in to them anymore. He had truly been specially chosen. For him to allow his lower nature to take over would be to make a farce out of the special favor he had been given, the gift of the Stigmata. He tried to close his eyes and ears to all the pettiness he saw around him. Some younger brothers complained that he always took his old friends with him on his trips. Francis told Elias that anyone could go with him from that time on. However, the old guard, those who had been with him from the beginning, were not about to let that happen. Their role was more than just taking care of the needs of Father Francis; they were also his protectors, his friends. They had committed their lives to his service.

Francis knew where he could get away from all of this squabbling, at San Damiano. He wanted to go back to his roots, to the beginning, and to his beloved Clare. He had not given her much time or attention these last twelve years. Again, it was a decision. He never had any doubts about his shortcomings. He always loved Clare; she always loved him. They both knew their love was a celibate love, one that transcended the lower nature of man. But he also knew how the devil can twist even the most beautiful relationships into something immoral. He had always kept a respectable distance from Clare and the Poor Ladies, as they were called.

Misunderstandings had cropped up over the years because of Francis' insistence that he stay away from the ladies. Two instances in their lives bring that point home very clearly. While it's true that Francis was only the catalyst Jesus used to bring Clare into His bosom, there was that attraction. But as soon as Clare joined Francis' band of disciples, she was *cut off* from him completely. Francis' reasoning was sound. He did not want even the slightest hint of scandal to cast a shadow on his movement, and that of the Poor Ladies. That was good, but Clare felt the need Francis' teachings for her *own* spiritual nourishment, as well as that of her ladies.

Clare was locked away in her little Convent at San Damiano, while Francis traveled about spreading the Gospel. She understood they were called to different walks, she was to pray and he was to preach, but she had a problem in that he always stayed away from her and her ladies. This one day in particular, when she heard that he had returned from a trip and was at Santa Maria degli Angeli, she sent word with his Friars, asking to share a meal with him.

Francis refused. Even his followers thought he was being too hard on Clare. They told him,

"Father, it does not seem to us that your way of acting accords very well with charity. Clare has given up all the riches of the world; she is a choice plant in your spiritual garden. Why then do you not wish to make her happy in so little a thing as allowing her to have a meal with you?"

In his heart, Francis knew they were right. He really looked forward to being able to share with Clare. He decided, however, rather than going to San Damiano, he would have Clare come to Santa Maria degli Angeli. He felt it would be good for her to get out. Clare and one of her ladies went to visit him. First she went into the Portiuncola to pray; then Francis took her on a tour of the little Community that had been built there. As she looked around, she recalled fond memories of that Palm Sunday evening when she first went there to join Francis.

They went into the woods. Francis laid out the meager *bread and water* dinner on a stone. But before eating, they began to pray. They were so filled with the Holy Spirit that the entire area became illuminated. There was such a bright light, it could be seen for miles around. Townspeople thought there was a fire in the woods around Santa Maria degli Angeli, and came running with buckets of water to put out the flames. When they arrived, they saw Francis and Clare, with their two companions, deep in prayer, covered by a brilliant aura. After their prayer was over, the light went out and the townspeople dispersed. Clare and Francis stood up, spiritually filled, never having touched one drop of food.

The second instance took place some time later. It was very dramatic, in that Clare got her *Italian* up. Francis went back to his old ways of staying away from the ladies at San Damiano. He would come from time to time, but only to peek in the door. He wanted to be sure they were living up to their vow of poverty, which they were. But he never gave them any spiritual direction, never talked about the Lord, nor shared on the joy of living the Gospel life. Clare felt deeply that she and her ladies needed this. She had never regretted trading the luxuries of her life for the way of the Gospel. If there was not enough bread to eat, she could handle that. If there was no wine, that was better yet. But there was a strong need for *spiritual* food. She could not allow her ladies to be deprived of *this*. Francis, on the other hand, felt the need to turn Clare and her ladies completely over to the Lord. To add fuel to the fire, he instructed the brothers who brought provisions to San Damiano, not to speak to the ladies of spiritual matters, only their physical needs. Clare felt it was time for action. She and her ladies went on a *hunger strike*! They would not accept any more food or oil from Francis. She told her ladies, "*If we are to be deprived of our spiritual nourishment, we will be able to manage also without their material help.*"

When word got back to Francis of Clare's decision, he immediately moved into action. He went over to San Damiano to speak to the ladies. They were all excited, having their spiritual father there to share with them. Francis was somewhat ill-at-ease. They formed a circle around him. They waited for his words. He meditated for a few moments. Then, filled with the Spirit, he spoke words that touched their hearts. The more inspired he became, the more beautiful the words that flowed from him. Then he went into a deep silence, after which he left them. He had not stayed with them long, but that short period was so dynamic, the ladies were in Paradise on earth for days. Clare said a prayer of thanksgiving to Our Lord Jesus for coming through once again, with this most special gift.

During late Spring of 1225, Francis went to the Convent of San Damiano to be nursed by the Sisters. He thought it would be acceptable, because he was considered a "*Crucified*

Christ." He was almost blind. He described the pain in his
eyes as *"great splinters of glass scratching against his pupils."*
He suffered in his side, hands and feet from the Wounds of
Jesus. His internal organs were disintegrating; his stomach
ulcerated from fasting, and his spleen destroyed by fatigue.
When he arrived at San Damiano, though it was bright
daylight, he groped as if he were walking in the dark of night.
Clare met him and gently helped him inside. While he
allowed them to minister to him inside the Convent, he
would not sleep there. A small hut was set up on a balcony,
outside the upper room, which is called today, the balcony of
the Canticle of the Creatures.

He never told the ladies how he suffered at night, when
all God's creatures, whom he loved so much, bit at his toes,
and crawled all over his open sores. But one morning, as
Clare went to see how he was feeling, she heard him singing
a Canticle to the Creatures.

Most High, Omnipotent, Good Lord.
Thine be the praise, the glory, the honor and benediction.
To Thee alone, Most High, they are due,
And no man is worthy to mention Thee.

Be Thou praised, my Lord, with all Thy creatures, above
all Brother Sun,
Who gives the day, and lightens us therewith.
And he is beautiful and radiant with great splendor,
Of Thee, Most High, he bears similitude.

Be Thou praised, my Lord, of Sister Moon and the Stars,
In the heavens Thou has formed them, clear and precious
and comely.

Be Thou praised, my Lord, of Brother Wind.
And of the air and the cloud, and of fair and of all weather,
By which Thou givest to Thy creatures sustenance.

Be Thou praised, my Lord, of Sister Water,
Which is much useful and humble, precious and pure.

Be Thou praised, My Lord, of Brother Fire,

By which Thou has lightened the night,
And he is beautiful and joyful, robust and strong.
   Be Thou praised, my Lord, of our Sister Mother Earth,
Which sustains and hath us in rule,
And produces divers fruits with colored flowers and herbs.

Francis also wrote the first part of the Canticle of the Sun, while at the Convent of San Damiano. When we consider all of the above, his deteriorated physical condition, plus his constant reminder of the distressing atmosphere just a mile away in Assisi, these were two of the most beautiful canticles that Francis ever wrote. How do you think he was able to write them, with all that was going on. We believe he received *affirmation*, and *love without motive* at the Convent of San Damiano. Clare had always been his number one advocate. She was the most ardent supporter of his Rule. If there was anyone in the world who could *out-poverty* Francis, it was Clare. For that brief time with her, he was young again. He was the idealist, who would go out to all the world, using his own brand of knighthood, and make it a better place.

But that time had to end. Reality clicked in. He knew he was sinking. He had things to do before the end. He left Clare and her Poor Ladies. She knew from the time he staggered blindly away from San Damiano that it was just a matter of time. But no matter how much time the Lord would give her to adjust to the fact that he would die, it was not enough. Clare could sense Sister Death closing in on Francis; she felt as though her heart were being ripped out of her body. Her whole world was crumbling.

"All Praise be Yours, my Lord, through Sister Death"

In the last days, the most frustrating thing for Francis, was to be blind and useless. The brothers, in an effort to save what was left of the carcass of their Holy Father Francis, scurried to send him all over Italy to various doctors, for treatments which didn't really work. He consented reluctantly, because, while he did not want to prolong his life, he wanted to be productive to the end. But this was not the Lord's plan.

In the last days of September, 1226, he was brought back to Assisi. It was enough now with the doctors and the cures. Francis knew the Lord was calling him, and he responded. He dictated his last Testament. He wanted to set things straight. While he trusted in God, he didn't trust in man. He wanted everyone to know exactly how he felt, what his concerns were for the Order, now that he was leaving them. In reading the Testament, it doesn't appear that Francis was trying to open an old wound, but that's exactly what happened. While he made a point of telling the brothers *not to interpret* what he was saying, this Testament became the ammunition for many who believed he did not accept the Rule of 1223. It became food for those who wanted to split from the Fraternity as it existed.

Francis did recap his values, and his commitment to the Rule. He warned the brothers not to be going off in all directions, but to be obedient to the legitimate authority. He ended his Testament with a blessing from the Holy Trinity, and from himself.

He dictated a letter to Clare and the Poor Ladies. He made a promise to them, which he kept. *"Let her know in truth that before she dies, she and all her sisters will see me again and will receive great consolation from me."*

His last commitment was as his first, to Lady Poverty. He wanted to go out of this world as he had come in, with no earthly possessions. He ordered[19] the brothers to take all his clothes off, and lay him on the ground near St. Mary's of the Portiuncola. He couldn't see, but he could hear. He

---

[19]ordered - Francis had to order them to do this, as they didn't want to. For some reason, they didn't think he would die.

recognized the sad voices of his companions. They had been such good friends. It was right that they should surround him for this last good-by, especially his beloved Leo. This was a special moment, this last one with his Fraternity.

Francis blessed all the brothers, those present, and those in far-off places. He forgave them all their offenses, and insisted they be advised of this. He lapsed into Psalm 142, David's lamentation in the cave. The brothers responded to his prayer. Finally, a heavy silence fell on the place. They waited for Francis to speak again; no words came. The silence was broken in places by weeping. The brothers looked one to the other, then back at Francis. A peace had come about him. His face was serene; his body limp. He had passed over.

Although the mood was, for the most part, one of sorrow, there were those from the town, who waited anxiously to parade the body of the Saint through the town of Assisi. But a promise had been made to Lady Clare.

"When word had come to her that they would see Francis, her Sisters were consoled. Clare was thankful to the Lord for this ray of hope that she would see him again. But seeing him once more was not enough! She wanted time with him. She wanted Francis alive! She needed the little poverello who had been her Jesus on earth. The journey to their dream had gone so fast. It couldn't end this way! But it did. She wished she did not have to set an example at this time. She wanted to be a normal woman for just an hour, instead of a Mother figure. She wanted to run out, away from San Damiano, over to Santa Maria degli Angeli. She wanted to cradle Francis in her arms; she wanted to bathe him in her tears; she wanted to take away his sickness; she wanted to make him better. She knew the Angel of Death was coming to take her Francis Home to the Father and she did not want him to go, not yet!

She wanted to stop Francis from dying!   But she couldn't.   The Lord mercifully gave her the gift of illness, which kept her a prisoner of her thatched bed, on the upper level of the Convent of San Damiano.   Her Master Jesus saved her from her own desires.   He cried with her, by her side, as she unleashed all the sorrow in her heart, crying uncontrollably, without stopping, until she heard the sound of the funeral procession coming to the front of the Church of San Damiano.   The body of Francis was brought into the church.

Francis had promised Clare she would see him again.   Now he was lying dead on a stretcher.   Half the town of Assisi was in attendance.   This was not what she wanted.   She wanted to be with him; she wanted to talk to him; she wanted to listen to his voice.   But that was not the gift the Lord gave her.   This was her gift.   She accepted it.   She stopped crying.   She opened the Grille.   The creaking sound of metal grinding against metal ripped through the silence of the church.   Everyone focused on the lone figure emerging from behind the enclosure.   She walked over to the stretcher.   Before her was her love, her role model, the instrument the Lord used to change her life.   He was broken.   The body was frail, gray, lifeless.   A cold chill blew through the church, ricocheting off the walls.   Francis' hair was tossed by the wind, as was his tunic.   It was the only movement on his body.   Clare looked at him.   For a moment, she thought he had blinked his eyes, but it was the wind.   Then the wind died down, and Francis was still again.   She bent over and kissed his wounded hands, his feet and side.   She painfully rose and took a long last look at him.   She tried to memorize every inch of him.   It would have to last her twenty seven years.   She turned and disappeared behind the iron Grille, among a sea of Sisters, weeping and moaning the loss of

*their spiritual father. Clare never looked back. Francis
had kept his promise."*[20]

We would like to make a final comment on the Rule. It
has never been completely resolved. It has been said that
there is no other Rule, and most likely will never be one that
had so many people trying to interpret. So, even in this,
Francis' last wishes were not to be followed. However, a
magnificent statement has been made about the Rule, by a
Jesuit, of all people. Sometimes we have to be outside a
situation to really understand it. Peter Lippert had this to
say about the Rule of the little Poverello,

*"The organizational principle that leads from Benedict
through Dominic and Ignatius to the newer
communities seems to have practically exhausted its
inner possibilities...The fundamental newness that is
precisely the thing being sought today by countless
souls...is to be found only along a completely different
line; along the original ideal of Francis. In other words;
in the direction of a freely chosen life style and freely
chosen bonds of love; in the direction of a life that
operates through spontaneous initiative of the self rather
than through great constructs of the will; in the direction
of a truly living and individual personality shaped by its
own inner laws and standards. If God should someday
deign to reveal the Order of the future of His Church...it
will surely bear the stamp of Francis' soul and spirit."*[21]

Simply put, all the great minds of the Church, all the
Doctors and Theologians and Philosophers, all the movers
and shakers of this world, have never come up with a better
mousetrap, and most likely, never will. The Lord worked
through a simple, humble, meager *giant!*

---

[20]*Saints and Other Powerful Women in the Church*, Bob and Penny
Lord, Journeys of Faith 1989, Pg. 33-34
[21]Living Our Future pp 172-179

The little town of Assisi has changed over the centuries. The entire original Fraternity of Francis and the Portiuncola has been enclosed inside a large Basilica at Santa Maria degli Angeli. There are hotels and restaurants, and railroad tracks, and a lot of noise from the cars and buses that frequent the road up the hill to Assisi. But as you look at the panorama of Assisi, two things are etched in the sky. On the one side is the Basilica of St. Francis, and on the other side, the Basilica of St. Clare. One gets the impression that they're actually looking at each other. And if you stay up late one night, until after all the automobiles have stopped running, and all the people have gone to bed, if there's a blanket of quiet all around you; and you listen intently, you might just hear the two of them, Francis and Clare, singing together, very softly, these simple, powerful praises to Our Lord Jesus.

> *"All praise be Yours my Lord,*
> *through all that You have made,*
> *And first my lord Brother Sun,*
> *Who brings the day;*
> *and light You give to us through him.*
> *All praise be Yours, my Lord,*
> *through Sister Moon and Stars;*
> *In the heavens You have made them,*
> *bright and precious and fair."*

Photo Credits *Basilica of St. Francis, Assisi, Italy*
All excerpts and quotations from *Francis of Assisi, Omnibus of Sources*

Left:
Francis instructed the brothers, *"Come back to the Portiuncola at least once a year. The Spirit of Jesus and Mary are very strong here."*

Below:
The Tomb of St. Francis, the final resting place of St. Francis, is one of the most venerated shrines in Christianity.

Above: ***St. Anthony holds the Child Jesus***   Below: ***St. Anthony made the sign of the cross, the foot became attached to the leg.***

St. Anthony of Padua

Finder of the Lost

There has always been an Anthony in my life, even before I knew who *Saint Anthony* was, and what part he would play in my life. My middle brother's name is Anthony, and although he is six years older than I, his job was to take care of *baby sister*. He grumbled a lot at having to drag the *pest* along with him and his friends, but he did. When I could not keep up with his long legs, he carried me on his shoulders. We fought as brothers and sisters do, but do not let anyone *else* try to hurt me; I could always rely on my older brother to defend me. As I grew into a teen-ager he became my advisor to the lovelorn. I didn't always welcome his counsel, but darn him, he was always right!

We each married and moved miles apart. But the Anthony of my intimate family was to be replaced, *as an instrument*, by another Anthony. Our precious son died and we died along with him. We turned off God and His Church and although we didn't know it, Bob and I were on the way to turning each other off as well, when *St. Anthony* came into our life.

The St. Anthony who appeared in our life, after almost four years of not asking *anything* of St. Anthony, of Jesus or any other member of our Heavenly family, was a curly-haired Sicilian-American. This Anthony persisted and persisted until he led us to Marriage Encounter and *new life* in Jesus and the Church. Even the Seminary where we went for our Marriage Encounter week-end was called, *right again*, St. Anthony's.

Of course, I was completely unaware, at the time that St. Anthony was interceding in my life. But that doesn't stop Jesus, His Mother or any of His Saints from consistently helping us. The pieces finally started to come together, when the fool (that's me) began to grow up. As we learned more about this wonderful, exciting Faith of ours, I began to realize St. Anthony was not merely a statue my grandmother had on her altar, in *our* bedroom. He was not solely someone you prayed to find lost items[1] or a husband[2]. I wanted to know more about this special man, this *St. Anthony*, and so, the search began.

Who is St. Anthony?

In the United States, he has been given the *obscure* title of "Finder of Lost Articles." Whenever we lose something, we ask St. Anthony to find it for us and, more times than not, he answers our prayers.

The St. Anthony, *I* had known over the years, is probably the one you know, as well. There was nothing I misplaced, I couldn't ask him to find for me that he didn't. One time, in Padua when I shame-facedly admitted turning to St. Anthony to find lost *objects*, a Franciscan reassured me, saying,

> "*Oh, St. Anthony doesn't mind. As a matter of fact, he likes to be part of your everyday life. You see, as you are calling him to ask him to find something, he really is taking you by the hand and leading you to Jesus.*"

This is not unlike the way St. Anthony lived his life. He was a brilliant man, but for most of his life, he chose to live

---

[1]This tradition began when a novice stole a book belonging to St. Anthony. As it had notes the Saint used for his homilies, he prayed for its return. The novice is said to have had an apparition which *compelled* him to restore the book to St. Anthony.

[2]There is a tradition, in some cultures - where young girls pray to St. Anthony, asking him to find them a suitable husband.

an *obscure life*, a humble life. And because of this, no one knew *who* he was.

He was proclaimed a Doctor of the Church. There are 32 Doctors of the Church[3]. In the 2,000 years since the Church was instituted, out of its millions of holy people, and *thousands* of canonized Saints, only 32 have been given the honor of this title. The Saint, we pray to for *lost objects*, is one of these honored people. But until the Lord decided to put St. Anthony into active ministry, he was a dishwasher and confessor to Franciscan hermits. No one had any idea what the Lord had locked up in the mind and heart of this great Saint.

Son of Italy, his beginnings in Portugal

Sts. Francis of Assisi and Catherine of Siena are the *co-patron* Saints of Italy. This is in no way, to belittle *them* or the place they hold in the hearts of Italians and Catholics, as a whole; but the Saint's statue, seen in *every* store, car or apartment, is that of *St. Anthony of Padua*, or as he is affectionately called, "*Il Santo.*"

Of course, the Portuguese would give them an argument; they call him St. Anthony of *Lisbon*, just because he was born there and lived there most of his life. Oh well!

This towering yet humble Saint is loved throughout the *world* by Catholics and non-catholics, including many Jewish people, as well. But, he is not really known for the fullness of who he was and is to us, the Church. Although, we believe this is really how he would like it, with all due respect to him and his wishes, we must nevertheless endeavor to share some of the discoveries we have made. This is not to further honor him, as he needs no added acclaim, but to encourage others to follow in his footsteps on their journey to Jesus.

---

[3]The Catholic Encyclopedia defines a Doctor of the Church as: A title conferred on eminent ecclesiastical writers because of their learning and holiness of life; they are always canonized.

Whenever our Church is in danger, and it looks like all the principalities of hell are about to level her, the Lord calls forth a Saint or two.

St. Anthony was born into a time of oppression: Portugal and much of Europe had been under Muslim domination for centuries. For over one hundred years, Portugal had been trying to liberate itself from its invaders. Piece by piece, pain upon pain, inch by inch their land was being reclaimed for Christ and His Church. Brave knights, many of them Crusaders, settled in Lisbon, after having fought courageously to oust the Saracens(or Muslims). St. Anthony was born of one of these knights, *Martino*. We are told in the most authentic biographies of the Saint, he came from a powerful family of the *nobility*.

St. Anthony was born on the Feast of *The Assumption of Mary* into Heaven, August the 15th, 1195. All his life, he was strongly devoted to our Lady and Her Assumption into Heaven. As he staunchly defended the Son, he championed the Son's Mother, as well. Show me a Saint and I'll show you Mary in his life.

His baptismal name was Fernando, which means *bold in peace*, and that he *was*, to the end of his life here on earth.

His religious education began where the most meaningful learning begins, from his parents. He not only inherited *worldly* wealth from his family, but a treasure that would hold him in *holy* stead the rest of his life, a heritage of the Faith that no one could ever take from him.

Although, there is little information about St. Anthony's youth, there are legends that have followed him, filling in the blank pages, for almost 800 years. One of these legends[4] takes place when Fernando was quite young.

His father Martino and Fernando loved to go to their farm on the outskirts of town. One day, Martino took his son with him to see if their crop was ready to harvest. Summer was here; God was good and the crop was ready! There was only one problem; the greedy sparrows had their eyes and bills on the crop, as well. Martino would have to get help from the neighbors, if he was to prevent the winged enemy from pecking away his entire harvest before he could gather it. He delegated the task of keeping the thieving birds away, to Fernando, until he returned.

Fernando began running up and down the hills, shooing away the birds, before his father disappeared from sight. But soon, his little legs tired. Not far off, a small country church was calling to him, inviting him inside to pray. The little boy, torn between his duty to his father and his desire to pray, kept running toward the church and back toward the hills. Finally, he had an idea! He called to the sparrows to come with him. He led them into a large room, in the house, and locked the door and windows behind them. The little boy, Fernando, went peacefully and joyfully to spend time with the Lord, he could *feel* present in the church, even at this young age.

His father, upon returning and not being able to find his son, became *frantic*. Combing every inch of the hillside, as a last resort, he thought to look in the church. There was Fernando deep in prayer! Before his father could scold him, Fernando took his father's hand and led him into the house.

---

[4]legend or *legenda*, in Medieval times, was a formal literary composition intended to be read and reread for the purpose of edification. Conventional norms, including an orderly exposition were expected of such a work. (We Were with St. Francis - Salvator Butler O.F.M.)

As they opened the door, the singing prisoners flew out to freedom and the crop.

As a priest, the older Fernando, later said, "*The waves of the sea, when they hit a rock, break, and the tempest of temptation which hurts you will break if it finds you united to Christ.*" Was this in memory of something that happened when he was still a boy? One day after Mass, Fernando, having stayed behind to pray, felt something stirring inside the church. He looked up toward the choir-loft; he saw a face so hideous, it made him tremble uncontrollably. It was the face of Satan; he was going to stop the boy from praying, if he had to scare him to *death*.

Fernando could no longer pray; he was frozen, paralyzed with fear. With all the strength he could muster, he traced a cross on the floor. As quickly as *he* had appeared, the vision disappeared. Tears of joy welled up in the little boy's eyes; the Lord, his Shepherd had frightened Satan away. The only sign of the encounter was the cross which *remained* on the floor.

Fernando and the Call to Arms

Although their land was reclaimed from the Saracens, real peace had not returned to Portugal. Alfonso, the king largely responsible for their freedom, died, and a new king ascended the throne. The new monarch, Sancio I, was an equally *just* king, whose focus was to bring stability and peace to his country. This was not in keeping with the aristocracy, who, for their own reasons, whether for adventure or personal gain, were always on the lookout for a confrontation. Fernando's father, of this class, advised his son to pursue the call to arms. With other young men of his station, Fernando developed an agile and strong body, a courageous spirit, and a boldness to do right, no matter the cost. Even though he and his father thought this was for the defense of country, we will see how God will use this training for defense of His *Church*.

Although very handsome and well accepted by his friends, at fifteen years old, Fernando began to feel an *emptiness* in his life. He had been in readiness for the eventuality of battle. At first, he found that exciting, but even that did not fill the void. All around him, his friends and companions were busying themselves with an idle life. Allures of the world were dominating and contaminating their minds, absorbing them with a need for more and more wealth. Self-love was consuming them. *Pride*, the "I" did this and the "I" did that, was blinding them. As a man, he later wrote,"...*the heart before engaging in luxury, emerges in pride which is the beginning of all sins.*"

The world was also tempting him with *good*: attachments and concerns tugging at him, pulling him apart. *His country and family needed him* (chivalry). *Why couldn't he marry and have a family* (pure love)? There was nothing wrong with all the world was offering; then why did he see it as flawed and lifeless?

The young cavalier felt more and more stifled by the life around him. Fernando later describes his struggle between the world and the Kingdom,

"If you do not resist the evil of luxury, at the end even the things which appear good will perish."

We often see a statue or painting of St. Anthony holding a lily, a sign of purity. This purity, like with St. Francis, was an ongoing *war* that could only be won with strict discipline and hard struggle, over many years. As he found himself being called more and more to the priesthood, he had to fight, not only his parents' dreams for him to take over the family estates and give them grandchildren, but the lure of ambition, his desire to *amount* to something. Only the whisper in his heart, that gentle tugging at his spirit, kept him on the road to the Lord and the priesthood.

Fernando leaves his family

His family had reared him, in keeping with his place in society, to care for people's physical and social needs. Then why were they so upset when he set out to work for the needs of their *souls*? Fernando joined the Order founded under the Rule inspired by St. Augustine. Unlike Benedictine monks, whose goal was *personal* sanctification through work and prayer, the Augustinians' charism was to help *other* souls.

Fernando's parents looked upon this son, who had shown such promise, with tears in their eyes. Their good-bys were, as if they would never see him again. He had demonstrated how dependable and mature he was, even for fifteen years of age; nevertheless, their grief was that pain, only another parent knows, of saying good bye to *their baby*. They were partly right; the Fernando who left the family would never be the same.

It was the year 1210 and Fernando walked through the door of St. Vincent's Abbey. He had won a hard battle, but the war was yet to be won! Perhaps one of his sermons best speaks, of the walk he had chosen, his walk to the priesthood and Sainthood:

"Whoever joins a religious Order,... is like the pious women who on Easter morning went to Christ's tomb. Considering the greatness of the tomb, they said: 'Who will move the stone away for us?' The stone is large, so is the harshness of convent life: the difficulty of entering, the long vigils, the frequent fasts, the sparse meals, the rough habit, the severe discipline, the voluntary poverty, the ready obedience...Who will roll the stone away from the tomb? Oh, you souls like those of the women, come near and observe and you will see that the stone has been removed. An angel came down and rolled the stone away and then sat on it. The angel is the grace of the Holy Spirit, who makes frailty strong, who softens

every hardship, who makes every bitterness sweet by His Love..."

The Abbey he'd chosen, was *too* near Lisbon, and all he had left behind. The pealing of bells from the nearby church, he and his family had attended, cut through and disrupted the peace he sought with his Savior. Memories became more and more *painful*. His well-meaning friends, convinced he had chosen unwisely, did everything they could to try to dissuade him from becoming a priest. *For his own good*, he must leave the Monastery. As they were of good social standing, the Monks did not dare refuse them visiting rights; Fernando had to take another *giant* step away from the world toward his vocation.

He requested, he be transferred to a Monastery, far from Lisbon. His prior granted permission; Fernando set out by foot, to his new life in the *Abbey of Santa Cruz* (Holy Cross), 100 miles away, in Coimbra.

Fernando, priest of Christ

Fernando was now seventeen years old. The *reason* he joined the Abbey of Santa Cruz was to follow a more *spiritual* life. God had other plans! Maybe, because Fernando wanted *only* to love God, purely, he was to be given other gifts as well, gifts he would later use. This Abbey *just happened to be* a center of important ecclesiastical study. At St. Vincent's, he'd read the literature of *pagan* philosophers. Here, at the Abbey, he would devote himself to Theology and the teachings of our Founding Fathers. He traced the History of the Church, delving into the religious controversies that our Church faced and survived over the centuries. Little did he know, he was being prepared for the battle, he would wage in her defense.

As he grew in his Faith, his love of Jesus in the Word grew. He wrote,

"Oh divine Word, admirable Word that inebriates and changes the heart, You are the limpid Source that refreshes the parched soul; the ray of hope that gives comfort to the sinner; the faithful Messenger that brings glad tidings to us exiles of our heavenly country!"

Fernando always had a *photographic*[5] memory. Every word he read in Sacred Scriptures, he placed in that library of his mind, never to forget it. He would use this gift from God, later, as a priest. He had an *unquenchable* love for learning; it came easy to him. The most talented and dedicated teachers were at his disposal. All the knowledge, derived from them and the Abbey's extensive library, would be an ongoing source of nourishment, for Fernando, the rest of his life.

Eight years flew by, at the Abbey. His joy was to be replaced by pain. Ten years an Augustinian, Fernando asked to *leave* the Abbey, and the Augustinians. He requested permission, to join the followers of Francis. Fernando never did things half way. Not one to compromise, his spirit was disquieted by the division and dissension that had arisen among the canons, at the Abbey of the Holy Cross. The Prior was compromising his commitment to the Pope and his canons, placing loyalty to the King before his vocation as priest and Prior. The Pope excommunicated him. Some canons rallied behind the *excommunicated* Superior and others behind the Pope. This *scandal* and increasing influence of the *world* on the Abbey, brought about unbearable sorrow in Fernando's soul. Many of his future sermons reflected his suffering. Referring to his Prior, he *warned* of the *responsibility* of one who would lead,

"The Superior is called the Father of the house, because under him the subject, like a son, enters the paternal house, where he finds shelter from the carnal

---

[5]*photographic* - recalling or retaining in precise detail

lust, from the tempest of diabolical persecution, and from the poverty of worldly prosperity."

He spoke with painful disillusionment, as he chastised certain canons who had sold out the Christian ideal, that of the Gospel,

"*The locusts, which jump so high, signify the monks, who, resting on poverty and obedience, must jump to the heights of eternal life. But, unfortunately, from on high they jump back down again. Today there are no fairs[6], (only) civil or ecclesiastical tribunes where monks are found. They buy and sell, build and destroy. In trials they begin the proceedings, they quarrel before the judges, they act as lawyers, they are witnesses ready to swear an important oath on unimportant matters.*"

These were Fernando's feelings, the night that five Franciscans stopped overnight at the Abbey of Santa Cruz. They shared, they were on their way to preach to the Muslims in Morocco. There is no explanation why they stopped *there*, rather than at the *Franciscan* Friary. Could this have been God's Way to help Fernando take the next step in his journey to the Kingdom? As he struggled between obedience to his Prior *and* loyalty to his Pope, had he reached out to the Friars at the neighboring *Franciscan Abbey of the Olives?* Had he gotten to know and love them, as he shared his bread and wine with them? We really cannot say why or how, but we do know he had become friendly with Franciscans Friars *before* the five came to visit.

Not long after their departure, the five Franciscans returned from Morocco. Their *remains* were interred in a Shrine at Santa Cruz; they had been martyred for the Faith. The gnawing at his heart began again, only now it was clear; he was called to go to Morocco and die a "*martyr.*" His Prior, although hardly a Saint himself, could see *his* holiness. He

---

[6]Fairs - just

sadly gave Fernando, now *Father* Fernando, the necessary permission to join the followers of Francis. All at the Abbey of Holy Cross, knew, with his intelligence and dedication, Fernando had been slated to do important work for the Order. Now, they had to let him go! I know this generous act was to their *credit*, as God considered this "*yes*," when passing judgment on their many *unwise yeses*.

"*You are no longer Fernando; I give you a new name, Anthony, that you might know that you are called to a new life.*"

Can you not hear the Lord speaking these words, as *Fernando* removed the white robes of the Augustinians, and *Anthony* donned the rough tunic of Father Francis? The Augustinian canons, he so loved and lived with these eight years, and the Franciscan Friars, he had *learned* to love, joined hands, praising God. In addition, we believe, there was a *heavenly* company, the Trinity, Mother Mary, the Angels and Saint Augustine. Saints do not have a problem with *who* gets credit for the salvation of God's Church. Although Fernando was leaving the Augustinian Order, St. Augustine knew what Anthony had learned amongst his friars, would be used for the glory of God and *His* Victory; that was enough for him!

Onward Christian Soldier - to Morocco and Martyrdom

One of the Augustinian canons bid *Friar* Anthony farewell saying, "Go, go and become a Saint!" To which Anthony humbly replied, "*The day that you are told that I have become a Saint is a day you will glorify God.*"

After spending a few months learning and practicing the Rule of Francis, Friar Anthony was on his way to *martyrdom*, as a missionary. He embarked for Morocco, in the footsteps of the five Franciscan *martyrs*, who had gone before him. Their work, conversion of the Muslims, was now left for Anthony, or so he thought.

The land he stepped foot on, the land made glorious by such as Augustine, was now a wasteland of non-believers. Christians faced danger, or even death, should they become detected. The churches were in a state of pitiful decay, unloved and unused. The utter spiritual desolation of this desert attacked Anthony's spirit. But *that* did not stop him! Instead, he was struck down by a high fever, which persisted. It not only debilitated him; it almost killed him. News of his condition reached his superiors; he was recalled to Portugal. Anthony started the long journey back; his mission, to bring the Good News of Jesus Christ to the Muslims, as dead as he physically felt. *He would not be a martyr for the Faith,* he cried. But, he would be martyred in another sense, saying each day, maybe each moment of the day, *"I do not know Your Will, Father, but Thy Will be done, not mine."*

He had offered his life to the Father, as a martyr; He didn't want it, or was it, He did not want him? These thoughts nagged at him. Although Anthony was a man of passion, he was also a man who thought things through. After much reasoning and more prayer, he overcame all the harassments and doubts of the devil. Anthony recognized he'd been hasty. He had tried to force the Will of God. We're supposed to let God push us into *His* Will. It's not for us to push Him into *our* will. Was Anthony supposed to be a martyr in the *spiritual* sense rather than in the physical sense, dying a martyrdom of desire and, above all, the heart? Anthony died in Africa, only it was to *his* desires, *his* will and *his* dream. Journeying *to* Africa and Morocco, he was *Friar* Anthony; returning, he was *Saint* Anthony.

Anthony's destiny was clearly not in Portugal, either, because a storm diverted the ship to the shores of Sicily. Anthony and his companion spent two months with the *Friars Minor* in Sicily; his health slowly returned. At this time, *it just happened,* a general chapter was called for the Friars to meet in Assisi. Anthony took this as providential;

God had not desired, he die in Morocco! He had used this to bring him into the presence of the beloved *poor one*, the Poverello, Father Francis!

The fourth general chapter of the Franciscan movement opened May 23, 1221. Anthony was not ready for the over two thousand Friars who had gathered, at the Portiuncola[7], from all over the world; nor was he prepared for St. Francis. This *magnet*, who had attracted so many souls to live the Gospel life, was barely able to speak above a whisper. All his sacrifices, having taken a heavy toll on Francis, *physically*, he'd chosen Brother Elias to be his voice.

His friars were, nevertheless, prostrate before *him*. His failing health did not weaken their commitment; they were there, with one heart and one spirit, to hear and do the will of their *Father in Faith*. Francis whispered, *they were called to bring a mission to Germany*. Anthony was part of the eighty who jumped to their feet! He stood there, excited, anxious to do Father Francis' will anywhere, and everywhere, he sent him. But, *no one* saw or noticed this enthusiastic, on-fire young friar, who, some day, would play such an important part in the Order and in the Church.

Friar Anthony, unwanted and unwelcome

Here, was Anthony in the presence of his hero, Francis. And *he* did not even notice him! Nevertheless, he could not return to Portugal; he had to remain near this man, who had touched, and would continue to touch, so many. Finally, he came to St. Francis' attention. He'd been told of Anthony's sacrifices, his giving up family, friends and country. Calling him an outstanding *asset* to any Friary, Francis *highly* recommended him to all the Provincials.

---

[7]Portiuncola - also called the *"little portion"* - first church of St. Francis, given to him and the Friars, by the Benedictines.

Anthony was *rejected* by most and *unwanted* by all. The young Friar, out of humility, had withheld all knowledge of his background, his education and training. No wonder, the Friars interviewing and considering him, were not enthusiastic about taking him in...*What would he do!*

Anthony offered to be an assistant in the kitchen, sweep floors, *anything*; nothing too menial, to do the Will of the Lord. And still there were no takers. His health, not totally restored, he was still pale and weak, decidedly not one who could take on the drudgery of convent life. And so, time passed, and no one would have Anthony! The Chapter was ending; everybody was leaving, and Anthony was still not chosen for anything.

I have to believe Anthony was now thinking, how am I to do the Will of God if no one will use me? Was the *enemy* telling him, he had made a giant mistake? Not giving up, in desperation, he turned and pleaded with a Father Gratian. *It just happened*, he needed a priest. In response to his question, "Are you a priest?" Anthony gratefully exclaimed, "*yes*!" And so, another "*yes*!" Maybe not the *yes*, he had planned; maybe, it was even a little disappointed *yes*; but as he scaled the mountains to obscurity, to say Mass for some recluses in a very small hidden house, he said "*yes*" over and over again.

There were two kinds of houses in the Franciscan Order; the large ones were located near the cities, to serve the needs of the poor in body and spirit; and the small ones, hermitages, were hidden away in the mountains, dedicated to prayer, fasting and contemplation. The house, Anthony was sent to, was one of those smaller houses, remote and removed from the outside world. It was nestled in mountains reserved for little birds and animals, who shared in the peace and quiet. Anthony was happy there. In addition to celebrating Mass, he begged for, and was allowed to help with the daily *menial labors* of the other friars. He deemed every task a *holy* honor.

His comfortable life of obscurity and peace, would not last more than a year. In March of 1222, he accompanied Father Gratian and the other Friars to an ordination in Forli, a nearby city. Although Anthony's talents and intelligence were getting more and more difficult to conceal from Father Gratian, Father was not ready for the surprise that awaited him at Forli. The Bishop at the ordination, asked Father Gratian to deliver an address to the candidates for the priesthood. Father Gratian deferred to the *Benedictines* present. Not prepared, they declined to speak on this, so solemn and important an occasion. There was a problem! Who could they get to address the future priests? Ask Anthony! If he made a fool of himself, it would not be as disastrous as if one of the more *illustrious* preachers were to fall on his face. He could crawl back into his hole, unnoticed; so the kitchen-helper from the little remote hermitage in the mountains, was chosen to speak!

At the hermitage, Anthony had become known for the simplicity and directness of his language, as well as for his loving compassion; nevertheless, he had never spoken publicly. To compound the trepidation he must have felt, he had not opened a book, except his Breviary and the Psalms, since he had become a friar. He pleaded he was unfit, much better suited for the physical labor, he did in the hermitage, but all to no avail! Father Gratian insisted!

And so, out of obedience, Anthony stood up; he began to speak. All his years of study, prayer and humility, empowered by his fiery love of Jesus, he delivered one of the most commanding and stirring homilies, heard in many a year.

All the Holy Scripture, he knew by heart, all the years of preparation for the priesthood, came bursting forth. The knowledge, he had kept so well hidden, which would raise him someday to Doctor of the Church, was being resurrected, never to be buried again, not even at death. To everyone's amazement, he was eloquent! His humble whisper grew into a power-filled, passionate, blazing, roaring fire. No longer able to hide, in his comfortable obscurity, he was plunged into the limelight, he abhorred. Anthony's time had come. He had been in the bullpen long enough. *This was the day the Lord had made.* Anthony, the kitchen helper, became this day, and for all time, Anthony the Preacher.

St. Francis, hearing of this gift, commissioned Anthony to preach, to bring the Good News of Jesus to the starving faithful, *everywhere.* Not aware of his extensive education, Francis ordered Anthony to study Theology, so he would be able to speak with the true authority of the Church. Anthony obeyed! He took in, chewed, swallowed and digested every morsel of learning, offered to him, as if he was hearing it for the first time. He loved it!

He tried to keep his former learning to himself, in an effort to remain anonymous and unnoticed. His ability to absorb so much so quickly, soon came to the attention of the other friars. When they had problems understanding Theology, he explained everything so simply and clearly, the other friars pleaded with him to teach *them.*

The Rule of Francis was founded on poverty, humility and contempt of all things of the world. *Would teaching be in opposition to his Seraphic Father's wishes? Would he be causing scandal to the Order if he were to instruct the friars?* Like St. Francis, who wanted to do the Will of Jesus, who wanted to do the Will of the Father, Anthony, knew, only by abandoning himself to his earthly father (Francis), would he be ultimately doing *God's* Will. Anthony wrote to Francis, asking his will. Francis' reply was,

"*It is my wish that you teach the brothers Sacred Scripture; yet not in such a manner as to take away from yourself and them the spirit of prayer and devotion, as it is prescribed by the Rule."*

Anthony spoke to the heart and the mind: *"To know, to love!"* To *know*, that one might love in a holy and never-ending love; to *love*, that one may obtain *knowledge* that is born of faithfulness, respect, self-sacrifice, and one vision. We seek that God Whom we love. So that we might *love* Him better, we need to *know* Him better. As Anthony spoke more and more, the Gospel, he spoke of the need of learning *Who* the Father is that you might *truly* love Him. For there is no true love without knowledge of the Beloved. We cannot love someone we do not know.

St. Anthony - Vessel of the Holy Spirit

St. Anthony's preaching was almost always followed by *Miracles.* The book, *Flowers of St. Francis*, calls him *"marvelous vessel of the Holy Spirit."*

It is said, he had the *gift of tongues.* You decide! While in France, he spoke to the French, and although he'd never studied the language, they understood him. In Italy, he *preached* in *Italian.* His limited knowledge of the language, which he'd picked up from some illiterate brothers at the hermitage, was hardly adequate to *preach* the Faith! To compound the complexity of preaching in Italy, in the time of Anthony, there were as many dialects as there were principalities (28).

St. Anthony once preached before the Pope and his Cardinals, including those who spoke only Greek, Latin, French, Slavic, and English, as well as, men of *other* languages. He spoke sweetly and clearly, to be sure; but how did each man understand him in his *own* language? On this occasion, the Pope called him, *"Ark of the Covenant"* and *"Vehicle of the Holy Spirit."* It was Pentecost revisited! St. Anthony spoke through the Holy Spirit, understood in every tongue, by every man, and we know that, as in the days of the Apostles, they would never ever be the same.

Anthony - Defender of the Faith

It was a time of *heresy*! We always seem to be writing that, as we journey back through the life of our beloved Church. Man has been, and I guess will always be, suckered by his desire to do his own thing. And once he takes that first step, he is on the road to *pride*, need of *power*, and his own little heresy. Recently, we were on a Retreat where the priest asked the important question, "What do you want?" I think you might add, and how *much* do you want it? Anthony, beautiful priest, wanted only to do the Will of the Father, as passed on by the True Church of the Son, and so life was simple. His rule was, *The Pope said it and it's so.* He believed in his Pope, the head of the Church here on earth, and did not feel the need to justify, only to obey.

Ignorance of our Catholic Faith was widespread and common among the faithful; consequently heresy was easily accepted by them. The heretics used the scandals of the clergy, of that time, to woo the *naive* away from Mother Church. These Judases distorted and warped the Word to fit their own lies, lies that promised a revolution (or Reformation, as they deceptively called it) that would result in a *new age* of well-being. Does this sound familiar? St. Anthony left behind pages and pages of text, lashing out at those who would lead innocent lambs astray. Armed with knowledge and sound doctrine, he defended the Faith simply and understandably; but his *sanctity*, and *the living example* of what he preached, were his shield and his sword.

As in times past and since, there have always been dissidents[8] in the Church, as well as, in the world. The affairs in Europe, State and Church, were in a sad and dangerous

---

[8]in Thesaurus - defectors, agitators, heretics, malcontents, traitors, troublemakers, insurgents.

condition. We discover, how the world goes, so goes the Church. Heresy had many names and espoused many lies. To cite a few, there were: the Partorini, Cathari, Waldenses, and Albigenses[9].

As in times past and present, there have always been *defenders* of the Church to combat the *dissenters*. The Lord had plans for Anthony. He became one of the most compelling homilists in Europe. He would use this gift of persuasion and instruction, to become *Defender of the Eucharist*. He fought in France, successfully preaching against the *Albigensian* heresy. He didn't hesitate to lash out at *anyone*, whether heretic or bishop, who posed a danger to the Church.

During the crusades against the Albigensian Heresy, a Synod was called in Bourges, the center of France. The Archbishop of this area was involved with protecting his feudal rights and maintaining the *luxurious* life of his court. As this required gaining more power and wealth, it caused more pain and consequently, more dissension. He became one of the tools, the heretics used, to draw the poor, innocent faithful away from Holy Mother the Church.

---

[9]Albigensian heresy- The Albigensianists were very powerful in 1226, especially in Southern France. It was "...an attack not only on religion, but on civilization, itself." "...also called Cathari, the poor ones." "The Albigensian heresy, which got it's name from the town of Albi, France, was spreading its false teachings throughout the southern part of the country. The heresy condemned all the Sacraments, especially marriage. Sexual permissiveness was promoted by the Albigensianists. The Eucharist was completely rejected. Albigensianism was a religion created to justify doing everything that was irreligious and blasphemous, even to the extent of civil disobedience. It was condemned by the Church as early as the Eleventh Century, but it wasn't until the Albigensianists began serious attacks on the secular governments that the heads of the countries where they had their greatest stronghold denounced and outlawed them. *Excerpt from This Is My Body, This Is My Blood, Miracles of the Eucharist*

St. Anthony listened, as the talks at the Synod, became simply exercises in futile "*academic oratory.*" Nowhere, was there mention of metanoia or *inner* conversion. No one, looking to *self*, for cause and solution, so crucial to stopping this malignancy (heresy) from spreading.

When the opportunity presented itself, Anthony did not waste time! He went right to the *head*, for if the shepherd leads on the right path, the sheep will follow. He told the Archbishop of the *inconsistencies*, the weaknesses and the injustices that existed in his Archdiocese. Because St. Anthony spoke with love and not judgment, the Archbishop *admitted* his mistakes and repented the self-love *that had prompted them. He promised to immediately initiate* the *necessary* reforms, beginning with himself.

St. Anthony belonged to that Army of Cross Bearers, who, never looking for the easy way out, boldly spoke the *truth*, passed on by Jesus, St. Paul and St. John. They all made sacrifices, whatever it took. Because his strength was *gentle*, force balanced by love, he was known to move the most *stubborn* souls to repentance. He taught,

"*The preacher must bear with 'patience and joy' the trials which test him. When he preaches the Word of God, he must strike the hearts of sinners with force; but when the preacher is made an object of insults, he must be sweet and amiable.*"

In Imitation of Christ, we read, "*Every time I have been among men, I have returned less a man.*" St. Anthony did not return a lesser man, when he left the company of men; on the contrary, he said, he became a better man through all those, he loved. It is true, if you place your *faith* in man, it can break you. If instead, you place the Face of Jesus upon the face of man, seeing Jesus, like St. Thomas Aquinas, you will say, "*I am doing it all for You, Lord.*" Then loving the Jesus you see in him, like St. Anthony, you will become a better man, transformed by that love.

Anthony and the Heretics

Anthony was called back to Italy. She was being contaminated by her invaders. Originally, these mercenaries came into this land of love and faith, by the invitation of the Italians themselves. These *murderers-for-hire*, were supposed to attack, or defend them from their *fellow* Italians. Instead, the blood shed, was not only that of Italian bodies, but of Italian *souls*. If you sleep with the snakes, you soon get bitten; and so, the *venom of the hired* soon poisoned those, who had hired them. The Italians not only took on the coldness of the killers, losing their renowned warmth and friendliness, but they lost their precious belief in the Faith. They began to adopt the customs of these new *friends*, and their lies. And so, heresy spread like a fire out of control throughout this once *terra firma* of the Seat of the Catholic Church. This land of Saints was fast becoming a stinking swamp of sinners. Was this why Anthony had to travel thousands of miles from home and dreams, to be ship-wrecked on these shores?

St. Anthony was thrust into the midst of battle, waging war against heretics and their malignant growth among the innocent, and often gullible, faithful. He took this mission of preaching very seriously:

"It behooves a preacher to lead on earth a heavenly life, in keeping with the truths he is charged to announce to the people."

St. Anthony not only preached; he *lived* what he preached. One day, he asked a brother Franciscan to accompany him, as he set out, to share the Gospel in the neighboring towns. Later, returning home, his companion asked St. Anthony why he had *not* preached. *"But,"* St. Anthony replied, *"we have preached."* He told his companion, it was their love of the Savior, their humility, and their dedication to the Truth that was the *living sermon*. For, all who had seen them, experienced Jesus *alive* in them.

Everywhere St. Anthony went, he drew crowds. Not only did he speak with authority and simplicity, but when he appeared, with all that love shining through his eyes, the faithful would rush toward him. They wanted to get close to him, to touch him, to kiss the hem of his habit or the crucifix on his rosary. This had to be a *martyrdom* of its own. Like Francis before him, Anthony knew and taught that he is nothing: Jesus is all, and Who they love is not him, but the *Jesus* that shines out of his otherwise lifeless body.

People have been searching for Jesus since the beginning of time. When we see someone, like Anthony, who so closely resembles Him, we are drawn and hopefully converted. This was the sign! People, after hearing him talk, returned to the Sacraments; reconciliation came about between states, neighbors and families; restitution was made by those who had taken unfair advantage of others; women and men, who had turned to a life of vice and sin, repented and started to live faithfully the life, to which Jesus had called them.

St. Anthony and the Miracle of the Eucharist

He was called back to Italy to fight heretics, but again God, writing straight with crooked lines, had another plan as well...*Prove to them, I am with them to the end of time.*

He went to Rimini, on the Adriatic Sea, to the southeast of Padua. He was not faring successfully there. The heretics made fun of him, and when he spoke of the Eucharist, they became hysterical, ridiculing him.

St. Anthony was known for his sharp temper. When the heretics poked fun at him while he spoke at the port of Rimini, he turned towards the sea, and spoke to the fish. The fish, for their part, raised their bodies out of the water, and perched, as it were, on top of the water, listening to the homily given by St. Anthony. When he was finished, St. Anthony blessed the fish, at which point they returned to the sea.

Above: *St. Anthony delivered his homily to the fish.*
Below: *The Miracle of the Eucharist of St. Anthony*

The enemies of the Church, on seeing this, were completely overwhelmed. Word spread throughout the town, and heretics by the droves were converted. But there was one man, Bonvillo, by name, who wasn't impressed with St. Anthony's persuasive ways. He said to him, "You, who hold fish spellbound, let's see if you can do the same to my mule." A challenge was made. The heretic would starve his mule for three days. At the end of that time, St. Anthony would stand on one end of the square, holding the Eucharist, and Bonvillo on the other, with a pail of the animal's favorite fodder. If the mule went to St. Anthony first, the heretic would stop persecuting Catholics.

The beast was starved for three days. St. Anthony fasted and prayed for three days. On the third day, St. Anthony celebrated Mass at the local church. After the Mass, he took a consecrated Host with him out into the square. The square was packed with heretics on one side, and those who had been converted on the other. Bonvillo, the heretic, had his mule by his side. He tempted the animal with the pail of fodder that was to be the bait. At the given time, St. Anthony went to one corner of the square, with the Eucharist in his hand. The heretic went off to the other side, with the pail of delicious smelling food in his hands. He tried to lure the mule with the food.

St. Anthony gave the animal a little sermon. He said, "Creature of God, in His name, I command you to come here to adore Him, so that it will give truth to all, of the Real Presence of Jesus in the Blessed Sacrament of the Eucharist."

The mule ignored his owner and the food, and went instead over to where St. Anthony held the Body of Christ. He knelt down on both legs, and lowered his head in reverence. When all were convinced that the Lord had won out over the heretic, St. Anthony blessed the mule, who then got up, and proceeded to eat all the fodder in the pail.

The heretic Bonvillo followed the example of his mule. He went down on his knees, head bowed to the ground, in adoration of the Blessed Sacrament. *He was converted back to the faith. Before St. Anthony left Rimini, he had converted all the heretics in that region. He was given the title* **Hammer of the Heretics**. *It's not known for sure if it was given him as a result of the conversions in Rimini, or simply because he had the reputation of beating down his opponents into conversion. Poor St. Anthony! For such a brilliant man, and fervent defender of the faith, he is given the strangest titles.*[10] *There is a shrine in Rimini, in honor of the Eucharistic Miracle of St. Anthony and the Donkey.*[11]

When preaching to heretics, St. Anthony always presented the Word of Christ in the *fullness* of the Catholic Church. As God is *positive*, he taught positively; as Jesus was *gentle*, Anthony spoke gently. The only time he was known to stray from this course, was when he defended the Real Presence of Jesus in the Holy Eucharist. In one of his homilies, he firmly said,

"Upon the Altar there takes place the transubstantiation of the bread and wine into the Body and Blood of Jesus Christ. That Body which the Virgin begot, which hung upon the Cross and was placed in the sepulchre, which rose again the third day, and ascended to the right Hand of the Father, this Body the Church today and everyday presents and distributes to her faithful.

When the priest speaks the words: This is My Body, the essence of the bread is changed into the Body of Christ."

His courageous and uncompromising defense of the True Presence of Jesus in the Holy Eucharist, to the heretics, has given birth to some of the very documents and teachings, used in Seminaries for almost eight hundred years, affirming and reaffirming the Heart of the Church, our *Lord Alive* in

---

[10]Such as Founder of Lost Articles, and Hammer of the Heretics

[11]Excerpt from *This Is My Body, This Is My Blood, Miracles of the Eucharist*

our midst, to our future priests, the shepherds that will lead us to the Father. This humble man, defender of the Faith, who never lost his gift of true humility, once hidden in a kitchen *"amongst the pots and pans,"*[12] earned the honored and respected title of Doctor of the Church, possibly more for this defense of His Lord and Savior in the Holy Eucharist than for any of his other discourses on the Faith.

St. Francis dies and Anthony is called back to Assisi

Arriving in Assisi, St. Anthony made his first stop at the tomb of St. Francis. As he prayed, mourning the loss of his Seraphic Father, Anthony could already feel the pain, the whole Order would suffer, as they became divided, brother against brother, some for keeping the Rule as left by Francis, and others for radically modifying it. Our Saint was thrust into the midst of this struggle that had to make the Angels weep. Although there were those, who would have split the Order in two, with dissension, Anthony was, like Francis before him, the *peacemaker.* He called for reconciliation and unity, while pleading to the friars to remain true to the Rule and dream of their Seraphic Father.

Elections were held. The little band, which had followed the *"poor one,"* had grown into *thousands*; organization was needed, with *headship*. Little known six years before, St. Anthony was nominated *Minister Provincial* of Emilia (northern part of Italy). The preaching that had taken him out of comfortable obscurity, had led many to convert and return to Mother Church. Through his *example* of Saintly life, his work spreading the Order, and his defense of the Faith, he had inspired multitudes to lay down their lives for the Gospel. *Now, he was being called* to lead young friars to a deeper commitment of mind, heart and soul to this radical life of Francis, as *Minister Provincial*!

---

[12]Quotation from St. Teresa of Avila - from Saints and other Powerful Women in the Church

As he was famous and highly respected, he was also, humble and considerate, more a *companion* to the friars than a *Superior*. He asked them to consider him one of them, to regard him as a servant, available to them at all times. Following the example of Christ, Anthony would wash the feet of his friars. He loved to go into the kitchen, in each of the Friaries, and help the brothers clean and cook. He wrote,

"A Superior ought to be loved, rather than feared. Love makes bitter things sweet and heavy things light; fear makes even easy things, burdensome."

And his living testimony, his words to bishops, could be counsel to *anyone* who would lead,

"The Prelate, who wishes to rule well the people entrusted to him, must be wise, humble and strong...must color his words with Christ's humility, commanding with kindness, love and understanding. The Lord is not in the fury of a wind, the tremor of an earthquake, nor in a roaring blaze. The Lord is in the quiet whisper of a gentle breeze."

St. Anthony and the Christ Child

One of the most beautiful paintings of St. Anthony portrays the Saint with the Christ Child in his arms. Like Blessed Mother, whom, he so admired, you see St. Anthony deferring to the Lord, as he looks at Him, lovingly. The tradition around this painting is *authentic*, as it was not only passed on by a responsible eye witness, but has survived the test of time, close to 800 years.

When St. Anthony's duties delayed him, and he could not return to his Monastery in time, he would accept the hospitality of friends or villagers. One such evening, after St. Anthony had long retired to his room for the night, his host became alarmed. He was awakened by a bright light pouring into his room, from underneath his bedroom door. Rushing into the hallway, he was startled to see it was coming from *St. Anthony's* room. He hesitated to knock, not wishing to invade St. Anthony's privacy. Worried, he decided to listen at the door, to be sure nothing was wrong. He heard noises. This further disturbed him. He thought, he'd better peer through a crevice. His eyes filled with tears. Never had he seen anything so radiantly beautiful, in his life. The light that emanated from the scene, blinded him at first and he thought that was the reason for his tears; but he soon *understood.*

St. Anthony was kneeling beside a table. There was a large volume, on it. It was open, and an *Infant* was standing on it. The Baby was *precious*; He was smiling, playing, turning the pages of the book beneath Him, with his tiny, chubby, exquisite Feet. If not for His breathtaking beauty, He could have been an ordinary child. A soft and misty aura hung in the air, surrounding Him. A heavenly fragrance of flowers came rushing toward the onlooker, intoxicating him with its blessed sweetness. The host felt a little heady, dizzy. The Child moved! He leaned upon the Saint's chest and caressed his face gently and tenderly. Heavenly music and the fluttering sound of wings filled the room. The Army of Angels was there! Were those tears spilling from St. Anthony's eyes as he beheld the Christ Child so close to him, touching him? Was it because, this moment was just for the two of them; no one in need of help; no one to call him away from this time *alone* with his Lord? The Child whispered in St. Anthony's ear: *there was someone there*! St. Anthony turned toward the door and the intruder. His host knew he had been detected!

The next morning, when his host greeted St. Anthony, he asked, "Father, what did Jesus tell you?" To which, St. Anthony responded,

"He told me that your house will flourish so long as it remains faithful to Mother Church; but that it will be

crushed by misfortune and become extinct when it goes over to heresy."[13]

St. Anthony - Wonder worker

People *were drawn* to St. Anthony. He was widely known as a *miracle-worker*. Like those before him, and after him, whom God chooses to bring hope into the world through miracles and healings, St. Anthony always pointed away from himself, to the Lord. It was He Who healed, Who went out of His Way to bring about *Miracle*, so they would know He was with them, to the end of the world, and they need not be afraid. Anthony looked upon himself, as only a worthless pipeline for the Lord to flow through. St. Anthony performed miracles during his lifetime, or better, he *obtained*, through his prayer and penances, Miracles from the Lord.

St. Anthony was a priest! And through his faithful *yes* to that priesthood, *Miracles* came about. A typical day in his life, would read much like that of one of our own faithful priests, in our own parishes, only multiplied a hundredfold. Hearing of him, many came in need, and he was *available* to that need. Between preaching, teaching and hearing confessions, the sun set on many a day, leaving him without having had an opportunity to eat. I think many a priest today, maybe your priest, would love to have that *kind* of pain.

Even in his day, St. Anthony's type of Christianity was not *easy*. Some of his fellow priests considered him unbending and stern; still, the faithful came in droves, for him to hear their confessions. The hours he spent in the confessional, thoroughly poured out and exhausted to the point of dropping, were *enough* to have taken his life at 36

---

[13]In the seventeenth century, the Lord of Chateau-neuf embraced the *Calvinists* and the prophecy that had been given to his ancestor (the host), four centuries before, was fulfilled; his house fell.

years old. Imagine carrying all those sins upon himself, as he took the place of Jesus, in the confessional. Maybe, the most moving quality, penitents saw in Anthony, was the *compassion* behind his unrelinquishing, uncompromising living out of the Gospel. With this, he could touch even the most stubborn. Maybe, as we pray for *our* lost loved-ones, we should try praying for *St. Anthony's* intercession.

Many miracles came to pass in the *confessional*. One day, he was reading a list of sins, written on a piece of paper, by a penitent. To the sinner's amazement, as the Saint read, the sins *disappeared* from the page.

And then there was the time, a young man confessed, among other sins, he'd kicked his mother so violently, she fell to the floor. St. Anthony, strongly detesting the outrage, burst out passionately,

"The foot that kicks the father or the mother should be cut off."

The young man, not understanding the *meaning* of his words, returned home, took a hatchet and chopped off his foot. People have always delighted in bad news. Results of the severe punishment meted out, *supposedly* by Anthony, quickly spread throughout the city. It soon reached the ears of the hero turned monster, Anthony. He followed the youth's grieving parents to their house. He made his way to the young man's bedroom. He prayed, holding the severed foot close to the leg of the misguided, but repentant son. St. Anthony made the sign of the cross, and instantly the foot became attached to the leg. The young man jumped up, giving praise to the Lord and thanksgiving to Anthony, who had healed his leg in this truly miraculous way.

St Anthony was a peace-maker. He was highly esteemed, not only *within* the Church but *without*, among civil authorities, as a mediator of *peace*. They called on him often, to bring about reconciliation. So, it was no wonder that families turned to him, *confidently*, to resolve their

Above: *Infant testified to the innocence of its mother, pointing to the husband as its father.*   Below: *St. Anthony and the Miser's Heart*

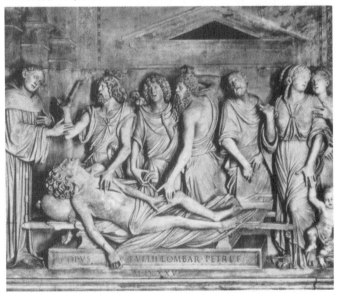

differences and bring harmony back into their lives. One day, a woman was accused of infidelity by her husband, their newborn was not his. *He wanted to leave her.* She turned to Anthony for help. He came and placed his hands on the couple's baby. The infant testified to the innocence of its mother, pointing to the husband as its father.

Another miracle, chronicled by Art over the centuries, is *the Miracle of the miser.* St. Anthony spoke out strongly against the *"tyrannical bondage"* of money. He never said *having* money was wrong, but having money *own* you was. Then, as now, money owned people in many ways; if you were not careful, you could not tell victim from victimizer. Times have never been *easy.* They certainly were not easy in Anthony's time. People worked very hard for very little. Most people depended on farming, raising sheep, and a little fishing. When nature was *hard*, very often, they had to turn to money-lenders to survive.

There were *those* who preyed on the desperation of the poor, *"...fierce beasts who rob and devour."* St. Anthony was asked to speak at the funeral of one such as these, a money-lender. Preaching at this miser's funeral, he referred to his (miser's) treasure chest,

"Don't bury this corpse in sacred ground. Bury it in any other place as you would the body of an animal, because his soul is already in hell and his heart is no longer in his body. In him the words of the Gospel have already been fulfilled: 'For where your treasure is, there will your heart also be.'"

Legend tells us, when they opened the body of the miser, his heart was *not* there, but, with his beloved *money* in his treasure chest.

St. Anthony goes Home to his Heavenly Family

Fifteen days before going Home to his Heavenly Family, St. Anthony *prophesied* his death. He told his companion, Padua would shortly receive a great *honor*. He did not disclose *its identity*, but his death and his entombment there, was indeed to bring fame and honor to Padua.

On June 13, 1231, St. Anthony was eating lunch with the friars, when he became suddenly very ill. Feeling life slowly ebbing out of him, he asked to be brought back to Padua. He knew, he was dying, and he wanted his body to remain among these Italians of Padua, he had come to love, so dearly. The friars reluctantly granted his wish. They knew, they were saying good-by to their friend and spiritual father, for the last time.

He and a friar set out, slowly and painfully, toward Padua. After a short distance, our Saint, visibly too weak to go on, his companion begged him to rest. He took him to a Friary near a Poor Clares' Monastery, in Arcello. No sooner had St. Anthony staggered into the Friary, the friars, immediately, helped him to bed. He grew rapidly worse, his breathing more and more labored.

They called a priest, who heard his last confession and absolved him of all his sins. Suddenly, the *angel of death* no longer seemed to be looming, in the room. Like a child, whose mother had just kissed away his fever, all the ravages of sickness and death left his face. St. Anthony began to sing his favorite hymn to Mother Mary,

O gloriosa Domina
"O glorious Lady, fairest Queen, exalted high in heav'n above! The great Creator, mighty Lord, by thee was nursed with mother's love. What sinful Eve had lost for us, by thy dear Son thou didst restore; the gate of Heaven thou hast been made, that we may entrance find and weep no more. Through thee the Savior came to us, to be our guiding Light and King. To Christ, our Life, of Virgin born, ye ransomed peoples praises sing. O Mother dear of grace divine, God's mercy for us

sinners plead, protect us from the enemy, in life's last hour to Heaven lead."

When he finished singing, his eyes went toward Heaven; he appeared to be staring intently at something or was it Someone! The friars asked him, "Father, what do you see?" He replied, "*I see my Lord.*"

Realizing the end was near, they attempted to anoint him with holy oils. He raised his hand as if to stop them, "*Brother, it is not necessary to do this to me, for I already have this anointing within me.*" Then yielding to his brothers, "*Nonetheless, it is good for me, and I agree to it.*"

He sang the penitential psalms with his friars, to the very end, his arms outstretched, as if on the Cross. Half an hour later, his soul was released from the prison of his earthly flesh and absorbed into eternity, to everlasting life with our Lord and His Mother. He appeared to be asleep. He was smiling. He looked, as he had described in one of his sermons, like "*a child (who) comes running to the arms of his mother; she comforts him and wipes away his tears.*" Anthony, the child and man, was Home. Pain and struggle, no more would hurt him. His Mother's arms were around him. She was leading him to her Son Jesus.

However, wherever there is truth, there, also, will controversy be. As in life, so in death, there would be struggle around St. Anthony. The friars tried to keep his death quiet, until they could grant the Saint his final wish, to return to Padua. Knowing of the devotion of the people, they knew this would be impossible, once the news got out. Man proposes, but...It seemed the very birds knew their preacher had left them; they stopped singing.

The cry went out! *The Saint is dead.* He has left us! No sooner had word reached the ears of the people of the area, that their beloved "*Santo*" had gone to the Father, they started to argue over his body. Since they never had the gift of him alive, the Poor Clares contended, it was only right they have St. Anthony, in death. They would *not* give up his body. The friars argued, they only wanted to carry out the Saint's last wish, they return him to Padua. The bishop was called in. Battles ensued; bridges leading out of town, toward Padua, were blockaded. But finally, the *Saint of Peace*, as he was known, must have gotten to everyone, Anthony was on his way to his final resting place, in Padua.

Miracles began immediately. The blind came to the tomb and they could see! The deaf prayed to the Saint and they could hear! The mute began to speak, the lame to walk. Broken hearts were mended and souls were saved; lives were made whole. The dead came to life.

The long followed tradition of *St. Anthony's Bread* began shortly after the Saint's death. A woman's son drowned. She ran to St. Anthony who had, as yet, not been buried and pleaded with him to bring her boy back to life. She promised, like the prophets who bargained with the Lord before her, if he did this favor for her, she would, from that day forward, give her son's weight in wheat, every year, to the poor. Her petition was granted, and now almost 800 years later, the tradition continues. Bob and I started to follow in this observance, when we heard about it, giving to a worthy Franciscan Apostolate which feeds the poor and the elderly, St. Anthony's Dining Room, in San Francisco. On our grandson's birthday, we send in his name, a gift equal to the sum of his weight, sometimes in petition, but mostly in thanksgiving.

Till today, when you pray at the tomb of St. Anthony, the evidence of the powerful and tender intercession of the Saint, is there; photos of crushed cars and twisted motorcycles, where lives have been miraculously spared; love letters in thanksgiving for favors received. Bob says that St. Anthony loves women best, answering their prayers more often than those of men. I don't know about that, *but* I must admit he has never let me down.

Right from the beginning, people testified they felt
something, like *a life force* coming from inside the tomb. I
like to think of myself as someone not too open to illusions
(as those who know me can attest); but I have to share, not
only I, but Bob too, cannot explain the *power* we have felt
coming from the tomb, as we have prayed there. There are
so many testimonies. On one of our Pilgrimages, sipping
Cappuccino at an outside cafe, across from the Basilica of St.
Anthony in Padua, Bob and I overheard a woman, who had
come in on a tour bus:

> *"I was a little annoyed when I discovered we were*
> *going into a church. I thought this was a tour. I*
> *wandered aimlessly around the Basilica, at first,*
> *appreciating the art and the architecture, when I found*
> *myself in back of St. Anthony's tomb. Before I knew*
> *what was happening, I found myself crying. I couldn't*
> *stop! I looked for a Confessional with an "English*
> *spoken here" sign, and went to confession for the first*
> *time in thirty-five years. I attended Mass and received*
> *Holy Communion. I feel as if I have been reborn. I*
> *have never been so happy in my life; then why can't I*
> *stop crying?"*

I have always been the spoiled brat of Jesus, but Bob
says I am also the spoiled brat of St. Anthony. On June 12,
one year, we were rushing to leave Padua, before being
crushed by Pilgrims converging on the Basilica[14]. The next
day was the Saint's Feast Day, June 13th, and it looked like
all Italy had arrived. Mass had just finished, and Bob gently
but firmly (out of necessity), asked, *"Well, Penny are you*
ready?" This is usually my signal, it's time to leave. *"I just*
wanted to say good-by, one more time," I weakly pleaded. The
tomb was surrounded by lines of people ten deep. It looked

---

[14]On the Feast of St. Anthony, literally hundreds of thousands jam
the little piazza and the Basilica of the Saint.

hopeless. All of a sudden, as if someone had come and ordered everyone to leave, they all filed out. We were all alone with our Saint. I cannot describe the emotions we have toward our friends and family, the Saints. Not even death can separate us from the love we feel *from* them, or the love we feel *for* them. And so, we hugged the tomb of our Saint, and kissed it till we would return, once more.

A Saint is proclaimed, for all time

St. Anthony was buried, as he wished, in the Church of Santa Maria in Padua, in 1231. In 1232, the present, magnificent towering Basilica was built over it. The faithful are still coming to their Saint, having their prayers answered. Miracles abound! Those same faithful and their love, raised Anthony to the glorious Communion of Saints. On May 30, 1232, in Spoleto, Italy, the bells peeled; Pope Gregory IX enrolled Anthony among the Saints. *Barely a year had passed!* The Pope read off the Miracles, which had begun immediately following his death. The merits of his life were proclaimed for all time. The Pope rose from his throne, raised his arms to Heaven and with joy, burst forth a proclamation, saluting Anthony, not only as Saint but *Doctor* of the Church:

"*O excellent doctor, light of Holy Church, blessed Anthony! Lover of God's law, be our advocate with God's Son.*"

A few days later, a papal bull announced the canonization of Anthony of Padua to the whole world.

At St. Peter's in Rome, under the ring of the Fisherman, on January 16, 1946, Feast of the Proto-martyrs[15], in the seventh year of his Pontificate, Pius XII officialy declared for the whole Church and world, *St. Anthony, Doctor of the Church.*

---

[15]Franciscan Proto-martyrs-the Friars who had touched St. Anthony when they returned martyrs from Morocco.

St. Anthony returns again

Bob and I have always been amused at how God uses the minds of the scientists, He has created, to prove what we, the Faithful, *without* proof, have believed for close to two thousand years. But God knows, we are very often an *unfaithful* people in need of signs. Instead of giving up on us, he makes *Miracles*, raises *Saints*, or uses *scientists* to furnish with us assurances, of which faith has no need.

The relics of St. Anthony were recognized and venerated on the 750th anniversary of his death. For those who might question the opening of the tomb of a Saint, today, with the highly improved technical instrumentation at Science's disposal, we can learn much on the lives of our brothers and sisters, who went before us. Through investigation of their remains, we can discover and affirm, how they lived and died. What kind of people were they? In this age of proof, God wants us to *know* our Saints, so we might imitate them as they imitated Christ.

At 7 pm, Tuesday, January 6, 1981, members of the Papal Commission presided at the opening of the tomb of St. Anthony. The coffin was taken out of the tomb, and brought to the foot of the altar of St. Anthony. The top of the coffin was removed. Over two hundred Franciscan Friars viewed and venerated the Holy remains, which had not been seen for over 700 years.

After the friars had sung two hymns of thanksgiving, *the Te Deum*[16] and *Magnificat*[17], they solemnly processed with the

---

[16]The first words of the Latin version, and the title of the most famous hymn in the Western Church. The words mean: "to You, God." It is a prayer, a hymn of thanksgiving, a solemn invocation for a blessing, and a profession of faith.

[17]This title has been given to the canticle spoken by the Blessed mother on the occasion of her visit to her cousin, Elizabeth, as recorded by Luke (1:46-55)

Saint's relics, into the cloister. St Anthony's remains were placed on a table, inside the convent, and examined by experts. The Saint's bones were found to be marvelously intact and would be a source of much *new* information and *affirmation* of traditions passed down through the centuries, of the Saint's life.

The Skull in the coffin, perfectly matched the Saint's jaw, which was brought to them from its reliquary in the Basilica Treasury. It had been found miraculously preserved in 1263, and the jaw has been venerated by the faithful, since then. Scientists ascertained, the skull and jaw were from the same man. In investigating the skull, they discovered St. Anthony had a large head. He is said to have had as much *grey matter* as Leonardo Da Vinci, who is known to have had more grey matter[18] than any human (whose measurements are known), on earth, including Albert Einstein. We have been told by Scientists that genius is measured by grey matter. Is this arguable? Frankly, to us, this is not very important. We believe, the *teachings* and homilies left behind by St. Anthony, speak even more authentically than this *physical* confirmation, of the gift God gave him, and is giving us. (Author's note: It's interesting that God gave genius to three men, St. Anthony, Leonardo da Vinci and Albert Einstein. History will remember each of them by *how* they used the gift and the fruits they left behind).

At his investigation, the Saint's vocal chords were found still intact. St. Bonaventure, in 1263, discovered the Saint's *miraculously* incorrupt tongue. It is still in a reliquary, for all the faithful to see. Both of these signs, *physical* evidence of God's *gift of tongues* to the Saint.

The scientists discovered he had been 5'7". St. Anthony would have been considered tall, in his day. He had deep-set

---

[18]grey matter - cerebral cortex - it controls human intelligence, as well as our senses: sight, hearing, taste, smell and touch. It is the most important part of the brain that sets us apart from other animals.

eyes and was generally well-built, a strong man. His exceptionally developed legs affirmed the history of the Saint, which speaks of St. Anthony travelling great distances, on foot, spreading the Good News and dispelling the bad news. They confirmed he was a man from the Mediterranean area. His enlarged knees pointed to the many hours spent on his knees in penance and prayer. Again science said, he was a man who died at or about 40 years old (the Church says St. Anthony was 36 yrs. old).

750 years had passed, but you would think the Saint had just died. Over 700,000 people lovingly and reverently processed in front of the remains, they still call *their Saint*. Although, originally 30 days had been set aside for the viewing, Church officials had to extend the time to 54 days. There were many testimonies. People said, as they venerated the remains, they began to question the *quality* of their life.

I think of all the powerful and famous men and women, who have lived in my lifetime. My grandson does not even know their names or for what they were famous. They recognized the world of *today*, never thought of the World of *Tomorrow*, and they are forgotten. Saint Anthony spent his whole life living, loving and bringing that World of Tomorrow, and its King, to this world that is quickly passing away. He has not only been remembered for almost eight hundred years; he has returned. Our Saint has returned. And he has something to say to *you*!

In case it is not obvious, I love St. Anthony; oh, not the way I love Jesus, but he's right up there. Can you tell me of someone, you know, who loves Alexander the great or Caesar or Hitler or Stalin or even Roosevelt?

Where is your treasure? Where is your heart? Who do you love? Who is the hero in your life? Who do you choose, today, to follow, to fashion your life after? Like St. Anthony, give your answer to Mother Mary to give to her Son.

As you are preparing to go Home, what will you answer when you are asked, *"What do you see?"* Will you answer, like St. Anthony:

"I see the Lord!"

†

Each day, as we pray our ongoing Novena to the Patron Saint of our Book Ministry, St. Anthony, we try to follow his words: *"In all you do, put God's Will first."*

St. Peregrine...The Cancer Saint

Cancer: the big "C", killer, feared enemy

When Cancer strikes your home or your family, a bolt of fear shoots your entire body. There is a sense of helplessness that deteriorates into hopelessness. You pray hope against hope, it isn't true. Then your prayers go from, "Please Lord, don't let it be malignant." to "Please let them get it all out." to "Please let the chemotherapy work." to "Please don't let him suffer." This monster strikes so rapidly, so brutally, it takes a healthy, virile, alive loved one and reduces him or her to a skeleton before your eyes. Your final prayer, in futile resignation is, "Lord, take away the anger I feel."

My first encounter with Cancer

My mother called, one day. She said something was wrong with my dad; he didn't close the kitchen cabinets after himself. They were alone for the first time; all the children had moved away. I said she was paying too much attention to *everything* he was doing. This did not seem like a major crisis, but I do remember having a funny feeling. Daddy was someone who could not leave a picture on the wall that was not exactly level! She telephoned the next day, and said she thought she better take him to the doctor. He was having a problem adding *simple* figures; he kept going over and over the bills. Now, I was starting to get worried. My dad was a mathematical genius who did long division and multiplication in his head! He used to poke fun at us, when we used adding machines or calculators. Then, Bob shared, one night, when they were coming to pick me up from the bus stop, Dad kept veering the car to the left side of the road. He hadn't said anything before, because he thought Dad was just tired!

I will never forget that day, waiting at home for their phone call. It was hours; it seemed more like years. The doctor called; Daddy had to go to a neurologist. I remember saying, "*But he'll be all right.*" This doctor, like everyone who knew him, loved my dad. It seemed like he was crying when he said, "*He's very sick.*"

The next seven months were a nightmare! I could think of nothing or no one, but that my Dad was dying and I had to hold onto every moment. We played games with each other, my father and the rest of us, pretending he wasn't dying. For the first time in his life, he told us off-color jokes, the ones Mama said he would never tell us, because they were so *bad*. Thank God you are not here, Mama and Daddy to see and hear what is rated PG in the movies, and said on daytime television, *today*.

One morning, my mother came to me with fear in her eyes. She was on the verge of tears. She said, Daddy shared a dream he'd had. It was of my maternal grandmother; he'd loved as a *real* mother, and she had loved him, in return, as a dear and precious son. He said, she told him she was waiting for him, and that Mama should pray to the Virgin Mary for consolation. Mama looked into my eyes for an answer. What had my father meant? He never talked this way. They were good people, but they never spoke of praying to Our Lady for *consolation*. They prayed to St. Anthony for lost articles; they prayed a novena during World War II that my brother, missing in action, would come home safe. They prayed for *things*. But pray for consolation, what did that mean? I had no answer, at that time, when Mama asked me what I thought Daddy meant. You see, we did not pray to Jesus through Mary or anyone else. *So, we didn't know St. Peregrine*!

Public Enemy No. 1 - Cancer

We read a book about Father Damien, heroic priest of Molokai, in the Hawaiian Islands. Someday he will surely be known as Saint of Lepers, we thought. Leprosy, a word that struck *terror* in the hearts of all who heard it, was not really a threat in our country or in our time. Little did we know when we read that book, there would be a new Leprosy - Cancer. Although Heart Disease is the No. 1 killer in the United States, somehow the "*C*" word, the diagnosis *Cancer* has the ability of rousing more fear and less hope.

After almost four years away from Jesus and the Church, when we came back, we couldn't stay away, especially from the Sacrifice of the Mass. No matter what town we visited, on business or pleasure, the first thing we investigated was where the Catholic Church was, and what time was Mass the next day.

San Juan Capistrano is a seaside village on the coast of California, made famous by the swallows that return each year. Like most of our state, this village was consecrated and named after a Saint, St. John the German[1].

We attended Mass in the Old Mission of San Juan Capistrano. When Mass was over, not anxious to leave this world of yesterday for the world of today, we kind of looked around. In an alcove, the size of a little room, there was a shrine with a statue of a Saint we had never heard of before, St. Peregrine. He was called *Saint of Cancer*. We picked up a small booklet which gave us a little background on this new Saint in our life, and how he came to earn his title.

The roster of victims who had fallen to this enemy, Cancer, had grown over the years, with my beloved mother joining the ranks. It was consoling to know there was

---

[1]John Capistran (foreign head) we wrote of him in our book "This is My Body...This is My Blood, Miracles of the Eucharist, in our chapter on Langenwiese, page 161.

someone in Heaven to whom we could pray to our Lord when we needed a *miracle!*

Who was St. Peregrine?

As we asked around, in the United States, we were quite shocked to discover there were few people who knew of him, not even Italian-Americans. This seemed strange as he was from Italy. Little did we know, at that time, how many Saints there are from Italy. But, if it appeared odd that Americans with Italian ancestry knew nothing, it was to be topped as we *adventured* to the town where he had been born and died.

In 1977, what with that sword of Cancer that hangs over the heads of every family, where Cancer has struck, mine being no exception, Bob and I thought this is a Saint we would like to know more about. We'd include him in our Pilgrimage itinerary.

Word got around! Bob and Penny were going on another Pilgrimage, and when it got out we were going to visit some *Saint of Cancer*, petitions started to pour in. Before we left, the Lord sent three people, in need of prayers. One was *terminal*; he had lung cancer and would not last out the year. *Another* was a young man around 38 years old. His whole body was riddled with cancer. He had gone completely downhill! The *third man*, a doctor, had an inoperable brain tumor (like my Dad had).

We prayed on that Pilgrimage, passionately prayed, not only at the Shrine of St. Peregrine, but at all the Shrines, pleading with God to have mercy. And, he did! Why does that surprise us? We ask humans who are sinners, often still sinning, to pray for us, and we believe or at least *hope* God will answer their prayers of intercession. Why is it so hard to believe He would not listen to someone like His Beloved and Perfect Mother, or to one of His Saints, who've earned a crown of holiness and dwell in His Sight.

When we returned, we discovered *change* had come about, for every one of the people we had prayed for at the Shrines. We cannot explain why. Could it be, we prayed, *believing* God would listen? Was this the faith of a child, Jesus spoke of, that was needed and is so needed today?

The man who'd *had* lung cancer, had new x-rays to compare with his former ones. There was no question; *there was no sign of Cancer.* His doctor said it was a miracle; not an enigma, but a miracle! Was it through St. Peregrine or could it have been through Our Lady of Lourdes? It doesn't matter; they don't care who gets credit, as long as *Jesus* does.

The *young man*, who had been helplessly bed-ridden, was up and about; his doctor said it looked like the cancer was in remission. The young man wasn't a Catholic, but he was on fire. He wanted to know more about St. Peregrine. We had a thought! Since he had been losing his life, would he *now* devote it to the Lord? He never answered that question. We never found out what he did with the remaining months of his life. Had he made that promise to the Lord? Had the Lord given him and his family more time to get ready? We don't know, but we found out, *he* did die.

The *third man*, with a brain tumor, not only had renewed energy, but returned to his medical practice. Oh, not to earn money; instead, he volunteered his time and talents to the Seminary, nearby. This, from a man who had been *away* from the Sacraments, and his Church, for years.

Thirteenth Century Italy

Italy and Italians have never been *moderate* in anything. If you don't know what we mean, watch two Italians arguing on a street corner. You think they're going to kill each other! Voices are raised! Arms are swinging expressively up and down, to the right and left, like a conductor leading a symphonic orchestra, flying in the air but never touching one another! Then, their *discussion* over, they walk away still talking, still friends, to share a cup of *cappuccino* or a shave at the local barber. It is a way of life to be passionate and noisy, to argue and make up, and sometimes, but not often, to *not* make up.

We are in Italy! It's the thirteenth century! It's a time of passion and anger. This era was pervaded by the privileged and the underprivileged; and who was *who*, was according to your perspective. Those who *had*, never had enough; needing to blame someone, they blamed the Pope! The Pope of that time was more like a King! *He* had lots: lots of political power, lots of land, lots of wealth, *lots of everything*. The upper class wanted what he had. When words did not work, and they had to use strong means, *well* so be it. Twenty-four years later, conditions deteriorated to such violence, the Papacy was forced to flee, for its life, from Rome to Perugia (near Assisi), and then to Avignon.

Forli, of yesterday and today, has always been a fairly large city. An ancient city, it has also, always been a *proud* city. Located near Bologna, where some of the finest and *first* universities began in Europe, it inherited much of this city's fame and *intelligencia*. But sadly, with these bed-fellows, *friend pride* often sneaks in, and with it, its companions *superiority and disobedience*, not far behind. This was the climate of Italy, her big cities in general, and *Forli* in particular, at the time of our Saint.

Italy, of the thirteenth century, was called *"Europe's hot-bed of creative genius, political rivalry and religious renewal."* It was 1260. A future Saint was to be born into this strange and contradictory time and climate. The well-to-do Laziosi family were actively involved in affairs of state. But more important, than all the squabbling over who owns what, was the little boy being born. Did they know what they were doing when they named him Peregrine, *Pellegrino in Italian*, or *pilgrim*? We think not.

†

Peregrine - Rebel and Rabble-rouser

By 1283, Peregrine had grown up in the narrow, self-centered world of the upper class, an oasis of wanting and getting. "*No*" was not a part of his vocabulary; especially when it pertained to something *he* chose to do or not to do.

It was a difficult time for Pope Martin IV. He imposed an *interdict*[2] on Forli. Because of Forli's open *anarchy*, priests of that Diocese were not allowed to administer the Sacraments[3]; and the faithful were denied receiving Them. This censure forbid celebration of *all* divine services, including the Holy Mass, punishing the clergy *and* the laity. Only the hearing of sermons was allowed. Although this did not constitute ex-communication, an interdict was only issued under grave situations, usually as a result of scandal against our Religion.

It was a time of hard heads and hard hearts. Things went from bad to worse. The people of Forli countered the Pope's actions with anti-clerical actions, to *even the score*. It became so critical, the Pope sent a mediator, future Saint Philip Benizi[4] to try to *move the hearts* of the warring citizens of Forli. St. Philip came; he delivered an impassioned plea, calling for peace and reconciliation.

A group of young rowdies *answered* for the entire mob. They made fun of him; they jeered; they mocked his every word; they ridiculed him to the point, some of the older people were *embarrassed*. When they could not provoke him into answering them, *in kind*, they responded by roughly pulling him down from the pulpit, as he was preaching.

---

[2]Interdict - A censure that deprives the faithful of certain spiritual benefits.

[3]except administration of the Sacrament to the dying if regulations are observed.

[4]called by Jesus and Mary, in two different visions to propagate the Servite Order

Pushing and shoving, *manhandling* him mercilessly they finally ran him out of town.

One of these rowdies was *Peregrine!* He belonged to the same political party as his parents. Forli was definitely anti-papal; his parents were anti-papal and so naturally, Peregrine was anti-papal! He was cocky, sure of himself, as only the young can be. He knew exactly what he wanted out of life and how to get it! Sounds like a thirteenth century *Paul*, before *he* converted, doesn't he!

Peregrine was eighteen years old. He was a man! He'd outdo the rest of his friends; he was bolder than the rest of them. *He struck St. Philip on the face.* Now, St. Philip Benizi was known to have an Italian trigger temper; his reputation for having lost it, many times as a youth, was not a well-kept secret. However, he just stood there and offered Peregrine his other cheek.

No sooner had Peregrine struck St. Philip, than he could feel the pangs of guilt and remorse. He ran after St. Philip. He begged his and the Lord's forgiveness. St. Philip's action had brought about *immediate* repentance in Peregrine. He needed to reconcile with him. St. Philip opened his arms and forgave him, absolving him not only of this sin, but others he had committed. As if he had showered and removed layers of skin, Peregrine felt like a new creation! The Lord had touched him, and he would never be the same.

He began to find it difficult to associate with his old friends. Their coarse ways and language repulsed him. What had been normal was now *unacceptable*. He wanted to cover their mouths, before they could again use the Name of the Lord abusively; the pain, hearing them blaspheme Him, was more than he could bear. They weren't funny, anymore. He and they were not one! They didn't speak the same language! It wasn't only he didn't know them; it was as if he had *never* known them!

Peregrine was confused! As he and his friends had been persecuting St. Philip Benizi, he had been praying for them, his *persecutors*! Maybe he would find his answers in *church*. Turning completely away from his old life and old *friends*, Peregrine began to spend more and more time praying in the Cathedral. Hours on his knees, his eyes riveted on the beautiful statue of our Lady in her chapel, Peregrine, our boy becoming man, was falling in love. He didn't understand it at first. He just couldn't stay away.

Come and serve - my son...Our Lady appears to Peregrine

While praying at Her Chapel one day, in the Church of the Holy Cross (now the Cathedral), our Lady appeared to him! He had been praying to her for *wisdom*, how to know the Will of Her Son, and knowing it, how to go about obeying it. She said,

"My son, go the Siena. Seek out my Servants (Servites). Among them, you will be able to close yourself off from the rest of the world and do penance for your sins."

Peregrine was hopelessly, passionately in love with Mary. He could refuse her nothing. It is impossible to describe his feelings. Many who have seen our Mother have tried, but there's just no way.

When they were trying to make a statue of our Lady as she appeared in Fatima, Lucy was never quite satisfied with any of them. The one agreed upon, the Pilgrim Virgin which is breathtakingly beautiful, is the closest anyone was able to come to duplicating her. But still, ...

How can you explain the tears that well up in your eyes as you look up to our Lady of Guadalupe, *divinely* left 400 years ago, in Mexico, miraculously preserved for us that we might get a glimpse of His and our Mother.

Possibly this excerpt from our book, *The Many Faces of Mary, a Love Story*, might, to some extent, explain Peregrine's

emotions. Bob chose this passage for his personal chapter -
"*Mary, My First Love*":

> *When I was young and innocent, I sought her.*
> *She came to me in her beauty,*
> *and until the end I will cultivate her.*
> *As the blossoms yielded to ripening grapes,*
> *the heart's joy,*
> *My feet keep to the level path because from earliest*
> *youth I was familiar with her...*
> *I became resolutely devoted to her...*
> *the good I persistently strove for.*
>
> *I burned with desire for her,*
> *never turning back.*
> *I became preoccupied with her,*
> *never weary of extolling her.*
>
> *For her I purified even the soles of my feet*
> *in cleanness I attained her,*
> *I gained understanding with her, such that I*
> *will never forsake her.*
>
> *My whole being was stirred as I learned*
> *about her;*
> *therefore I have made her my*
> *prize possession.*
>
> *Submit your neck to her yoke, that your mind*
> *may accept her teaching.*
> *For she is close to those who seek her,*
> *and one who is in earnest finds her.*
> *(Sirach 51:13)*

Was it so for Peregrine? Here is Peregrine, young,
passionate, with emotions he doesn't know what to do with,

confused, being pulled from one direction to the other; and *then*, the most beautiful, most perfect Lady who has ever been born is there, for *him*, before his very eyes.

He had seen the Mother of God and all mankind, and like the children of Fatima, his toys had no longer any meaning for him. Although he, too, felt unworthy and unqualified, as had Juan Diego, when our Sweet Mother commissioned him to go to the Bishop, *he could not refuse the Lady anything*.

And, if I may, as with my Bob, when he was in the room with the seers in Medjugorge, believing Mary was appearing to the children, seeing and hearing nothing, he *knew* she was asking him to write about her love for us. Against all the strongest, most loving, most *well-intentioned* advice, he was so touched by what and Whom he could not describe, he wrote about his Mary; so, it was with Peregrine.

No matter what the cost, he said "*yes!*" Mary sent an Angel to accompany him to Siena. Peregrine put his house in order. Leaving no loose ends, he set out for a new life; and with him, his *Lady*, the light that would guide him through the dark nights, he would walk, for years to come.

Radical to Religious

As he approached the city of Siena, he must have felt that catch in his throat, we always have when we spot the ancient towers and majestic dome that loom up in the Siena of contrasts and contradictions - land of Saints and Miracles and Etruscan mystery - land of spirituality and sophistication. As he walked up the cobble-stoned hills of Siena did he feel the excitement of the new tomorrows, Mother Mary had prepared for him?

He rang the bell of the house of the *Servants of Mary* or as they are also known, the Servites. Did you want to run, at the last minute, Peregrine? You must have thought: *Was it Mary or had it all been my imagination*? That bell made such a *loud* sound. A heavy door opened. The face, that peered out from the long, black habit, was serious but friendly. Wasting no time, he was brought before the *Prior General*.

Who do you think Peregrine saw, as he looked up from his bowed head, but the very man whom he had slapped, St. Philip Benizi.[5] That moment, when St. Philip had withheld his temper, could he have known that this one act would result in the conversion of a soul and the gift of that soul to the Church! He accepted Peregrine into the Order with much joy and thanksgiving, our Lord's Word coming to life before his eyes, "...this son of mine was dead and has come back to life. He was lost and is found." (Luke 15:24)

Peregrine entered the Order around 1290, as a *choir-brother*. Our attitudes never change, but if you hand them to the Lord, through the Hands of Mary, then *He* will take those same flaws and turn them into fruits for His Garden.

Peregrine was born a radical and he would die a radical. He did nothing half way! He loved passionately and *he hated* passionately.[6] He adored this God and His Church, he so had hated. He *ardently* loved the poor people, he'd held in disdain. With the same conviction and determination, he had defied the Lord and His Church, he now defended and obeyed Them!

A latter day St. Paul, running the good race, not stopping for anything until his goal was reached, Peregrine never rested. But also like St. Paul, with this *other* zealot, the race was never done. They say, once he received his habit,

---

[5]St. Philip Benizi was not only a priest-maker, he was a Saint-maker. Notably good men he called to the Lady's service were: St. Peregrine, Bd. John of Frankfort, Bd. Joachim Piccolominin and on and on, over seven powerful men who have been beatified, and in addition the well-known *Saint* Juliana Falconieri from which sprang up the third order regular of the Servants of Mary.

[6]from St. Peregrine. The Cancer Saint - Rev. Stephen Gibbons, O.S.M.

he did not allow anything to get in his way. He truly, untiringly lived as he spoke, "*one must never rest in the way of virtue.*"[7] It is said, he never sat down for thirty years. But he did take whatever free time available to observe silence and solitude, his *wonderful* time alone with his Lord and his Lady.

Peregrine, Servite and priest - returns to Forli

After approximately five years, his superiors sent Peregrine, now a priest, back to Forli, to open a house, there. He was available to everyone who called on him, never too tired to counsel whoever came to him. Because of this, he earned the name, "*Angel of Good Counsel.*"

An authentic and outstanding priest, he approached all the works of his vocation as *gifts and privileges*. His life was salvation of souls, and consolation to the suffering and impoverished. And this, he did not only with much devotion, but delight!

He was fervent, as he celebrated the Sacrifice of the Mass. Beginning reverently with the Word, he went on to passionately *reliv*e the Eucharistic Prayer. He was back in Capharnaum, with Jesus, as He is telling his followers, He will give them bread and they will never die; he is in the Upper Room with Jesus, as He is giving us the means by which we could have Him until the end of the world; and Peregrine is saying *yes*, to being that means through which Jesus would be brought to life, to the faithful of *his* day.

We know Peregrine was a zealot, but he was first and foremost, a servant of God. Jesus said, "Feed My lambs," and *that*, Peregrine did with the last ounce of his strength. The same qualities, he had shown as a brash young man, fighting *against* the Church, he now used fighting *for* that Church's people.

He ministered tirelessly to the sick. A plague had broken out in Italy and had spread to Forli. No one was

---

[7]Butler's Lives of the Saints

safe, or excused, from the spreading ravages of the disease. Peregrine would not even take time out to be sick. Now, a very tired and sick *sixty years* old, he could barely stand. A cancerous growth, on his right leg, had spread dangerously, and there was no way out. He had to be operated on!

He had worked among the sick, ignoring his own pain and the seriousness of *his* illness, for years. Now, it seemed, the Lord was saying, through the doctors, there was nothing that could be done; the leg had to be amputated! Or was that the Lord talking?

All his life, his greatest struggle had been *obedience*. That was the room of his heart, he would have to hand over to Jesus, again and again. No sooner did he allow the Lord into that part of his will, he would, at the next crisis, shut him out again. He always judged himself the reluctant giver. But the Lord really does not care how you do it; He loves reluctant and willing, the same.

The Lord was waiting for his total surrender! Peregrine turned the entire matter over to Jesus. But, it wouldn't hurt to pray! If, the next day, when he awakened from the operation, he was to be in the Presence of Jesus and Mary, in his Heavenly home, what better way to prepare for the journey? *They* would not reject him, as even those he'd helped had. The sight of his sore, and the stench emanating from it, *repulsed* them. Did he surrender all *those* hurts over to the Lord and His Mother?

The night before he was scheduled to be operated on, he went into the *chapter room* of the Priory. He was all alone. He prayed before a fresco of Jesus Crucified. He fell into a deep sleep. He had a vision of the Lord. Our Lord came down from His Cross and reaching out to his cancerous leg, He touched it, ever so gently, with His Healing Hand.

The next morning, he awakened, resigned to the operation. Like with so many of us, the Lord had been just

Above: *Fresco of Jesus that came alive and touched Peregrine's cancerous leg.*   Below: *Choir loft where the miracle took place*

waiting for his *yes*. Peregrine was amazed! His leg didn't hurt. He could stand, he could walk, without pain! He was completely healed!

The operation never took place. When the surgeons investigated the leg, they reported there was not a trace of the illness. As Bob likes to say, tell an Italian and you tell the world; news of this miracle spread. People, who knew and loved him, had been following anxiously the progressive deterioration of Peregrine's health. Imagine when they heard, he had been completely cured! And overnight!

Peregrine lived for another *twenty* years. People continued to come to him, for help. Before, it had been for spiritual direction and healing of the soul; now they came seeking miracles of the *body*. Like with his Lord, he didn't care why they came, he said *yes!*

There were miracles, even before his death. As we say, in Lourdes, no one went away disappointed. Many were healed of the cancer that attacked their bodies, but we are sure as many, if not more, left cured of the cancer that spreads and kills the *soul*. Through the Sacrament, he so lovingly administered, that of *Reconciliation*, they went away with new life. Remembering that Jesus *first* said, before healing *physically*, "Your sins are forgiven you," imagine the next twenty years for Peregrine in the confessional. It had to be the culmination of this faithful priest's life!

Peregrine was eighty years old, but when he looked upon his Lady, it was like the first time; he was young! The young cavalier in the old priest's body was ready to ride gallantly forth with his Lady. On May 1st, 1345, consumed now by fever, with his last spark of life, Peregrine's spirit soared, like a *rocket of fire*, to his Lord and to the Lady he so loved. She had called him from the world, to life as a *religious*. Now, Mary was calling him out of the world, to live eternally with her and her Son, Jesus.

All his life as a *religious*, had been a preparation for this, his entrance into eternal life. We know, as Peregrine called out, "*Jesus! Mary!*" They lifted him and carried him *Home*.

Their Saint was dead

The faithful filed by, for days. Their Saint was dead! So many continued to come, they left the gates of the city unlocked at night. This was unheard of because of the danger of neighbors, invading. (Author's note: When Pope John Paul II came to Los Angeles, California, September of 1987, crime was *down* 40%. Although we have an average of three murders a day, in Los Angeles, during the three days the Pope was here, there were *no* murders committed!)

They came, those he had loved and helped, those he had visited and served! First, the poor! Then the sick! They testified how he had been an *instrument* by his example, as well as, by his words. Testimony after testimony came forth, from the faithful, who had come to witness to St. Peregrine's *sanctity*! A delightful aroma of flowers, from the body of St. Peregrine, filled the church. People said they could smell a fragrance of flowers unknown to them, strong but not sickening, *delightful*!

Days passed. They had to say good-by to their old friend. The Servants of Mary placed the body of St. Peregrine in a coffin or sepulchre. But they could not place it in the cemetery. The fragrance continued, and the body showed no signs of decomposition. Instead, they kept it above ground in the Chapel of *Our Lady of Sorrows*, next to the Lady he had loved for over sixty years of his life. *It remained there until 1639.*

They wanted to canonize him immediately! In many parts of Europe, the people proclaimed a holy person a Saint, long before they were added to the Calendar of Saints. The faithful brought evidence of the multitudes of miracles, through Peregrine's intercession.

News spread rapidly of the *Saint of Forli.* Devotion to the Saint began, long before he was canonized. As early as from 1350 to 1375, a fresco was painted by the school of Lorenzetti in far-off *Siena.* In Italy and to the four corners of Europe, devotion to this holy Saint began. Miracles, through the intercession of St. Peregrine, were being proclaimed, from almost every corner of the earth.

Something interesting happened, at the Servite Church in Barcelona. Pilgrims gathered, from all parts of Spain, to honor, to petition St. Peregrine to intercede for them. The sick would receive three *Hosts.* On the first Host was imprinted the words: "*Christ is born.*" On the second Host: "*Christ has died.*" And on the third Host: "*Christ is risen.*" Through this, the priest was telling the sick that Jesus in the *Eucharist* is alive, and Jesus in the Eucharist is the *Healer*! St. Peregrine, and all those known to have the gift of *healing,* go through Jesus Christ. And here, in this church in Spain, Jesus tells us again, "I am in your church. Come to Me all you who are weary..."

So many miracles were reported after his death, they stopped recording them, after awhile. Over 300 miracles occurred, before he was canonized. Pope Pio V, in the 16th century, approved the cult of praying to Peregrine for his intercession, and declared him a *Blessed.*

His cause was brought to Rome. All historical testimony of his life as a *religious,* and miracles attributed to his intercession, were examined by the Sacred Congregation of Rites. These affidavits were carefully scrutinized, under the supervision of such as St. Robert Bellarmine, who was then a Cardinal and Jesuit.

In response to the investigation of the Sacred Congregation, in 1609, Pope Paul V issued a Papal Bull *officially* approving the cult (devotion) of venerating Peregrine, allowing the use of *Beato* or Blessed before his

Right:
Peregrine had a vision of the Lord. Our Lord came down from His Cross, and touched his cancerous leg with His Healing Hand. He was completely healed!

Left:
A beautiful chapel was added to the Church.
On May 16, 1639, St. Peregrine was solemnly processed from the Cathedral. They investigated his remains, and discovered his body had never decomposed. They placed him in a glass urn, so the faithful could venerate his body.

name. He added his name to the Roman Martyrology[8] with permission to celebrate Holy Mass in his honor, May 1st of every year.

A beautiful chapel was added to the church in honor of the new *Blessed*. On the 15th of June in 1626, the first stone was laid.

On May 16, 1639, the body of Blessed Peregrine was solemnly processed from the Cathedral to the church where he is till today. They began in the Chapel of the Blessed Mother, where She had first appeared to Peregrine, directing him to a new life in Her Son through Her. His urn was placed in his new Chapel, which had been made so lovingly, in his honor.

The Process of Sanctification, of Peregrine, began in the 17th century. On the 27th of December, 1726, Mother Church *officially* added Blessed Peregrine to the Communion of *Saints*. Pope Benedict XIII, on the High Altar of St. Peter's Basilica, declared, the Church had a new Saint, for all ages, *Saint Peregrine!* The servite custodian of St. Peregrine's Shrine proudly says, *he* was the first Saint to be officially canonized from the Province of Romagna.

May 1st is the Feast Day of Saint Peregrine. It is also the day my Daddy was born.

Three hundred years after his death, when they investigated his remains, they discovered his body had never decomposed. At that time, they placed him in a glass urn, so the faithful could view his body when they venerated him. He was then placed above the altar in that side chapel that had been constructed when he was Beatified. This has been a place of Pilgrimage, for most of Europe, since that time;

---

[8]Roman Martyrology, a liturgical book, is the listing with readings of the Saints honored in the Church, and the names of newly canonized Saints are added to it. It first was published in 1584, and now numbers more than five thousand entries.(Catholic Encyclopedia-Broderick)

but until now, not for Americans who were unaware it was there.

St. Peregrine of Today

The Forli, we found, looked like a sleepy little city, unlike that of the Forli of the past, which we have since discovered. It had a silence about it, that first time we visited. It was like the Saint had covered it with a blanket of his spirit. It was as if he was protecting it from the outside world. Maybe, unlike during the epidemic, when he ministered to the sick *infected* by the disease, he was now, at the town gates, *blocking* modern day epidemics of the soul from entering.

The day we arrived, it was *Saturday*. Like many European cities, on Saturday, it seemed everyone was asleep behind those shuttered windows. It was great! There were no cars! But to every positive, there is always the negative. How would we find the Church and Saint Peregrine? We finally spotted someone with a loaf of bread under his arm, and we asked.

The Church was around the corner from a large hospital. Could it be the Saint arranged this, so the suffering, the ill and their families, could still come to him for hope? The Mass was over. There were some people left in the Church, still praying. We passed the side Chapel where his body had been placed. We could tell by the many *hearts of thanksgiving*[9] that hung from the Chapel's walls.

As we walked up the center aisle, we were amazed to find a glass coffin, *there*, containing the body of Saint Peregrine. It was on a small pedestal, rather than above the Altar where it always is. We discovered, through the priest, it was because, unknown to us, we had arrived during the octave of the Saint's Feast Day! It is the custom to place his

---

[9]hearts of thanksgiving-a practice in Europe and Mexico, the faithful bring signs of their giving thanks for petitions granted.

body in a special place, where the faithful can file by, and venerate the body, for eight days after the feast day.

The priest told us, although most of his body, over 500 years old, was now little more than a skeleton, the leg our Lord miraculously cured, was still completely intact with *flesh* on it. We went up to the coffin, placed our hands on the glass and we prayed! We prayed *believing*, and as we wrote in the beginning of this chapter, the Lord answered our prayers through St. Peregrine. Or so, we believe!

The priest's name is Father Brighetti. Like all the priests in Europe, he has become a very dear friend. It was plain, he loved his Saint. He gave us a tour of the Church meticulously explaining, in the strong dialect of his region, when the Chapel had been constructed; and how the Chapel was *extended*, when the Saint was raised from *Beato* to *Santo*.

He pointed out how *faithfully* the Altar and its choirs stalls, had been restored to their original state. We go into all this detail at *this* Shrine, because all these things, the Altar, the choir lofts, the paintings and the fresco, all from St. Peregrine's time that are so carefully preserved, are a part of this Servant of Mary, this *St. Peregrine alive, today.*

He continued, with us trying to keep with his Italian and his energy (although he is way up there in years), and him striding proudly ahead, leading us to the back of the altar down a long corridor, into the *Common Room*, where the Lord had healed St. Peregrine. The fresco of our Lord Jesus Crucified is still there!

He pointed with pride to the photos, in the corridor; on the one hand, evidence of how badly the Shrine had become a shambles; and then, how it had been restored. Years before, the local government had *taken* it from the Church and had allowed it to fall into ruin. When the Servites were able to reclaim it, this restoration began, and the miracle before us, was due to this priest's love and hard work and that of his fellow Servants of Mary's !

At our priest's insistence, we listened to a tape made by an Irishman, a few years before. It told all about the restoration, which the priest had so carefully explained to us, in *Italian*. He wasn't sure, we understood, and he didn't want to miss an opportunity to spread this Saint and his Shrine to the United States.

We knelt and prayed in front of that same fresco of our Lord Crucified, before which St. Peregrine had prayed. We cannot describe the feelings, we had. To the mind's eye, it appears to be a *plain* room, a room most would not pay much attention to. But it was not just a *room*. The Spirit of the Lord is here. He never left. He touched our Saint *here*. These walls remember it well; and they echo what happened, over and over again, when the helpless come crying, Science having failed them, without hope, their hearts breaking.

We never want to leave the Shrines. And that's the truth! But we had another Shrine to discover and another adventure into the world of Church to begin, and so, we had to say good-by. We didn't want to go and our priest didn't want us to go. As we were walking down the street from the Shrine, it seemed, our priest was crying. And then before we could round the corner, Father Brighetti caught up with us. He had a book containing all the Servite Missions in the world. He pointed out the ones in the United States, and insisted we write down the ones in California, that were not as yet in his book. And this, we obediently did. As the priest left us, he was wiping his eyes. He had been crying!

Dear *Father Brighetti*,

Maybe, you were crying because you thought we wouldn't return. Well, little did we and you know, we would return, not alone, but with Pilgrims, and now with a copy of this book which contains a small sharing of our great Saint's life.

Left:

St. John of the Cross is best known for his poem, *The Dark Night of the Soul*. It tells of lover encountering Lover, only to become one in heavenly communion. In 1726, he was Canonized. Two hundred years later, he was declared by this Church, he so loved and obeyed, Doctor of the Universal Church.

Right:

Ana de Jesus went on to prepare a convent for St. John to found in Segovia. He built this convent with his bare hands. He stayed there from 1589 to 1591.

St. John of the Cross

Saint, Spaniard and Poet

St. John of the Cross is best known for his poem, *The Dark Night of the Soul*. Not a poem of tragedy and storms, St. John and all his poems spoke of love and joy, that happiness that only the Father can provide! *The Dark Night of the Soul* tells of lover encountering Lover, only to become one in heavenly communion. Like with St. Teresa, his only true desire was to achieve that complete *union* when he and the Lord would be one.

As we turn the pages of St. John of the Cross' story, you will discover a *powerful woman* in this *powerful man's* life. Like with St. Francis of Assisi, whose *Sister Moon* was St. Clare, the story of St. John cannot be told without St. Teresa of Avila. God was to use her to change the course of his life. He loved her with a powerful celibate love, the gift we will all bring to the Father as we face Him on our last day. Almost thirty years older than he, at times she led him; at other times, she *leaned* on him. Born into a strong *macho* society, he was free to recognize, love and follow this controversial woman who, with him, would unseat and ruffle the feathers of the Church and world of sixteenth century Spain. Working *through* the Church, always loving and obeying Her, even when they did not always agree with Her leaders, Sts. John and Teresa brought about *Reform*.

Keeping His promise that Hell would not prevail against His Church, our Lord raised up another Saint to save *Her*. It was a time of heresy and division. There was a storm brewing over Europe which would destroy everything in its path. Good people were doing bad things, and the Church would bear the scars for centuries to come.

St. John of the Cross, known in Spain lovingly as *San Juan de la Cruz,* was born four hundred years ago into a time of darkness and disgrace. God always balancing the scales, there was an excitement that filled the air of Spain, as well. It was a time of pathos, not knowing when to cry and when to rejoice. It was the year 1542. After hundreds of years under the oppressive yoke of the Moors, a golden age was emerging for Spain.

Fifty years before the birth of St. John, Catholic Queen Isabela, believing in Columbus, had backed up that belief, financing him and his expedition. He set out to open a new route to India. His discovery of *America* for Spain, instead, opened an early gateway to the Americas, gaining a sizable advantage for Spain and her navigators. Her Treasury swelled as her ports buzzed with traffic from the sea.

Spain has always been made up of soldiers of fortune and men in love with God and His Church; one moment, planning the possession of more land and more gold, for the glory of *Country,* and the next, building churches and spreading the Gospel to their newly discovered colonies for the glory of *God.* They were a contradiction within themselves, an enigma. Subjected to cruelty and slavery for centuries, they became a nation of men who could be as cruel to those *they* conquered. St. John would write and suffer for his opinions, for his desire to reform this unruly Spain gone proud and haughty, this Spain he so loved.

He was born of little estate

He was born of peasants in a land where the land and the weather can be an enemy. But to the poor, of which he was a part, it could be a *killer.* He was placed by God in a village called Fontiveros in the Castile section of Spain. Here, the villagers he grew up with lived simple, hard lives.

John, along with his two brothers and widowed mother, were colder and hungrier than most, his mother unsuccessfully trying to eke out a meager living doing some weaving. With not even her husband's relatives willing to help, the little family had to move to Medina del Campo or starve. *Here,* the little band would know some relief; they would be able to find some work and therefore, some food.

John, the youngest son, found work in a hospital serving men suffering from tumors. This brought some money into the house and still enabled him to go to school. All the deprivation, he had known, physical and emotional, had not affected his will or his mind. Right from the beginning, he showed himself to be enthusiastic *and* brilliant.

God, His plan in the works, began molding John through a new company of men dedicated to Him and His Church. The teachings of these holy men, already known as the *Society of Jesus*, would remain with him the rest of his life. But whereas they left an indelible imprint on his mind with their character, he had a problem with some of their methods. The structure of this company very clearly projected that their founder was a Spaniard and an officer.

The founder of the Society of Jesus, *Ignatius Loyola,* was the prototype of Cervantes' Man of La Mancha, the dreamer of impossible dreams, the believer of a new world somewhere. And the new world Ignatius Loyola dreamt of was his love, the *Church.* He was a knight; but the treasures *he* would bring to his Queen, the Church, would be men's souls. He would *champion* the Woman clothed with the Sun, his Mother Mary. All he had been trained for as a soldier for his country, he would use to form this army of the Church.

Although this would influence St. John and his walk to the Lord, his road was to be different. He was being called to be a *new* Saint, one who would touch lives that possibly Loyola could not; so God would use his training under the

Company of Jesus, but would fashion him uniquely and authentically through Himself and for Himself, a one of a kind!

St. John enters the Carmelites

In St. John's day, a quarter of the population of Spain belonged to Religious Orders. Either a young man joined an Order, or he went adventuring by sea to far-off lands and conquests. Therefore, it was not surprising for a bright, gifted young man like Juan de Yepes (St. John) to enter a religious house. He sought and knew he would receive *support* from other members in the *religious* community. The strict rule, under which they lived, appealed to him. The tradition of those who had gone before him, strengthened him; it offered him the *security* he needed, that it was the one *God* wanted him to take.

The object of the *Carmelite life* was to meditate night and day on God's Law and His Word. Their houses were purposely found in places far removed from the distractions of the world, very often in the desert, in hermitages. They would practice long and severe fasts. Their life was spent *communing* with their Lord in contemplation, meditating on this King of all Who loved them. In a word, they were to live austerely, centering on the World *beyond*, and their Creator.

At least that's what they *had been* and were called to be.[1] This is what St. John thought he was joining, but the Carmelites of St. Teresa and St. John's time were being invaded by the *world*. Literally thousands of lay people trafficked in and out of their houses, affecting and infecting those within, with the world and its standards. The convents less resembled houses of prayer and more reflected opulent houses of the *world*.

---

[1]According to the Rule written by St. Albert in 1209.

St. John leaves behind his old life and begins a new life

Everyone loved St. John. His family was no exception. The night he made his decision to leave, to start his new life in the Lord, he waited till the house was dark and quiet. Fearing his family would try to dissuade him, not knowing if he could resist them and the love he felt for them, he left the only way he could, not even saying good-by. What did the young man feel, as he ran through the night? Was he sad at all he was leaving? Was he excited at all that was ahead?

Months passed quickly for John, as a novice. He found his life full, each day bringing new excitement and joy. Many hours flew by in the worship of God and the reading of the Word. He loved it all, the reciting of the solemn offices of the Church, the long passages they read of the Bible, the chanting of the solemn office of the Eucharist where and when God once again came to him, Body, Blood, Soul and Divinity.

Unlike much of our vision of contemplative life, contemplation is often through *action*, caring for the household of a convent. There are rooms to be cleaned, meals to be cooked, tables to be served, dishes to be washed, provisions to be gotten; all in all, hard work making the hours fly. St. John not yet fully professed, like novices before and after him, was always being tested. It is so important that the religious die to the ego, or as we say in the ministry the "*I*" this and the "*I*" that part of our life.

It is imperative that the *religious* understand, as in any relationship, the courtship and the attraction period does not last forever. The life is lived in the everyday saying of "*yes!*" In every matter requiring obedience St. John excelled, joyfully proclaiming his *fiat*, his act of faith each day. This would be a stronghold for him in later years when that "yes" would be so painful.

After six months of the *novitiate*, he professed his final vows, donned the scapular of the fully confirmed Carmelite and left to study Latin and Philosophy in Salamanca. His professor, the one who would nourish his mind and spirit, drew *crowds*. Through him, students discovered learning could be stimulating. The professor's lectures were simply stated, clear, yet balanced with humor. He was everything the young man, from the little town in Medina, needed.

Was his professor too popular? Was his teaching too innovative? Whatever the case, the Inquisition was to rear its ugly head and he was arrested! There is nothing as deadly and angry as the self-righteous. His jailers made sure he had barely enough to eat, sometimes nothing at all. Alone, no one permitted to visit him (they probably would have been too frightened to do so, if they could), it was hard to hold on to any sanity.

His spacious room, at the university, had always been brightly lit by the noonday sun that streamed through its picture window. The burning embers of his fireplace cozily warmed him during the day and into the night, glowing long after he had fallen contentedly asleep. Now, he was in a foul-smelling, damp, grey dungeon. The only measure of comfort he found, was in a knife (with a blunt point he could write with), some books and writing paper, which in a moment of weakness his jailer had given him.

This kind, bright, good humored professor, tried to meet all these trials bravely; but, he finally found himself drowning in nervous exhaustion. Depression, hopelessness, and fear were his constant companions for five long, long years. Suffocating summers cruelly, slowly, moving into freezing winters, he was brought before the Inquisition, trial after trial. Accused and maligned, threatened and tortured, repeating over and over again his loyalty to Spain and the Church, *finally*, he was found innocent!

He was given back his *chair* in the University of Salamanca and it is said he began his first lecture with, "*As we were saying yesterday.*" Although this was not the end of the accusations and threats lodged against the professor, his poetry continued to speak *heart to heart*, praising the Creator and all the miracles of God's creation that so revealed His Glory and Presence.

This professor and poet would influence St. John and his writings during his formative years in the University, but the greatest impact on him would later come from a cloistered Carmelite nun, St. Teresa.

Life in the University - Heaven and Hell

Although, I am sure, many times St. John wished he could fade into the background, as Jesus said, *"you cannot hide a light under a bushel basket"* (Matt. 5:15). Whenever one in a community shines more brightly than the others, there is bound to be envy, and that envy will not rest until it puts out the light, whether it means killing mind, heart or spirit. Sadly, the ones who, with a generous heart, affirm and accept this light as a gift to the community, are not as persistent in their *praise*. And so, it was with St. John.

As we wrote in our chapter on St. Teresa of Avila, convents were in dire need of reform. Could it be this young friar, striving toward living the strict Rule of their founder St. Albert, was a threat to others in the community, reminding them of what they could be and were not? *They scourged him!* Three times a week, St. John bared his shoulders, so the friar in charge could discipline him, for his own good, of course.

Did he gather strength as he was being chastised? Was he being asked to accompany Christ, following the path He had walked, that of humility? Did St. John see his Savior before him, as he took *his* blows, his Lord Who did not defend Himself? Was this his way of sharing the Lord's Passion with Him? Rather than flee from the pain, St. John embraced suffering, refusing every comfort. His peace came, not through *personal* satisfaction, but was sown by each new flower of sacrifice he could place in the basket he, like the little boy at Capharnaum, could offer His Crucified Lord.

Four years of studying with the greatest minds, at the University of Salamanca, no longer held the young friar. Medicine, astronomy, law, philosophy, even theology no longer fulfilled him. He longed for a more intense life, a closer encounter with his Lord. A romantic, St. John had a yearning to be silent and know his God. He would seek this God in the silent Order of the Carthusians.

He set out for Segovia. He would, in the quiet and the remoteness of Mother Nature find this elusive God he so loved. He would study Denys the Carthusian who said "*Love makes us like the Holy Spirit, so wisdom makes us like the Son: but contemplation is an immediate working of the Three Divine Persons on the soul.*"

St. John wanted to know *not the gifts of the Lover, but the love of the Giver, not anything, even the highest, accorded by God, but God Himself.* His plan to reach Paradise on earth, the young Carmelite set out on another expedition in the dark of night. He was all set! The only thing he didn't count on was a woman, a nun named Teresa.

St. John meets St. Teresa-his world would never be the same

God, the Great Chess Player, has been moving His pieces into position. He has a great battle to win! He will begin by placing His queen (St. Teresa) in the path of His knight (St. John). Together they will check-mate the *black knight* who threatens His Church. And so, while St. John is returning from Salamanca, his dreams and future plans neatly defined, probably whistling happily as he arrives in Medina, who should be there having arrived from opening her first convent of San José in Avila, but St. Teresa.

St. Teresa wrote, "*For my part, I believe our love is the measure of the cross we can bear.*"

Luis de Leon, St. John's professor had been his first hero and the first powerful influence in his life; but he was a theologian. Teresa, who he would meet now, and love, was not that. She was a mystic, a woman and a nun who lived and died for the Church and the true Carmelite life. Even before St. John *entered* the Carmelites, St. Teresa had already been battling to reform her Order.

Now, in Medina, she took a broken-down building, and made it into a *religious* house. Never at rest, the Wind of the Holy Spirit always at her back, her next step was *reform* of the friars of the Carmelite Order. She would need some men who would help her achieve God's Plan. She'd heard of the young Carmelite, John. When she heard he had arrived in Medina, she eagerly summoned him. He didn't have a chance!

What St. John saw was a nun who, although fifty-two years of age, could not hide that blinding spirit, that haunting magnetism even under her *coarse* habit. As he looked down at her sandals, he knew her soles of hemp rocked the earth as she walked. Her large, expressive eyes swallowed him up, blinding him, piercing his very soul, and he was a goner.

St. Teresa later wrote of St. John,

"I realized that he was a saint, and had always been a saint." Before her was a figure tiny in physical stature, as the world measures, but a towering giant in the Eyes of the Lord. She recognized the same fire burning in him that raged inside of her.

She was fifty-two; he was twenty-five. She, a nun twice his age! He, a young friar with a dream to become a Carthusian hermit. But, as he looked at her, he knew he would do anything she asked of him. And ask she did! She implored him to wait to join the Carthusians until the Lord had given them a Monastery. She continued, he was, at this time and place, to serve the Lord by working change within *his* Order, as she had begun amongst the *nuns* of the Carmelite Order.

What could he do? As he later wrote, his was "*a heart of one that had fallen in love.*" He promised he would help and agreed to wait, to join the Carthusians, if it didn't take too long. (Author's note: It reminds me of Brother Joseph who came to *help* our ministry and never left.)

St. John waited until autumn. He was restless. He wanted to be about his dream! He struggled! Determined to fight the magnetic pull of Teresa on him, he set out toward Salamanca. His journey over, he looked upon the towering magnificence of the University of Salamanca and knew he had to say *good-by* to all his memories. He would use all he had learned there, but the gnawing inside him, clearly told him he had to return to Medina and his promise to St. Teresa.

So, back again, in Medina, he meets up with St. Teresa! She asks him to join her, as she is on her way to found a house in *Valladolid* for her sisters. She had promised to do this in the hope of rescuing the soul of one Don Bernardino from Purgatory. The first Mass celebrated there, she saw his soul rising to Heaven, and Don Bernardino thanking her for what she had done for him.

This accomplished, she remained in Valladolid for the winter, sending St. John ahead to Duruelo. He stopped at Avila to pick up a workman. He arrived in Duruelo. The *house*, St. Teresa had chosen, that he was supposed to make into a house for *religious*, was a broken-down *shack*.

This young man, who had studied in Salamanca, in one of the finest Universities in the world, who had enjoyed the company of fresh, young minds and been surrounded by great thinkers, who'd been cradled in the glory of God he saw evidenced in the fine churches of Valladolid, was standing in front of a hovel which, with God's Mercy would fall apart before he had to enter it. But it did not fall down.

Left:
St. Teresa of Avila was fifty-two;
St. John of the Cross was twenty-
five. But, as he looked at her, he
knew he would do anything she
asked of him. She implored him
to wait to join the Carthusians
until the Lord had given them a
Monastery. They opened the first
Male Discalced Carmelite
Monastery in Duruelo.

Right:
St. John of the Cross wrote
the first two of his treatises
on Mysticism, *Dark Night of
the Soul, and Living Flame
of Love,* at the Convent of
Beas.

He began to clean it, dispossessing the bugs and vermin that had been its former tenants.

Jesus calls him by a new name-John of the Cross

Like the Saints before him, in Duruelo, the Lord asked him for everything! No more consolation! He had been *born* Juan (John) de Yepes y Alvarez; he *became* Juan de Santo Matía, when he was professed; now he would *earn* a new name: Juan de la Cruz, John of the Cross. Jesus had said, "Deny yourself, take up your cross and follow Me," and John said, "*Yes, Lord. Here I am, Lord. I have come to do Your Will.*"

He was on the road, to *live* what he later wrote,
"*In the Cross is holiness in perfect beauty*
There is no safety to the Soul,
No hope of life eternal
Save in the Cross.
Take up that Cross and follow Jesus."

How often we do not recognize our afflictions as blessings! The remoteness, the poverty of Duruelo, whose potential St. Teresa could foresee, became a *center* of religion. Not only did the local peasants come, but this little household drew others from far and wide. A few weeks after his arrival, St. John was joined by another Carmelite St. Teresa had *invited* to make a sacrifice. As St. John was young, all of twenty plus, Friar Anthony, the new recruit, was *sixty* years of age. He and St. Teresa had been friends for years. Do you get the idea it was dangerous to be her friend or to get within range of her and her vision? What makes a friar who lives in a comfortable house, with all the rewards of having been in an Order for many years, leave it all for the hard life of Duruelo? She said of Friar Anthony,

"*God had inspired him with more valour than He had me, and so he answered that not only there would he dwell, but in a pigsty.*"

When St. Teresa returned three months later, she found the little community singing and laughing. Seeing the former Prior, Anthony, broom in hand, St. Teresa could not help but tease,

"How is this? What has become of our dignity?"

The peasants, one by one, came and brought others. Was it, these friars were infectious with their joy and the obvious love they had for God and through Him, for one another? In any case, not only the poor came, but the wealthy as well. Among them was a lord who would build a house for the now *fourteen* novices, in the village of Mancera.

It was lovely! St. John was to take charge. They had everything conducive to, at last, getting closer to God through *nature*. The groves, the brooks, the flowers, the Sierra mountains, he was in Heaven on earth. Now, he could get about communing with his Lord as he had planned, *before...St. Teresa*!

Meanwhile, the Lord and St. Teresa were planning *new* projects. I guess St. John was too happy. Not to be the way, evidently, for John of the *Cross,* he was summoned by St. Teresa to be superior of a *new community*!

St. John's stay in the new community would not last a year when, *right*, Teresa again! She sent him to a *house* in Alcalá de Henares. Here, as superior he would be instructing students from the university in things of the faith; and from this intellectual input, lead them to higher plains of spirituality. Was he happy! Here we go again! St. John receives disturbing news of abuses coming from a man who had been placed in charge of novices in *Pastrana*. Off, St. John goes to straighten things out.

Although forms of mortification were used as a means of reaching perfection at that time, the man in charge who had taken the name, Angel de San Gabriel, was carrying things too far! Being himself a *victim* of melancholy, he relieved his frustrations on the novices, scourging them. Their bare backs, scarred from the frequent beatings, were not only to be tortured inside the Monastery, but in the *public square.* There they could be abused mentally and emotionally, as well as physically. The young men of the town, made a pastime of *taunting* the novices, as they were being chastised.

Friar Angel's lust for cruelty held no bounds. Pointing to people who are guilty of spiritual gluttony, who for their own pleasure kill themselves (and others) with their penances, St. John admonished,

"This, was the penance of beasts to which they are attracted exactly like beasts by the desire and pleasure they find in them."

St. John told them the devil is always there to deceive good people into doing bad things. When doing anything, the question must always be, am I pleasing God or myself? St. Francis of Assisi would not allow the brothers to practice forms of *physical* penance to the degree he did, because he said some were too immature, and others *enjoyed* it too much! When there is any form of spiritual gluttony, there is less tendency of it resulting in virtue, more in vice.

St. John hardly had time to shake the dust of the road from his habit, back in Alcalá de Henares, when *yes,* St.Teresa called him to *Avila*! She needed him, she said, to act as spiritual director to her own convent of the Incarnation where she had been named Prioress.

St. John is called to direct St. Teresa at the Incarnation

Since her departure from the Convent of the Incarnation, ten years before, things had regressively become worse, if that was possible. There were still a hundred nuns there. The need for Reform that Teresa had seen, ten years before, was even greater than it had been. Life in the Monastery had become easier and easier, to the point of hardly resembling the original Rule. Their parlor was now not only frequented by female family and friends, with their worldly priorities, but now *young men* came, with little regard for the nuns' station in life. The nuns represented an unattainable prize for these playboys, a feather in their cap. Soon the nuns began to look forward to the compliments they received. No way, were they about to allow St. Teresa and her restricting Reform into their lifestyle; so enlisting the aid of some of their more strong-arm *don juans*, they tried to physically bar her from entering.

The new Pope, Pius V had ordered the Reform, but it would take, sadly, more than his decision to allow this to come to pass. It took the Provincial and another friar's help to bring the now sixty year old, very tired St. Teresa into the convent. St. Teresa spoke *lovingly*, responding to her sisters' fury with a gentleness so powerful, they were bowled over. She assured them, placing an image of the Virgin Mary before them, that it was the Mother of God who would be the Prioress and not she. She overpowered them as she said,

> "*I come only to serve you...to this end, I hope the Lord will greatly help me. For as to the rest, any of you can teach and inform me...what I can do for each of you, I will do it willingly, even to the shedding of blood, and giving my life. I am a daughter of this house and a sister...Do not fear my Rule, for although I have lived till now amongst Discalced nuns, by the Lord's mercy, I know well how those who are not should be governed.*"

Even the most hot-tempered nuns had no quarrel with this humble speech. Everything would go as before, or so they thought. They became sharply aware, this would not be the case; St. Teresa reverted to self. A young and very foolish *gay blade* came calling, as usual, in hot pursuit of one of the young nuns. Can you imagine the look on his face when looming ominously before him was the foreboding, terrifying St. Teresa. She boomed, if he so much as thought

of coming to the convent again, she'd know; she'd report him
to the King and *have his head cut off.*

Needless to say this did not endear her to the other
nuns. She became *really* more like a prisoner than a Prioress,
no longer feeling at home in the convent of her early days.
She was so *alone.* Possibly worse than the attacks of silence
she had to endure, as one after another turned her off, she
missed not having a spiritual director! So, who does she call,
but St. John, from Alcalá. She knew she could count on this
eager, well-balanced, uncompromising mystic to not only
direct *her*, but she knew she could trust him to counsel the
other nuns in her care.

St. John was to guide all the nuns in the convent, wisely,
for the next five years. *St. Teresa was so proud of him!*
Although he was only thirty years old, in some cases as
young or younger than the nuns he directed, he gained their
confidence and respect.

"I have found a man after God's heart and my own"...Teresa

St. Teresa and St. John of the Cross were two different
people with two different personalities, definitely not clones
of each other; no carbon copies these two, but *originals*!
Whereas she had great administrative abilities, she knew he
did not. And she playfully chided him about his little defects.
They liked one another, one not envious of the other's gifts,
but such a precious balance one to the other; truly as St.
Paul said, different members of the Body, each with his and
her own gifts.

What she so deeply admired about him was his lack of
guile, his gentleness in handling sinners, his patience.
Sometimes these attributes attracted women whose focus
was not his own. One day one such young woman forced her
way into his cottage. She had fallen violently and more than
a little *demonstratively* in love with him. Little is written how

he handled the situation, but it is recorded she left in peace, tears streaming down her face.

Path of Self-renunciation

Nothing that St. John of the Cross would write, in later years, was as uncompromising as the standards he set for himself and St. Teresa, of self-renunciation. He wrote,

> *"Let us therefore put the love of Jesus above all things. He that clings to a creature shall fall with what is frail; but he that throws his arms around Jesus shall grow for ever stronger. He will never leave you. There is no surer road than that of the Holy Cross. Come unto Jesus and He will refresh you."*

They influenced each other's writings, Sts. Teresa and John. *She*, infused and taught by God Himself, used the everyday evidence of God's Presence among us, for example: *God is among the pots and pans.* *He*, the learned poet, wrote, influenced by much of his theological and philosophical wisdom. *They inspired one another;* each contributing insights to the other.

Treachery and Scandal invade the Convent

There is always a price to be paid. Jesus paid with His Body and Blood. Teresa would pay with accusation and rejection. As St. Teresa was writing her *Interior Castle*, sharing her gifts of contemplation, she *knew* her joy and exaltation would be short-lived. The way to Resurrection and Heaven has always been through the sharp ascent up that stony mountain called Calvary, with all its pain and persecution. Teresa saw in a vision, "a great storm of tribulation." The Papal Nuncio denounced her, calling her journeys founding new houses, *"gadding about."*

Each house put yet another nail in her coffin. She was tired! At one of her houses, in Pastrana, a widowed Princess coerced a Carmelite into clothing her in the habit of a Carmelite. She then forced her way into the convent.

Receiving as many men as she judged necessary to console her, in her widow's grief, she not only brought scandal to herself, but the Inquisition's suspicion upon *St. Teresa*. They accused her of being in accord with the Princess' wishes and behavior. And so, our two mystics, Teresa and John, her spiritual director, found themselves in hot water again!

By the grace of God, the Princess was judged solely responsible. St. Teresa could now go about choosing a *superior* for her community at Pastrana. She chose *Gracián*, a young man of the Spanish Court who had renounced everything to become a priest and a Carmelite. That would surely put her mind at rest. Not really!

There was a war declared between one set of good people and another. Sound familiar? The General of the Carmelite Order got his feathers ruffled when Gracián failed to inform him of his every move. He didn't have time for all these formalities. It seems, Gracián not only went about bringing much needed peace and sound balance in the convent, he concerned himself with the business of *undoing* some great harm, in the *reform*. The General of the Order, judging he was usurping some of *his* authority, wrote to Teresa, *demanding* an explanation. The letter, didn't reach her; he got no answer. Silence angered him! She was evading him! How dare she! Something was wrong!

"Patience wins all!"...only words by St. Teresa or cries from the very depth of one's heart? With every petition to the Lord we know there is a trial, a test. What was behind St. Teresa's words and how did it affect St. John? Tostado, Vicar-General of the Carmelites for Portugal and Spain, and feared *head honcho* of the Inquisition, had been completely swayed by the General of the Order against her. This Tostado would do everything to prevent her from being re-elected as Prioress, even to the point of ex-communicating the fifty nuns who chose to support their mother, no matter

the cost. Meanwhile, the eyes of her soul strictly on her Crucified Lord, St. Teresa was finishing her *Interior Castle*.

Such was the state of the convent in Avila. Tostado was furious with the nuns who would not back down, even with his ex-communicating them. He needed someone to blame! Let's blame Friar John, their spiritual director. He enlisted the help of Maldonado, a Prior from Toledo. Failing to *persuade* the fragile director, they took St. John, arrested him and his companion, had them beaten, and locked them in different cells. St. John escaped the next morning, just long enough to destroy some papers, when he was recaptured.

Tostado was respected and feared by everyone, except Teresa! She protested his treatment of St. John and his companion, right to the King, himself. She pleaded, she feared for the fragile St. John's life.

Meanwhile, Tostado and Maldonado's actions were plain: terrify them; break their wills! They threw St. John into a cell too small for even his tiny body. He was allowed to leave only those rare moments when he was given some bread and water to eat from the *floor*. When he finished his allotted portion, food not fit for the dogs, not ones to waste *any* opportunity, his jailers bared his back and mercilessly scourged him over and over again, the whips ripping at skin already hanging.

When we walk into our Church, should we ever stop to reflect on the price paid for this Church, by the communion of Saints before us, we would tremble!

Mental abuse was added to physical. The Spaniards had been good students; when they were occupied, they'd learned their lessons well. All the degradation, physical and mental completed, they sent St. John and his companion back into the *aloneness* of solitary confinement, again!

Imagine the pain! Although his road was different from theirs, he, choosing the road to God through strict contemplation, he *believed* as they did. He spent hours praying the same prayers they did. Was he not a Carmelite, like they were!

As he journeyed through prayer and reflection, St. John discovered: even in a life of prayer, many of the habits of our life *before*, surface, and we are walking away from that narrow path to the Lord. Like our Bob says, St. John knew and had to accept: "*there was only one God.*" How much disillusionment did he endure, as he became aware: "*some pious people stop short, at times, of even being kind; some old priests are domineering; some young ones are puffed up by their own importance; many virtuous people are self-righteous.*"

As he spent eight long months, now in a prison in *Toledo*, he observed how even men of prayer had the potential of wickedness. Conveniently tucked away in their hearts, it would surface brutally when the occasion presented itself. And on *this* occasion, of course, it was for *the good* of the Church!   No wonder, St. Teresa spoke out so uncompromisingly, that "*not even the smallest evil was to be done to bring about the greatest good.*"

No amount of lies, no amount of threats, not even deadly monotony nor food so foul he thought he was being poisoned, no amount of beatings that even a strong healthy man could not survive, could make St. John give up his allegiance to St. Teresa and the Reform!

In his pain and torment of "*body and soul,*" St. John of the Cross began to compose one of the finest verses in Spanish literature:

> *The silence laid invisible hands upon my heart*
> *And the night knew me.*

The Love of a human and his love of God

As we read the lives of Sts. Paul and Francis, we can only *try* to understand how, with their pain and hurts, they could have written so lovingly *of* the Church *to* the Church, but they did! And so, it was with St. John of the Cross. His poems contained the Spaniard's love of adventure and romance; but the adventure and romance he most wrote of was, his *journey of faith* to the Father!

Was it that the beloved becomes like the Lover? St. John wrote, *"Love produces a resemblance."*

The quality of a man's love is greatly influenced by what he loves; when it is by Whom he loves, he is empowered by that Love. These souls who love, love not only the beloved or the Lover, they love love. In the case of the love affair with the Author of all Love, He fills the lover with so much love, the beloved cannot contain it and he is changed. The love of the Lord takes over the heart of the human who loves Him. Then, the mind begins to enter that mystical romance that human drama cannot begin to experience or understand.

Was this revealed to St. John, as he suffered the torments of prison, the hours slowly ticking away into days, into weeks, into months, into what must have seemed, at times, *eternity*?

On August 15th, Feast of the Assumption, St. John was so weakened by the intense heat in his cell, he did not recognize his jailer and torturer Maldonado. He asked St. John what he had been thinking. St. John asked for the consolation of saying Mass. Maldonado ran true to form and refused.

That night, our Lady appeared to St. John and promised him he would escape. One week later, loosening his bolts, he escaped! Opening the door of his cell, he walked past the cruel Tostado and another jailer, *sleeping* soundly in the hall. He lowered himself down the wall. Fleeing through the night, not knowing where he was going, his only guide a dog who ran ahead of him, he found himself at the Convent of San José, St. Teresa's first foundation.

He remained there for a couple of months. Things did not get better for this little remnant of the Lord. Gracián, who had been appointed Head of the Reformed Carmelites, was relieved of his powers by the *Papal Nuncio* and was in hiding. Teresa was forbidden to move from Avila.

God runs interference

One of the novices at Pastrana during the time of St. John, was a Catalan who had taken the name of *John of Jesus*. Later appointed Prior of Mancera, he was on his way to Madrid to settle some legal questions. He *just happened* to go through Avila and he *just happened* to visit St. Teresa. After listening to her, he vowed not only to do battle with Tostado on her behalf, but with the new Papal Nuncio, Monsignor Sega, himself. The Papal Nuncio, being a fair man and of open mind, *imprisoned* him.

We are not sure why the Nuncio *finally* agreed to see John of Jesus. Could it have been, the Court was keeping a close eye on all that was going on and was kindly disposed to St. Teresa? The Nuncio and John of Jesus were like two bulls locking horns. The Nuncio was an Italian, *proud* of his ability and experience to access a situation. He had long since made up his mind; he supported Tostado, backing him *unconditionally*, in his vendetta toward Sts. Teresa and John of the Cross.

The Nuncio described St. Teresa as: "a restless, roving disobedient female who under the pretense of devotion to the Lord and His Church, was instead inventing *evil doctrine*..." He accused her of going against St. Paul who said women should not teach. Although John of Jesus was able to temper the Nuncio's opinion of St. Teresa, their troubles were far from over.

Everything was against Teresa and John of the Cross; too few friars with too many enemies, their houses taken away from them, there was little hope. Or was there! There was the Royal Court! Teresa not only had the King in her corner, but many of his court were favorable toward her. Besides, the King did not appreciate an *Italian* interfering with the affairs of Spain. An order was issued suspending all action against the Reform and a warrant was issued *relieving* the Nuncio of any further authority over the matter.

The Nuncio *demanded* to be allowed to appear before the King! Although the King was mindful of the necessity of having the Pope's support in his pending battle with England, he was a *Spaniard* first, and would not allow Teresa to be sacrificed. He did, however, concede to reprimand one of his officials, who (at his orders) had put the Nuncio down. Giving the Nuncio, what he judged, his pound of flesh, the King coldly and positively ended the audience by stating the Nuncio's support of a certain party (Tostado) was very *unpopular* with him.

The Reform, with Gracián still in hiding, again decided to declare themselves a separate order. Although this was not received favorably by *episcopal* authorities, the King was on their side and so a new chapter was held.

Enter St. John of the Cross! He arrived, drawn, emaciated, ill, never having recovered from his ordeal at the hands of Tostado and Maldonado. St. Teresa, worried about this little cavalier of hers, wrote:

"The life Friar John has gone through, that he should have been allowed, being so ill as he is, to go there at once had distressed me deeply. See that they take good care of him...I assure you that if he dies, there will be few left like him."

He attended the chapter. He came out *strongly* against the disobedient steps they were taking; but with the King behind them, they would not listen to him.

The dark night of the memory-to the dark night of the will

John of the Cross had endured the long dark nights of imprisonment in Toledo; now, over, he expected and *found* no consolation left for him. No joy in his poetry as his mind went blank, his heart robbed of every *human* solace, St. John turned to and found his sanity in his loving and faithful God;

at times, clinging only by his fingertips to the Lord's Promise He would never leave him.

God never leaves us alone. The Lord had prepared St. John with a mission and He would have His Way. He had given him a brilliant mind, filled it with philosophy, theological training centered in the Bible, placed him in a country on the move, needing not to lose its way. He placed him in the path of a brilliant, contradictory, powerful, saintly woman - St. Teresa, who would help him put together all the Lord had given him.

He had been living in community for seventeen years. For ten years, he had spiritually directed either friars or nuns. He had been the pain-filled victim of his brother friars' anger and envy. He had graduated the school of trials, a school he never willingly applied to. He was ready! Spain and the Church of Spain had the same sickness: too much world, not enough God.

After that rebellious Chapter, where the decision had been made to separate disobediently from the other Carmelites, the leaders of the Reform found themselves in trouble! Friars Antonio, Gracián and others had been thrown into prison! St. Teresa was a prisoner in her convent in Avila. The King stepped in and got everyone pardoned by the Nuncio, but Gracián. Therefore, the battle was not over! The matter went to Rome. A General Chapter of Carmelites was called. St. Teresa's prayers had been answered! The Reform was admitted *into* the Carmelite Order!

When news reached Spain and St. Teresa, not to leave even one of her chicks deserted, she set about not only having Gracián *pardoned*, but elected as *Provincial*!

While all this was going on, St. John was separated from St. Teresa and his many friends. Although the countryside where he was staying, had been all his heart had desired, a perfect place to go away and know his Lord in the silence of the Sierra mountains, it only served to remind him painfully of all he had been through and his Reform family was suffering still. With this, haunting him, he began writing *The Dark Night of the Soul.*

The Dark Night of the Soul

In his third book, St. John speaks of self-renunciation, the death of the memory which we might call today *healing of memories,* to raise the will above itself to the heights where it can glimpse God and begin to know Him. *The Dark Night of the Soul,* he writes, is but another name for the narrow way by which certain souls pass to the perfection of love, which is blessed union with God.

Like with St. Francis, who wanted nothing to weigh him down from going to the Father, St. John prescribed, we let go of our *memories.* For they, as good as they may be, hold on to us, keeping us from freely soaring to our Lord and His Kingdom. He says, the more the mind is given to God, the more the *memory* will act under His Guidance and not under our ability or choice. There is a light, airy feeling that comes about us as we see ourselves shedding all our cares, as we did as children to our earthly father, only now to our Heavenly Father.

He goes on to say, only by making *God* the center of our life, giving over to *Him* the four passions that pervade in our life: joy, hope, grief and fear, then, and then alone, can we love the Lord our God with all our heart, and mind, and soul and strength.

He warns, there are certain dangers that can accompany certain gifts: healing, miracles, prophecies, interpretations, visions. He explains, God permits and gives these for His children's sake here on earth. But unless these are used for bringing glory to *God* and hope to His children, they are of little profit and great harm. When people set their hearts on *gifts* they've received rather than *He* Who gave them, getting puffed up by the attention *they* receive as a result of these gifts, He does not take them away from them. But, the devil is waiting to use this vain *"I" centered* glory to pull them to himself.

There are those who judge, even contemplatives, that St. John's teaching is hard and depressing, bordering on a puritanical harshness. He, himself, said it would take time for his words to sink in. But, when you place yourself in Spain and the Church of his time, his words begin to come alive! Reading on and *praying*, you begin to discover they were not only for that time, but history forever repeating itself, you can see the little giant, St. John walking and talking in *our* midst.

The Dark Night of the Soul was written by a man who took the Cross as his *sign*, who lived and wrote through that sign. But although he only spoke of *holy* things, he was far from depressing, definitely not *a sour-faced Saint*. He did so with so much joy, the friars he directed, loved to hear him, seeking out his company, even during their free time walking in the garden. They said, "He would make us all laugh!"

St. John was a man who loved *passionately*. He had learned to love, and to be free to write of this love, from *Song of Songs* in Holy Scripture. He wrote to his Lord, his Love:

> *If I see not Thee,*
> *What use have eyes*

Two Friends part

God is always moving things and people gently; although, at the time, we find it hard to believe.

St. John of the Cross' life was full, what with the friars he had to train and govern, mixed with the *hustle bustle* excitement of University life. All his suffering a memory, God's little cross-bearer was finding, once more, his God in the beauty of His Creation around him.

Then, in 1580, an epidemic broke out, spreading over all of Europe; it claimed his mother. When it hit Baeza, the village where he was staying, he became involved with the townspeople, setting up a hospital in his Carmelite College. Through his concern for them, his cheerful, uncomplaining disposition as he tended them, the hope he always brought them, they began to come to him, only now to have him hear their confessions. They continued to do so, even after the epidemic.

For St. Teresa, her Reform was now *legitimate*; she was so proud of everything her friars were doing; it all seemed like a wonderful dream. But, her work completed, her battle fought and won, Teresa was feeling the cost of all those years of struggle. She was getting ready to go Home! If only she could see St. John of the Cross, once more. She wrote to her Provincial asking to see her little friar, once more. Her request was denied.

St. John longed to return to his beloved Castile and Teresa. The work of Baeza had begun to become more administrative than instructive and it was starting to get him down. His poetic soul longed to be free to communicate with his Lord.

At last, his and St. Teresa's wish would be granted. It had been suggested a house of nuns should be founded at Granada. It was decided, *St. John* would be the best to send to Avila to beg *St. Teresa* to found the house in Granada. So, now, five years from the last time they had seen each other, the two friends would meet. This friar, she so loved, was her single greatest consolation; she had become *lonely* in Avila. She missed visiting her houses, the excitement of new places and new hopes, the adrenalin-pumping battles fought and won. Her body was worn out; *it* had grown old, but not her spirit. With her ever-young friar St. John here with her, even her old bones seemed young again.

St. Teresa had struggles and disappointments till the end, only now with those she loved *within* her Reform. She died on her way, once more, to straighten out problems and to put one of her houses in order. Too sick to go on, at Alba de Tormes, a very tired Teresa gave up her spirit to the Spouse she had always loved.

On October 4th, her face took on a youthful brilliance. She was beautiful! Her words, "*At last, at last, a daughter of the Church,*" her last act of faith and obedience uttered, she recited the *Miserere*, and her spirit took flight, like a butterfly that had been locked in a cocoon.

St. John is on the Road

St. John of the Cross was elected Prior of Los Mártires (Martyrs) in Granada. The foundation was located on a hill overlooking one the most breathtaking scenes of all Spain. There, before him, he had the shining rivers, the blooming orchards, vineyards whose vines bent from the weight of grapes ripening, waiting to be picked. He could see for miles around, the poplar-lined roads leading to and from Granada on to the picturesque villages beyond. Surely, nestled here in the Sierras, he was as close to Heaven as any human could be. It was enchanting!

Granada and the foundation of *Los Mártires* was to be St. John's home for the next six years, the place he would come back to, the Wind of the Holy Spirit at his back, as he journeyed far and wide. He climbed the hills, walked through the valleys and all to found new houses. He went from Málaga, to Córdoba, to Caravaca, to Buljalance and as far west as Lisbon. St. Teresa was not dead; this disciple of the Cross would carry on for her. But the way would not be easy. If you would know someone's life, read between the lines of his writings.

St. John wrote, a soul was not to follow the desires and designs of the *heart* (feelings always ready to betray you);

rather you must deny your very self, allow yourself to be humbled, and *pray*, always ready to take up and follow Jesus as He carries His Cross, carrying your own. And what will be your reward? You can *count* on this from the world: you will be unpopular; you will lose your friends, your credit, your reputation, and even your worldly goods. The tongues of people will rise up against you; they will make fun of you and ridicule you. They will try to tempt you to go back to what you had been and where they still are. They will use your heart against you, your logic, your pride, your intellect, your strengths and your weaknesses. And very often, all in the Name of God or at least for your own good! But Jesus' Promise, "I am with you always," will sustain you, because *"the Lord will deliver you out of it all."*

St John of the Cross was passionately in love with his Lord, and there was no turning back. We find part of the answer to his walk and love affair with the Lord in this passage based on St. Thomas Aquinas' Summa Theologica:

"Contemplation is dark and for that reason is called by its other name, mystical theology, which signifies secret and hidden wisdom of God wherein, without noise of words and without the service or aid of any bodily or spiritual sense, as in the silence and quiet of night, hidden by darkness from all that is of the senses and of nature, God teaches the soul without her knowing how."

The Living Flame of Love

The Living Flame of Love is St. John's last account of his life. One of St. Teresa's early supporters of the Reform, the now-widowed Doña Ana de Peñalosa, placed herself under the spiritual direction of St. John of the Cross. She totally surrendered herself to the Lord and then went on to prepare a convent for St. John to found in Segovia. Having filled the terrible void left by St. Teresa's death, she seemed to be closer to him than any other; so he poured out his life to her:

his renunciations, his acceptance of trials and tribulations. He wrote of the rewards of sacrifice: the rapture, the *calm* that comes about from the Spiritual Life. This was probably the last letter he wrote.

In his poem, The Living Flame of Love, he explains why people who walk closer to God call themselves sinners, finding more *imperfection* and less perfection in themselves. He says, as souls advance toward perfection they discover deficiencies of which they knew nothing. Again, is it not, *who* can appear before that illuminating *Perfect Truth* and see *themselves* as perfect? He cautions, wisely, that:

"God leads each soul along different roads, and there shall hardly be found a single spirit who can walk even half the way that is suitable for another."

So many times, pilgrims come to us and cry, "What's wrong with me? I find I want things of the world more now than before I gave my life to Jesus." All we can reply is, "When was the last time you gave your heart to Jesus? If it is longer than two seconds ago, that's the problem." St. John speaks of that unending walk *towards*, that ongoing *recommitment* to, that union that is never final, until we meet our Lord face to Face, in our Heavenly Home.

At the end of *The Living Flame*, St. John sums up, in one short passage, the mystery of God in the soul of man:

God dwells secretly in all souls, hidden in their very being; for otherwise they would be unable to exist. But like the measure we shall know him in Heaven, how different is the manner in which He dwells in each soul:

"For in some He dwells alone, and in others not alone; in some He dwells contented, in others displeased, in some He dwells as in His house, ordering it and noting everything, while in others He dwells as a stranger in the house of another, where He is not allowed to do anything or to give any commands."

St. John of the Cross prepares to go Home

With St. Teresa, it was right after she finished writing *The Interior Castle*, she faced her worst persecution. St. John of the Cross would not be denied his share of the *cup*. All hell broke loose, no sooner did St. John complete the final passages *of The Living Flame of Love*!

St. Teresa had her battles with Tostado and the Nuncio; for St. John, now without Teresa, it would be with his new superior.

Gracián had been replaced, not even by a Spaniard but by an Italian! Brothers of his own order voted against him! They had questioned his ability, when they'd voted the first time. He had won the election, as superior, by *one vote*. Hardly a vote of confidence! Now, Gracián was a diplomat, always trying to please everyone, not make waves. In leading, there are times one must be unpopular. This, Gracián could *not* do, and so he, trying to be fair to everyone, weighing and reweighing every decision, made none.

They needed a strong man, one who could make up his mind and *follow through*. They did not consider what living with this kind of man would mean. My dear mother would say, when you buy a vicious watch-dog, beware he does not turn around and bite *you*! Whereas Gracián was an idealist, Doria, the new Italian superior was a pragmatist[2]. Gracián, with his idealism had made many mistakes. Doria with his cold calculations made none. Gracián was loved but not trusted. Doria was trusted but not loved.

During Gracián's time as Provincial great projects were openly accepted and encouraged, but nothing came of them. In Doria's nine years of office, it was simple, none were approved and so none had to be executed.

---

[2]pragmatist-one who is basic, business-like, hard-headed, practical, sensible.

Although he knew well the faults and shortcomings of Gracián, St. John felt impelled to warn the friars, who smacked a little more than ambitious, how they were called to an *uncompromising* life-style. I am sure he echoed the words of St. Teresa, warning them *the smallest evil cannot be justified by the greatest good.* No amount of pleading, quoting of their Mother Teresa, warnings, could change the minds of the friars. They voted Gracián out and Doria in. And then, it began!

Doria proved to be a tyrant! If he terrorized the Order as a whole, he reserved special venom and vindictiveness for Gracián! To quote the new superior, Doria, in his first Chapter, said, "Let us cut off the rotten limb, and the body will recover its strength." If he could have, he would have expelled Gracián, but he couldn't, so he sent him to a post, across the Atlantic to the yet unexplored and feared, wild, mountainous Mexico.

Jesus had not been popular, and he promised we would be persecuted, as well. The mob, like in the time of Jesus had chosen Barabbas (Doria), but he knew they could as quickly turn against him, back to Gracián. *Kill him! Kill him!* Mexico was not far enough!

Doria had won the favor of the King. He would bring Gracián before the Inquisition; that would finish him off! Doria began by securing a decree, from the Court of Spain, giving him *absolute* authority to expel anyone he judged rebellious from the Order. And so, bringing Gracián before the Inquisition, he accused him of publishing a pamphlet without permission. In case that was not enough, he added Gracián was having intercourse with the nuns!

Gracián was *expelled* from the Order! He should have fought, but he was a man of peace; besides like St. John, he desired only to be united with the Lord in the Spiritual Life. If they allowed him to do that, *well*...Instead, he was *relieved* from his post in Mexico, and not answering the charges against him, he was run out of the Order in disgrace!

Not satisfied with destroying the living, he went after the dead; it was St. Teresa's turn, now! Teresa's nuns! Attack them! Get rid of them! Since St. Teresa was the *rule* rather than the exception, these strong Spanish women did not lie down and die. St. John of the Cross fought to preserve the Reform and St. Teresa's work. He got up in the assembly, and spoke, defending St. Teresa and her nuns. *Doria lay in wait.* As he listened to St. John brilliantly extol his Foundress, Doria hatched another plan; send him to Segovia as *Prior.* That's how he'd silence him, at least for now!

St. John waited from 1589 to 1591, in Segovia, for the other shoe to drop; he knew Doria would never be satisfied until he was gone for good! He built his convent with his bare hands. He was content, but his good friend Ana de Jesús was not going to let it go at that. She pursued St. John's cause to Rome! As the Holy See was favorable toward St. Teresa and all her work, Ana de Jesús used that to defend St. John. She testified that Doria, with his actions, was really going against Teresa's Reform. Her petition was granted! St. John would be exonerated!

When news got back to Doria, at first he ranted and raged; then he *plotted.* The Pope was too ill to put through his decree, so Doria would make the most of this time; he would strike before the ailing Pope could act. He tried scandal, he tried smearing Sts. Teresa and John's names. When that failed, he exiled St. John to Mexico!

St. John would not go peacefully to Mexico. Not content to escape with his life, justice and fidelity uppermost in his mind and heart, St. John not only defended the nuns whose good names Doria had tried to destroy, but Gracián's as well. St. John was deprived of his offices and made again a simple friar. With his words, "*I shall be thrown into a corner like an old rag,"* St. John was sent into exile, to lonely, remote La Peñuela on the mountainous ranges of Sierra Nevada. Here he would find *peace*, but this was not to be his gift the last years of his life.

First they had tried to discredit St. Teresa, now they were trying to disparage him, so like with Gracián they could expel him from the *Order*.

In his last letter, he wrote,

"They cannot take the habit from me, even for incorrigibility and disobedience, and I am quite prepared to amend my ways in all wherein I have strayed, and to be obedient, whatsoever penance they give me."

He remained in La Peñuela until another enemy struck, now, a *physical* one. The friars had to take St. John to Ubeda. He had a raging fever and they thought he would be able to get some help there. His trip seemed endless, as his aching body bobbed up and down on a mule, his tongue stuck to his pallette as his temperature rose, ulcers ripping away at his stomach like ground glass, unable to eat anything but a little asparagus.

When he arrived at Ubeda, the Prior, remembering how he had once been reprimanded by St. John, put him into the tiniest, coldest, dampest cell he could find. The Prior would have more purely enjoyed his revenge, but old Antonio de Heredia, who had been with St. John in Duruelo, came to the rescue. Our Little Saint's suffering was so excruciating, a kind friend sent in some musicians, hoping they might sooth some of his agony. St. John refused any relief.

The weeks painfully passed until December the 7th, when he was made aware, he was dying. The Prior had witnessed the willing suffering of this servant of God, who'd never complained, but instead *praised* the Lord for allowing him to share in His Sacrifice. He repented his treatment of St. John and *wept* at the foot of the dying Saint's bed.

On December 14th, St. John grew silent. There was an aura of peaceful light surrounding him, enveloping and cradling him. He exclaimed, "*I shall be to-night in Heaven.*" As he said the words, "*Into Thy Hands, oh Lord, I commend my spirit,*" the friar, who had been holding him, saw a triple crown encircling his head. As a sweet perfume filled the air, St. John no longer suffered. He had breathed his last. His face was radiant. So, went the little Carmelite, friend and helper, on his last journey, to his last House.

Loyal son of the Church, faithful to the end

St. John of the Cross loved and died, a son of the Church, and that Church was the Body of Christ, *alive* continuing His Incarnation, *alive* as a witness of His Resurrection and Ascension, *alive* in that moment in the Mass when the priest raising the host and the chalice, all Heaven unites with earth and we have God among us.

St. John of the Cross was a Catholic, a *Spanish* Catholic, a priest, Confessor and a Friar, and a Poet. No amount of rejection, persecution, and injustice could dissuade him, from the call that he had answered. No matter what the cost, he lived and died a Catholic son faithful to his vocation, to his Sacrament. He loved Mother Church. He loved *everything* about his Mother, the Church, but especially the Sacrifice of the Mass.

The Church not only had no quarrel with Her son, She raised him to the communion of Saints. In 1675, he was *Beatified.* In 1726, he was *Canonized.* Two hundred years later, he was declared by this Church, he so loved and obeyed, *Doctor of the Universal Church.*

Although I tried to keep this a recounting of the life of *St. John of the Cross,* living and breathing between the lines, sometimes bursting forth like a rocket, had to be St. Teresa.

The contrasting personalities and gifts of Sts. John and Teresa *complemented* each other, creating a harmonious

Song of Songs like the angels, as they praise the Lord during the Mass, singing Glory to God in the Highest. And because they were free to accept each other and their gifts, as they were, their songs still fill the air. She had the courage, strength and determination of a conquistador. He had the sensitivity, the gentleness, the intuition and excitement of a *newlywed* drinking the honeymoon experience with his Lord.

He was sent by God to a land of captives to help set them free. They knew him not and so, they killed him! His crucified body has been raised! He now dwells with the Eternal! At last, he communes with the Lord he always sought.

†

John of the Cross-Poet and Actor in the Drama of Church

But St. John communes with us, too. His two treatises on *mysticism*, he left us, were based not only on his study of Theology and Scripture, but on his *own life experience*. He was not an apathetic bystander but an active participant, in all he wrote of Mother Church. In *The Ascent of Mount Carmel*, he reminds us *"how different from the Infinite and Eternal Power Who creates are all the finite things which are created."* With the world preaching, illogically, we are to have faith in *things* rather than in the One Who *created* them, St. John's words are as alive today as in the sixteenth century. He said, *"created things are like crumbs falling from God's table."*

When speaking of *images*, he clarified, in the sixteenth century, some misconceptions we still have in the *twentieth* century, not only those of our brothers and sisters who are non-catholic, but also those of some of our mis-informed Catholics. He explained, it is not that statues and paintings are wrong. It is our dependence on *them* which obscures the fact they are only symbols that is wrong, and as symbols are meant only to draw us towards our Lord Whom they symbolize. He simply was saying, depend on nothing, or no one, but that God, Whom you can depend on. Things and humans, of their own power, can do nothing without His Will.

Jesus asked His closest disciples, "Can you drink of the chalice that I shall drink?"

St. John explains, the chalice *"is to die to our own nature, stripping it and annihilating it, that one may go by this narrow path in all that pertains to sense and soul: that is in understanding, in enjoyment, and in feeling."* He spent his whole life trying to drink from that chalice.

As with the disciples before us, we want the *feelings* connected with following the Lord, but we do not want to pay the price, necessary. We wear a crucifix around our necks, but refuse to do as the Savior teaches, that is to take up our cross and follow Him. St John of the Cross, not only bore the name, but the cross, itself.

He said, he did not mean his writings for everyone, that he wrote for St. Teresa and those who would ascend Mount Carmel, *barefoot.* But if you are someone who would like to begin saying *"yes"* to the cross Jesus hands, lovingly, to each of us, it is true you may find the path narrow, but the rewards are great! The conditions of the cross, when you look at them all at once, might cause you to want to run, but that is why the Lord reveals them to you, one at a time.

The most important rule St. John speaks of is, if you should decide to embark on this road, you keep nothing for yourself. All that you are, have been or ever will be is from God. If you claim, for yourself, anything as your *own property*, whether it is a gift from God or *anything* else, you are not stripped and denied in all, and so you will never ascend the narrow path toward things *above* and our Lord, Who awaits you.

Pray with us, as we try to live his words as he did, in his company and that of all the Saints who walked before us, journeying: naked, transparent, casting aside all reserve, opening every room of the castle, giving over to the Lord, our very souls. Wanting to find all, we know we must seek nothing. It is in this nothingness, St. John tells us, we will find the *secret* of the All, this Lover Whose Love magnetizes, drawing us closer and closer to Him. And when we have arrived, like a butterfly, we will beg to be consumed by His Fire.

St. John best described this nothingness with,

In order to arrive at having pleasure in everything,
  Desire to have pleasure in nothing.
In order to arrive at possessing everything,
  Desire to possess nothing.

In order to arrive at being everything,
  Desire to be nothing.
In order to arrive at knowing everything,
  Desire to know nothing.

St. John Vianney, Cure of Ars

Patron Saint of Parish Priests

When something meaningful has happened in our lives, we can recall *where* we were, *who* we were with, and *what* was going on at that time.

One of those times was April 14, 1967, when God sent us an angel, a blonde, blue-eyed baby weighing barely five pounds. Our grandson was almost swallowed up in his blanket; he was so tiny. We couldn't keep our eyes off this precious bundle. Suddenly, the nurses seemed to be having a problem with him. Seeing us, they quickly drew the curtains shut. The doctor finally came out from the nursery; he told us, our baby wouldn't last the night. Numb, we replied helplessly, *"You mean he is in the Hands of God."* He looked at us, kind of strangely.

We ran to St. Patrick's Cathedral. It was locked! The *last* thing we remember doing that night, was going to our parish church, out on Long Island. *It was locked*! It was dark; all we could see was a lighted statue of Jesus in front of our church. I knelt before my Lord and begged Him to save our precious grandson.

The next day, we went to the hospital; they told us our baby took his first nourishment at 6 a.m. When I tried to thank the doctor, for saving our grandson, he replied, "We did all we could, with the scientific knowledge we have; it was your *God* who saved him." And this, from someone who claimed to be an atheist.

The day Robby was Baptized, we raised him up before a beautiful statue of Jesus, "He is Yours, Lord. You gave him to us, twice. Now we consecrate him back to You." I had always loved that statue; Jesus had red Hair and blue Eyes, like my father, my first *earthly* Jesus. My earthly father now in Heaven, I talked to *this* Jesus. I related to Him. I liked

255

Him. I trusted Him. I didn't know, at the time, why He had a Heart, with a crown of thorns surrounding It, outside of His Body, on His Chest. You see, I didn't know much about my Faith, no less the *Sacred Heart* of Jesus.

Robby was the only baby who did not cry, when he was Baptized with holy water. A Jewish friend with us, said this was a sign he was to do something special for the Lord. Our grandson has grown up into a fine young man. He has been close to Jesus and His Mother Mary all his life. He is a part of this book and this *chapter*, in particular. You see, the name of the church, where we had prayed for our boy, on the night he was saved, the same church where he was Baptized, was The Curé of Ars (St. John Mary Vianney).

Lord, You placed us in the path of one of your great and faithful servants, *twenty-three* years, ago. Little did we know why, then. The first time we journeyed to the Shrine of St. Jean Vianney in Ars, France, with our family, in 1979, we did not know *why* we were there! As we studied the life of this Curé, and brought pilgrims there, year after year, we still did not have the answer. Priests on our Pilgrimages, always asked to serve at the Altar where St. John Mary Vianney had celebrated Mass. Still, we did not grasp *why*, what the Lord was doing all those years. They say, the moment you understand the Lord, you have lost your faith. Every time, I think I've got a handle on *what* the Lord is saying and doing, He says "*Surprise!*"

We were giving a talk on the Miracles of the Eucharist, one night. As we spoke of This Treasure in our midst, our Lord Alive in the Blessed Sacrament, we found ourselves going to the instruments He uses to be with us in this unequaled way, our priests. We called our brothers and sisters to affirm our priests and the holy role they play in our lives, how they are representatives of Our Precious Lord and Savior with us, and when we love and respect them, we love and respect Him. They are a lifeline; without them we have no Jesus in the Eucharist, no healing from the forgiveness of our sins. When we finished speaking, a priest came up to us. He said,

"Thank you for your words. I didn't know you could feel our wounds, our loneliness, our need for affirmation. Tonight is my birthday. You gave me the most precious gift. Oftentimes, when I look out at the congregation, from the Altar, I see a sea of boredom, their eyes glazed over. Sometimes I wonder what judgment of me, it is, I sense on their faces. There is so much scandal, so much pain. How do I say, 'I'm none of those things; I love you; I love Jesus and His Church, and I want to serve Him by serving you?' Instead I keep these feelings to myself and keep a safe distance from those I love, God's people."

This chapter is about a *priest*, who was raised up to the communion of Saints as *Patron Saint of all Parish priests.* This chapter is for those unsung priests, those Curés who are taken for granted, unloved and often crucified. This is for the many hours, week after week, they have sat alone, waiting for us to come to be reconciled with our Savior, through confession, and we have *not*. This is for every Holy Mass they have celebrated, joining with our Lord as victim upon the Altar. This is for their "Fiat," their *yes*, especially on those *dry* days when they felt nothing.

Who is St. John Mary Vianney?

St. John Mary Vianney was a humble priest, hidden away in a small remote village, too small to appear on most maps of France. This priest, like the mustard seed, could not be hidden in obscurity; the gifts of the Holy Spirit he received were to bring thousands and thousands to *him*. It is no wonder he comes from that section where over a century later, the *Charismatic* Renewal of France began. The Holy Spirit goes where He wills, when He wills.

It is also no coincidence, he was born close to where our Lord showed His *Sacred Heart* to St. Margaret Mary Alacoque. Jesus told Margaret Mary, He was more *deeply* hurt by the Crown of Thorns pressed on His Heart by His *friends*, than by the One His enemies mockingly placed on His Head. How many times, Curé did your heart get pierced from a crown of thorns thrust there by friends? Did it wound you, like it did Jesus?

Here again, like with Mother Mary's Apparitions and Miracles of the Eucharist, we have *clusters* of Heavenly happenings. Could it be, the Lord *goes* where there is much need? You could definitely say that of Ars and of France, at the time of John Vianney. Ars was a village of sin and apathy. The Curé would spend forty-one years of *dry martyrdom*[1], as Pastor of Ars, the only parish he would ever serve.

John Mary Vianney was born in France, the France of *Heritage*, eldest daughter of the Church. This France, in his lifetime, would be ripped apart and aborted by revolution. That malignancy of the spirit was not only to eat away at all the magnificent old traditions of France, but would spread right into the heart of the Church. As anger cannot be contained, those spoiling and destroying did not stop at the aristocracy, but forgetting why they had begun in the first place, turned on Church, guillotining priests and nuns. We share this because, as in the time of St. John Mary Vianney, if faith, like a garden, is not cared for and nourished, it will die. And die France did, and the Church along with her. Only in places like French Canada and our beloved Louisiana can you see evidence of the glorious Heritage of the France of Yesterday. There, the old traditions and pride in France and the Church flourish, side by side.

---

[1]Archbishop Fulton J. Sheen speaks of this type of martyr in his chapter. One who suffers each day pledging and living his Profession of Faith, loyally each day, each hour, sometimes sixty times an hour.

John Mary Vianney was one of six children, born in a little village, Dardilly, five miles north of Lyons. His family's reputation for *charity* became so wide-known, beggars would pass their name on to other fellow travellers of the highway. There is an expression, *angels unaware*. Well, one of the beggars they so generously gave to, was a *saint*. St. Benedict Joseph Labre, affectionately called the *beggar saint*, stopped at their home sixteen years *before* John Mary was born. However, we can be assured, the prayers and blessing this holy man bestowed on the family, would be an instrument to bring another holy man unto them, who someday, like himself, would be declared by Mother Church, *a Saint*.

John Mary, child of Mary

From his mother's knee, John began to pray. Helping his little hands to make his first signs of the Cross, she would patiently and joyfully have him repeat, in his sing-song way, the Apostle's Creed, the Lord's Prayer and the Hail Mary. His two greatest treasures, as a small child, were his Rosary, a precious gift he received only to have to give it to his younger sister, and a little wooden statue of Mary his mother gave him, to compensate for giving away the rosary. This statue was to be at his side most of his life, a source of strength, a reminder his Lady was with him. Years later, the Curé, nearly seventy years old, still spoke of the Lady he loved, "*The Blessed Virgin is my oldest love; I loved her even before I knew her.*"

The neighbors seeing this little boy, first to drop down on his knees each day, when the Angelus bells rang, would prophesy to his mother, "*Your John Mary will become a priest or brother.*" One of his greatest delights was to accompany his mother to church. She tried to go to Mass each day, her little boy pleading and winning, trailing after her. He listened intently, as she explained the Mass, sharing with him the Divine Mystery, what was *really* happening. No wonder he developed early, a love and passion for the Blessed Sacrament in the tabernacle. He discovered at a young age, this Lord Who was alive, and He would become for John Mary, as a priest, his Strength and his Fulfilling Love.

John Mary loved attending school, but his learning did not end there. As soon as he arrived home, he opened books on the Lives of the Saints. Religious worship was one of the *fatalities* of the Revolution, the authorities leveling all sorts of threats. It was strictly forbidden! In spite of this, the Church was alive in the Diocese of Lyons, which included Dardilly. The Church was underground, but flourishing! Priests disguised themselves as artisans and *secretly* conducted their ministerial services throughout the parishes. One of these priests who passed himself off as a *cook*, visited the Vianney home, one day. After blessing all the children, he turned to John Mary. He liked the boy. "How old are you?" the priest asked. John Mary replied, he was eleven. The priest asked him how long it had been since his last confession. Before John Mary could finish replying, *"I've never been to confession,"* the priest had him in tow, and John Mary was making his first confession. Then the priest turned to the family, "Now it's time for him to study Catechism, so he will be ready to receive First Holy Communion."

No sooner said, John Mary was off to live with his aunt, in Ecully. There were two nuns there, disguised in lay clothes, who were preparing fifteen other children; so he could join them and prepare for his First Holy Communion. Although his companions *learned* to love this young boy, his life in Ecully began with painful jibing. Being short and a little plump, they would taunt him with: "Look at the little fat boy wrestling with his angel."

He was thirteen years old when he finally received His Lord in His Body and Blood, his First Holy Communion. The shades were drawn to prevent detection by the authorities. The only light, outside of the lit candles on the

Altar, was the New Light of John Mary and his Savior, now *one*.

As a grown man, he was still not able to speak of that day, without tears coming to his eyes. He had not wanted to leave; he had wanted this moment to last. Or was it, as he explained, years later,

"When we receive Communion, we sense something extraordinary...a great joy,...a great consolation,...a well-being that permeates our whole being and makes us tremble...We cannot but say with St. John, 'It is the Lord!' O my God! What joy for a Christian to get up from the Sacred Banquet and go forth with all Heaven in his heart."

Call to the Priesthood

The young Corsican general who led **the** *coup d'état* on September 18, 1799 not only overthrew the Directoire, restoring peace to France, but Napoleon, upon entering into negotiations with Pope Pius VII, ended the persecution of the Church, temporarily. The church bells peeled loud and strong, bringing life back to France. "Come back! Come back!" they tolled and they came. First, the priests returned. Churches which had become *buildings* were now churches again, for with the priests, the Mass returned and with the Mass, the Eucharist! And then, the faithful came. They cried. They were so happy, but no one was happier than John Mary.

He had worked in his family's vineyard with his older and stronger brother. Whenever he had a problem keeping up with him and the work, he would take the little wooden statue of his childhood and pray to the Mother of God. *"Always put your trust in the Blessed Virgin Mary. I prayed hard to her today and she helped me. I was able to keep up with Francis, and I wasn't tired."* (Authors' note: Whenever the work at the Ministry is ten times what we can handle, we too, turn to the Queen of the Angels and *They* come down and help. How else do you explain it when four do the work of forty?)

He was now sixteen years old and the thought of becoming a priest persisted. He would tell his mother and his aunt, *"If I were a priest, I would want to win many souls!"* He was a simple country boy, with only an elementary school education; the idea was ridiculous. His mother wept for joy; she knew he could do it! His father fumed and stormed, resisting all his son's pleading for two years!

God to the rescue! His little troops, mother and son, not faring too well, He sends a priest to Ecully to promote *vocations.* Father Balley, in addition to being pastor of the church in Ecully, turned his rectory into a *school.* He had three students preparing for the priesthood.

John Mary's mother, finally able to *persuade* her husband, went on to Father Balley. *He was not very sympathetic.* "It was not logical. The boy was nineteen, with very little education! Sorry, but no!" They pleaded and begged and reasoned, all to no avail. Only John Mary's brother-in-law's suggestion, "Meet him! When you see him, I'm sure you will take him," was able to move the priest's heart.

Father Balley not only accepted him, but this man, who would "make any sacrifices for John Mary if there was need," was responsible for preparing the heart of a Saint and priest. Although not named in the Communion of Saints, we know Mother Mary is saying to him right now, "Father Balley, John Mary could not have done it without you. Job well done!"

John Mary was not stupid. He had a keen mind. But he had a problem *memorizing.* And when what you have to remember are fundamentals of *Latin,* well the brain becomes like a leaky pot and nothing stays in there, especially not declensions and conjugations. Little boys, in his class, couldn't understand or empathize with his problem. *It was so easy!*

One of the brightest pupils, Matthias Loras, tried to tutor John Mary with his Latin. One day, he lost patience; furious, because John Mary could not retain what he had just taught him, he *slapped* him in front of the other students (all much younger than John Mary). Now, John Mary, almost twenty years old, also had a trigger temper, and here was this *twelve year old* slapping him. To everyone's surprise, *he went down on his knees and* begged forgiveness from the boy who slapped him. This unexpected response from John Mary completely disarmed Matthias. John Mary had returned his slap with humility and love. They became lifelong friends.

Remember angels unaware? Well, this friend, who had hit a future Saint, John Mary Vianney, went to the United States and eventually became the first Bishop of Dubuque, Iowa. *His* holiness was so great and widespread, there is a movement to start his *beatification* process. Do we have a *cluster* of Saints in this school of saint-makers?

Father Balley, head saint-maker, had his hands full with John Mary; but he never gave up on him, not even the time he came to him, tears in his eyes, crying he wanted to go home. John Mary insisted, God didn't want him to become a priest. If He did, why couldn't he learn? Father Balley knew John Mary's soft spot: his love for the Church and its Mystical Body. "Well," he said, "when your father sees how dejected you are, you will never be able to return. You can say *good-bye* to the priesthood and to the souls you wanted to help." Father's plan worked. John Mary stayed!

John Mary Vianney - Call to Arms

As if all the struggling to learn was not enough, in the fall of 1809, John Mary received orders to report to a *military* barracks. A special provision had been granted the Bishop:

all *seminarians* and priests in his Diocese were exempt from serving. Father Balley, the Vicar of Religious and others of the Diocese tried to help; they fought the decision, insisting John Mary should be exempt. Strange as it seemed, John Mary *had* to answer the call to serve in the Army.

Two days after he arrived at the military depot in Lyons, he became seriously ill. When his family and friends visited him, all he spoke of was doing God's Will. *Two weeks* later, he was discharged from the hospital and transferred to a convoy stationed in Bayonne. His legs barely able to support him, he wasn't able to travel farther than Roanne. There, he landed in a hospital again, only now for *six weeks*. Not fully recovered, still weak from his illnesses, he was ordered to join his company, which was now in *Spain*. Out of obedience he started the hike up the Pyrenees Mountains. The steep ascent was more than he could make, physically. John Mary soon became exhausted and was unable to go on. He met up with a deserter who offered to help him: John Mary could hide out with him, until the war was over. John Mary didn't want his brand of *help*. Wanting to obey his orders to rejoin his company, but too weak to refuse the deserter's proposition, he very reluctantly followed him to town.

Still unsure of his decision, John Mary went to the mayor of the town. Not too impressed with the Empire and their aims, he hid John Mary, deciding he could teach school in the town. The hard first few months became joy, as the townspeople learned to love their teacher. This could not make up for the anxiety John Mary felt: *Were his parents suffering because he had deserted? Were they worried about him?* The woman who was giving him shelter went to his parents to tell them their son was safe. His father who had suffered reprisals because of his son's defection, demanded to know where he was living so he could go get him, and bring him back. She told him in no uncertain terms, "Even if you were to discover where I live, I would hide him somewhere else. He's worth more than anything you own."

The situation was finally resolved and John Mary came home. No one ever thought he had acted wrongly in this matter, with the possible exception, for a short time, of his father. John Vianney never apologized for his desertion; he knew he had not offended God in any way and that was his primary concern.

John Mary Vianney, at last the Junior Seminary

His teacher and mentor prophesied John Mary would become a priest. One day, when his mother had come to him, worried, Father Balley reassured her, "Mother, don't worry about your son. He is neither dead or sick. He will never be a soldier. He's going to be a priest."

His mother never lived to see the prophecy fulfilled. Soon after John Mary returned to Dardilly, she died. But before she left to go with *the* Father, she convinced John Mary's father to have him continue his studies at Ecully with Father Balley. Father Balley continued to work closely with him, especially with his Latin.

It was October, 1812, and John Mary was off to the Seminary in Verriér. In the days of John Mary Vianney, seminarians were required to have one year of philosophy and two years of theology. Considering these and all his other subjects were taught in Latin, he was having a hard time. He was hardly a top student. Now, 26 years old, he was the oldest in his class. One of his *professors* was younger than he was. You can see how compounded the problem was. John Mary just could not get it in Latin, so they took him, along with seven other students, and taught them in French. That really did not alleviate the problem to any great degree, but John Mary wrote to Father Balley, "*My studies are progressing a bit better than I had expected.*" God can work with that kind of clay. From this He would form a priest. John Mary remained at the bottom of the scholastic curve, his only consolation and affirmation was with and through our Lord in the Blessed Sacrament.

Another step toward the Priesthood - the Major Seminary

Although this was the next step toward the priesthood, for John Mary, it was to be by way of the Cross. His studies, still in Latin, were no easier than they had been in the Junior Seminary. Several of the seminarians, when asked to testify at his Beatification Process, would comment on outstanding qualities they had seen in him: his devotion to Jesus and Mary, his vocation, his humility, his total abandonment to the Will of the Father, and his frequent failure but persistent struggle to keep up with his courses.

A priest later spoke of him as a simple man, nothing extraordinary about him to make him stand out, but nevertheless a *Saint*!

Although his subjects, when presented to him in French, were less threatening, he found tests *terrifying*. He would freeze, forgetting everything he had learned. His failure to get passing marks caused him to be dismissed from the Seminary. *He thought he would never become a priest!*

Well, if he could not become a priest, he could follow the religious life as a *brother*. He went to one of his friends who had become a Christian Brother and told him of his inability to master Latin. He pleaded, "*I have come to become a Brother.*"

He went back to Ecully and told his friend and teacher of his decision. Father Balley knew God had need of this young man for the *priesthood*. The Church of France desperately needed priests, but it went beyond that; Father Balley could see the qualities of the faithful priest etched on the heart and soul of his young protégé. He directed John Mary to inform the Christian Brothers, he would not become a brother; he would study with *him*. And they began, *again*!

When he was at his lowest ebb, he heard a voice, "*Come now, don't worry! You will be a priest some day!*" Fortified by this Divine intervention, he studied harder than ever with Father Balley. Three months later, at Father Balley's insistence, he took the test at the Major Seminary, *again*. He froze! Wanting to pass, so very much, he could only helplessly stutter, unable to utter the answers he had so diligently stored in his brain. *He failed miserably.* But, because of the high regard they had for Father Balley, they decided, although they could not possibly accept him in the Archdiocese of Lyons, they would okay him applying to another diocese. Father Balley, believing in his protégé, insisted John Mary be tested in Ecully where he had confidence.

When the panel of priests came to Ecully, they were taken aback by the obvious miracle before their very eyes (and ears). John Mary, supported by the love and affirmation of his teacher, friend and mentor, answered the questions to the satisfaction of the panel. When the administrator made the final decision whether he would be accepted or not, although there was desperate need of priests, the deciding factor was *holiness.* "Is Abbé Vianney a devout man? Does he have a devotion to the Blessed Virgin Mary? Can he recite the Rosary?" When the response was, "Why yes, he is a model of piety," he was accepted. Father Balley had won his battle, and the Church of France, as well as the Universal Church, had a Saint!

He entered the sub-diaconate, the first of the major Orders, on July 2, 1814. He took a vow of celibacy and committed himself to reciting his breviary everyday. He was giving himself totally to God and he was taking his first big leap toward his dream, the priesthood. A priest, present at his ordination, said,

"*I had the good fortune to be very close to Abbé Vianney that day...His face was radiant. Inwardly, I applied to him the verse: 'And you, child, shall be a prophet of the Most High!' thinking to myself: he has less knowledge than some others, but he will do great things in the Sacred Ministry."*

John Mary continued to study and prepare for the priesthood for the next year with the patient and persistent Father Balley.   In this way, he was sheltered from the upheaval of Napoleon with Waterloo, and the chaos of the second Restoration now under *foreign* occupation.   The seminarians had been distracted by these worldly events, but again, our Lord intervened that his future priest might be focused on one battle alone, that of the soul. Five days after the fateful battle of Waterloo, another battle was fought and won. John Mary was ordained to the diaconate, receiving the Order which confers the Holy Spirit and the spirit of strength. It was June 23, 1815.

At last, the Priesthood

When he was given his final examination, all his years of prayer, persistence, courage and loyalty paid off. He was *accepted* for the priesthood! But as a precaution, because of his past poor marks, they would only ordain him with the faculties to say Mass, this priest who would spend sixteen to eighteen hours a day in the confessional!

How did John Mary Vianney, now Curé Vianney feel about the priesthood? Let him speak for himself:

*"Oh! How great a person is the priest! The priest will truly understand himself only when he gets to Heaven...
If we understood what the priesthood means, we would die, not from fright, but from love!"*

And so, on August the 13th, 1815, thirteenth Sunday after Pentecost, John Mary Vianney was ordained a priest *forever*, according to the order of Melchizedek.   Truly: *Sacerdos alter Christus!*...The priest is another Christ! One man, a brother in Christ, a priest, believed John Mary

Left:
St. John Marie Vianney, the Curé of Ars, patron saint of Parish Priests, was a humble priest, hidden away in a small remote village, too small to appear on most maps of France.

Below:
Incorrupt body of St. John Vianney

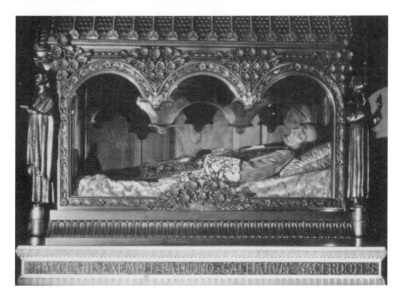

Vianney had a vocation; and through that belief in action, he received a brother *who became a priest*; and priests, especially Parish priests, received, as a gift, a *Patron Saint.*

Abbé John Mary was appointed to be the curate at Ecully! Not only did his heart swell as he celebrated his first Mass, there, but it was to continue as he served with *Father Balley*! He could further learn by word and example from this holy priest. He spent two and a half years as curate of Ecully, practicing with his friend, Father Balley, rigorous penance, spending long hours praying, and learning the doctrines of the Church, as well as other spiritual matters.

In the rectory at Ecully, their reading consisted of The Holy Bible, the Lives of the Saints, and the Lives of the early Desert Fathers. Through these inspired readings, they were able to live a life that would terrify most of us today. In fighting their *French* love of food, as well as their barest needs of comfort and of the flesh, they never depended on their own strength and faculties. They placed all their trust in the Lord, believing His Grace was enough!

When asked how he resisted and overcame temptations against chastity, John Mary replied, it was the result of a vow he had made in 1816, when he was a curate in Ecully. It was a commitment to daily recite the *Regina Coeli* (Rejoice, O Queen of Heaven...) and six times a day, the prayer, "*Blessed be forever the most holy and Immaculate Conception of the Blessed Virgin Mary, Mother of God! Amen.*"

When word got out of the *extreme* penances practiced by Father Balley and his associate curate, they were reported to the Chancery! The reply from the Archbishop's office was, "People of Ecully, you are indeed fortunate to have priests doing so much penance for you."

John Mary was soon granted the faculties to hear confession. As soon as he began, people flocked to him. They not only returned, but added to their number were others who, upon hearing of the great spiritual food derived from this holy confessor, came from miles away.

Father Balley was not envious of the devotion to his former student. He was, instead proud of the progress the humble curate had made. He knew, as well, all those years of hardships, during the Revolution, were at last taking their heavy toll on him. He felt he would be going *Home*, soon; God had indeed provided a holy and competent successor. When we speak of the relationship of Father Balley and the Curé John Vianney, we remember what a very holy priest once told us, "Our sons are those who through some small way have become priests through us." This same priest once wrote, "It is said, if you are responsible for the salvation of one soul, your redemption is assured."

In December, 1817, the little curate administered Last Rites to his pastor, his teacher, his *"father"* and friend. It was time for Father Balley to join the communion of Saints. I am sure there has to be a *special* place for priest makers, and he was surely one personified! As Ecully was, like Nazareth, unaware of the Saint in their midst, they did not want the young curate as their pastor. The priest who took Father Balley's place felt there was no need for an assistant, therefore, less than two months after his friend's death, John Vianney was being assigned to *Ars*.

The priest who assigned him, prophesied, "There isn't much love of God in that parish. You will put some love of God into it!"

John Mary Vianney, Curé of Ars

Ars was the poorest of parishes, more a mission than a parish, impoverished spiritually as well as materially. The people were not *hostile* to the Church. The Curé would almost have preferred this to their *apathy* and *indifference*. No one, with the exception of one devout, very charitable and very influential lady, wanted or cared if there was a priest or a church there in Ars. Their fame for dances and drunkenness was widespread. People came from miles around, even on Sundays and holidays, to join in with the townspeople, to go wild in the four taverns in town. The village was too small for even their one church, they claimed, but not for four taverns. And *this* is where The Curé was to practice his ministry!

The Curé, John Vianney, looked older than his thirty-two years. He was thin and emaciated, short, shorter than the average Frenchman (5ft. 2in.). His auburn hair, the only remnant of his youth, would soon turn prematurely white as he carried the weight of his spiritual children's sins and lack of love for the Lord.

He was helplessly lost. He spotted a young shepherd and asked him the way to Ars. As the young boy directed him, the Curé spoke the words that revealed his purpose, and that of His Father in Heaven, for coming to Ars,

"You have shown me the road to Ars; I will show you the the road to Heaven!"

Right from his first Sunday Mass, he spoke of his love for them, how he longed to bring them the Food with which they would never know hunger or thirst or death. The mayor, who would become his staunchest advocate and support system in Ars, recognized his holiness immediately: "We have only a poor church, but we have a holy pastor."

The benefactress of the village, in a wave of appreciation, bestowed the most beautiful furnishings for the Curé's lodgings. He returned everything but the strictest necessities.

This village, mockingly looked upon as the bottom of the barrel, became the focus of world-wide *pilgrimages*. When questioned about the miraculous conversion of Ars and the flow of thousands of pilgrims to that afore unknown village, he would always attribute it to the intercession of St. Philomena, a young unknown martyr of the early Church.

Lest we give you the impression that this came about right away, it was bought with *ten years* of blood, sweat, suffering, tears, rejection and struggles. Although in a small physical frame, the Curé was a *giant* of prayer and penance. And this is the formula! This is how the glory of Ars and its Church, and the recognition of this holy confessor, came about with prayer, and faith in that prayer. Whenever we feel overpowered by what there is yet to do and how little time there is to do it, and as a *last* resort we turn to God, we need to recall, with the Curé of Ars, it was the *first* resort:

"I am nothing, God is everything. I can do nothing of myself, God can do everything. The souls of men belong to God, they were made for God. And the reason I came into the world, the reason I am here is to give them God!" St. John Vianney.

When the going got tough, he never gave into the horrible temptation to run! Obedience always held him back, obedience to his vocation, and to his spouse, the church, given to him by the Lord. It didn't matter if she didn't want the love he had to give her. Rejected often and humbled, he accepted this as a gift from the Father, one he could hand back to Him, as victim-priest.

He trusted in the Lord, saying, we are sure, over and over again, *"I trust You; I trust in You and Your Plan for me and Your children."* Another strength was his unfailing loyalty to God, His Mother Mary and to His Church. He lived in God, with Him and for Him. He literally *"lost"* himself in God.

Over the years, his parishioners observed him, at all hours, early morning and late night, entering the church, prostrating himself before the Tabernacle and the Blessed Sacrament and praying. His persistent or was it pestering prayer went something like,

"Dear God, I beg you to convert my parish. I am willing to suffer anything you want and as long as I live!"

In later years, when a priest came to him, asking for his secret, how the conversion of his parish came about, he replied,

"My friend, the Devil cares very little about discipline and other instruments of penance. What really puts him to rout (or gets rid of him), is sacrificing one's need to drink, eat and sleep. These are the penances the Devil dreads the most and that are therefore most pleasing to God. Oh! How I experienced it! When I was alone, as I was indeed for eight or nine years, I was free to follow my bent. (No one was around to check up on me). In fact, there were times when I didn't eat for whole days at a time... Then God would grant me everything I wanted for myself as well as for others..."

Curé Vianney, Preacher

Father Vianney considered preaching from the pulpit one of the most important charisms of his apostolate. Although his preaching was not considered eloquent, people thronged to hear him bring the Word of God to them. He preached, like Jesus, clearly and simply, using the countryside, and things familiar to them and himself, to explain the message and the *Messenger*. Souls were touched. Their hearts were pierced by the arrow of the Father's Love that sailed through the air as he preached. He brought them His Love and His Mirror to look into and they were converted into the Image before them. He loved them and they loved him, and it was this love and holiness that converted them, more than his arguments. If it is true that the best preacher is the one who loves *God* most, then that surely would have to apply to the Curé of Ars. The love he had for God and God had for him, was the love that spilled out of him and covered everyone who heard him. And yes, people were converted!

Above: *Interior of church*
Below: *The humble parish church, made famous by its curé, St. John Vianney.*

As we know, when the Curé came to Ars, the greatest moral evils were dancing and the drunkenness that pervaded this small village. He waged an ongoing battle against the too many temptations with the too many taverns. Never needing to be popular, he came out boldly and passionately, never giving up until they were closed down. He had little sympathy for dancing and was not above attacking with a bit of biting sarcasm:

"One day, I happened to be passing in front of a great fire. I took a handful of dry straw. I threw it unto the fire, telling it not to burn. Those who witnessed this action said to me mockingly: 'You are wasting your time telling the straw not to burn, that won't stop it from burning.'

"And how is that?" I answered, since I told it not to burn?"

"What do you think, good mother? Isn't that what you told your daughter: to be a very good girl, when you gave her permission to go to the dance?..."

His voice, never growing tired, roared through the church, penetrating their minds and hearts:

"The Devil surrounds a dance the way a wall surrounds a garden."

"Dancing is the rope which the Devil drags most souls to hell."

"Everyone who enters a ball leaves his Guardian Angel at the door, and a devil takes his place. And so very soon there are as many devils as dancers in the ballroom."

The problem he had, was not so much with *dancing*, but with what he knew the dancing would lead to. And we only need to look around, now in our own time, to *where* dancing has progressed or should I say regressed: to the teen-age pregnancies, to drug and alcohol addiction, to music which promotes sex, despair and dope. He doesn't sound archaic, now, does he?

A Parish - won for Jesus

In addition to the prayer and penance practiced by the Curé, actions that helped to bring about the conversion of his parish were: visits to his parishioners; his sermons; the living example of all he preached, his own life; his generosity to the poor, giving often at the cost of depriving himself from life's very necessities. Such were his weapons, as he fought, day after day, waging war against sin. Transformation and conversion is a slow, painful process. But change was coming about. The faithful came from all parts of the countryside on Sunday and Feast days to attend Mass. They recited the Rosary, attended Vespers and the Curé's catechism classes. But that was not all! They wanted more! They had discovered the treasure that was Church and they came, even during the week, with an appetite that could not be quenched.

Their devotion spilled over to the fields, as a farmer said his Rosary, fingering his beads as he plowed the land. All who could, gathered in the church in response to the tolling bells calling them to prayer. Families came and prayed together. Instead of swearing and foul language, *hymns* could be heard coming from the fields. At table, before and after meals, grace was said in thanksgiving.

At the sound of the Angelus, all work stopped; they dropped to their knees and prayed. The Curé taught them to "bless the hours," to say a *Hail Mary* as the hour struck. This custom, which had ended with the bloody Revolution, was now being revived by their priest; they were so happy!

To quote a visiting Bishop, "Their faces reflected a holiness that we have rarely noticed elsewhere to the same degree. A serenity, a sort of radiant blessedness made them stand out among thousands." When considering this little giant, the Curé of Ars, I dare say *this* was probably the most powerful evidence of his sanctity, that which *reflected* from the mirror of his parishioners' souls.

The Curé founds a School for Girls

The full extent of education after the Revolution, in most villages, but especially in Ars, was a visiting teacher who would teach some classes to boys and girls. It was spasmodic, at best; its lack of continuity providing poor education, making it more dangerous than having no education, at all. Poor, with no money of his own to start a school, the young Pastor forged ahead. The Lord had planted the *need* in his heart and all he had to do was say *Yes*!

He searched for a site and some suitable women teachers. First there was Catherine Lassagne, who would play an important part in the Curé's life and the other was Benoite Lardet. He trained them himself. In November, 1824, the free private school opened in Ars. From the start the school was a success. People came from surrounding towns to bring their children. Soon, it was too small. Because of the distance the girls had to travel, he would have to find them a place to stay overnight. He opened a shelter for little orphan girls and for daughters of the poor. Father Vianney called the newly organized institution, *Providence*. The name and the institution are still there. (We visit it when we pilgrimage to Ars, each year.)

The Curé was a living example that a priest does not give up having a family, but has instead, a *large* family. The students and the teachers were his most precious children. He carefully gave them as much time as he could. He ate his meager meals with them, the few moments he spent "*feeding his cadaver*" (as he liked to call eating). These little girls became *prayer warriors*. He would ask them to pray for all the intentions dear to his heart. To them, he brought his brokenness, and the weight of his deep concern for the welfare of the poor sinners who came to him. And they prayed! And miracles abounded!

Ten years before his death, the Curé was forced to give up supervision of the Institution he so loved and founded. This almost broke his heart. There had been complaints: there were sixty students in a space meant for twenty and worse, the wealthy did not appreciate their daughters going to school with the poor and the orphaned. So, grievances were lodged and the Bishop asked the Curé to turn the school over to the Sisters of Bourg. Catherine Lassagne did not reveal *her* broken heart, but I am sure it rests alongside that of the Curé when she says,

"It was a great sacrifice for him, because after he had turned everything over, he felt he could not and should not interfere in the affair of others. He completely withdrew from it. Several children were kept on for a short time, then they were sent away. The children of the Parish, that is the little girls, continued to be given free schooling."

Boys not holding a second place in his heart, he also started a school for boys, a foundation for *the Brothers of the Holy Family.* He carefully chose a teacher, known for his integrity and holiness, who later became a very close friend and co-worker of the Curé's. After the Curé's death, the teacher testified, a principal witness at his cause for Beatification.

The Curé taught Catechism

His catechism classes were more like little sermons. The fire of his love of God, and of them, the children, shone through his words. When he gave instructions in the church, he was acutely aware of the Lord in the Blessed Sacrament, never able to talk with his back to the Tabernacle. Although he had a pulpit placed on the right side of the sanctuary, so his back was not to the Tabernacle, Christ was so present to him, in the Blessed Sacrament that his voice would tremble with emotion as he spoke.

The making of a Saint - his trials and triumphs

There is no Resurrection without the Cross. As we *journey in faith* to the Father, we find, as did the Saints before us, there are no triumphs without trials. In Ministry we discover our walk is like riding a giant roller coaster with the highest highs and the lowest lows. You're on Mount Tabor, one day, and on to Calvary, the next. And so, it was with the Saints. The deeper we study, we learn: as go the trials, so go the Saints; as the measure of the trials, so the degree of the Saint. Is it that God can trust great trials to great Saints? Or is it that great trials *make* great Saints? In any case, the little Curé of Ars suffered the greatest trials balanced by the greatest consolations. As with Mary and all the Saints before him, he did not ask to be spared and spared he was not.

He had made many *enemies*: tavern owners, dance hall proprietors, as well as their patrons, all wanted to kill him. But he was so loved by most of the townspeople, they could not come outright against him, and so they grumbled and whispered and plotted. Had the youth, outside of the village, decided it was their duty to put this Curé in his place? In any case, they accused him of *misconduct*. When that was too ridiculous for anyone to accept, they began by singing obscene songs about him; if you can't kill someone, *ridicule* him. When that failed, they sent anonymous letters threatening him; maybe they could scare him to death, or at least silence. They posted all sorts of vulgar, disgusting signs on his door. They would not even allow him to sleep the little time he set aside for rest. Although he called this time when he was persecuted the best time in his life, he did *suffer* from the onslaught of attacks. He was even denounced to his Bishop! Not without feelings, he cried; not for himself, but for those he could not reach.

In later years, he shared,

"If I had known when I arrived in Ars all that I would have to suffer there, I would have died on the spot."

He seriously considered leaving the parish. Certainly, this discord was not good for the parishioners, especially the children. At his Beatification, witnesses said,

"He was so tired of all the evil rumors that people were spreading about him that he wanted to leave his parish. Indeed, he would have done so if someone had not come to him and convinced him that his departure could appear to confirm these sordid attacks."

He stayed on, although he later confided he was afraid he would end his days in *jail*. The more he was threatened, the more fear assaulted him, the more hurts he bore, the more he abandoned himself to the Lord and His Will. When his friends came to him with a new attack, he would reply, *"We must pray for them!"*

The Devil was not satisfied with the results; the devious back stabbing not succeeding in getting rid of the holy priest, he went all out. You always know when the Devil is frustrated and is losing the battle, he gets *obvious*! The next attack: the Curé began to hear voices telling him he was destined to go to hell! The voices deep inside of him, tortured him, taunting him with: his accusers might be right; maybe, he was going straight to hell!

The Devil's nightly visits usually occurred when there were sinners, repentant, eager to return to the Sacraments of the Church. They almost always arrived after he had suffered the worst attack by the *Evil One*. The Curé, through his faithfulness to the confessional and to the Word of God, was calling many to *new life*, and the Devil was furious! Like the Curé, we can have confidence, the Devil can only attack to the degree, our Lord allows. And He never leaves us alone!   *And* on our side, we have our Guardian Angel and the Blessed Virgin Mary as well, to help us fight and defeat the *enemy*!

As if all he suffered was not bad enough, his fellow priests poked fun at him. Some priests, staying in a rectory in Saint-Trivier with the Curé, heard strange noises coming from his room, one night. When they complained to him, he answered them with his usual straightforwardness.

"It's the Grappin²," he replied. *"He is furious about the good that is being accomplished here."*

Annoyed, his fellow priests' snapped , "You don't eat, you don't sleep. It's all in your head! You have rats running around in your brain." The Curé judged it useless to answer, *"If it is in my head why do you hear it?"*

The next night there was such a racket outside the rectory, all the priests (except the Curé), as well as the housekeeper, shot up from bed. The rectory shook as if a huge carriage, laden down with a heavy load, was passing by. They all panicked; the house felt as if it were going to cave in. They heard such a battle ensuing, coming from the Curé's room, they were positive he was being *killed*. They charged into the room. The Curé was sound asleep but his bed had been dragged into the center of the room! When they wakened and questioned him, he apologized,

"The Grappin dragged out the bed. I'm sorry. I should have warned you. But it's a good sign: we'll catch a big fish tomorrow."

Imagine the fun his fellow priests had with him when *tomorrow* came and nothing unusual happened! But the day was not over; when evening came, there was a knock at the door. Monsieur des Murs, a nobleman, who like the rest of his class had long ceased receiving the Sacraments, had come to have the Curé hear his confession. Needless to say, there

---

²The Curé's nickname for the Devil

was no more kidding their fellow priest. The obvious sign of the nobleman made them all believers. They now said, "The Curé is a *Saint!*"

The Devil even followed him into the Confessional using the body of a woman confessor. Taunting him, the Devil said, "I have beaten stronger men than you. You say you're leaving why don't you! If it were not for the B....(referring to our Blessed Mother, using a vulgar word), we'd would have gotten you a long time ago! But she protects you too much, and that big dragon at the door of the church...(the chapel of St. Michael and the Holy Angels at the entrance to the church)." Gradually, the visits and the attacks of the Devil became less and less frequent; but they did not stop until a year before the Curé died.

"The Devil did not come back anymore, and Father Vianney had no regrets at the loss of such a comrade. He did not disturb him during his last agony, as had happened in the case of other Saints. Even before his death, the Curé of Ars had inflicted a definitive defeat upon Satan."[3]

His greatest Joy - the Holy Eucharist

We have spoken of pain and trials. Like with the other Saints, the Curé embraced his daily Cross because of the *joys* in his life; the greatest of which was the Holy Eucharist. For the Curé, the greatest sign of the Lord's triumph in his parish, was the effort the people of Ars put into making the procession of the Blessed Sacrament, on the Feast day of Corpus Christi, so extraordinarily magnificent.

These celebrations later were called the *"pilgrimage of Ars."* Ranking with the Shrines of the Blessed Mother at Lourdes and La Salette, this pilgrimage to Ars, in the nineteenth century drew Frenchmen from all parts of France to this formerly unknown and remote village.

---

[3]from Abbé Trochu's biography of the Curé of Ars

It is important to stress, without devotion to the Holy Eucharist which originated on the Altar, as the Curé celebrated Mass, none of this would have come to pass. They had come to know their Lord and Savior in the Eucharist and it was to Him and His faithful priest they were doing homage.

An anonymous writer described his experience during a *pilgrimage of Ars* celebration. He said he came *by chance* to Ars. He was not ready for what he saw before him. There was a procession advancing, a canopy of gold cloth sheltering a gilded Monstrance. An old man, the Curé, walked slowly and solemnly, carrying the *God* of all! The voices of the pilgrims, accompanied by Angels filled the air, singing hymns in praise of this God alive in their presence. The canopy stopped! Over two thousand people dropped to their knees in adoration of their Lord. The priest, hands trembling with emotion, raised the Monstrance and blessed everyone in the Name of the Father, and of the Son, and of the Holy Spirit!

These were the days our priest lived for. His face was almost transfigured, as he looked upon his Lord and the people this Lord so loved, He left them His Body and Blood. He seemed to them what every priest is called to be, another Jesus Christ, a mirror of Jesus with them. How he reflected this Lord he so adored! People gravitated toward the light that emanated from his face. They saw Jesus in him, and they had come to trust this representative of His, as they had Christ, in Galilee, when He had walked the earth.

The Curé loved and envied - Magnet of God

"Monsieur le Curé, other missionaries run after sinners, even into foreign lands, but it seems that sinners run after you."

The Curé answered his parishioner, with a gleam in his eye, *"That's not far from the truth!"* And it was not far from the truth.

From the very beginning, the clergy, his brother priests were not only *unsupportive* of this mass movement of the faithful to the holy Curé, but they did everything in their power to stop it! Again, as with the other Saints, their envious and hurting thoughts were: *Why him? He has very little formal education and knows no Theology. He could mislead them, this ignorant nobody.* They did everything to prevent their parishioners from going on pilgrimage to Ars, even to the point of speaking out against him from the pulpit. Is this why the whole world does not know Jesus Christ? With all the souls who need to learn about Jesus, I cannot, for the life of me, understand a member of the Mystical Body of Christ trying to silence another, unless he is not speaking the Word of Christ faithfully, according to the Church. No one could have accused the Curé of that, but they tried!

He received *anonymous* letters insulting and condemning him. Again, they threatened to take him to his Bishop! A young Pastor of a nearby village wrote, what could be used as a sample of the kind of letters the Curé received:

"Monsieur le Curé, anyone who knows as little Theology as you should not enter a confessional."

Father Vianney answered the young priest. Thanking him, he reflected the attitude which drew so many to him:

"My very dear and very revered colleague, I have so many reasons to love you! You are the only person who has really known me well. Since you are so kind and charitable as to take an interest in my soul, please help me to obtain the favor I have been asking for so long that I may be replaced in a post of which I am unworthy because of my ignorance, so I can retire into some little corner to weep over my poor life. I have so much penance to do! I have so much atonement to make. So many tears to shed!

Always generous, loving and truly humble, he disarmed his enemies and was finally accepted by his brother priests.

A day in the life of a Priest called John Mary Vianney

He would rise from bed, most often, at one in the morning, when his day would begin. Lighted candle in his hand, he made his way to the church. The many people who had slept in the belfry, during the night, were waiting for him. After a while, it became necessary to enlist guards to keep the faithful from pushing, rushing to be first to enter the Confessional. There were so many, so many who had waited days, they would sometimes forget the *real* reason they were there: reconciliation was with *God*, not with the Curé. The humble priest would have been the first to tell them to take their eyes off him and place them on God!

Before he entered the Confessional, he would go to the foot of the Altar, kneel down and pray to the Lord, his Strength and his Wisdom, for the grace and love necessary to be His instrument of mercy and compassion. He would remain in the Confessional for as much as seven hours straight, interrupting this Sacrament only in order to celebrate the other Sacrament, the Holy Eucharist.

He would go home to eat a very small meal, spending most times not more than five minutes. He considered eating a *nuisance*, and if it were not necessary, he would not participate in this waste of time. Like Jesus before him, he had an *urgency*. His joy was in the people of God, anxious to know their God more and to be reconciled with that God. After gulping down his food, he would take a cat-nap, for not more than a few minutes. Refreshed, he quickly returned to hear confessions until eleven o'clock. He would, very often, ask the penitent to remain quietly in the Confessional while he read his office; this being the only way he could find time to do so.

Above:
The humble bedroom of St. John Vianney
Below:
Kitchen in St. John Vianney's Rectory

At eleven o'clock, he would then teach catechism for approximately forty-five minutes. After he was finished, he would try to slip by the crowds, often by way of the garden; but soon he was spotted by the waiting throngs of *needing* souls, and it was necessary *again* for guards to keep them back.

Once more, back in the rectory, he would take a bite to eat, rest for a few minutes and then return to the church and the confessional. In the winter, he was known to be in the confessional until seven in the evening. In the summer, when the daylight hours were longer, his hours with his penitents were longer.

In between hearing confessions, he would go to the pulpit and lead the waiting faithful in reciting the Rosary and other prayers.

There is little known how long he actually slept. But we do know his vocation as a priest and his little church were his *whole* life. He needed and wanted little else: therefore this is where he received his refreshment. He spent as *little* time as he could resting. Toward the end of his life, he was not to know even those few moments of rest; his nights were filled with pain and raging fever.

His mind and heart had made their choice. Or had the Lord chosen *them* when He chose John Vianney for the priesthood? It was said best in the *Album du Pèlerinage*:

> "*His heart has never been touched nor his mind tormented by arrogant knowledge, riches and human honors for which the crowd strives, laments, and constantly aspires... The God Who rewards and sustains love of neighbor, Who relieves and consoles-this is all the good priest knows, and especially all that he teaches...* "

It was a publicly well-known fact, the Curé spent between sixteen and seventeen hours in the confessional. So, his young associate Pastor thought it only reasonable, since the Curé used his bedroom so little, *he* should have it, instead. This bedroom so coveted by the young priest was at best austere (a polite word for hardly livable). The walls were bare. His total belongings consisted of an old chest, a few treasured pictures of Saints, some old threadbare books on Theology and on the floor, a mat upon which he slept.

Hundreds of thousands passed through the curtain of the Curé's confessional. He faithfully and tirelessly carried the cross of men's sins and sorrows for thirty years. Never too tired, too disillusioned, too broken to say *yes* one more time and listen; loving with the Heart and speaking with the Mind of his Savior, he brought the words of absolution to everlasting *life*.

The Gift of Prophecy

In our day of excitement and renewal in the Church, with so many returning to the Church, as *adult* believers, with new love and joy, many gifts are being received from the Holy Spirit. Some which we know and some which we do not know or understand. One, which is more often than not misinterpreted, is the Gift of Prophecy, people often calling it the gift of foretelling the future. I prefer St. Paul's letter to the Corinthians (1 Cor 14:3):

"The Prophet...speaks to men for their upbuilding, their encouragement, their consolation."

Such a Prophet was St. John Vianney, Curé of Ars. He could read men's hearts. One time, a man accompanied some friends to the Curé's church. He had no intention of confessing. The Curé asked him if it wasn't *time* he confessed. The man said it had been thirty years. The Curé said, "*How about, thirty-three years!*" He looked at the man, now overcome with shame. The man meekly followed the Curé, confessed his sins and twenty minutes later was filled with a joy and a peace he said was unexplainable. He had never known anything like it in his whole life!

There was a woman who regularly came to the Curé to have him hear her confession. One day, becoming seriously ill, she went to a *sorcerer* for a healing. The healer gave her a a potion, sure to heal her. On her way to Ars on foot, she thought it best she hide the vial containing the potion, before entering the church. She knew enough *not* bring it into the house of God. As she finished confessing her sins, instead of the Curé giving her absolution, he asked,

"My good child, you aren't telling me about the vial you hid in the bushes."

She confessed her grave sin. The Curé gave her absolution. The woman, weeping now with relief, ran to where she had hidden the vial and threw it away.

A man came to the Curé. Pointing to his crippled child, he begged, the child be cured. He asked for his prayers. The Curé led him into the confessional. Having been away from the Sacraments for many years, the father *reluctantly* confessed his sins. The Curé absolved him of his sins. With that, the child stood up and walked, not showing a trace of the illness that had kept him a prisoner of his crippled body.

There were many healings through this powerful confessor and his tireless administration of the Sacrament of Penance. Like in Lourdes, more often than not, they were healings of the spirit, but that did not preclude the many *physical* healings. Jesus always first said, "Your sins are forgiven." He knew their bodies could not be healed if their *souls* were not first healed. And so, faithful servant and royal priest, Father John Mary Vianney, each moment of each day, became a willing prisoner of the confessional, joining Jesus in the Garden of Gethsemane, as he, too, suffered the pain of their sins.

It was a time of Miracles

As with gifts of the Holy Spirit, which do not necessarily constitute sanctity but are *gifts*, so it is with the granting of

Miracles. They are gifts freely given by the Lord, *signs* of holiness, but not necessarily holiness of the person or persons receiving or experiencing them. The few Miracles we wish to share in this segment are different from the ones required for the canonization of a candidate for Sainthood. These have been recorded as taking place during the Curé's lifetime. Those required and accepted by the Church were those obtained after his *death* through his intercession.

There was the *Miracle of the Multiplication of the Flour*. Once, at *La Providence*, there was not enough flour to bake even an oven full of bread. The mill couldn't grind the wheat that had been sent over. There was just enough flour to bake three loaves of bread. When they had seen there was not enough flour to feed all the girls in the school, they went to the Curé. He told them to use the little they had. They took the small amount of flour they had, and began to knead it. The trough filled, overflowing with dough as on days when they had a *large sack* of flour. Had the Curé prayed? Did he ask the Lord to multiply the loaves as He had, on the Mount of the Beatitudes? It is definite that a Miracle was granted by the Lord for the Curé's spiritual children. Was it by his intercession? What do you believe?

Then there was the *Miracle of the Wine*. One day, the Curé came to his people, advising them a full cask of wine had split and the contents had spilled onto the sand floor. Sure enough, when they investigated, the cask was empty. They tried to retrieve whatever they could of the clearest wine from the sand. They were barely able to collect two little pails of clear wine. They poured what little they had into a cask which was nearly empty. To their amazement, they kept drawing from the cask for *days*, till there was nothing left!

Beside the now empty cask was another cask of wine, half full. They decided to pour the 50 liters of wine from the half full cask, to the empty one beside it, which had a capacity to hold *200* liters of wine. Jokingly, one of the women teased, "See if the cask is full!" Imagine the look on her face when the other woman replied, "It is! Look, I can touch the wine with my finger!"

When the Curé had mentioned the cask was empty and they should see about it, wasn't he, like Mother Mary before him, really speaking to Jesus! And then, turning to the women, wasn't he really saying, like Mary before him, "Do whatever *He* tells you!" And our Jesus Who never tires of feeding us, Who is always available to answer our needs, responded and gave him and us, a Miracle! In the Lord's Humility, He acted as He has always done, through one of His children's faith and petition.

As we read the lives of the Saints, the words of Scripture come alive. If the Lord cares for the lilies in the field, as He does, what will He not do, if we ask in His Name? Why do we question, wasting time on worry, where we will live, what we will eat, what we will wear? The Lord of all, knows our hearts and *He* answers us!

When people came to the Curé sharing all the Miracles and phenomena occurring in the Parish, he always pointed to God and the intercession of the Saints, especially his Saint Philomena. In an effort to draw people away from praising him, he would give credit to this little know early Christian martyr. Through him, this heretofore unknown Saint became so popular throughout France, many parents chose Philomena as a Baptismal name for their little girls. All the pilgrims would not be *fooled*. They insisted, if the Miracles were from the intercession of St. Philomena, it was because the Curé had asked her. He persisted,

"I do not work miracles! I am only a poor ignorant man who once tended sheep...Turn to St. Philomena. I have never asked for anything through her without receiving it."

And this was and is, the kind of *leaven* the Lord can and will work with. How do we know the authenticity of a Saint while he or she is still on the earth? Well, the Curé, St. John Vianney, placed no importance on Miracles bringing about bodily cures unless they aided in great measure to the conversion, the *transformation* of souls.

In speaking of Miracles, we must agree with his biographers before us, the greatest single Miracle of Ars was the *living out, day by day, of who he was,* John Mary Vianney, Curé, holy priest and shepherd.

The Curé's Spirituality

The Curé followed the example and teachings of the Early Fathers of the Desert and that of Saint Sulpice. In that of the *Fathers of the Desert,* he not only derived inspiration from their teachings, he followed them to the letter, often quoting them verbatim.

The Curé had many friends but he had enemies as well, who were always trying to discredit him. Those who loved him, wanted him to answer his accusers, to defend himself. In response, he told this story, from the *Sayings of the Desert Fathers:*

"One day a Saint commanded one of his monks: 'Go to the cemetery and say insulting things to the dead.' The monk obeyed and when he returned the Saint commanded him: 'What did they answer?' 'Nothing.' 'Well then return and praise them.' The monk obeyed once more and came back. 'Did they answer you this time?' 'Still nothing' 'Well then,' answered the Saint, 'whether people insult you or praise you, do the same as the dead.'"

Another time, making reference to the *lukewarm*, those who just go through the motions, *mouthing* prayers, *attending* Mass, distracted by the world and its attractions rather than centering on Him, without Whom there would be no world no less its beauty, he again used teachings from the *Sayings of the Fathers:*

"Flies do not settle on boiling water. They fall into cold or tepid water."

He was warning: Unless when you are on fire: you continue to stoke up the fire with spiritual reading, attend Holy Mass daily, receive the Sacrament of Penance often, fast, practice abstinence, make use of the crosses handed to you each day of your life; unless you become a contemplative in action making every thought, every action, every step, every beat of your heart in adoration of the Lord and His Sacred Wounds, you will become as tepid or cold as the stagnant water flies like to habitat.

Father Vianney was not one who lived in the past, *the good old days*. True, he was influenced by the lives of the Saints before him, using forms of their spirituality and wisdom to more closely portray Jesus Christ in our midst. But he was a man for all seasons. He tried to walk boldly in the footsteps of the Desert Fathers while accepting and using the available gifts of the Church of the nineteenth century.

These two spiritualities were closely fused into the man-priest that made up Father John Mary Vianney: one from the ancients and the other from the Church of his day. He loved this Church on the move. He revered this Church which stood on the foundation of centuries of faithfulness and martyrdom. Right from his days in the Seminary and with Father Balley, strength was formed within him which would last and sustain him throughout his entire priesthood. He had Jesus as the center of his life and the Blessed Mother as *his* mother and intercessor.

From the spirituality of *Saint Sulpice*, he developed an acute awareness of his Lord in the Holy Eucharist. From this 7th century Saint, he learned, the one perfect Adorer of His Father was Jesus, the Eternal priest, in the Eucharist.

The burning love Father Vianney had for the Savior was manifested as he *prepared* for the Sacred Celebration of the Eucharistic Liturgy. But although the Eucharistic Liturgy was the high point of his Mass, he carefully *balanced* the Liturgy of the Word with the Liturgy of the Eucharist.

He could *feel* his Savior's presence in the Tabernacle, so he took every opportunity to adore Him in the Blessed Sacrament. His Presence brought tears to the Curé's eyes. This passion he felt for the Lord was no on-again off-again affair. Speaking of the Lord in the Holy Eucharist, he said:

"If we had a lively faith, we would certainly be able to see Him in the Blessed Sacrament. There are priests who see Him every day during the Holy Sacrifice of the Mass."

Many who saw the Curé during the Mass, believed he was speaking of himself as one of those priests, but the Curé would never have admitted that, never wanting attention brought to himself. He would have considered this *consolation.* He not only did not seek consolation, he distrusted it:

"When we have no consolations, we serve God for God's own sake. When we have them, we are in danger of serving Him for ourselves."

The Curé and the Blessed Mother

This account of the Curé having an apparition of Mother Mary, did not come from him, but from an eye witness. When we speak of apparitions, like in the case of charisms, they do not constitute *holiness*, but a gift from God. When the mother of God appears to one of Her earthly children, she is choosing to use them strictly as a *conductor* of a message she is bringing to all her children. The Curé, like St. Bernadette and other visionaries, never wanted the emphasis on himself. He called himself a poor, ignorant priest; she called herself a broom to be cast aside.

On May 8, 1840, a Mlle. Durié came to see him, to donate some money for his parish missions, an apostolate dear to his heart. When she arrived at the rectory, she heard voices coming from the Curé's room. One of them sounded like a lady's voice. Plainly curious, she quietly ascended the steps and listened at the door.

"What are you asking?" the voice said.

"Good Mother, I ask for the conversion of sinners, the consolation of the afflicted, the relief of the sick, especially a lady who has long been suffering and is begging either to die or to be cured."

"She will get well," the voice answered. "But later on!"

The lady at the door knew *she* was the sick person, the Mother of God was referring to, as she had been suffering a long time with cancer. She rushed into the room. Before her, standing in front of the fireplace, was a lady of medium height, breathtakingly beautiful in a white dress, upon which rested white roses. Upon her delicate feet were slippers, soft and white as newly fallen snow. Her hands sparkled from the most perfect diamonds the lady had ever seen. A crown of stars glittered, forming a crown upon her royal head. It was hard for the lady to catch her breath, but catch it she did; she pleaded, "Good Mother, please take me to Heaven."

The Blessed Mother replied, "Later on."

The lady insisted, "It's time, now, Mother!"

Mother Mary consoled her, "You will always be my child and I shall always be your Mother!"

And the Blessed Mother disappeared! Although the lady did not hear what she *wanted* to hear, the Mother of God had spoken to her and that would last her a lifetime. When she regained her senses, she looked over toward the Curé. He was standing in front of a table, his hands clasped in prayer upon his breast, his eyes still, motionless. He looked dead. She pulled at his cassock. She told him she had seen the Blessed Mother. He assured her, he had seen her, too, but cautioned her to tell no one what she had seen.

Mlle. was cured of cancer three and a half months later, on *August 15th.* This testimony was given at the Curé's Beatification Process.

What was important about the Curé seeing the Mother of God? Well, it is hard to see and recognize someone you do not know. The Curé knew and loved the Mother of God; and like the Saints and other holy priests before him, he came to Jesus through His Mother. Mother Mary had been his first love and he had never gotten over that love.

Home at last! The Curé goes Home to his Lord!

What makes a Saint? A total *abandonment* to the Will of God, in union with an unconditional love for His children's souls, no hours too long, no sacrifice too great, the Curé lived, breathed and worked solely to love God and to bring others to know and love Him.

As Jesus was crucified *for* the salvation of souls, so the Curé was crucified *by* sinful souls. At the end of his life, he said, "*Oh! The sinners will finally kill the poor sinner!*"

The Curé spoke of going Home! The hours spent as prisoner of the confessional, the fasting and penances, and his victim-hood with Jesus on the Altar were taking their final, merciful toll. The little, humble priest, God had chosen to do such great work on earth, was to, at last, have his heart's true desire, to spend eternity loving Him!

A reporter, who had visited Ars, wrote,

"It was four o'clock in the afternoon when I entered the church. The Curé of Ars was in the confessional. I had just knelt down to pray when I heard a sob I cannot describe. It was coming from the confessional." He reported, the sob could be heard every ten minutes, a choking sound seemed to be coming from the Curé. When he saw him, he said he was frightened how much the Curé resembled the picture of our Lord hanging on the Cross. Was the Curé suffocating, like the Savior he so adored and wanted to emulate? This day was no different from all the other days of his priesthood. How many times had he suffered for the sins of those who had come to be forgiven?

Summer came and with it cruel, stifling, choking heat. The doctor said if the heat wave did not subside, the Curé would not make it. The heat wave continued, but the Curé *did* make it. Oh, not like the doctor meant, but he did make it! The Curé asked for his confessor. He reached out hungrily for the last Sacraments. He began to cry. When asked why the tears, he replied,

"Ah. When I think I am about to receive the Lord for the last time!"

And then, touched by the generosity of his King, he whispered,

"How good God is! When we cannot go and see Him, He comes to us!"

He kissed the Crucifix and as his confessor came to the words, "May God's Holy Angels come to meet him and bring him into the heavenly Jerusalem," the Curé fell into the sweet sleep of eternity. Without struggle, he gave up his spirit to the Angels who surely had come to bring him Home.

August 4, 1859, there was a groan, as from Heaven, for all the faithful he would leave behind. *Their Curé was dead!*

The Curé was dead, but the pilgrims came! The funeral was held on August 6th, at eight o'clock in the morning. They counted more than 6000 pilgrims. It was not until August 14th that the Curé's body was buried in a niche in the church. It remained there until 1904 and then was placed in a glass sarcophagus.

Till today you can see and venerate the incorrupt[4] remains of the Curé of Ars. A humble priest, who lived and

---

[4]incorrupt - never decomposed - bodies which have not suffered the decay process which normally occurs after death. With Saints and Blesseds, whose bodies have not decomposed, no preservative chemicals have been injected into their bodies, no embalming or

died for God each moment of his life, was specially honored by God's Church.

His Beatification Process began in 1862 and closed in 1865.

The Curé was Beatified in St. Peter's Basilica, on Sunday, January 8, 1905, forty years after his death.

On May 31, 1925, on Pentecost, Pope Pius XI canonized John Mary Vianney, *Saint* John Mary Vianney. France had a new Saint! Parish priests had a Patron Saint, one whose life would be *simple* to follow, but difficult to live.

When writing of the Saints, we look for a word, a *special* word to set them apart. We find the *word* we have that makes one a Saint is usually flowing through the life of another. If there were only two words I would be allowed to use for St. John Mary Vianney, they would have to be *Humility and Trust*.

The Curé always kept his eyes on Jesus Crucified, on his Savior Who allowed Himself to be *humbled*, even to death on the Cross. He opened his arms wide to love like the Lord he adored, Who before Him, loved as His Father in Heaven loves. And he *trusted* in that Love to bring him through the daily trials temptations and hurts of his victimhood as a *priest*.

---

mummification; nor have any chemicals been found which the bodies could have produced *naturally* to cause this preservation. In these cases, there has been no medical or scientific reason why the body has not decomposed. (from Saints and other Powerful Women in the Church...by Bob and Penny Lord.)

Above: ***Prophecy of Don Bosco: May 30, 1862 - Vision of the Body of Christ, the Mother of Christ, and the Vicar of Christ***

St. John Bosco

*"When you speak or preach,
always insist on frequent Communion,
and devotion to the Blessed Virgin Mary."*

The Lord sends us special people to handle special needs, at crucial times in the history of our Church and our world.

From the time of Jesus, the *little ones*, the children, have been dear to the heart of the Father. We recall the words of Jesus in Scripture, *"Let the little ones come unto me, and do not hinder them. It is to such as these that the Kingdom of God belongs."* (Mk 10:15) Again, He spoke of the children as being *important* in God's Plan. *"For what you have hidden from the learned and the clever, you have revealed to the merest children."* (Mt 11:25)

Children have always been uppermost in the mind of the Father, as they have been helpless and in need of protection. There have been orphans and street urchins from the beginning of time. Over the centuries, the Lord has provided for these little ones, by sending men and women to take care of them.

An epidemic of exploitation of children began at the end of the eighteenth century, with the dawn of the Industrial Revolution. Inventions, such as machines for spinning thread, the power loom, and the steam engine, created a new way of manufacturing goods. It also created a need for massive *cheap* labor. Families were lured off the farms and brought into the cities to work in factories, under the deception of living a better life.

In the name of progress, a new term had to be phrased, *slums*, to accommodate the unbelievably poor living conditions, to which these families were subjected. Mothers and fathers worked long hours, as did the children who were old enough to work. Those children who could not find work, or were too young to work, were left to roam the streets, on their own. Satan had a field day, turning these little ones into *street gangs*. Left to their own devices, many embraced lives of crime. There was no one to curb their behavior, or focus them in the direction of God. *But God is in charge; God is always in charge.*

From God's vantage point in Heaven, He could see the entire history of civilization, past, present and future. He could see the crisis, building in the lives of His children, in the wake of this new wave of materialism, this frenzy to possess more goods, better goods, no matter what the cost in human lives and souls. God knew, He would have to send a very special person to combat this wholesale evil in the world and save the children. That person would have to be so charismatic, he could draw young and old alike. He had to be able to soften hearts of stone and convince others that the vision, the Lord had given him could be accomplished. He had to have a "*can do*" personality. He had to be a mover and shaker. He had to be a super-yes man. He had to be a **Don Bosco!**

Don Bosco was God's gift to the Church of the nineteenth century. He was one of the most powerful men in our Church of that time. The magnetism of Don bosco reached out and touched souls all over the world, even to this present day. He was one of the most multi-faceted diamonds, the Lord has ever given us. In addition to being a pied-piper to the young, attracting them, embracing them, protecting them, guiding them, he founded a *Religious Order*, was an author, a super church-builder, as well as a visionary and prophet. His accomplishments were so great, he was *loved* by millions of God's people and *hated* by God's enemies. He gave all credit to Our Lord Jesus and to His beautiful mother, Mary's active intervention, under the title of Mary, Help of Christians.

When I was a little person, the good nuns in my Catholic elementary school, filled my spirit with beautiful tales about Don Bosco and his work with children. Interspersed with the stories were accounts of miraculous happenings, to which Don Bosco gave credit to Our Lady. She was his best friend; she became my best friend, possibly as a result of these marvelous stories. When I grew up, naturally, I believed that all the stories the nuns had told me about Don Bosco, as well as other saints, were just that, *stories*. That is, until I came back to the Church at age 40, at which time the Lord gave me the gift of believing as a child again. I remember sadly, a young priest, in his early thirties, sharing how devastated he was when he entered the seminary and was told that all the stories he had learned in Catholic school were not true. I wanted to embrace him and tell him it's not so. They are true. You just need the *freedom* to believe. But he's not ready yet. Perhaps someday, the Lord will free him enough to believe.

In researching the incredible life of this modern day role model, we found the same problem exists, even among his own biographers. Some of them feel that supernatural aspect of Don Bosco's life has been blown out of proportion, that the instances of miraculous intervention in his life have been overstated, and we should focus on the man and his accomplishments, rather than the power of the Lord to work in men's lives, *in whatever way He chooses*. On the other hand, there are those who picture Don Bosco as an empty vessel; they give full credit for every good thing in his life to the intercession of Mary, Help of Christians. To be honest, that's the way Don Bosco felt about most everything.

We realize, though, there has to be a balance, that some of the incidents in his life make him so unique that no one could feel capable of imitating him. In the interests of keeping the man on a plain where he remains touchable, we will attempt to keep our enthusiasm, for how much the Lord worked in his life, to a minimum. But if we don't expound on the miraculous in his life, we fail to give glory to God, who is the moving Force behind all of it. We also fail to give honor to this man, who allowed himself to be emptied completely, that he might be filled with the Holy Spirit. We have to give serious consideration to the words Pope Leo XI said of him, "*In his (Don Bosco) life the supernatural almost became the natural and the extraordinary ordinary.*" We really have to address that profound statement.

†

Out of the Darkness

It was the year 1815, Napoleon Bonaparte had just been defeated, but his iron grip on the Piedmontese area of northern Italy could still be felt. He had bled the country of all its natural resources. The people were left to their own devices to survive, or starve. Dead bodies were found strewn all over the countryside each morning, having starved to death the night before. It was hard times for the common people, who had nothing to do with the political upheavals of the day. But they were the victims. They looked for a place to begin again.

Masses of migrants descended on the big city of Turin, Italy. They had deserted their farms, fresh air, and the fragrances of the land, in exchange for the sweat and stench of close quarters in these newlyfound slums, all in the hopes of a new life. But some were still holding on to the lives, their families had lived for centuries in the little hamlets, the rolling hills of northern Italy. One of these villages, Becchi, was to be the birthplace of one of the most powerful men in our Church. On the day after the Feast of the Assumption in 1815, our Lady gave us a gift, in the birth of John Melchior Bosco, in this unknown place, which is still not on the map of Italy today.

He was born of strong peasant stock, Francis and Margaret. Theirs was a large household to feed. Francis' invalid mother, as well as a son by his first wife, plus John and his brother Joseph, created a major financial burden on the young couple. The fruits of their land were not enough to take care of the family, so Francis worked at other jobs to bring extra income into the house. It was while he worked for a landowner that he contracted pneumonia and died. John was barely two years old. John always remembered his mother's words, although he could not remember his father: *"You have no father, Johnny."*

With the father and main breadwinner gone, many families would have fallen apart, but not the family of Margaret Bosco. She had been given special graces by the Lord, to hold onto and provide for her family's welfare and growth. She used them. She took care of her bedridden mother-in-law, a step-son, and her own two children. She had the greatest influence on Don Bosco. While he has been given the honor of being among the Communion of Saints, his mother has to be right there next to him, sharing the glory.

Penny has always shared her amazement at how much scripture her mother knew, although she never went to High School. She was always quoting scripture. The same would apply to Margaret Bosco. She could not read or write, yet she taught her children their Faith. A natural question might be, *"Yes, but how much could she have taught them?"* The response would be to point to the fruits of her teaching, Don Bosco. Case closed!

There has been an ongoing dispute about the value of absorbing huge amounts of information, compared with the simple, uncluttered teachings of our ancestors. Francis of

Assisi distrusted books and learning. Don Bosco, on the other hand, was a great proponent of learning. We have to believe that a great deal has to do with faith. Where is the information coming from, and how does it glorify God? Margaret Bosco was very clear on that point. Whatever she taught her children was to point them towards God.

The children were not spoiled in any way. It would have been impossible. Hers was a monumental task. There was no place for frills in their lives. Margaret believed that she was training her children for the difficult world they lived in. They all worked hard. Simple proverbs like *"Idleness is the devil's workshop"* guided her in every step of their upbringing. They ate little. They put up with all the hardships imaginable. But they became strong, physically and spiritually. John began working at four years old. The whole family pitched in with the housework. It was good training for the life John would live as a religious. We can't help but think, Our Lady had a direct hand in raising John.

The First Dream

Don Bosco was gifted with many dreams, visions and prophecies, during his lifetime. Actually, it's very difficult to distinguish between them. We believe, his dreams were prophetic visions. There is a great deal of accuracy attached to Don Bosco's visions, both for his time and for the Church of today. Penny and I always open our talks by focusing on one vision of Don Bosco's in particular. We'll talk about it later in the chapter. He actually became very famous, while he was still living, for the dreams, visions and prophecies he was given. In 1858, Pope Pius IX[1] ordered Don Bosco to write down all his dreams *"word for word"*, for the posterity of the community.

---

[1]Pius IX - Gave us the Dogma of the Immaculate Conception in 1854.

Don Bosco experienced his first dream at age nine. He wrote it down in his autobiography. It impressed him so much, he never forgot it. Years later, he could recount the dream exactly as it had happened. In his own words,

"When I was about nine years old, I had a dream that left a profound impression on me for the rest of my life. I dreamed that I was near my home, in a very large playing field where a crowd of children were having fun. Some were laughing, others were playing and not a few were cursing. I was so shocked at their language that I jumped into their midst, swinging wildly and shouting at them to stop. At that moment, a Man appeared, nobly attired, with a manly and imposing bearing. He was clad with a white flowing mantle, and his face radiated such light that I could not look directly at Him. He called me by name and told me to place myself as leader over those boys, adding the words,

'You will have to win these friends of yours not with blows, but with gentleness and kindness. So begin right now to show them that sin is ugly and virtue beautiful.'

"Confused and afraid, I replied that I was only a boy and unable to talk to these youngsters about religion. At that moment the fighting, shouting and cursing stopped and the crowd of boys gathered about the Man who was now talking. Almost unconsciously, I asked:

'But how can you order me to do something that looks so impossible?'

'What seems so impossible you must achieve by being obedient and by acquiring knowledge.'

'But where, how?'

'I will give you a Teacher, under whose guidance you will learn and without whose help all knowledge becomes foolishness.'

'But who are you?'

'I am the Son of Her whom your mother has taught you to greet three times a day.'

'My mother told me not to talk to people I don't know unless she gives me permission. So, please tell me your name.'

"*At that moment I saw beside Him a Lady of majestic appearance, wearing a beautiful mantle glowing as if bedecked with stars. She saw my confusion mount; so she beckoned me to her. Taking my hand with great kindness, she said:*

'Look!'

"*I did so. All the children had vanished. In their place I saw many animals: goats, dogs, cats, bears and a variety of others.*

"*'This is your field, this is where you must work.' the Lady told me. 'Make yourself humble, steadfast, and strong. And what you will see happen to these animals you will have to do for my children.'*

"*I looked again; the wild animals had turned into as many lambs, gently gamboling lambs, bleating a welcome for that Man and Lady.*

"*At this point of my dream I started to cry and begged the Lady to explain what it all meant because I was so confused. She then placed her hand on my head and said:*

'In due time everything will be clear to you.'

"*After she had spoken these words, some noise awoke me; everything had vanished.*"[2]

The next day, when he shared this dream with his family, everybody came up with a variety of interpretations of what the dream might have meant. However, his mother zeroed in on the message immediately. She said, "*Who knows if some day he may not become a priest?*"

---

[2]Memoirs of the Oratory - John Bosco

In this, the first of many dreams, the pattern of John Bosco's life was set, his vocation and his work within his vocation. He would be a priest, and he would work with children. While he was a normal child, he was very focused. Once his goal had been given him, he worked feverishly towards that end. He learned to read, which was a great accomplishment, in that time and place. But the great value of learning to read, was that he was in great demand during the cold winter months, to read to his friends *and* their parents. He had a captive audience; so they had to play by his rules. He began each of his performances with two solemn signs of the Cross and two Hail Mary's, reverently prayed. Then he would read to them.

During the summertime, on Sunday afternoons, when the children were all out playing, John Bosco found another way to keep their attention, entertain them and lead them in prayer. He became a juggler, acrobat and clown. He was so smart. The Lord told him exactly what to do, to captivate the children, who were to be the goal of his life. But he was given an extra added gift. Children of *all ages* came to watch the show. He set up a corner of the field near his home, with a rope tied between two trees. He performed sleight of hand tricks; he juggled; he walked the tightrope; he did cartwheels. But he also led them in five decades of the Rosary and gave them a short talk, which he'd borrowed from the priest's homily at Mass that morning. He shortened the homily, changed it a little and made it his own. He gave them insights, they had not received at Mass that day.

Don't get the impression that John was perfect at his avocation right away. He watched every performer that came into the public squares of the town, then went home and imitated them. But in the learning process, he fell many times from the tightrope, landed on his face doing cartwheels and walking on his hands, and missed many a card trick or sleight of hand. But he got up *every time* and continued on, until he perfected his act.

While there's no question that he was bringing the Lord to the people in a simpler way, sugar-coated with the antics he performed, he was also being trained in preaching to people and bringing them closer to *Jesus*. He learned how to capture their attention, by using everything he had ever learned and then turning it in the direction of the Lord. As far as he was concerned, he was giving everything over to the Lord; but at the same time, the Lord was preparing him for a mighty apostolate.

John's love for God and his Church, was well-known throughout the entire area. Priests, as well as lay-people, could see the special qualities in the boy. He wanted very much to receive Our Lord Jesus in the *Eucharist*. But the rule was, no one could receive until he was at least twelve or thirteen years old. An exception was made, however, for John. He knew at age ten, what many people never know all their lives. Jesus was there in the consecrated Bread and Wine, alive and present, nurturing. John wanted that union with his God, *desperately*. When the priests realized the spiritual depth of the boy, they allowed him to receive his First Holy Communion at age ten.

John's vocation was a foregone conclusion. Everybody knew, he was meant to be a priest. He had written that at age nine, he believed he was called to the priesthood. If there had ever been a doubt in any one's mind, even his, it was wiped out, when he met his mentor and future teacher, Don Calosso. It was 1826. John was not yet eleven years old. The year before had been the Holy Year. Hundreds of thousands of pilgrims had converged on Rome. But this year, the Jubilee graces of the Holy Year, were extended to the local churches. There was a week's course in Buttigliera, about two and a half miles from Becchi. There were two sermons in the morning, and two courses of instruction in the evening. It was the most exciting thing to hit the area for John, since he was born.

Keep in mind that John had never gone to school. He had a hunger to learn, especially anything that had to do with the Church. He had a brilliant mind, a photographic memory, and the ability to remember sermons. He had learned to read over a summer, but there was nothing *else* to challenge him intellectually in his surroundings. So when the opportunity to *learn about Church* was presented to him, he grabbed at it.

The only way for poor people, like John and his family, to get to the next village was to walk. And walk they did, two times going and two times coming, a total of ten miles each day. It was on this road that John met the priest, Don Calosso. The older man, actually in his seventies, took an interest in the eleven year old. The only reason we can think of was that he saw something in the boy that was not ordinary. It's also very possible that the Lord touched the priest's heart to put young John on the right road to the priesthood. But he had to test him first. He asked John if he understood what the priest had been saying during the sermon. John answered eagerly that he did. The priest asked him to repeat what he understood of the lecture. John repeated both sermons, word for word. This knocked the older man for a loop. They had a very brief conversation which went like this:

"What is your name, my son? Who are your father and mother? Where do you go to school?"

"My name is John Bosco. I lost my father, when I was two. My mother has five to feed. I can read, and I can write a little."

"You haven't yet begun your grammar?"

"What is that?"

"Would you like to learn?"

"Oh, yes."

"Why don't you then?"

"My brother Antony is against it,"

"Why?"

"He says we always know enough to till the fields."

"Why do you want to learn?"

"To become a priest."

"And why do you want to become a priest?"

"To get children to come to me to teach them religion and to keep them from being bad.   I can plainly see they turn out bad because no one cares for them."

Meanwhile they had arrived at his village.

"But excuse me, Father. This is my home."

"Can you serve Mass, little John?"

"I know a little about it."

"Then come and serve mine, tomorrow.   I have something to say to you."

This was to be the beginning of John Bosco's training, which would lead him to the seminary and ultimately, the priesthood.   At first, he went to the priest in the mornings to receive instruction.   He had to be available to work the fields, in the afternoon.   Even at this, his step-brother, Antony, was furious about the whole thing.   He resented John terribly and did everything he could to block his path to *learning* and the *priesthood*.   Antony was much bigger than John and thought nothing of *beating* him up at every opportunity.   He even vehemently opposed John's mother, who had the fortitude of a bull.   But Antony was growing each day, and Margaret was not sure how long she could control him.   In an effort to maintain peace in the family, she made John stop his lessons.   But that was not enough for Antony.   He was always after John.

Finally, Margaret felt it dangerous for John to stay at home.   She made the ultimate sacrifice.   She sent John away.   She knew the Lord would provide for him and protect him, even though he was only twelve years old.   If anyone ever had doubts, as to how actively the Lord guides our lives, they have but to read the adventures of Don Bosco, especially as a child. It was as if he was under the constant protection of a number of Guardian Angels, with Our sweet Mother Mary in front, leading him on the road that Jesus had chosen for him. He went to stay with a relative for a short time.

Through the intercession of his uncle, his mother's brother Michael, John was able to return to Don Calosso, to be taught, but also to get to know what a priest is like. He learned to love this old man so much. But their time together was only to be enough for him to learn how he should act, when the honor of priesthood would be bestowed upon him. Shortly after they began their lessons again, the priest died. He wanted to leave all his earthly possessions to John, to insure that he could afford his religious education. But when John realized the problems he would have with the priest's relatives, he gave them his inheritance and walked away.

Why did the Lord allow John so much conflict, in his quest for the priesthood? Was it to make John appreciate, no, *embrace* the gift he would be given? Do our priests today go through the unbelievable hassle that John Bosco endured? Might it make them cherish the favor more, if they had to work so hard for it? The struggle for him to become a priest, was so difficult, others without his tenacity, would have given up *early* in the game. He suffered every humiliation possible. He was much older than his classmates. They considered him a buffoon. He was a country hick. He dressed like a farmer. Even his instructors belittled him. He returned their insults with a smile and a blessing. But he didn't always want to be this *kind*. He had a fierce temper, that if he let fly, would have knocked them all down, like a tornado. But he prayed for the strength to hold down this weakness, and the Lord gave him that.

In the course of his pursuit for the priesthood, John Bosco learned and worked at more trades than a dozen men work, in a lifetime. At any time during his studies, he was a candymaker, shoemaker, restaurant manager, tailor and of course, his great love, a clown, acrobat and juggler. He excelled in everything he did. He probably could have taken up any of those trades and been successful at them. But his heart longed for the *priesthood*.

A moment of truth was to come for John Bosco. He finally reached a *dead end*, a brick wall, which he could see no way of overcoming. During his years of study, he could always work at these odd jobs we've mentioned, which gave him the money he needed to survive *and* pay for his education. However, once he entered the seminary, he would not be able to do that. There was no time, and he couldn't leave the seminary to pursue part time work. He, quite honestly, didn't know what to do. For the first time in his life, he feared he might not be able to achieve his lifelong goal of being a priest.

Then he thought of the Religious Orders. While he did not want to be an order priest, he also didn't want *not* to be a priest. If he joined a *Religious Order*, he wouldn't have to worry about money. They would pay for his seminary training. So, he embraced the Franciscan Fraternity in Chieri. But this was not the Lord's plan. At the eleventh hour, as he was preparing to take vows, a young priest, Don Cafasso[3], who was to become very much a part of Don Bosco's life, advised John to wait until he could join the diocesan seminary. Once John said yes to that, money came from all quarters; not a lot of money. John Bosco would never have enough money for anything he wanted to do in his life. But the Lord opened the hearts of just enough

---

[3]Joseph Cafasso is one of two major figures of the nineteenth century, from the area of Castelnuovo, to be proclaimed saint. The other, of course, is St. Don Bosco

people to provide just a *little less* than John needed, to keep him on the edge. He never wanted John to become comfortable. To make up the difference, John won partial scholarships for excellence in conduct and studies, was given the job of Sacristan, which carried a salary with it, little things which put him over the top. Everything he had was donated to him. This was really good in a sense, in that everybody played a major role in his vocation. That's the way the Lord wanted it.

John learned a very strong, very painful lesson in the seminary. The superiors maintained a great distance from the seminarians. John knew the need he had, for spiritual warmth from his superiors. If he needed it, he was sure his companions needed it as badly, if not worse. There was a wall put up between the seminarians and the priests. This was a hangover from the Jansenist heresy[4]. Many saints of the eighteenth and nineteenth century, were victims of scrupulosity. In addition, Communion was only available on Sunday and Feast days in the seminary. John, who had a hunger to receive the Eucharist more often, had to sneak out of the seminary and attend Mass at a local church, in order to receive Our Lord.

John complained to his mother on many occasions, how these priests were missing such an opportunity to mold souls, and the souls of *future priests*, by these practices. He wrote in his autobiography,[5]

---

[4]Jansenism - a heresy from the 17th century, which stated that all men were unable to resist temptation, and unworthy of redemption. It denied that Christ died for the sins of all men. It created an elitist group of those who were worthy, as opposed to most of the rest, who were not worthy. A bad premise was compounded when a belief was spread that without perfect contrition, a sinner was not worthy of the Sacrament of Penance and Communion. A by-product of this was Scrupulosity, which caused many to believe they were guilty of serious sin where no sin existed.

[5]Memoirs of the Oratory

"I may say that this was the greatest sorrow I felt at the seminary. How often I wanted to speak to them, to ask for advice or to submit a perplexity to them: it was impossible. And worse than that: if one of our superiors happened to cross the playground while the seminarists were enjoying themselves, though we knew not why, we scurried away to right and left. It is an ill wind that blows nobody any good."

He vowed that he would never allow himself to be aloof from his flock.

"This sort of thing had at least the advantage of kindling my heart more warmly with the desire of becoming a priest more quickly, to mingle with young folk and to get to know them intimately, so as to help them in all circumstances to shun what is bad."

God knows exactly what to teach and how to teach. John Bosco learned as much, if not more, from his negative experiences in the seminary, as he did from his studies. The Lord knew the work, He had planned for this young man and what kind of *training* it would take. John, for his part, was open to *whatever* the Lord wanted to teach him.

We can't leave John Bosco's seminary days, without making mention of a very influential companion, Louis Comollo. In addition to being close friends, the Lord allowed them to perform the function of spiritual director for each other, since they had no priest to turn to. John and Louis shared their dreams together. Louis was very close to the Lord. He knew, he would not live out his seminary days; he predicted that he would die before ordination. He fulfilled this prophecy on Easter Tuesday, after six weeks of agonizing illness.

John and Louis had made a foolish, adolescent pact that whoever died first, would come back and assure the other that he was in Heaven. After Louis' death, John was inconsolable. *But in the back of his mind, he wondered if his friend would be able to keep the pact they had made. Many other seminarians, who were aware of the pact, were wondering the same thing.* The day after Louis was buried, two days after his death, a strange thing happened, which was witnessed by over twenty seminarians. It was late at night, probably around midnight. Everyone was in bed. John was unable to sleep. His mind kept going back to that *silly* pact he had made with his friend. All of a sudden, a low rumble started, which built to a great roar. The entire building shook so violently, John thought it would snap from its foundations. All the seminarians were jolted from their sleep. They were frightened, as they had never been before, including John Bosco. They thought, it was the end of the world. They couldn't tell what direction, the tremor was coming from, when *suddenly*, the doors of the dormitory blew open and a great wind entered, followed by multi-colored lights of a surrealistic nature.

The noise died down. All that could be sensed were the lights, which became more intense. A hush filled the room. As the lights became brighter, a voice could be heard, clearly. It was Louis Comollo. It was not eerie, or ghostly. He called out three times, *"Bosco"*; everyone heard it. Then he finally said, *"I am saved!"* The lights became brighter; the roar started up again, grew to fever pitch and then whooshed out of the room, as quickly as it had entered. Silence returned. The only sound that could be heard was the blood, pounding in the hearts of each of the seminarians, trying to burst out of their bodies.

No one knew quite what to make of it. Their fear didn't leave them, when the vision ended. Many heard the message, but didn't understand it. Others understood, but the knowledge of what had happened, didn't calm them. *Fear* reigned in the dormitory the entire night. No one slept, including John Bosco. They cringed in corners, jumping at every sound that was made. John went around to each of the seminarians during the night, assuring them it was Louis Comollo, coming back to tell them he was in Heaven. But it wasn't until dawn that they all breathed a sigh of relief.

Louis Comollo was with John Bosco all his life. Once, in 1847, eight years after Louis' death, Don Bosco's mother heard him conversing with someone, in his bedroom at night. The following morning, she asked him to whom he was talking, the night before. Don Bosco answered matter-of-factly, *"With Louis Comollo."*

John Bosco is pointed in a direction

Towards the end of his seminary days, John Bosco had *another* dream. It was similar to the one he'd had at age nine, only much clearer. He was in a great valley back home in Becchi. Abruptly, the valley turned into a large city, overflowing with young people. They were running, playing, shouting and cursing. His ears couldn't stand the sounds of their cursing. He went over to them, in an effort to get them to stop. They wouldn't pay any attention to him. Anger rose up in him. He began to shake some of them. They retorted by hitting him. He hit them back. Then he retreated; they were too much for him. He could actually feel the pain of his bruises, in his dream. As he ran away from the youths, a mysterious Man stopped him. He ordered him to go back to them. John just showed the Man all his bruises. The Stranger pointed to a beautiful Lady, who was coming closer to John. "This is my Mother. Listen to Her." She looked at him, with eyes that bore deep into his soul. The warmth of her love mesmerized him. "If you wish to win over these boys," she told him, "do not hit them; be kind and appeal to their better selves."

He did as she told him, and another transformation took place. As in his first dream, the children first turned into wild animals, then into sheep and lambs. After he had wakened, John knew, this dream was the Lord's way of affirming the vocation, He had chosen for him, from at least age nine, and possibly from before he was born. John had only to say *"Here I am, Lord. I come to do Your will."*

John Bosco becomes Don Bosco

John was chomping at the bit. He wanted to get out of the seminary and get about the business of doing the job, for which the Lord had commissioned him, saving the souls of the young people of Turin. To this end, he attempted a near-impossible feat. At the end of his third year of study, he asked Bishop Frassoni, Bishop of Turin, to give him permission to study his entire fourth year of Theology over the school holidays. He gave his advanced age (24), as the reason for the request.

He was given permission. He studied dilligently the whole summer. When he returned in the autumn of 1840, he was tested on the entire fourth year of Theology. He passed with flying colors and was advanced one full year, to his *fifth year*. In his autobiography, Don Bosco did not advise those who followed him, to do what he did, in this instance. He said that while it was good for him *intellectually*, he felt that emotionally, he was not as prepared as he should have been. The fifth year was one of taking final vows and although John Bosco had no doubts as to what his vocation was, he was not sure he was mature enough to make those vows.

Saturday, June 5, 1841, was the first Saturday of the month, Mary's day. We have to believe that a Heavenly contingency, led by our Lord Jesus and His most special Mother Mary, were there at the forefront to congratulate their son, John Bosco, as he was ordained a priest in the Cathedral of Turin. Nevermore to be called John or Johnny, (except of course, by his mother Margaret) he was given the title which he used the rest of his life, and by which he is famous the world over, **Don Bosco.**

Don Bosco was not the only one who was anxious for him to become a priest. Almost immediately after his ordination, he was besieged by offers to serve in various capacities all over the Diocese of Turin. He was somewhat overwhelmed by this. He appealed to his spiritual advisor, Don Cafasso, for help. Don Cafasso was Don Bosco's senior by only four years, but in the priesthood, he had preceded him by eight years. Don Cafasso was a very saintly man, who had to have a direct line to Our Lord Jesus and His Mother Mary. He had the ability to cut to the core of a given subject. This is exactly what he did with Don Bosco. He told him not to take any of the offers he had received, but to stay in Turin and continue with his theological studies.

A Salesian, John Cagliero, later wrote of Don Cafasso, *"We love and reverence our dear father and founder, Don Bosco, but we love Joseph Cafasso no less, for he was Don Bosco's master, adviser and guide in spiritual things and in his undertakings for over twenty years; and I venture to say the goodness, the achievements and the wisdom of Don Bosco are Don Cafasso's glory."*

Don Cafasso was extremely instrumental, on a *continual* basis, in focusing Don Bosco in the direction of his apostolate, the children.

Don Bosco gathers his flock

At the time of Don Bosco's ordination, Italy was very anti-clerical. A lot of this stemmed from the clerics' Jansenist behavior, which caused them to remove themselves physically and emotionally from their flock. Don Cafasso fought to end the grip *Jansenism* held on northern Italy. One way was to have the students in the Theological Institute walk among the people, in an effort to become more aware and involved in what was going on. For Don Bosco, this was a revelation. He knew, his apostolate was children, but he really had no conception of their plight, until he began to walk the streets of Turin.

The charming city with the beautiful boulevards had become a *hell-hole*, a giant ghetto for the working class. Two and three families lived together in a single room, under the most unsanitary conditions. He could walk anywhere in the slum section of the city and see the horrors of the young who were left on their own. One time, during an evening walk, he came upon a field. Hoardes of children were running around, filthy, half-clothed, screaming, cursing and generally acting offensive. For a moment, his mind flashed to the dreams he'd had, first at nine years old and then again in the seminary. It was as if he were standing in the middle of his dream. He tried to reach out to them, but they ignored him. This was not the way the dream ended; *they* had all turned into little lambs. What was happening here? They were not working with the script. Then he realized that he was not approaching them with a kindness and love they had never known before. He was on the brink of jumping into his life's work, but he was not ready yet.

His real beginning came, as it should, on the Feast of the Immaculate Conception, December 8th. He was waiting to begin Mass, when he noticed a sacristan chasing a dirty young boy in rags *out* of the church. Don Bosco made him bring the boy back. He tried to put the nervous youth at his ease. He asked him many questions; could he read or write, were his parents alive or dead. The boy stiffly tried to answer. Then Don Bosco, with a straight face, asked him could he sing or whistle? The boy let out a big smile. Don Bosco had broken the ice.

He began to teach this boy catechism. At the end of an hour, he asked if he would like to return the next week? The boy answered yes. Don Bosco told him not to come alone; bring a friend. That was how it started. The next week, he had nine, and then twelve. Pretty soon, he was the *pied piper*

Above: ***Don Bosco had a great devotion to Mary, Help of Christians.***
Below: ***Don Bosco's vocation was always children.***

of Turin. He had over a hundred children coming to him every week. *Where was he going to put them?* This became his battle cry for the rest of his life. He had too little room, and too little help. This is also the cry of our ministry. We have so much work to do and so few to do it. And we are quickly running out of room. We always wondered what it was that drew us to Don Bosco so strongly. We have so much in common.

Don Bosco brought these young people together each Sunday, for Mass and Catechism. But in addition, there was much fun, playing, picnics, a version of the acrobatics and juggling that the younger John Bosco had become famous for. It was relationship. It was someone caring about these young people, in a world where they were barely tolerated. They had street smarts. They could tell very quickly who was sincere, as opposed to who wanted to exploit them. And they reacted accordingly. They could see *love* in this young priest. He genuinely wanted to make their lives better. It was their souls he was after, but he was not beyond helping with their physical necessities in any way he could. He called the meetings *Oratories*[6]. To Don Bosco's way of thinking, an Oratory was an actual building or complex, with a playing field, classrooms and a chapel. But for many years, the Oratory only existed in his mind. However, Don Bosco was a man of *vision*, and great *faith*. He knew what he was being called to do, and the Lord would provide the means to do it. It was just that simple!

Don Cafasso helped, as long as he could. He allowed Don Bosco and his boys, to use the courtyard of the Institute, at great sacrifice to the resident priests. The priests looked forward to Sundays, as their one opportunity each week, for peace and quiet. They had to give it up to

---

[6]Oratories was a term coined by St. Philip Neri, as he gathered Roman boys together for instruction and singing. Don Bosco borrowed it from St. Philip Neri, and made it famous.

the more than hundred very lively, very vocal young people. But at the end of three years, Don Bosco had completed his studies at the Institute, and so he and his roving band of young people had to leave. By now, he was up to one hundred and fifty.

Bishop Fransoni was extremely pleased with the work Don Bosco was doing with the young. He encouraged the young priest to continue. But we don't read anywhere that the bishop offered any concrete assistance of any kind. However, sometimes, just the knowledge that the bishop is behind a project, gives people the *push* they need to step out and help. Many people did try to help Don Bosco and his scamps, by offering facilities for their meetings. For the most part, however, after just one meeting, the group was asked to leave and never come back. You really couldn't blame the benefactors. The noise of so many young people, allowed to let loose after a week of *whatever*, was more than most people could endure. Put yourself in the position of the neighbors. Looking forward to a quiet Sunday, all of a sudden, four hundred young people converge on your peaceful neighborhood. What would you do? That's what *they* did.

Don Bosco tried everything! He would gather all of them together, then walk them out of the city, to a place where they had been given permission to celebrate Mass. After the Mass, they would walk together again, to a field where they could let loose. Then, again as a group, they came back to a Church for Benediction. *Remember, we're talking about four hundred children, parading en masse!* It was as if this man walked around with an appendage, only it was four hundred children long!

Satan had to find ways to stop Don Bosco, and he was not beyond trying anything. Don Bosco was called a *revolutionary*. He was accused of preaching treason to his young people. Undercover police followed the group to the field on Sundays, trying to catch the priest in revolutionary activities. Although the police tried to be inconspicuous, it was very obvious who they were. Don Bosco kept his voice down during his sermons. The police had to draw closer to hear him. He wanted this. The sermons were meant for *them*! One commented that Don Bosco was some kind of conspirator. Three weeks more of this, and all the police would be going to confession.

It was suggested to Don Bosco that he disband his group, and send them to their local parishes for spiritual nourishment. On paper, this sounded good. But none of these children *had* a parish. *They were street people!* They had never gone to church anywhere before Don Bosco picked them up out of the gutter. And if they did have any association with a church, there were no priests who would reach out to them and love them. This was a unique *situation*, because Don Bosco was a unique *Saint*.

Rumors flew that Don Bosco had lost his mind. He was constantly talking about this oratory, this building, with a chapel and a field and classrooms, that didn't exist. Even some of his supporters thought that he was going off the deep end. Word got to the diocese. Investigators were sent to question Don Bosco. Although it was obvious, he was brilliant, he couldn't convince them that he was not *crazy*.

The investigators left. They instructed two priests to come and trick Don Bosco into going to an asylum with them. But how could you trick someone, the Blessed Virgin was talking to all the time? They were very courteous, very congenial. They invited him to take a ride. He consented gladly. As they approached the coach, he insisted they enter first, as they were senior to him. As soon as they had gotten into the coach, he slammed the doors and shouted to the driver to go immediately to the asylum.

This had all been planned in advance, so the driver thought the crazy man was in the coach. He raced to the

asylum, which was very close by.   The attendants were
waiting to accost the *quack* in the coach.   When the driver
stopped at the entrance to the asylum, the attendants
pounced on the doors of the coach.   To their surprise, they
found two crazy priests, instead of one.   They didn't think
much about this; they dragged the two screaming priests out
of the carriage and prepared them for straight jackets.   It
took some time before the priests could convince the
hospital officials that they were sane, and the insane one had
tricked them.

We're writing this 150 years after the fact.   Don Bosco
has been raised to the Communion of Saints.   He has been
proven by the test of time.   These escapades seem amusing
now.   But we wonder how Don Bosco reacted to them,
during the actual occurrences.   All he could see was that he
was being attacked by *his very own.*   They thought he was a
revolutionary, or *crazy.*   He and his children were being
rejected, everywhere they turned.   Was he depressed?   Did
he believe he was a failure?   In reflecting on this bleak time
in his life, he wrote:

"As I looked at the crowd of children and the thought
of the rich harvest they promised my priesthood, I felt
my heart was breaking.   I was alone, without helpers.
My health was shattered and I could not tell where to
gather my poor little lambs any more."

We always talk about our *eleventh hour God.*   He is so
available, especially in the life of Don Bosco.   I guess He
likes to test us, though, to see just how much we can take
before He has to come in, like *gangbusters* and save the day.
This is what happened *again* with Don Bosco.   He had
rented a field, where he could bring the boys on Sunday.
But the local people complained so fiercely to the landlords
that they broke the lease.   They gave Don Bosco two weeks
to find another place.   *Two weeks!*   It was impossible to find a
place in two weeks.   One week passed; nothing happened.

Above: ***Don Bosco wrote over 130 books, pamphlets and articles.***
Below: ***Don Bosco and the Oratory band***

Two weeks passed; still nothing. Don Bosco brought the boys to the field for what might very well have been their last Sunday together. He had reached the end of his rope. As he walked among them during playtime, he prayed, "*O my God, show me where I must gather them on Sunday, or tell me what I ought to do.*"

If we could imagine, for a moment, with our mind's eye, what might have happened, it could have gone something like this. Don Bosco's Guardian Angel grabbed his pleading petition, and zoomed up to Heaven, faster than the speed of light, heading straight for Jesus. Mother Mary intercepted the Angel at the gates of Heaven, grabbed the petition and bolted past any interference, going directly to her Son, Jesus. He might have looked at her beautiful, imploring eyes, then at the petition she held before Him. He might have said something like, "*I know, Mother. I was just about to take care of it.*"

Whatever the scenario was in Heaven, down on earth, Don Bosco had no sooner made his prayer of petition than an elderly man came up to him on the field and offered him a site for the Oratory. Don Bosco went with the man to look at it. It must have been near, where he was with the children. What he saw was a beat-up barn, a hayloft. Not only was it not at all what he envisioned for the Oratory, but he had to bend down to get in the door. The roof was full of holes. When Don Bosco brought this to the man's attention, he was told, it was no problem. "We'll dig out a couple of feet of earth and put down a floor. Then you will have the use of the land around the shed, all the lot (everything) for twelve pounds a year. What do you think of it?"

Don Bosco had been hurt a lot, having been thrown out of five locations in ten months. He may have been a little *gun-shy.* He asked mildly, "On lease?" The man replied, "On lease and everything ready by Sunday." *Praise you Jesus!* Don Bosco ran back to his boys, who were still playing in the field. He told them of the miracle that had happened, that they now had a *permanent place*, which would not be taken away from them, and they could begin there the following Sunday. The cheers from the little people could be heard all over Turin. They all prayed a vigorous, super-reverent Rosary of thanksgiving to Our Lady. They knew she was the one who did it.

Don Bosco was physically and emotionally worn out. His dilemma, what to do with his brood, was only one of the many pressures, he was under all the time. In addition, he spent all his spare time trying to take care of their *problems*. He went to the jails, when they got into trouble. He tried to get people to help house and feed them. He tried to get them work. He acted as intermediary for them with their bosses. It was a full time, twenty four hour a day, seven day a week job for about ten people, and he tried to fit it all into *his* regular schedule as a priest, while holding down a position in an orphanage at the same time. His expertise as a *juggler* was not enough to handle this situation.

As soon as the question of a permanent Oratory had been settled, and some of the pressure was relieved, his body *shut down*. It often happens this way. When the stress is at a peak, the body works overtime to handle all the problems. But as soon as the situation is somewhat alleviated, the body breaks down. Don Bosco came down with a deadly case of pneumonia, the same illness that killed his father. He was put into bed, on the critical list. It got so bad he was given the last Sacraments of the Church[7].

He had taught his young people well. They went to the local churches and bombarded Heaven with prayer. Deals were sent up to Heaven, with promises of good behavior, weekly attendance at Mass, confessions, love of neighbor,

---

[7]The Last Sacraments, Reconciliation, the Anointing of the Sick, and Viaticum (Holy Communion).

anything and everything they thought might touch the Heart of God. The battle cry that went up to Heaven was, *Don't let Don Bosco die!*

At the darkest hour, when it appeared that Don Bosco was at the end of his life, one of his friends, Fr. Borel, who had stayed at his side throughout the illness, spoke softly to Don Bosco. "John, these children need you. Ask God to let you stay. Please, pray this prayer after me, *'Lord, if it be your good pleasure, cure me. I say this prayer in the name of my children.'*" Don Bosco weakly whispered the prayer after his friend. The following morning, the fever broke, and he was back in business again.

Meager Beginnings

Don Bosco had dreams, on three different occasions, in which he saw the house, the chapel and the grounds of the Oratory. This barn, the Pinardi property, definitely was not it. At best, it was a stopgap measure. So says Don Bosco; but not necessarily the Lord. Don Bosco complained of the house, which was part of the property. *It was inhabited by prostitutes!* This was no example for his young people. *The Lord decided Don Bosco would live in that house.* It was a *scandal* for a priest to live in a house with prostitutes! The Lord made it necessary for Don Bosco to have someone live with him, whose reputation was above board, beyond question. Who could that have been? Margaret Bosco was the perfect choice. The *Heavenly* plan went far beyond what Don Bosco had envisioned, and a person like Margaret, no, *Margaret herself*, was needed to put it into effect. It was not an easy task, to convince her to leave her beautiful little home and move into the big city. But when it was determined by Margaret and her son that this was the Lord's will, she moved without hesitation.

The children took to Margaret immediately, dubbing her "Mamma Margaret." If she had thought her work was finished, after having raised her sons and put this one (Don Bosco) into the priesthood, she was in for a surprise. She embraced the four hundred, which soon became five hundred and within a year, the little Oratory was bursting at the seams with seven hundred children. Don Bosco began to educate them. Little by little, word of this marvelous work spread throughout Turin. Other priests joined him in the work, by teaching the children. Although Don Bosco would not turn anyone away, it became obvious there was just no place to physically *fit* one more child. That's when they began to spread out. Without any money *(what's new?)*, they rallied enough support to open not one, but two new Oratories in Turin.

A most important phase of the Lord's work, through His servant, Don Bosco, began one rainy night when Margaret Bosco opened the door to find a soaking, half-starved orphan, standing in front of her. Naturally, she let him in, and before very long, one multiplied into ten, and on and on. Don Bosco wound up renting the entire house from Signor Pinardi, which was not an easy feat, considering the prostitutes had set up a solid business in that locale. But the Lord wanted to accomplish two goals at once, get rid of the *ladies* and bring in the homeless children. There were some holdouts among the prostitutes, who were just stubborn and wouldn't leave. But eventually, Don Bosco bought the building, and they had to leave.

In many ways, Don Bosco was his own worst enemy, especially where it applied to help. He wanted priests to help educate the children; he needed them desperately. But he was such a hard act to follow. Try as they might, they didn't have the one ingredient that Don Bosco fought all his life to maintain, patience. He had a way with the children, which was uncanny. None of the others could duplicate this God-given gift; after a while, they tired of trying and left.

The Order of St. Francis de Sales, the Salesians

Don Bosco knew, there was only one way to combat this constant shortage in quality help. He knew he was called to begin his own Order. He had known it, from the year after he was ordained, but every time he tried to institute it, he was blocked. The timing was just not right, or the people were not right. In 1852, when he actually planted the seeds of what was to become the Salesian order, it was the *worst possible time*, not only to start a Religious Order, but to even consider priestly vocations. It was at the height of anti-clericalism and anti-Catholicism in Europe. The Jesuits had been thrown out of Piedmont. An order of nuns were also ejected. *The Bishop of Turin was living in exile in Lyon, France!* Even Rome was cutting back on Religious Orders. They were seriously considering combining Orders, to make them more manageable and less troublesome.

So, naturally, this was the *best possible time* for Don Bosco to *begin* a Religious Order. If it were successful, no credit would be given to him, because it was an impossible task. Perhaps, that's why the Lord blocked any attempt, before this time. People might have a tendency to give credit to Don Bosco, who was too famous for his own good, anyway, so they thought. He began with four. He brought them into his room on June 5, of that year. He really didn't spell out what he had in mind. He asked for a commitment to work with him over a period of time; he wanted to train them for a special mission. They all agreed. This was the nucleus which formed the Salesian society, a year and a half later, in January 1854.

Don Bosco picked the octave of the feast of St. Francis de Sales, to have his young men formalize their commitment. He asked for a *promise*, which might eventually become a *vow*, which might lead to the priesthood. Everyone who agreed, was given the name Salesian, after the great Doctor of the Church, St. Francis de Sales. We have been asking why he chose St. Francis de Sales as his patron, from the very beginning of our research of Don Bosco. There's no mention in his own writings, or in his biographies, about a significant event in his life, which had anything to do with the Bishop of Geneva; nothing which would give any reason why he chose St. Francis de Sales. Yet there was never a question that his Order would be named after this saint.

Don Bosco had always been a great *admirer* of St. Francis de Sales. His writings were brilliant. He was a *workaholic*, as was Don Bosco, who fought tirelessly against all the heresies of his day. But possibly the most attractive trait in St. Francis de Sales, which Don Bosco wanted his followers to possess, was his *gentleness and understanding*. The apostolate of Don Bosco was of a very special nature; one where the qualities of gentleness, patience and understanding were as important and possibly more important than any other. He prayed that his benefactor, St. Francis de Sales, would help from Heaven, in instilling these virtues into all his people.

(Author's note: We have only known two members of the Salesian order to any degree. They possess many admirable virtues, but their greatest qualities are those their founder prayed for, gentleness, patience and understanding.)

As word got out among the religious and political community that Don Bosco intended to begin a Religious Order, there were many bets taken as to how *successful* his venture would be. But he possessed one asset, which helped in pushing him over the top. His charism, that of taking care of the poor children, orphans, etc., without taxing the church or the state, made him a very popular cause. The king was in favor of his apostolate, as was his bishop. The Pope had great *respect* for what he was doing.

The way Don Bosco got most of his support was *hilarious*. People in high places *actually suggested* that he begin an Order. As far as they knew, he was just following their suggestion. Naturally, this also encouraged them to come to his aid. For example, there was a very powerful man in the government, Urbano Ratazzi, who was an anti-cleric, but a fervent supporter of Don Bosco.

At one meeting in 1857, Ratazzi spoke to Don Bosco. How would his work be carried on after he was gone? He said, *"My dear Don Bosco, I wish you could live long, yes, a very long time, to educate and teach all these poor children. But you are not immortal. What will become of your Oratory after you? Have you thought about that?"*

Don Bosco smiled, but said nothing. Ratazzi continued, *"You ought to associate with yourself more intimately, a few of your young fellows or of your clerical helpers in governing and teaching your young people, in handing on your methods and spirit and finally in gathering them into an Association which will go on."*

Don Bosco answered him, trying desperately to hold back a grin, "Your excellency, it is you who are speaking to me of a Congregation, whereas the Law..."

"Oh, the Law, the Law," replied Ratazzi, *"well I know it thoroughly, and I know its bearing. It is directly against....the old orders living outside the scope of legislation. But give me an Association in which all the members retain their civil rights, submit to the laws of the State, pay their taxes personally, an Association of free citizens living together for some beneficent purpose, and I guarantee you that there is no regular settled Government which can interfere with you. On the contrary, if it is just, it will have to protect you in the same way as it protects other Associations, whether they be commercial, industrial or for mutual assistance. So you can settle your affairs in all security. You will have the support of the State and the King, for it will be a question of a humanitarian Institution in the front rank."*

Don Bosco mumbled a "Thank you Jesus" under his breath and said, "Very well, your Excellency, then I will think it over." He knew, he had the State behind him. His bishop was in his corner. All he needed was the Pope. So, when the Lord gave him the sign, he went to Rome.

Don Bosco left for Rome on February 2, 1858. He had his first audience with the Pope, on March 9th. You and I know that Mary was roaming the earth at that time, talking to a little French girl in the Pyrenees, who would become a Powerful woman in our Church, Bernadette Soubirous. Now, Don Bosco didn't know about it. The Pope might not have heard about it at this early date. But we're sure Mary was there at all the meetings Don Bosco had with the Pope, especially the first one. While he was still very poor, Don Bosco had attained a great deal of popularity. He was famous in many circles. The Pope admired him greatly. At this first meeting, after listening to all the projects, Don Bosco had been working on, he said to Don Bosco, "*How many undertakings you have started, my good Father, but if you happen to die, what will become of them?*"

It was as if the Lord had put the words into the mouth of the Pope. Don Bosco *just happened to have* a whole outline of his proposed *Congregation* in his pocket. The Pope gave him some important direction, then asked him to put it all on paper, and bring it back to him. Twelve days later, Don Bosco placed the rule of the Salesian Society in the hands of Pope Pius IX. As far as he was concerned, he was in business. The actual *approval* took some sixteen years and much agony for Don Bosco and his followers. At one point, he said, if he had known at the outset all that he would have had to go through, he probably would not have had the courage to do it. The politics of putting together a Religious Order at that time were horrendous. If he had not had the support of the King and the State and the Bishop in exile and the Pope and more than that, of our Lord Jesus and His Mother Mary and most likely St. Francis de Sales and all the Angels and Saints, it never would have happened.

But he did have their support, and it did happen. At last count, Don Bosco's followers number 22,000 worldwide.

Dreams, Vision and Prophecies of Don Bosco

The chapter on Don Bosco would not be complete, without delving into the marvels of his dreams, which were more like visions and prophecies. We know from the Bible that dreams have been one of God's ways of speaking to His children, from the earliest days. The dreams of Joseph, in the Old Testament, changed the course of Jewish history. The dreams of Joseph, in the New Testament, assured him that Mary had conceived a child by the power of the Holy Spirit. Another dream warned him of Herod's plot against the Child and thus saved the Baby Jesus from the slaughter of the Innocents.

The Lord used dreams in Don Bosco's life to guide him, direct him, assure him, and affirm him. Don Bosco never denied any of these dreams. Naturally, we wouldn't know anything about them, if he hadn't divulged them. At one point, he was instructed by Pope Pius IX to write down all his dreams. When the Pope reminded him of this nine years later and learned that Don Bosco had not written them, he ordered him to do so. He said to him, "*This task must have priority over everything else. Put aside the rest and take care of this. You cannot now fully grasp how very beneficial certain things will be to your sons when they shall know them.*"

The parallels between his dreams and how the Lord orchestrated his life, are uncanny. This is why we call them prophecies. In one form or another, they all came to pass. Very often, it took *decades* before the pieces fell into place. Even Don Bosco would be amazed when an action affirmed a dream, he might have had years before.

Don Bosco was a very *humble* man. He never wanted attention focused on *him*. When he talked about his dreams, he never played down their importance, but it was obvious he was *uneasy* about having been the recipient of such honors. Sometimes, he would take on a playful tone, or speak in a very matter-of-fact way about the dreams. Some of his dreams *frightened* him, especially when they came to pass. He dreamt about people's deaths, and they died. But more important than that was the insights he received about sin and how good confession was so crucial. Very often, sharing his dreams about sin with his young people, had more effect on them than a retreat. They made sincere confessions, with a firm purpose not to sin again.

Most of Don Bosco's dreams had to do with his life, his mission, his boys and his Religious Order. Our Lady was a part of *most* of his dreams. For a good deal of his life, Don Bosco went around with overwhelming confidence, as to how his life and ministry would work out. Even when others thought they were at the end, that the bottom was falling out of everything, Don Bosco kept that belief that his life was guided and orchestrated from above. We believe his dreams had a lot to do with this positive outlook.

There is one dream of Don Bosco's that Penny and I use in all our talks, to accentuate the focus of our ministry and what we believe has to be the direction the Church has to take, in order to survive. He shared this vision with his boys, on May 30, 1862.

"A few nights ago I had a dream. True, dreams are nothing but dreams, but still I'll tell it to you for your spiritual benefit, just as I would tell you even my sins - only I'm afraid I'd send you scurrying away before the roof fell in. Try to picture yourselves with me on the seashore, or better still, on an outlying cliff with no other land in sight. The vast expanse of water is covered with a formidable array of ships in battle formation, prows fitted with sharp, spearlike beaks capable of breaking through any defense. All are heavily armed with cannons, incendiary bombs and firearms of all sorts -

even books - and are heading toward one stately ship, mightier than them all. As they close in, they try to ram it, set it afire and cripple it as much as possible.

"This stately vessel is shielded by a flotilla escort. Winds and waves are with the enemy. In the midst of this endless sea, two solid columns, a short distance apart, soar high into the sky: one surmounted by a statue of the Immaculate Virgin at whose feet a large inscription reads: Help of Christians; the other, far loftier and sturdier, supports a Host of proportionate size and bears beneath it the inscription Salvation of believers.

"The flagship commander - the Roman Pontiff - seeing the enemy's fury and his auxiliary ships' very grave predicament, summons his captains to a conference. However, as they discuss their strategy, a furious storm breaks out and they must return to their ships.

"When the storm abates, the Pope again summons his captains as the flagship keeps on its course. But the storm rages again. Standing at the helm, the Pope strains every muscle to steer his ship between the two columns from whose summits hang many anchors and strong hooks linked to chains.

"The entire enemy fleet closes in to intercept and sink the flagship at all costs. They bombard it with everything they have: books and pamphlets, incendiary bombs, firearms, cannons. The battle rages ever more furious. Beaked prows ram the flagship again and again, but to no avail, as unscathed and undaunted, it keeps on its course. At times a formidable ram splinters a gaping hole into its hull, but immediately, a breeze from the two columns instantly seals the gash.

"Meanwhile, enemy cannons blow up, firearms and beaks fall to pieces, ships crack up and sink to the bottom. In blind fury the enemy takes to hand-to-hand

combat, cursing and blaspheming. Suddenly the Pope falls, seriously wounded, He is instantly helped up, but, struck down a second time, dies. A shout of victory rises from the enemy and wild rejoicing sweeps their ships. But no sooner is the Pope dead than another takes his place. The captains of the auxiliary ships elected him so quickly that the news of the Pope's death coincides with that of his successor's election. The enemy's self-assurance waned.

"Breaking through all resistance, the new Pope steers the ship safely between the two columns and moors it to the two columns; first, to the one surmounted by the Host and then to the other, topped by the statue of the Virgin. At this point, something unexpected happens. The enemy ships panic and disperse, colliding with and scuttling each other.

"Some auxiliary ships which had gallantly fought alongside their flagship are the first to tie up at the two columns. Many others, which had fearfully kept far away from the fight, stand still, cautiously waiting until the wrecked enemy ships vanish under the waves. Then, they too head for the two columns, tie up at the swinging hooks and ride safe and tranquil beside their flagship. A great calm now covers the sea."[8]

Most of Don Bosco's dreams were realized during his lifetime. He made predictions about the events of the Franco-Prussian war, which were so accurate, it was as if he read a script. He also predicted the death of Pope Pius IX. But the dream about the two columns has struck us from the first time we read it, as being more for today's church, then for the time of Don Bosco. Could Don Bosco see what would be happening in the Church of today, how we would be floundering so badly in a violent storm, not knowing what

---

[8]Dreams, Visions & Prophecies of Don Bosco

to believe, or who to listen to? Was this dream or vision or prophecy to help us see clearly, what and where our loyalties must be, if we are to save the Church? We like to think of this vision as being a directive to follow the great strengths of our Church, the Body of Christ, in the Eucharist, the Mother of Christ, through the Vicar of Christ.

After Don Bosco shared his dream, he asked his priests and students to comment on its meaning. None of them, not the priest, nor the students, said anything at that time, about one Pope being killed and being replaced immediately by another. Was that a prophecy of an event that took place in our time, when Pope John Paul I died after only 33 days in office, to be replaced immediately by Pope John Paul II? Or was the Lord telling us through Don Bosco that the Papacy does not depend on a man, but solely on God? Was that prophecy for Don Bosco's time, or for a hundred years later?

Il Grigio (the gray one)

Making the statement, "*The chapter would not be complete without....*" becomes a pat phrase, when speaking of Don Bosco. Il Grigio, the gray dog, really had nothing to do with Don Bosco's ministry, but very possibly, it had a lot to do with his ability to perform his ministry. Don Bosco actually devoted the last chapter of his autobiography, *Memoirs of the Oratory*, to his good friend, il Grigio. So if it was important enough for the master to talk about him, we can also share about the gray dog.

We have to preface it by telling you that a lot of people didn't like Don Bosco, probably more *hated* him than *loved* him. Attempts on Don Bosco's life became a commonplace event. Either dissident *religious* groups wanted to get him, or *political* groups. But between the two, he really had to be on his toes. It got to the point where he could pretty well sense when he was being set up for an attempt on his life. Usually, someone would come and ask him to go to the home of a sick person, to administer the last sacraments of the Church. That's where he was most vulnerable. Most times, he would try to bring two or more of his four strong young people with him for protection. But there were times, when he was alone on the street, or was not able to bring anyone with him. That's when he would find *Grigio*. No one ever knew where he came from, or where he would go after the incidents.

One instance took place in 1854, when he was coming home late at night. He was in a very bad section of town. He saw two men in front of him, walking slowly, keeping up with his pace. He wasn't sure they were after him, but as he speeded up, they speeded up; if he slowed down, they did the same. He crossed to the other side of the street. When they did the same, he knew he was in trouble. He turned around to retreat, but they jumped him and threw a black cloak over his head. He tried to fight them, but it was no use. They were attempting to jam a cloth inside his mouth, when all of a sudden, out of nowhere, a huge, gray, hideous looking *mastiff*[9] emerged from the darkness, and came charging at them. His growls sounded like those of a wolf or a bear. He *lunged* at Don Bosco's attackers. They were frightened right down to their toes. They pleaded with Don Bosco to call him off. He agreed to when they agreed to stop accosting passersby. They ran for their life. Grigio didn't chase them. He stayed by Don Bosco's side.

From that time on, whenever Don Bosco came home late, after he passed the last of the buildings, Grigio would come from out of nowhere, to walk him home. Many people from the Oratory saw Grigio. One time he barged into the Oratory. Everyone was frightened. But then he ran up to Don Bosco, nuzzled his face into his friend and ran off. Don

---

[9]Mastiff - a mixed breed - a large, powerful, smooth-coated dog with hanging lips and drooping ears - very often used for watchdogs.

Bosco never made a big deal about Grigio, who he was, where he came from, why he stayed around for *thirty years.*

Don Bosco writes that the last time he saw Grigio was in 1866. But he finished writing his memoirs some years before he died, so he did not chronicle all his adventures with Grigio. There is a recorded incident that Grigio accompanied Don Bosco on the road to Ventimiglia, near the French border, as late as 1883. When Don Bosco shared this with a friend, she marveled, because dogs just don't live that long. Don Bosco smiled and said, *"Well, maybe it was his son or grandson."* He didn't want to get into it with her. The Salesians sisters testified that they experienced Grigio's protection, on three occasions *between 1893 and 1930.*

Who or what was Grigio? Many Salesians said, *they* had seen him. Did he protect Don Bosco and the Salesians for 80 years? His origins have never been officially investigated, but there are theories. In 1870, Don Bosco commented, *"It sounds ridiculous to call him an angel, yet he is no ordinary dog..."* Our only comment is, *why not an Angel?*

Don Bosco wears out

Don Bosco spent his entire life *running* at ninety miles an hour. In addition to working with hundreds of boys, running a school, running an orphanage, running a Religious Order for men, starting a Religious Order for women, plus a third order for laity, building churches, he managed to write some 130 books and articles. He was a *bull* of a man, who played football with his boys up into his late fifties. And while we think his mind raced until the very end, his body began to give out. He never had any real ailments, until he was stricken with phlebitis[10]. He had to have Salesians on either side of him, walk with him to keep him steady.

---

[10]Phlebitis - Inflammation of the vein, or veins, a very painful ailment.

He couldn't resist an invitation from Pope Leo XIII, to go to France and beg for money, for the completion of the Church of the Sacred Heart in Rome. Don Bosco was a great beggar. He had had a lifetime of experience at it. He had ulterior motives. His movement, the Salesians, had spread their wings into France and Spain and Don Bosco wanted to visit them. He could never afford to do it on his own. This way, he could beg for the Pope and visit his people. In January, 1883, the *sixty-eight* year old Don Bosco headed for France, by way of Nice. He was not aware how famous, he had become. Everywhere he went, huge crowds of people followed. By the time he reached Paris, the excitement had risen to fever pitch. A little girl was cured of a malignant tumor through his intercession, which hit the secular newspapers. The crowds were tumultuous! It was said that not that many people had turned out to see a priest, since Pius VII had visited Paris in the early part of the century. They knew they had a living saint in their midst. They called him, *"The Italian Vincent de Paul,"* which was a great honor. Needless to say, he collected more than enough money to finish the Church of the Sacred Heart in Rome.

Was Don Bosco on a roll, or did he know that his days were so numbered, he had better do all his traveling, as quickly as possible? It took him three years to gather enough strength to go back out on the road, but in 1886, he went to visit his congregation in Barcelona, Spain. A repeat of his French trip took place. Throngs of excited people greeted him wherever he went. *Miracles*, all of which he attributed to the intercession of Mary, Help of Christians, took place. He was a huge success. But he was fading fast.

His doctors claimed he needed rest. He said that was the one thing he could not give them. When the doctors were asked, by the Salesians, what was ailing Don Bosco, they were told it was no great illness, or disease. He was just out of steam. He was like an oil lamp without oil. He had worn himself out.

During the last days, Don Rua, who had been chosen by Don Bosco as his successor, had all the brothers come into the death room to bid farewell to their father in faith. Though Don Bosco couldn't speak anymore, and his right side was paralyzed, he blessed each of them.

On January 31, 1888, Don Bosco turned his life over to Jesus, through His beautiful Mother Mary. In 1934, forty six years after his death, Don Bosco was officially raised to the Communion of Saints.

There is no way that we could tell the story of Don Bosco, without speaking of divine intervention, the supernatural events which guided his life. There are so many areas, we didn't get to talk about: his bouts with the devil, the miraculous healings, multiplication of food. But by the same token, we only *touched* on the great humanitarian efforts of the Salesians, which have grown steadily from its humble beginnings to this day. Read about this powerful man in our Church. There are so many good books. Check the bibliography for those *we* used, to research his life. Don Bosco is as important today, as he was at this time a hundred years ago. He has so many things to teach you, and he's not beyond pulling a coin out from behind your ear, or making flowers disappear, while he winks at you with that twinkle in his eye and leads you into the arms of Jesus and His beautiful Mother Mary.

†

Photo Credits Don Bosco Publications
All excerpts and quotations taken from
Memoirs of the Oratory
Saint John Bosco
Don Bosco, Life and Work
Dreams, Visions and Prophecies of Don Bosco

Blessed Miguel Pro

"Viva Cristo Rey"

There is a law in Mexico, which states that no religious ceremony may be held outside of a church. The same law exists in many communist countries, or at least did exist, until the revolutions in 1989. Mexico and perhaps a few other *hard line* countries still maintain that law.

There are only two times in the last twelve years that an exception to that law has been *allowed*, and that was when His Holiness, Pope John Paul II, came to Mexico in 1979 and 1990. At those times, Masses were celebrated *openly* in large outdoor areas. But with those exceptions, the law is very clear and very strict.

However, on September 25, 1988, a fairly large group of Mexicans, led by a priest, walked to the National Lottery building, located on a busy thoroughfare in Mexico City, and celebrated Mass there. The crowd was large enough to attract the attention of the police, and we're sure the police *did* notice. But the faithful were not stopped, or hindered in any way. We were very surprised to hear of this, until we were told of a little bronze plaque on the wall of that building. It reads very simply, "This is the spot where Padre Miguel Pro was executed on November 23, 1927." And the day the Mass was celebrated was the day Miguel Pro was *beatified* by Pope John Paul II, at St. Peter's Basilica in Rome.

Mexico is such a contradiction. How can a country which is 97% Catholic, and 99% Guadalupean[1], be ruled by Anti-Catholic governments since *1825*? And how has the

---

[1]Comment made by Pope John Paul II in 1979, while at the Shrine of Our Lady of Guadalupe in Mexico City. It was in reference to the almost unanimous veneration given to Our Lady of Guadalupe by the people of Mexico

Catholic Church been able to survive, under the heel of such domination?   We, in the United States, find it almost impossible to believe that only 75 years ago, there was such wholesale persecution and slaughter of Catholics, just south of the border, down Mexico way.

†

The situation between the State and the Church had been going downhill for many years.   To make matters worse, the Constitution of 1917 took away the Church's official standing in Mexico.   Priests were not allowed to wear clerical garb.   Previously, all church property had been confiscated by the State.   *Now*, the church was forbidden to accumulate any new private property.   The priesthood was classified as a profession, like a doctor or lawyer.   Priests had to have *licenses* to practice their profession.   If they had no license, they could not preach.   If they *did have* their license, the government had its finger on them at all times.   Foreign missionaries were banned in Mexico; and native Mexicans were forbidden to train in the Mexican seminaries.   So the faithful were not allowed to have Mexican priests, and not allowed to have foreign priests come in.   The idea was to kill off Catholicism in Mexico, by eliminating the *priesthood*.   When none of this seemed to work, the president, Plutarco Elias Calles, issued an order that all clergy were to leave their duties and report to Mexico City.   None of them left their parishes, which made them *outlaws* in the eyes of the State.   God only knows what Calles would have done with them, if they had all come to Mexico City.

Most of the world knew very little, or nothing, of what was going on in Mexico.   Those Catholic priests, nuns and lay people who had been murdered, might have remained unknown statistics of man's inhumanity to man, and Satan's hate for God, had President Calles not made a move that *backfired* on him, and all of Mexico.   The execution of Miguel Pro, and the publicizing of that execution, was a huge mistake on the part of the Mexican government in 1927, which they have never been able to live down, or sweep under the carpet. It highlighted the persecution of the Church by the government. Padre Pro just refused to go away, and based on his recent beatification, he never will.

Who is Padre Miguel Pro?

Miguel Agustín Pro was God's *clown*. He was born on January 13, 1891. His early days remind us very much of St. Francis of Assisi. Miguel came from a well-to-do family, which was a feat in itself, at the turn of the century, in Mexico. His father was an executive in a small mining village in the state of Zacatecas. Miguel grew up, embracing all the beauty of his surroundings. He was of the upper class, but he never thought of himself that way. His greatest love, as a child, was to wander down into the mines, to be with the workers. To Miguel, this was the best way to spend his life. It gave him a chance to meet and become close to those unfortunates who *had* to be in the mines, working long hours, under terrible conditions. But when Miguel was there, he cheered everyone up. All was fun.

He was a natural *comic*, which would be of great help to him in his unorthodox priestly ministry. He was a very happy boy in school, the leader of the crowd. We would call Miguel a very normal boy; yet there was a sensitivity in him that his mother noticed from his earliest age. Not that she didn't have to do some heavy duty disciplining of Miguel. He had an uncommon love for sweets. Most young people do, but Miguel's appetite for anything of a dessert nature, bordered on craving. He was always at the candy store, buying and eating sweets. When he ran out of money, he told the storekeeper to put it on his mother's bill; she was good for it. But when the mother received this outrageous bill for her son's dipping into the candy jar, she tanned his hide, in the way only a mother can do. It hurt her more than

Left:
**Blessed Miguel Pro,
natural *comic*,
a caricaturist,
God's clown,
the unofficial mascot
of his little
Jesuit Community.**

Right:
*During the
Consecration
of the Mass,
as he held the
Consecrated Host,
a brilliant light
surrounded him.
His vestments were
illuminated.
His face and hands
were gleaming;
he levitated.
He was transfigured
as Our Lord Jesus
on Mount Tabor,
before him.*

it did him, so she said. She cried, as she punished him. But she would not spoil her children!

He went to work for his father in the office of the mine, before he had finished school. That was fine with Miguel. He would rather be around the mines than at school, anyway. He adapted beautifully to the office. His natural talents emerged. He picked up all the office procedures, especially details, and mastered them. He was great on the typewriter; he could type 100 words per minute. But whenever he could, he would sneak down into the mines. He became friendly with the miners. He picked up their colloquial language, which was different from what his parents spoke in the house. You can see the Lord's hand in everything that young Miguel did. He would need this knowledge of the people's language, in his priestly ministry. So, as he grew up, he picked up *this* attribute, then added *that* quality, until he was just what Jesus needed, at the time He needed him. The Lord groomed Miguel, from the day he was born.

One talent Miguel acquired early in life, which would be extremely important to him later on, was as a *caricaturist*. He was able to capture, in exaggerated form, the peculiarities in people's faces. At first, he sketched them on paper; they were hysterical. He would embellish noses, thick bushy eyebrows, long chins, funny eyes, buck teeth. He had an aptitude for these things. But he grew from drawing them, to disguising himself in the same theatrical masks. This ability to disguise himself was to prove *crucial* in later years.

His focus was not on spirituality, at all. He was having too much of a good time. He learned to play the guitar and mandolin, as was required of a young man of his station. He loved his family very much, especially his two sisters. While he took part in all the family religious activities, Mass, the Rosary, the Angelus, no one would ever have considered him as a candidate for *religious life*, least of all, him. His two sisters decided to join the convent. Miguel became furious! Things were changing. He didn't want that. He was enjoying his family. He wanted things to remain the way they were. Miguel became very angry. He blamed it on the Jesuits. They had been the girls' spiritual directors. He developed a great animosity toward the Jesuits. He really didn't believe his sisters would go through with this insanity; he thought for sure he could count on his mother and father to step in and stop them. *But they didn't!*

On the day, his sisters left for their new life in Christ, an irate Miguel bolted out into the woods. He was gone for days. His mother was really worried about him. *Anything* could happen in the woods. He was not experienced in hiking or camping. She went out looking for him. When she found him, as she knew she would, she spoke very gently to her son. She was concerned about the way, he had reacted to his sisters' entering religious life. Miguel couldn't understand either, why he had reacted so angrily. He just knew it bothered him terribly.

His mother made a suggestion that she knew would not go over *well* with Miguel. She asked him to go on a religious retreat, just for a few days, to try to come to terms with what was bothering him. She was right; he was not *happy* with the idea. But, praise God, he went anyway. No one knows for sure what happened on that retreat. The best comparison we can make is Paul's conversion on the road to Damascus. It was about as complete a turnaround as Paul made. This young man, a hothead like Paul, impetuous like Paul, came back from this retreat, *converted like Paul,* his vocation to the priesthood, sealed. And most unbelievable of all, he was going to be a *Jesuit!*

The parallels with Paul are so clear. We have to believe that Miguel Pro was given some insight on that retreat, some vision, whether physical or spiritual, which lifted him to the heights of Heaven. This young man, who had embraced life with such a passion, and all that life had to offer, took that same passion and zeal, and turned it in the direction of the service of *God*. Miguel was a *determined* man. Had he decided to become president of Mexico, he probably could have accomplished it. But the Lord had greater plans for Miguel. We don't know how difficult it was for him to tear himself away from everything he had known and loved, for this strange new world; but on August 11, 1911, he left his home and family, and entered the Jesuit seminary in El Llano, in the state of Michoacán. He was twenty years old.

†

The Church and the State

The relationship between the Church and the State had plunged to its lowest depths. The conflict had begun about a hundred years before Miguel Pro *entered* the seminary. Ironically, the actions of a well-meaning priest, Miguel Hidalgo, brought about *revolution*. He had only wanted some equity for the Indians, who had been mistreated at the hands of the Spanish from the days following Cortez' conquest. The priest was about social *justice*; what he accomplished was social *uprising*, against the wealthy landowners, and (not part of his plan) against the Church. The leaders of the Church have always been associated with the *establishment*. It was that way during the French Revolution; it was the same during the *Mexican* Revolution.

Farmers and peasants, without weapons other than pitchforks, knives and the like, rallied round Hidalgo, and marched on the towns and villages of Mexico. The force swelled to over a hundred thousand, at which point, Hidalgo lost control of his followers completely; it became a bloodbath. Hidalgo was not a military man; he became the dupe for ambitious men, who would use him for their own ends. Finally, he was killed, a year after his ill-begun revolution. He has been called the "Father of the

Revolution" in Mexico. And from that poor beginning, revolution upon revolution has *continued*. The Spanish regained control of the *towns* after Hidalgo was killed, but they never quite controlled the *country* again.

After a period of ten years, many guerrilla attacks and much back-stabbing, a shrewd upstart took control of the country, and proclaimed himself its Emperor. His empire lasted less than two years, but accomplished two things. Spain *was banished* from Mexico, including its soldiers and governors, but also its money. The Emperor bled the country of what remained of its treasury, setting the stage for many to continue doing, down through the years. The bloodsuckers remained; only now they were home-grown Mexican opportunists, rather than the Spanish Overlords. In a period of fifty five years, from 1821 to 1876, Mexico was ruled by *forty* presidents, *two* emperors, and a few provisional governments. Everyone took their best shot at raping the people. It was also during this time that Mexico lost a good deal of her territory to the United States in the Mexican War of 1846: Texas, California, Nevada and Utah, in addition to parts of New Mexico, Arizona, Colorado and Wyoming.

The country had been looted of all its treasury *systematically* by Santa Anna, who had been in some degree of power for almost twenty five years. While he was exiled from the country *three times*, he was also asked to come back *twice*. Each time he returned, he wiped out the treasury again. Finally, in 1854, the people had had enough of him, and he was exiled his third and last time.

The country had been ruled for so many years by military men, who kept increasing and increasing their own personal fortunes, the people looked with hope to a strong non-military man, a full-blooded Indian, *Benito Juarez*. He was the only one who seemed to care about the people. During his eighteen years in power, he brought his country to financial ruin; not because he was crooked, he just didn't know how to run a country. Juarez, who has been called the "Thomas Jefferson" of Mexico, because of his reforms, was also most instrumental in persecuting the Church in Mexico. This seems strange for a man who was taken off the streets as a young boy and given his education through the generosity of a priest.

As soon as Juarez had attained even a small degree of power in the Mexican government, he passed a bill, *forbidding* the Church to buy property. He followed this with another law, called the Reform Laws, which *confiscated* all church property, *broke up* monastic orders, *dismantled* convents, and *prohibited* seminaries. Religious were not allowed to wear *clerical vestments* on the streets. The Reform laws of Benito Juarez, and his attitude, that of crushing the Church in Mexico, have existed in one form or another until this day. Once begun, the persecution never ended. Sadly enough, this man would not have remained in power, if it were not for the support he received from the United States.

Miguel Pro struggles on

From 1872 to 1913, when Miguel Pro took his first vows, tensions between the Church and the state had cooled somewhat. The fact that Miguel Pro attended a Jesuit seminary in Mexico, is proof of this. But the fire between Church and State was never put out. In the years to come, it was to be rekindled into a great blaze. The attitude of many people was, the country had been under some form of revolution since before their birth. They had survived thus far; they would continue to survive. But the balance of power affected the *common man*, in a devastating way. During the Revolution of 1910, Miguel's father had to flee from his home, as did his mother, and his younger brothers and sisters. His mother went to Guadalajara, while Miguel's father went in a different direction. Financially, they had lost everything.

Miguel put all his trust in the Lord. He had made a commitment; he was going to live by it. He tried, hard as he could, to keep himself on the track that he'd been following. While he was able to control his mind, his body began to give way. He contracted an agonizing illness, which would be with him, the rest of his life. But being who he was, he couldn't let on that he was ill. He was considered the jester of the seminary, as he had been in his hometown. Anyone who knew him, when his name was mentioned, smiled at his memory. But very few knew what lay behind his cheerful exterior.

Very shortly after he began his novitiate, he was playing football with the other young men. At one of the goal posts, he began to make a mock-speech, imitating one of his professors. The more his audience cracked up, the funnier Miguel became. More and more young people gathered around him. He was on a roll. All of a sudden, as he was at the height of his comedy, the Novice Master walked up, and asked what everybody was doing. Not knowing what to say, one of the young men pointed to Miguel, and blurted out, "*A sermon!*" The Novice Master, who had come to know Miguel pretty well, held back a grin, and said, "Indeed. I am sorry I missed it. Perhaps the preacher will oblige again?" And naturally, Miguel had to repeat his performance.

With all of his comedy, he was very firm on his observance of the Rule, and his studies. His superiors could *trust* him. He was actually very good for his peers. He was able to break up the stress, caused by the intensity of the training. His superiors allowed him to instruct the students, when a professor fell ill.

The Persecution intensified

Conditions in the country were approaching *disaster* proportions. Law was virtually *non-existent*. The military ruled by intimidating landowners, confiscating their possessions, and then *shooting* them. Miguel spent much of his spare time at the outer edges of the seminary, listening to stories from passersby of how bad things were going in the rest of the country. That was how he heard that his mother and father had to flee their home. In addition, it became very obvious that a new wave of persecution was being aimed at the Church. Now *Miguel* was a part of it. Pope Pius XI termed this period in Mexico as *"exceeding the most bloody persecutions of the Roman emperors."*

War stories of *Religious* being beaten, and strung up to die, found their way back to the seminary. The possibility of becoming a martyr for the Faith, became very real for the first time. How did Miguel handle that prospect? A fellow student testified that during the Carrancista epoch[2], Miguel expressed *"that ardent wish which he felt to suffer persecution for justice' sake."* We have to believe the seed was planted in his heart during these early days, so that when the Lord called on him for this greatest act of love, young Miguel was equal to the challenge.

A heavy blanket of tension covered the Seminary towards the end of the school year. The superiors were aware of the atrocities that were going on all around them, but were not saying anything to the students, in order not to frighten them. The students, for their part, were aware of the problems, but said nothing to their superiors, in order not to alarm *them*. There had been a skirmish with the guerrillas, in the next town, in which the head of the village

---

[2]the rule of Venustiano Carranza when armed thugs went around the countryside, terrorizing and murdering priests and nuns.

was killed by the general[3] in charge. Finally, what they had feared came about. One night, these pistol-shooting, drunken, vicious men found their way into the seminary. They broke down doors, chopped up furniture, shot up the building, and generally terrorized the superiors. The Lord spared the seminary of any serious damage. No one was beaten, or hung, or shot; but they knew their days were numbered. They didn't have to wait long; shortly after, wholesale persecution of all religious orders went into full force. It was determined they abandon the seminary, and flee for their lives. They were given civilian clothing to wear.

On the Feast of the Assumption, they left the seminary. The priests and novices went by twos, sporadically, in different directions, to avoid attracting attention. Miguel went to the nearest town, Zamora. The plan was for all of them to *mix* with the local population, and stay undercover until they could regroup as a community. For some reason, everyone in Zamora knew that Miguel and his companion were priests, or about to become priests. This didn't present a problem until a few days later, when the churches were closed; and everyone who had anything to do with the church, from a sacristan to a bishop, had to appear before the head of the town. Miguel and his friend didn't go. All who *did* were thrown into jail, manhandled and tortured.

But for Miguel, a very important chapter of his life began. He knew that he had to fool the soldiers and police. In order to do this, he began to practice his art of elaborate *disguise*. This was to be his salvation during his active ministry; no one could identify him. One evening, he disguised himself as a *peon*, dressed in cotton pants, wrapped in a serape, with a large sombrero on his head. He walked casually through the town, past all the armed revolutionaries,

---

[3]General - a very loose term given to any bully who could gather enough of a gang to terrorize and intimidate. It diminished the integrity of some really brilliant military men, by giving all the same title.

who were on the lookout for *religious*. Granted, the revolutionaries were distracted by pretty señoritas and their minds were clouded by too much tequila; but let's also give credit where credit was due! We believe Miguel Pro was camouflaged by the wings of Angels, who covered him and protected him. According to the plan set by his superiors, he made his way to Guadalajara, to meet up with the rest of the community. There, he found his mother and his brothers and sisters, living in the poorest of conditions. But they were *alive*; that was all that mattered. Word came to him that his father was definitely alive and safe, though they didn't know where.

This time in Guadalajara was a beginning of Miguel's becoming a heroic figure. There was an excitement in playing hide-and-seek with the authorities. He felt the thrill of the challenge, to perform his religious functions, and at the same time, elude the authorities. The more the danger, the more Miguel enjoyed it. No sooner had celebration of the Mass been forbidden than Miguel assisted at a Mass as server. He took up his mandolin and guitar, playing for his friends. He cheered up the despondent ones. He became the *unofficial mascot* of the little Jesuit community in hiding.

Risk-taking became a way of life for religious in Mexico. At one point, the bishop met with a group of five hundred faithful on private property, and celebrated Mass. During the service, the house was surrounded by *armed* revolutionaries, and all were placed under arrest. However, their plans were foiled by a huge group of people who surrounded *them*, and demanded, they free the Bishop. The revolutionaries backed down, in the face of such a mob.

It was becoming more and more difficult to function, under the suppressed circumstances. Finally, word came by *code* for Miguel and the other seminarians to leave Guadalajara, for Los Gatos, in California; there they were to continue their studies. It was a very heart-breaking experience for Miguel at the Guadalajara railroad station. His mother and brothers and sisters saw him off. He knew he was leaving them in an impossible situation, but he had to continue in his commitment to the Lord. He knew, as he bid his mother good-by, that he would never see her again on this earth. *He never did.*

Miguel in exile

Miguel and sixteen other companions, from the Jesuit seminary in El Llano, traveled together through Mexico, which was now enemy territory for them, across the border at Nogales, Mexico, and up through California to Los Gatos, some fifty miles south of San Francisco. Although he had never visited this country before, he knew that at one time, it had belonged to his beloved Mexico, and now, he was a *foreigner* here. But he was an *outcast* in his own country, an *outlaw*, a *deserter* from the cause, whatever that cause might be at any given time. Still, it *was* his country; his mother and father, his sisters and brothers, were still there. The people, the Lord had commissioned him to minister to, were all there. But Miguel was given the gift to know that if he felt down and out, and depressed, his brother seminarians had to feel the same way. So he used his God-given talents to submerge his *own* feelings, and continue perking up the spirits of his comrades.

The Jesuits at Los Gatos were extremely hospitable. Though they were filled to capacity, they found room for their sixteen Mexican brothers. Language, however, was a major problem. The Americans didn't speak Spanish; the Mexicans couldn't speak English. To make matters worse, Miguel's superiors had not taken into consideration one thing, when they planned the escape from Mexico, books written in Spanish that the students could use.

They were given a floor to themselves, at the top of the seminary. They had complete access to the library, although there was only one book in Spanish, which they could use. They felt out of place. It was extremely difficult for them to study. In addition, bad news from home was followed by worse news, always leveled at the Church. Carranza had written the devastating Constitution of Querétaro in 1917. In it, no foreigner was allowed to possess *anything in Mexico*. Religious vows were forbidden. All ecclesiastical property was to belong to the State. Priests could not practice their ministry. They had absolutely no rights, at all. Hundreds of priests, a number of bishops and nuns were *expelled* from the country. Two thousand Catholic schools were closed.

The situation in Los Gatos was not working out for the Mexican students. It was very doubtful, they would be able to reopen their seminary in Mexico, at least in the forseeable future. They decided to send the Mexican students to Spain to finish their studies. After all, Spain was the home of the Jesuits. And so, the sixteen packed up again, made the long trip to New York by way of El Paso and Miami, and boarded a ship for Spain. They arrived in Granada, in July of that year.

Miguel spent five years in Granada, Spain. While he was very sad inside, to be so far from his home and family, and while his internal illness gave him fits of agonizing pain, he maintained a great, cheery exterior. He became the ringleader of most of the students of his group, but definitely all the Mexicans. As a means of entertaining his friends, he put into practice a prank which gave him the nickname, "Rubber face." He had the ability to contort one side of his face, while the other side remained motionless. He would sit in the front of the room, facing the students. The left side of his face was in the professor's view, completely composed. With his right side, he would make the most outrageous faces. The students who could see him, rolled in the aisles with laughter. The professor couldn't figure out what they were laughing at. He couldn't prove it; but he knew that somehow, Miguel Pro was behind the joke.

Miguel wanted to go home to Mexico, or at least close to home. So when, in 1920, at the end of his studies, he was sent to Nicaragua, to teach at a Jesuit boy's school, he felt better that he had at least put 4,000 miles behind him. He was that much closer to his loved ones. He threw himself into the work, teaching the younger students drawing. He put together games, plays, anything to amuse them, and at the same time, keep him going. His heart was in Mexico, not far from Granada in Nicaragua. But after two years there, he was sent back across the ocean again, to attend Theology school in Barcelona. He never made any contact with anyone he knew in Mexico.

It was 1921; Miguel was thirty years old. For whatever reason, maybe he was growing up, or he was allowing his depression, or the pain of his illness to overcome him, he gave up being the clown of the seminary. Friends who had known him over the years, remarked that something must be very wrong with Miguel, if he was not cutting up. No one really knows why Miguel changed his personality in Barcelona. The only hint we get is his comment to one friend, "I'm staying in the shade. I don't know how a Catalan[4] temperament will take my fun." He studied very seriously in Barcelona until 1924, when he was sent to Enghien, Belgium. You'd think he would have been intimidated at Enghien. He didn't speak French at all, and the French spoke Latin differently from the Spanish. But that wasn't the case at all. He reverted back to the old Miguel, if not more so. He charmed all the Europeans at that college. He became the clown again, the joker of Jesus. Everybody loved him.

---

[4]Barcelona is in the Catalan section of Spain. They consider themselves a separate country, with their own language and customs. It's hard for a foreigner to know quite how they will take to him.

But this was also a time of intense reflection for Miguel. He focused on what his apostolate would be. He would work with the people, the commoners. He didn't know if he would ever be allowed to return to his beloved Mexico; things just kept getting worse. But that could not stop him from working for the Lord! To this end, he studied the Encyclicals of Pope Leo XIII on the working man. He delved into anything of a sociological nature that might help him in his quest to do the Lord's work. It was in Enghien that he was *ordained* on August 31, 1925. At long last, after fourteen years of preparation, he was given the gift he hungered for, bringing Jesus to the people through the ministry of the priesthood.

His illness became worse. He was sent to the hospital for an operation. It didn't take. He had to submit to a second operation. For some reason, they were not able to use anesthetic for this operation. Miguel asked for a book on Canon Law. During the entire, excruciatingly painful procedure, he studied the book on Canon Law, translating it from Latin to Spanish. A third operation was performed, which didn't help much either. He was sent to the south of France to a convalescent hospital for priests. He stayed there from the spring of 1926 until June. While it didn't help his physical condition, he found ways to practice his ministry.

We have to realize that for someone like Miguel Pro, who was a *doer*, this business of being an invalid went against his nature. He had a reason for entering the seminary. It was not to sit around schools or hospitals or nursing homes for the rest of his life. He felt he had a major contribution to make to his people, and he wanted to get about the job of doing it. He was chomping at the bit. As a matter of fact, during his time in Belgium, he began working with miners. He went down into the mines with them. He walked with them; he talked with them, looking as filthy from being in the coal mine as they. He spoke to them of Jesus, of His love for the working class; he won them over. Not knowing if he would ever get back to Mexico, he wrote his provincial in Mexico, asking for permission to work with the miners in Belgium. He didn't want to be a wanderer, a shepherd without a flock. He wanted to dig his heels in, and get to work, some work, somewhere.

The response was long in coming, but when it came, it shocked him. *He was to return to Mexico!* He couldn't believe that was possible, considering conditions there. Calles had taken over as president, and the reign of terror for the Church was at its worst. All the persecution that had preceded him was like child's play, compared to what Calles was determined to do to the Church. But Miguel was relieved that it was settled. His ministry was in Mexico, and that's where he was going, no matter what.

Miguel returned to Enghien in Belgium, to prepare for his long trip back to Mexico. Then he did something, before leaving Belgium, which anyone in the world would have thought was rash, but we understand it. He had an urgency to go to Lourdes, in the south of France. Now, he had just returned from the south of France. He could have gone to Lourdes from there in a day, by train. But the urgency didn't hit him until he had returned to Belgium, in the north.

Once Our Lady had given him the mandate, nothing could stop him. He begged for the money to go, from a friend. He went without food or sleep for two days to get there and back. He arrived at Lourdes, early in the morning, and went directly to the Basilica of the Rosary. He was able to celebrate Mass at nine a.m.; from there, went to the Grotto, where he stayed *on his knees* from 10:30 a.m., until he went back to the train station for the 4:50 p.m. train to Paris. At about three p.m., an abbé came up to him. "If you continue to kneel, you will faint. Go over to the baths. There is shade there." Miguel just stayed at the Grotto, talking to his mother, our mother, Mary. He didn't *do*

Lourdes. He didn't see any of the sights, or go to the Way of the Cross, or look at the river Gave. He went there for Mother Mary. His own mother had died earlier that year. Perhaps, he was asking his Heavenly Mother for courage for the days ahead. We are sure she gave it to Miguel. He wrote of this time to the friend who gave him the money:

"I have been, therefore, to Lourdes. And if I did not visit the Calvary, nor see the river banks, nor the outward shape of the Basilica nor what it contains? All the same I went to Lourdes! That is, going there for me, was meeting my Mother in Heaven; it was to talk, to pray, to her. And I met her, I talked and prayed to her. At 8:30 (next morning) I was back in Paris and at nine said Mass in the house. I could not sleep even for an hour. Tomorrow morning at 8:30 I leave, and arrive at St. Nazaire at 5:30 in the afternoon. The liner leaves at midnight.

"My crossing will not be as hard as I thought, since Our Lady told me so. Ay, Padre, it was very painful to my wretched natural self to return to Mexico without health, without finishing my studies[5], to find my poor country ruined by its Government, not to find there any mother, that saint to whom I owe my life and for whose death, I still weep. . . But my journey to Lourdes has given me courage, and this journey I owe to the charity and delicacy of you and your family."

Miguel Pro returns to Mexico

Miguel sailed for Mexico on the feast of John the Baptist, June 24, 1926. He was joyful after his time in Lourdes. He was actually *anticipating* his return to his native land. What happened there with Mary, that day that he knelt before her at the Grotto? We know that Miguel Pro is a Saint. Did she say things that he had to hear, in order to

---

[5]He had not finished his theological studies in Enghien, Belgium

give him the strength he would need for the days ahead? Was it the same as when she appeared to James the Apostle in Zaragoza, Spain, and told him to go back to Jerusalem to be martyred? Did Mary tell Miguel Pro to go back to Mexico to be martyred? We only know what we know. She was his last contact in Europe, and he returned to Mexico, with courage and joy. Praise You Jesus for Your mother Mary.

He wrote a prayer to Mary. We don't know for sure, if it was during this time, but it might very well have been.

May I spend my days near thee. What I ask on my road of life is not the joy of Bethlehem; it is not to adore the Infant-God in thy virginal hands; I do not want to enjoy in thy humble house of Nazareth the happy presence of Jesus Christ, nor to join the choir of Angels in thy glorious Assumption. I ask to have in my life the mockery and jeers of Calvary; I ask the slow agony of thy Son; the contempt, the ignominy[6] and the infamy of the Cross. What I ask, O sorrowful Virgin, is to be close to thee, to stand near thee, to strengthen my soul by thy tears, to consummate my sacrifice by thy martyrdom, to sustain my heart by thy loneliness, to love my God and thy God by the immolation of my whole self."

Miguel Pro had a deep devotion, and intimate relationship with the Mother of God. It was the same as the saints, before him, enjoyed. Why would she not have spoken to her son of the great works that would be accomplished through him in that next year and a half in Mexico, and also of his giving up his life for his people? His prayer to her would indicate his willingness, if not his knowledge of what his life and death would be like. It's almost as if he had been on the sidelines for fifteen years, preparing for the most

---

[6]Loss of one's honor

important part of his life. And she gave him the eagerness to *go for it!*

Miguel's trip home was such a contrast to what he could look forward to, in Mexico. On board the ship, the priest and his sacraments were well accepted. He celebrated Mass, daily. The ship's officers attended Mass. First Friday had almost the entire ship of 525 passengers, taking part in the Mass. But always in the back of his mind was the fact that he was getting closer and closer to his destiny, as he joined the ranks of his fellow priests, to minister to a nation under siege.

To any human, logical mind, the question has to be asked. Of all the priests who might have been brought back to Mexico, why did they bring Miguel Pro? How could he possibly benefit the Jesuits in Mexico? He was extremely sick; he had spent most of his time in Belgium in the hospital. What could his superior have been thinking? Or did his superior have anything to do with it at all? Was he urged on by the Holy Spirit to bring this man back? Originally, the plan was to have Miguel spend his time in the mountains, giving retreats. *He didn't even know how to give retreats!* In any event, that never happened.

Even his entrance into the country was like something right out of Scripture. It was reminiscent of Peter being released from prison by the Angel[7]. When Miguel left the ship, no one asked to see his passport. He wasn't questioned by the health department. His bags were not searched. It was as if he was invisible; he walked right through them. He no sooner got off the boat, than he was brought into the capital, Mexico City. He never left again.

Mexico Clandestinamente (Mexico underground)

What was Miguel Pro coming back to? Wholesale massacre was the order of the day. While the atrocities in

---

[7]Acts of the Apostles 12: 1-12

Mexico did not reach the heights of Adolf Hitler and Josef Stalin, it wasn't because they didn't try. They just didn't have the perception of how to do it. Also, they were not trying to build a power base, as much as line their pockets with *gold*. There was no unification. All the generals were taking care of "*number one*". And if four or five or ten sets of bullies agreed on the same methods, for however long, they were allies. Once they disagreed, they turned the pistolas on each other.

The aim of these terrorists was the weak: priests, old people, young boys, girls and women. They were the easiest. They couldn't defend themselves, or so the thugs thought. The clergy, the young people, the old men and women, decided it was time to fight back. And so they did. The bishop closed all the churches in Mexico. There was an *uproar* from the people against the government. An underground youth group was formed, which became the force behind the people of the country. A boycott was begun, in protest against the persecution of the church. People just stopped buying. Banks *failed*, and closed down.

Underground printing presses churned out anti-government propaganda. Balloons were sent into the air; thousands of pamphlets filled with propaganda material, attacking the government, cascaded to earth. President Calles countered with his *iron fist*. That was all he knew. He had not an iota of an idea how to put his country back together. So, like his predecessors, he ruled with force, and piled up as much money as he could, in anticipation of the day, he would be forced to flee the country.

This vast city was to be Padre Miguel Pro's parish; these catacomb Christians were to be his parishioners. Never in two lifetimes, could anyone have asked for anything as exciting as the time Miguel had, to minister to his hundreds of thousands of parishioners, in secret, in constant hiding, running from the police. *And he relished it!* He began his ministry, the day after he arrived in the capital. First, he found his father and brothers and sisters. Then he mapped out the lay of the land, and the method of operation. Then, he went to work! Every trick he'd ever learned, every disguise, was put into use. He began playing cat and mouse with the police. He organized *Communion Stations* all over the city. They were houses where the faithful would come to receive the Lord. He never distributed less than 300 Communions. On First Fridays, the figure swelled to *1,200*, and all under the noses of the police!

Masses were celebrated all over the city, before dawn. There were private homes, different ones all the time, with watch-dogs looking out for police, passwords, being changed constantly. The rich and the poor gathered together, in these small rooms, to adore their Lord, and receive the nourishment they could only get at the hands of their priests. Those who wanted to confess, had to arrive at the appointed places earlier than the Mass, sometimes at 5:30 in the morning. It was truly a *catacomb* Church.

What about the illness that had kept Miguel Pro in hospitals and convalescent homes so much? He wrote to his Provincial, "*Here the work is continuous and hard. I can only admire what the great Chief lets me accomplish. Illness? Minor complaints? Care of them? I have not even time to think of such things; and yet I am so well and so strong that in spite of slight, very slight, setbacks, I could go on like this to the end of the world...I am ready for anything, but should there be no major objection I would ask to stay here.*"

A crack underground organization had been put into effect. The police tried to smash it. They found out who a given set of leaders might be, arrested them, tortured them and killed them. They were no sooner arrested than they were replaced by those under them. The movement never slowed down for a minute. Calles bore down *harder*, hoping this might stop the nightmare which he had caused. Every now and then, the police would find the printing presses. They smashed them to pieces. New printing operations would start up almost immediately, so smoothly, so secretly, none of the spies Calles had employed, could keep up with them.

Padre Pro wrote a letter, describing his first run-in with the police:

"In spite of the strict Secret Police surveillance (there are in Mexico more than 10,000 agents), I can baptize, marry, and take Viaticum[8] to the dying. I have even come across the dying in places where I have been called for other duties. My first incident had for its theater one of my Eucharistic Stations. It was six o'clock in the morning; I was half way through the Communion when a maid rushed in crying: 'The police! The police are there!' The faithful were terrified. 'Keep calm' I said to them; 'conceal your religious emblems and disperse into the different rooms of the house; above all, no noise.' I was wearing that day a cap and a light gray suit that from long usage now verged on dark gray. I took out a cigarette and inserted it in an enormously long holder. Then I hid the Blessed Sacrament on my breast and received the intruders.

"'There is public worship going on here,' the police said to me.

"'There is not,' I said.

"'Yes, yes. There is public worship here.'

"'Well, this time you will have to own up you have had your legs pulled.'

"'How pulled? We saw the priest come in here. Anyhow, we have orders to visit and search the premises. Follow us!'

---

[8]Viaticum - The Sacrament of Holy Communion when given to a sick or dying person. At such times, the Communion Fast is waved.

"*'I like that! That is the last straw! Follow you? And by what right can you try and make me? Show me your warrants. However, if you are bent on it, go all over the house and if you find public worship going on, come and tell me so that I can hear Mass.'*

"*They started going over the house and to prevent worse happening I went with them telling them beforehand what they would find behind every door. But unhappily it was the first time I had seen the other rooms, so that it happened to me to announce a bedroom and to fall into a study.... 'This is a work-place' - and it turned out to be a dressing room...But they did not find the Curé[9] and the clever Secret Service then set themselves to guard the door of the house; I left them, pretexting my occupations, which alone prevented me from staying with them to assist at the capture of the priest in question who mocked their vigilance with so much cynicism. I went at once and distributed Communion at other 'stations' and that done I returned to see them (the police) but there was still no Curé...*"

Why do we have to be in such danger of losing our Church before we stand up to defend it? Why does it have to be taken away from us, in order for us not to take it for granted? The Mexican Catholics, who had been apathetic about their Church, now stood up for it. The bishops and priests could see them joining as "*one*", becoming stronger and stronger, against this attack by the government.

One bishop, who was arrested for the statement, said at Mass, "Let Catholics repair their sins of *omission*, affirm their civic rights; let them courageously resist the destroyers of the laws of humanity....Let all, old and especially the young, sacrifice pleasure and fight the fight of God, never retreating until all confiscated liberties are reconquered." In days gone

---

[9]French for priest

by, a homily like this would have gotten yawns for a reaction. But at this time, and in this place, they rose to action. The response was instantaneous and magnificent. They came out of their lethargy. They were there; give them something to do.

Miguel was put in charge of a group of leaders. With two others, one of whom was a young engineer named Luis Segura[10], they set up a network of young people who would give talks to large groups. In short order, they had over 150 members. Miguel was their advisor, spiritual and corporal. They received advice on all matters to do with the Faith. They were a powerful group of young men.

It was this excitement, this drive to stand up for their beliefs, under pain of death that brought about the balloon incident we mentioned before. On December 4, 1926, *six hundred balloons*, about three yards in diameter, were sent floating over the city, at about noon. Each balloon carried the symbol of the youth organization, and the word *Boycott* on it, both of which made president Calles' blood boil. This was followed by thousands of multi-colored pamphlets, falling from the buildings, with caustic anti-government comments. The people ran all over, trying to catch the pamphlets. The police, in turn, ran all over, trying to catch the people. Wholesale arrests took place. Although Padre Pro was not known by the police, his brother Humberto was, and so one evening, the police arrested Humberto, Miguel, his other brother Roberto, and a host of young men.

Miguel was not upset about this until, once inside the jail, a lieutenant commented, "Tomorrow we shall have Mass." Miguel could feel a pang of fear run through him. Had they found him out? All the young people shouted as one, "Mass?"

---

[10]Luis Segura was executed with Miguel Pro

The lieutenant answered, "Yes, for there is a priest among you."

This was a moment of truth for Miguel. He had played over in his mind thousands of scenarios of how his final capture might take place. Somehow, it wasn't like what was happening. He had to hold up. "Dear God, help me," he prayed. "Don't let me weaken now."

The lieutenant continued, "He is a Miguel Agustín".

Miguel stood up. His legs were shaking, but he couldn't let his voice crack. "Stop!" he said. "That Miguel Agustín is I. But it is as probable that I shall say Mass tomorrow as that I shall sleep on a mattress tonight."

"And what about this?" the lieutenant pointed to the name Pro.

"That only means my surname; it is not the abbreviation of *presbítero*." In Spanish, and Mexican, a priest uses the term Pbro. after his name, which means presbítero, or priest. Miguel laughed off the accusation, and was able to get out of the prison. But it was too close for comfort. His superiors caught wind of what had happened, and suggested he lay low for awhile. He bravely shrugged off their suggestion, until twenty five days later, the police burst into his apartment again, and wanted to arrest everyone. He begged, pleaded, and finally bribed the officer in charge. But he knew he and all his relatives had to leave the apartment and not come back. When his superiors heard about this, they changed their suggestion to an *order* to stay out of sight for awhile.

Miguel managed to keep himself under cover for two months, but he was itching to get back into action. He wrote a heart-rending plea to his provincial, which could not possibly have been turned down. In it, he said,

"...*folks have such need of spiritual help; every day I hear people have died without the Sacraments; there are no more priests to defy danger; from obedience or fear they stay home. If I gave my little contribution of a grain of sand, as before, it would be to expose myself; but to do it with discretion and measure does not seem to me rash...Between rashness and fear there is a middle course; and between excess of prudence and audaciousness, there is a middle course. They fear for my life! My life?...But what is that? Would it not be saving it to lose it for my brethren?*

"Certainly one must not expose one's self idiotically. But the sons of Loyola!..."

He got them with that one. Actually, Miguel hit them where they lived. By reminding them of their fearless founder, Ignatius Loyola, a military man, who laughed in the face of danger or death, he gave them no choice but to put him back in action. A lot could be said about Miguel's statements in contrast to his actions. He talked about discretion, *"between rashness and fear... between excess of prudence and audaciousness... expose one's self idiotically."* A case could be made as to whether he practiced what he preached, because he put himself right back in the middle of the battlefield. He went into prisons, disguised, "for they are brimful of Catholics," and laughed at how he got away with it. He walked around with a cane, as a cripple, with a police dog, and on a bicycle. His mastery of facial contortions made him the man of many faces. *He was playing Russian Roulette!*

None of this frightened him. What did make him extremely nervous was giving retreats. *"To tell the truth I was rather frightened; it is a ministry which I had never exercised."* He started with old ladies. But he wasn't right for them. Their moaning made him want to burst out laughing. He was afraid he would not be able to contain himself. So he chose, instead, fifty *drivers*. We're not sure if they were truck drivers, or motorcycle drivers. It took place in a yard. They surrounded Miguel. He was dressed as a mechanic.

Typical of the danger he put himself into, was when he gave a retreat to eighty *government employees*. They had been brainwashed pretty good. When he started with them, they believed the soul was mortal, and there was no hell. At the end of the retreat, all of them received Communion, and he counted twelve conversions. But that's not the point. These people were working for the *enemy*, the government. What would it have taken for any of them to have turned him in? Suppose one of the eighty had not been convinced, not converted. What would have happened to him then? But his greatest fear was not of getting caught, but not giving a good retreat.

The retreats were organized in a very systematic way. Usually, they happened in the following way. Some courageous Catholic ladies would gather a group of friends, and the exercises would be given in different houses; usually beginning at daybreak. In the evening, the priest would give the location for the following day, always, always a different house. Tickets were issued. You couldn't get in without a ticket. When they went, it was like they were attending a business meeting. The Rosary would be recited, and the priest gave his homily. All of this, keep in mind, was done with full knowledge that any minute the police might break in and arrest all of them.

While it sounded very romantic, and adventurous, and most likely was, there was a price to pay. The police had thousands of spies, out looking for information as to who was running these things, and who organized them. It was not unusual for a leader to be sold out by what he thought was a good friend and faithful follower. We're not sure if the pay was good, or if the informant was intimidated; but the results were the same. Leaders were arrested all the time, tortured and murdered.

On Good Friday of 1927, Miguel was giving a retreat to a large group of people in the capital. A young man, Manuel

Bonilla, aged twenty three, had been arrested for being one of the members of the youth group. He was a typographer, which made him suspect of working with the underground printing press. On this day, they took him and hung him from a tree, arms and legs attached, in the form of a cross. This was done right near Mexico City. They kept him like that from noon to three o'clock, at which time, he was taken down from the "cross", and shot to death. He, like Our Lord Jesus, had been sold out for money by a farmer, with whom he had had dinner. The parallels are incredible.

Padre Pro wrote many letters, chronicling his activities in his country, during this terrible time. But he wrote as he lived, joyful, cheerful, always the joker. Very often, we don't really get a true picture of the outrages that took place. We want to share just a few actual experiences.

A young girl led a revolt in a small town, Ciudad Victoria. She and some other brave women had been able to run off a small group of soldiers. A regiment was sent back to the town to deal with her. They arrested her, insisting she shout "Long live Calles." She refused. They asked where the priests were. She remained silent. They began to beat her with a whip. Before they were through with her, they ripped each of her fingers off her hand, then cut her arms off in pieces. As she went through this torture, and even up to her death, she kept up the cry, "Viva Cristo Rey", *Long live Christ the King.*

One old priest was totally deaf. He was accused of conspiracy. He couldn't hear the charges, so he couldn't respond to them. He was shot to death, immediately. Another priest was shot in his vestments as he celebrated Mass.

But not all the soldiers were animals. One priest was being led to his death. He couldn't walk too well, so an officer offered to let him ride on his horse. The priest refused. The officer said, "I cannot shoot an innocent man."

The priest replied, "My poor friend, you will only expose your own life if you do not." The officer refused to shoot the priest. He was shot *alongside* the priest.

A young lawyer in Guadalajara, Luis Padilla, was arrested and tortured for six hours. He was hung up by his thumbs, and stabbed with bayonets. He watched his companions shot before his eyes. His teeth were crushed. By the time he was taken down, he was a mass of bleeding meat. The soldiers then shot him in front of his young wife. When his body was brought to the cemetery, three workmen there praised the young man for his courage. They were arrested and shot.

These are just a few of the thousands of atrocities committed by brother against brother, in the name of God knows what. Miguel Pro never wrote about these things. There can be any number of reasons why he didn't. Possibly he wanted to lift up the spirits of those to whom he wrote, by focusing on the positives. Another might have been that he was afraid he might be called out of the battle field. Very possibly, knowing the humility of this great saint, he didn't want people to be aware of just how brave he was, in the face of the same retaliation, his colleagues had received. He would not make a *big deal* about the ongoing dangers he faced daily. He didn't want us to know he was a Saint. But naturally, God had other ideas.

Miguel feeds the poor

The economic state of Mexico was deplorable. Unemployment was high; poverty was a way of life. Many of the people Miguel ministered to, belonged to the poverty class. In addition, many of the young men who could *work*, were off in the state of Jalisco, *fighting* to protect the people against the government hoodlums. He began finding ways to feed and clothe them, and put a roof over their heads. He kept a set of figures in his head, of what was needed, and for whom. Just when he would be ready to do some heavy duty begging, he would get hundreds of pounds of sugar, chocolate, biscuits, wine, whatever he needed. People would come up to him, offering him money for the work he was doing. He'd tell them, "Send fifty piasters[11] to...., twenty five piasters to ....., and another twenty five piasters to ....."

Because his ministry was so diverse, rich as well as poor, he was able to appeal to the *rich* to help the *poor*. He was also not beyond selling goods at prices higher than they were worth, to provide money for food and clothing. He once wrote to his Provincial,

"May Jesus be praised! I have not time to breathe, I am in work up to the neck, giving food to the hungry - and there are many. I go off like a water-spout and with a light foot (the privilege usually of pickpockets), so much so that I do not worry when I get a message like this: the family says they have nothing in the larder (cupboard); there are twelve of them; their underclothes are in bits; three of them are in bed. In general my purse is as flat as the spiritual part of Calles, but that is not worth a thought, because the Overseer of Heaven is so magnificent!"

He even made a game of finding and distributing goods to the poor. His *staff* consisted of about six good men and women, who weren't working. He called the women "*The Section of Investigation and Supply*" in front of people, but among themselves, "*The Beggars on the Make.*" The men he called "*The Directing Committee*" in public, and "*The Supply Blackmailers*" in private. These volunteers begged from anybody and everybody, in a way that was almost like blackmail. The people were shamed into giving to the poor.

Very often, Miguel would be seen running around the streets of Mexico City, carrying sacks of goods. He had no

---

[11]Denomination of money, possibly a dollar

problem carrying live chickens and turkeys to his clandestine destinations. People laughed at him, called him crazy. He kept going at breakneck speed. One time, he got on a bus with six live chickens. Through his natural comedy, he got away with anything. But while he put up a false bravado, he was embarrassed by begging. It was one of the most difficult things he could do, so naturally, he threw himself into it with a fervor. *"...though cereals are abundant this is due to my crimson face. Because you cannot imagine the shame there is in begging, always begging...Happily that He for Whom one does it is not parsimonious (penny-pinching). May He be ever blessed!"*

The Way of the Cross

Miguel Pro had become very popular, very famous. At the same time, he had become notorious and infamous. Calles wanted him dead. Warrants were issued for his arrest. They were out to get him! There was, however, a major problem. They didn't know what he looked like. He was always able to slip by the police. His plastic face enabled him to disguise himself in so many different ways, and his flair for the theatrical gave him the inclinations to wear the most flamboyant costumes. But Calles was adamant. The cat and mouse game intensified.

There is a tradition about Padre Pro. We're told that it was given in testimony, at the process of his Beatification. We really believe it is so in keeping with whom the man was, and how loved he was by Our Lord Jesus, we feel it important to share it with you.

He celebrated Mass every day in secret. On the day before he was arrested for the last time, he was celebrating Mass in a home, attended by a small number of people. It is said that during the Consecration of the Mass, as he held the Consecrated Host, a brilliant light surrounded his entire body. His vestments were so bright that people had to turn their heads away. His face and hands were gleaming; he levitated[12]. He was transfigured as Our Lord Jesus on Mount Tabor before him. We like to think of this as a *Miracle of the Eucharist* of Mexico.

A plot had been hatched. We don't know if it was directed against Miguel Pro, or former president Obregón. Some think it was Calles' way of killing two birds with one stone. Obregón had been motoring in the area of Chapultepec, when a car came alongside him, and bombs were thrown at his car. He escaped with minor injuries, but his guards chased the four terrorists, who had run from their car. Two escaped. One was shot dead, and the other through the temple. He was brought to the hospital. His wife stayed with him until he died, and testified he never regained consciousness. However, the police claimed an undercover policeman got into his hospital room, disguised his voice as the assailant's brother-in-law, and spoke to him. The assailant supposedly put the blame on Padre Pro, his brother Humberto, and Luis Segura.

Miguel and his family knew nothing about the plot. As a matter of fact, he had felt somewhat of a lull in the police intensity to get him. He had even moved back into his father's house. When he heard about what had happened to Obregón, he was sure it would keep the police occupied for some time, and they wouldn't be bothering him. The lady, at whose house Miguel had stayed, prior to moving back with his father and brothers, was arrested. The police were looking for the Jesuit priest. Somehow, they managed to trip her up, and she told them where Miguel was. Early the next morning, before anyone was up, the police raided Pro's father's house, and arrested Miguel, Humberto, and his other brother, Roberto. They were all carted off to jail.

---

[12]Levitated - to rise and float in the air

Miguel actually thought what the police was doing was *hysterical.* There was no way, he thought, the plot against Obregón could be connected to him or his brothers. They were nowhere *near* the scene of the crime when it happened. So he went about his normal routine of clowning around and joking. He made friends with the guards, gave them cigarettes. He even converted one while he was in prison.

They stayed *incommunicado* for three days. There was questioning and brow-beating, but no charges were made, and no trial was set. Miguel insisted upon a trial, to prove that he and the others were indeed innocent. Meanwhile the head of the prison, General Cruz, issued a statement that all three had *confessed* to the crime. Miguel had supposedly been one of the organizers of the plot, while Humberto and Segura had been in the car from which the bombs were thrown. But the prisoners knew nothing of any of this.

Article 20 of the Mexican Constitution, (which President Calles had written) states that within 48 hours, a prisoner must be able to make a declaration of his innocence or guilt. At the end of 72 hours, the judge decides whether to free the accused, free them under bond, or give a formal order of imprisonment for the accused. None of this ever happened in the case of Miguel Pro and his companions.

On a parallel course, former president Obregón was conducting his own inquiry. Not for a minute did he think the priest or his friends had anything to do with the attempt on his life. He was *convinced* it was political, which it might well have been. But he was getting mixed messages from the investigators. He sent his lawyer to the prison to get to the bottom of it. There was nothing in the way of a police report, other than one made prior to the investigation. "And what does the chief of police, General Cruz, think of the guilt of the prisoners?" the lawyer asked.

The secretary said, "The Pro brothers have not confessed any connection to the crime, and we have no proof against them."

But the following morning, without benefit of an examining judge, or lawyer, or anything, sentence on Miguel Pro and his three companions, was to be carried out. Keep in mind that none of what was going on was known by Miguel Pro. He and his friends were sure they would speak to a judge, or *someone*, and this whole charade would come to an end. This was not the first time he had been in prison, nor would it be his last. It was just another nail in the Cross.

He was most likely relieved when the guard came and told him and his brother Humberto to follow him. Miguel bounced up, leaving his vest behind. When the guard sent him back to get his vest, something clicked in Miguel's mind. Possibly a sinking feeling went through him. Was this it? Was it his time to follow in the footsteps of his Savior, to walk his Way of the Cross? He went back into the cell, and put on his vest. His brother Roberto, helped him with it. Miguel squeezed his arm in a way that shot fear into Roberto's heart. He looked at his brother. The eyes were knowing. Roberto panicked. Miguel turned to the other prisoners in the cells, and with a bravado, said "*Good-by my sons, my brothers.*"

The guard, Mazcorro, asked Miguel's forgiveness for his part in what was about to happen. "*Not only do I pardon you, but I thank you. I will pray for you.*" Then he and his brother, without any handcuffs, followed the guard out onto the courtyard. Miguel went out first.

The cold, biting air of the November morning sent a chill across his face. His hair blew in the wind. The sun was shining brightly. It was a *glorious* day. Miguel surveyed the situation in the courtyard. It was as he feared. Soldiers were lined up for a firing squad! All the eyewitnesses, various generals and dignitaries, as well as members of the press,

Above: *He went down on his knees, folded his arms, and closed his eyes. He prayed for the courage to be strong.*
Below: **He held a crucifix in his left hand, a rosary in his right. His last words were, *"Viva Cristo Rey."***

came to attention as they saw for the first time, the famous Jesuit, who had made such fools of President Calles and his entire police force for so long. Cameras began clicking photos for posterity of this man, who looked more like a student than a conspirator. Miguel walked straight as a rod into the center of the courtyard. It was as if he was running the show, as he had always done. He was asked his last request. He asked to pray. He went down on his knees, folded his arms, and closed his eyes.

What did Miguel say to the Lord on this, the most important moment of his life? Did he ask for strength and courage, to set an example not only for his brothers, but for all those who were yet to come? Did he ask for help from his founder, the fearless Ignatius Loyola? Did he speak to Mary? Did he ask her to help him now? He needed her so much. He wanted to do this right. He wanted to give glory to her Son, Jesus, and to her. He wanted them to be proud of him. He wanted all the martyrs before him, to look on him with pride. He wanted, by his last simple act, to make the plight of his countrymen, worthwhile.

He stood up. His communication with Jesus and his Heavenly Family gave Miguel the strength he needed. Eyewitnesses report, his face was aglow, shining as if a reflection of the sun. He raised his arm to his executioners in the form of a blessing. He shouted in a loud, strong voice, *"May God have mercy on you! May God bless you! Lord, Thou knowest that I am innocent! With all my heart I forgive my enemies!"*

The command was given the soldiers. "Prepare!"

From his breast pocket, Miguel took out a brass crucifix that he was given on the day of his ordination. In his other hand, he held the rosary he had gotten in Lourdes. He held both outstretched, at arms length, in the form of the Cross. He said, in a voice which was not loud, but could be heard by everyone in the assembly, *"Viva Cristo Rey."*

"Fire!" The sound from the blast of the rifles, ricocheted against the walls of the courtyard, shattering the tense silence. Bullets ripped through Miguel's chest, pushing him backward, but he remained standing. Cameras went off like crazy, catching the image of the dead man, who wouldn't go down. Finally, he slumped into a heap on the ground. The captain came over to him, and shot him in the head, to end his torture. Miguel Pro was dead, but never forgotten.

A Martyr for Mexico

Word had rumbled through the underground of *Catholic Mexico* that the priest was to be murdered. Peasants, business people, hundreds, thousands of people gathered outside the prison, waiting to see what would happen. When the word went through the crowd that Padre Pro had been killed, seething anger against the government filled all of them. They began shouting and screaming. The police formed a barricade. Machine guns were set up on top of the buildings. They didn't know what they might be in for.

After the other three, Miguel's brother Humberto, Luis Segura, and a young boy, Tirado, who had been unfortunate enough to be an eyewitness on the attack of General Obregón, were killed, the bodies were brought to a van outside. The crowd moved in slowly, but in short order, surrounded the van, so that it could not move. The driver started up the engine, revved it to frighten the bystanders to move aside, but no one budged. The driver didn't know what to do. The crowd knelt in front of the van, and prayed. Finally, the van was able to move very slowly through the streets, to a hospital, where Miguel's father claimed the bodies of the two brothers. The fifth intended victim, *Roberto Pro*, was saved from execution.

The bodies were brought back to Miguel's father's house, where they lay that day, November 23, and the next. Roberto had been told he would be able to come home to venerate the bodies of his brothers, and so the Blessed Sacrament was brought to the house. They put the pyx on Miguel's chest. Roberto was not released that night, so the Blessed Sacrament remained on his brother's chest.

Thousands of people filed by the bodies of the two martyrs. They kissed the caskets, touched the brothers, as if touching saints, with linen, rosaries, and other objects. *Miracles* began to descend on the people of Mexico while the bodies were still warm. An old woman, who had been blind for six years, had wanted to pay her last respects to Padre Pro, but couldn't leave her house, because of her blindness. A friend in her home suggested she pray to Padre Pro for recovery of her sight. She claimed that no sooner had she finished her prayer than her eyesight returned to her. The friend who had made the suggestion, couldn't believe what she was saying. He asked her to read a newspaper, which she was able to do without any problem.

A woman in great financial problem, had given all her papers to Miguel to try to help her. When she learned of his death, she ran to her lawyer, not knowing what to do now that the documents were probably lost forever. She told her lawyer what she had done, and that Padre Pro had been shot. He said to her, "*That's not possible. Not ten minutes ago, he came himself and brought me your papers.*" Miguel Pro was still in rare form, only now he wasn't encumbered by space and time. Miracles abounded from that time on, in the tradition of St. Thérèse, the Little Flower of Lisieux.

Tribute to a Saint

Perhaps the greatest miracle was his funeral procession. Miguel Pro, from Heaven, gave each of his followers a special gift, *courage*. The caskets were carried down to the hearses at 3:30 p.m., on November 24, for the procession to the cemetery. Miguel had a white hearse. Masses of people were on hand to follow the hearses through the city. But as the hearses progressed, more and more people followed. They got off streetcars, and joined the crowd. Five hundred automobiles formed walls to block crossing traffic; the crowd processed between the blockade of cars, on the busy Paseo de la Reforma. More than twenty thousand people marched down the main street of Mexico City, pushing their way past soldiers with fixed bayonets. The streets were carpeted with flowers. Balconies all along the procession route, were filled with mourners.

But the climate was not at all that of mourners. They were jubilant. As the crowd swelled, the voices, as one, began singing, "*Viva Cristo Rey*", "Long live the martyrs! Long live the Pope! Long live our bishops! Long live our priests! Long live religion!" It reached fever pitch; it never ended. After the procession got out of the main part of the city, the coffins were taken out of the hearses; men took turns carrying them the rest of the way. When the throngs in the automobiles saw this, they left their cars, and went the rest of the way on foot. The body of Miguel was interred in the Jesuit vault, while his brother Humberto, was buried nearby. All the followers deposited flowers at both grave sites. It was like two mountains of flowers. The people broke into song, and continued late into the night, until the cemetery doors were finally closed. Miguel had never witnessed such homage paid to a human being. Now he was the center of it.

God will have His way. If Miguel Pro and his fellow victims had been judged guilty of attempted murder of the ex-president Obregón[13], they would have been put in prison

---

[13]As far as Obregón was concerned, whoever wanted him killed *(Calles?)*, got their wish less than eight months after the attempt on his life, which cost Miguel Pro his life. A month after having been re-elected president, Obregón was victim of an assassination plot in July of 1928, while dining with friends at a restaurant.

for eight to twelve years. Most likely, they would have died in prison, or in any event, never be heard from again.

But President Calles had to do it his way! He executed Miguel and his companions, and *photographed* the murder. Then he made sure the photos were *plastered* all over the newspapers, as a stern warning to anyone who would dare to disobey him.

What he managed to do was create a national hero, a martyr, a role model so strong that the people of Mexico would rally behind the banner of this young Jesuit, until all brothers and sisters could enjoy religious freedom in this land of 97% Catholics and 99% Guadalupeans.

We really believe, however, it was God's plan all along to raise Miguel Pro as a *martyr* for Mexico, a national hero, and a *Saint*, whose light blazes across the sky of his homeland. There were many priests executed under Calles' regime, some fifty. There were over five hundred lay people tortured and murdered by his home-grown Gestapo. Why was this one man, Padre Miguel Agustín Pro, singled out as martyr, hero and saint?

We've said it from the beginning, and the Lord bears us out. In times of crisis, *God sends us Saints and Other Powerful Men and Women in our Church.* God gave us Miguel Pro, not only for the Mexican people, but for God-loving people everywhere, to let us know loud and clear, *God is in charge!*

There are many messages in the story of our modern-day martyr, Miguel Pro. Perhaps the greatest lesson, the most important truth we will ever learn, is Blessed Miguel Pro's battle cry, the victory cry of Catholics everywhere, for all the world to hear, *"Viva Cristo Rey!"*

Left:
Maxmilian Kolbe,
man of many titles,
Saint of World War II,
Holy Prisoner,
Saint of Concentration
Camps, Saint of the Press,
Saint of Aviation,
Saint of Progress,
Saint of the Poor,
but above all,
"a Catholic Priest."

Right:
"Good-by, friends; we will meet
again where there is justice,"
was joined by another sobbing,
"Long live Poland!"
"Good-by! Good-by,
my dear wife; good-by,
my dear children,
already orphans of your
father," cried out Sergeant
Francis Gajowniczek, (right)
the man for whom
Fr. Maxmilian Kolbe
gave his life.

Left:
**Maximilian Kolbe
as a young Franciscan.**
*"I knew right from the beginning...
he would die a martyr."*
**These were his mother's words
to his fellow Franciscans ,
after he died.**

Right:
*Father Kolbe working
at his desk on the
Knight of the Immaculata.*
Below:
*Within a decade after
beginning the
City of the Immaculate,
over 800 brothers joined him
in his publication.*

St. Maxmilian Kolbe

"I am a Catholic Priest."

How does a man give up his life for someone he never met before? This *man* has been called by many titles: Saint of World War II, Holy Prisoner, Saint of Concentration Camps, Saint of the Press, Saint of Aviation, Saint of Progress, Saint of the Poor. But I think the one he would prefer is "Catholic Priest."

The devil uses any means to kill us. For so many years, in the United States, the Polish people have been the brunt of very poor ethnic jokes. It is true, every new group coming into our free society inherits the suffering, the minority group before them endured. It's like being a freshman in college. The only difference is, growing up out of the persecution is swifter, the freshman only degraded for a year not a lifetime. It gets so bad that the minority, to become one of "the guys," often pokes fun at *itself!* And then, most tragically, everyone believes it and the world is cheated of an extraordinary people.

But God loves us! God sent us a *Pole*, a charismatic, powerful, intelligent, talented, loving leader, our Pope. Through him and the interest the world has in him, we have become aware of the history of a brave, faithful, bright, true people of God. We find ourselves getting upset when someone tells an *innocent*, cutting joke about a *Polack*. It's like they're attacking us!

I would like to dedicate this chapter to our Pope and a young man whose name is *Robert Ziminsky*. He happens to be our grandson. We have tried to share with Robert, the centuries of *Italians* in his life who make up part of the fine man he is becoming. Now, Rob, we pray this will bring you a part of your ancestry we knew nothing about. Through the life of this Polish, Franciscan priest, we bring you hope in what man can be, and the courage to bring that hope to others.

It is with much thanksgiving to our Lord and His Mother, Mary Immaculate, *Niepokalanow* who play such a great and integral role in this chapter, that we begin our walk alongside our brother Maxmilian Kolbe.

The boy and his family

Maxmilian Kolbe, or *Raymond* as he was called when baptized, was born into a divided Poland. As had happened before and since, poor Poland, unfortunately located, had been a battleground, and the two powers, Russia and Austria, took what they wanted, leaving nothing for Poland itself. But to a Pole, it was and always would be Poland.

Like with most of their compatriots, life was hard for Father Kolbe's parents. They worked hard and long hours. They never complained; instead, they considered hardships and hard work as a necessary road to eternal life. As a young girl, his mother Maria pleaded with the Lord, she be allowed to become a *religious*. When she became resigned, she couldn't enter a convent because she didn't have the necessary dowry, she prayed: "O Lord, I do not want to impose my will on you if Your designs are different. Give me, at least, a husband who does not curse, who does not drink, who does not go to the tavern to enjoy himself. This, O Lord, I ask you unconditionally."

God answered Maria's prayers and she married Jules Kolbe, a fervent Catholic, everything she had prayed for. In addition, he was a leader in the Third Order Franciscans!

The young couple started a workshop in their one-room flat. In this all-purpose living, sleeping, working, praying room (with an altar in the middle of the room), a baby destined to become a Saint, Raymond (later, Father

Maxmilian) was born on January 8, 1894. His brother Francis was the first to be born, on July 25, 1892, then Raymond, and then a third son Joseph, and yet another child Valentine, who died in infancy.

The living quarters became too small for the growing family, and so they moved to a nearby town where they not only got a larger home, they opened a store! You can see the hard-working, progressive foundation upon which God would build the man Father Maxmilian.

Even as a boy, Father Kolbe was known as gentle and kind; so much so, they nicknamed him *"Marmalade."* His mother later said of her son, he was always quick in obeying, the *most* obedient of all her sons. He kept their home spotlessly clean while his parents worked, never complaining. He was the first to bring a switch, to be punished with, when he had been involved in some harmless prank. His parents not only stressed the spiritual, praying and going to Mass together, but the physical. Their father toughened the boys by bringing them into the snow covered yard to play *barefoot.* Sounds a little extreme? This would help and prepare Father Maxmilian for his later years, and what he would have to face.

Two Crowns - one White and one Red

"I knew right from the beginning...he would die a martyr." These were his mother's words to his fellow Franciscans after he died.

She said, one day, when he was about ten years old, she had become displeased with him, and as we all foolishly do, said, "Raymond, who knows what will become of you?" He didn't answer, but she began to notice a change coming about in him. He spent more and more time praying in front of a small hidden altar. She noticed tears in his eyes as he raised them toward the Crucifix.

His mother became worried. He was so quiet, always going off to be by himself. She approached him; worried, she appealed to him to tell her everything! Trying to keep the tears from spilling from his eyes, he told her that when she had scolded him, he went to the Madonna and asked Her what was to become of him. She appeared to him, holding two crowns in Her hands. She told him, one meant he would remain *pure*, and the other he would be a *martyr*. His Madonna asked him which one he chose. He told his mother, he had chosen *both*!

Raymond finished his elementary education, but could not go on to high school. Under Russian domination, the cost was too prohibitive for a family like the Kolbes, so they decided the eldest son would go for the higher education. It was determined Maxmilian would remain at home and take care of things there. And this, he did, with an abundance of joy, even to the point of surprising his mother with one of her favorite dishes, when she wearily arrived home from work.

Although he was a normal boy, loving to play with other youngsters, joining in with their loud boisterous laughter, when he was in church he was always respectful and reverent, aware of where he was and Who was there. He knew *that* God, and loved Him, serving Mass *willingly* whenever he could.

The Making of the Franciscan

His father, a Franciscan Tertiary had given his son the life of St. Francis to read. As young Raymond began to know the little "*Poor One*," he became attracted not only to him but to the Franciscan friars in a nearby village.

The Franciscan church of that village was dedicated to St. Anthony. After pilgrims venerated Saint Anthony, they would go into the crypt of Venerable Father Raphael Chylinski.

The venerable Father Raphael's life was a glowing example of what happens when the Virgin captures a man's heart. He had formerly been an officer in the Polish Army. The ravages of war and epidemics had eaten away at the people of Poland. This soldier showed such tireless compassion and charity to the helpless victims, the faithful continued coming to him, long after his death, only now in *veneration*. His deeds lived after him, and now would touch the young boy Raymond. He was fascinated by the life of this soldier who had given up the sword for the sacred habit of a priest.

Like Saint Anthony before him, Raymond was quite humbly hidden in the kitchen. One day, this was to change! His mother sent him to the pharmacy to fetch some medicine for a sick woman she was tending. When Raymond asked for the medicine by its *Latin* name, the pharmacist asked him how he knew the powder's Latin name. Raymond explained, he was learning Latin from the local parish priest.

The pharmacist asked the boy to tell him more about himself. Raymond told him about the situation at home, that his brother was the only one the family could afford to send to high school. When Raymond finished with, "*My brother will be a priest. I can do my part by staying at home,*" the pharmacist made a decision, "Come to me and I will give you lessons. By the end of the year, you will have caught up with your brother, and then you can both continue." At the end of the year, Raymond and his brother were promoted together and went on to business school.

His parents did not share the pharmacist's confidence or enthusiasm. Raymond becoming a businessman, ridiculous! His mother's vote, "When you are a merchant, I will be a queen," was seconded by his father's, "And I will be a bishop." Of course, time will prove his parents *and* the pharmacist right, but in God's way and timetable.

In Northern Poland, under Russian domination, the Franciscan Orders were suppressed. All friaries were closed down, but two; they were left open so the old Franciscans, there, could *die* off. But in the south of Poland, under the Austro-Hungarian Empire the Franciscans were flourishing. There was a revival of the Spirit and the superiors in the southern part of Poland believed it was the time to *reopen* the friaries.

It was Easter, Day of our Lord's Resurrection, 1907, two Franciscan missionaries announced the opening of the *new Seminary*. The thorn planted in Raymond's heart, the day our Lady had offered him two crowns, was blooming. He saw, in the missionaries' words and in the life that Francis had passed down, the two crowns of his Lady. He and his brother Francis went right up to the Franciscans and asked how they could enter the Order.

They were on fire! But they were told they would have to wait and finish out their school year in *Business*. In October of 1907, the two brothers arm in arm, said good-by to their parents and left for the Friary in Lwów.

Raymond proved to be intelligent; he was diligent in his studies of the humanities; he excelled in Mathematics; he progressed rapidly but never at the cost of his prayer life. All was going better than well, when on the night before his investiture, he was attacked by doubts and indecision. Was he supposed to enter the religious life? Was *this* what the Lady meant by the two crowns? Prostrating himself before Her, he promised to fight for Her. Would his "*Mamina*," as he called her, please tell him if this is what She wanted for him.

We read that at this time in his life, Raymond was suffering from *scruples*. Believing he was unfit for religious life, he would not accept his religious habit. He even tried to convince his brother Francis not to take this step.

This time, his *earthly* mother came to the rescue of her son. She had been living with the Benedictine Sisters[1] in Lwów and had just happened to visit him. We do not know *what* his mother said; but with all doubts gone, on the 4th of September, 1910, Raymond became *Friar Maxmilian*. All his life, he remembered this pivotal part of his life with gratitude to his mother.

His brother Francis left the Order! Friar Maxmilian grieved! All the memories they shared came rushing to the surface of his head and heart. He was remembering: how they had gone to school *together*; the day they had received First Holy Communion *together*; the days and nights, their hopes and fears, they'd lived through *together* in the novitiate; and the day they made simple vows, *together*. He cried, remembering: how *Francis* had not weakened when Maxmilian tried to convince him to leave the novitiate, the night before their investiture, how *he* had been strong when he (Maxmilian) had been weak.

But then he became consoled; his Heavenly *Mamina*, had sent his earthly Mama to him, to prevent *him* from leaving when he wanted to run. She had taken over in his life. She loved him! She was preparing him for his two crowns. Francis had been a part of Her plan. He would pray for this special brother all his life, here and beyond.

On September 5, 1911, Maxmilian made his simple profession, the vows of poverty, chastity and obedience, according to the Rule of St. Francis and the Constitution of the Friars Conventual.

---

[1]Not long after all her sons left home to join the Franciscans, she asked permission of her husband to follow her childhood desire to enter the religious life. This done, she entered the Benedictine Sisters temporarily, in Lwów, so she could be near her sons.

Friar Maxmilian sets out for the Eternal City

Maxmilian waited in Lwów for another year before going to the "*professed house,*" where the newly professed go to complete their studies in philosophical and theological studies.   When he finally arrived, he was surprised and a little overwhelmed. Instead of completing his studies there, he had been chosen, one of seven candidates, to go to the International Seraphic College, in Rome, to pursue his studies there! His health always having been poor, he at first was able to convince his superiors to take his name off the list. Later that day, fearing he might be blocking the Will of the Lord, he went before his superior, "*Father, do with me as you wish.*"

What the superior wished was, "Well son, go to Rome," and Maxmilian was off to the *Eternal City*, where he remained for seven years. He said, he saw nothing in Rome, but the Pope, "*all the rest was foreign to me.*" It was not that he did not see the splendid ancient ruins of Rome's grand history, and appreciate it. It was, he was so repulsed by all the decadence he saw. It was like ancient Rome revisited, the anything goes Rome. All the years of hate against Mother Church and her priests, had left its mark on poor Rome. It was as if the Tiber that flows through Rome had polluted its inhabitants and they had died. They were back into the Rome before Christ, before Peter and Paul.

Maxmilian looked around. Where was Christ? Jesus' words, "*Who do you say that I am?*" reverberated through his head. Who do *they* say You are, my Lord? And so, Maxmilian kept his eyes on Vatican Hill. *That*, and the protection of his *Immaculata*, would bring him through to his Apostolate and to his two crowns.

On November 1st, 1914, Friar Maxmilian made his final vows. On that day, he asked that the name of *Mary* be added to his religious name. This day when he consecrated himself totally to God and His Provident care, this was his way of going to Him in the arms of Mary.

On April the 28th, 1918, he was ordained in the Church of S. Andrea delle Valle. He celebrated his *first* Mass at the altar of the miracle recalling the apparition of the Virgin Mary, which brought about the conversion of the Christian-hater Alphonse Ratisbonne[2].

When he wrote to his mother, after his ordination, he said, "*For the future, therefore, I place all my trust in her (Mother Mary). If God wills it, if I live, I will tell it by word of mouth. I only repeat that in everything I recognize a particular benevolence[3] of the Immaculate Mother.*"

Love that has no limits - the knight and his Queen

Father Maxmilian wrote to his younger brother Joseph, only now Father Alphonse,

"*May God be thanked and the Immaculata glorified for all the graces that they shower upon us despite our unworthiness. I am most happy to learn that you feel enthused to procure the glory of God. In our days, the worst poison is indifference, which finds victims not only among the people, but even among religious...*"

He told his brother, the only important ideal was the salvation of souls, beginning with one's own. He advised that only through God can we learn what we have to do. And how can this come about? Through His representatives on earth. He said,

"*The superiors can make mistakes, but we in obeying can never make a mistake. There is only one exception: if a superior should ever command a thing clearly evident to be a sin, even the smallest sin...In such a case,*"

---

[2]This is connected with the Miraculous Medal. You can read more about this in The Many Faces of Mary, a love story, by Bob and Penny Lord.

[3]benevolence-contribution, donation, favor, gift, grant, present.

the superior would not be the representative of God, and we would not be obliged to obey him...we cannot trust our reason, which can make a mistake. Only God, only He, infallible, most holy, most loving, He is our Lord, Father Creator, End, Reason, Strength, Love...our Everything!"

Father Maxmilian stressed, *obedience* was the only way, adding, *"If there was a different way, Jesus would have pointed it out to us. Sacred Scripture says it clearly: for thirty years of his life, 'He was obedient to them.'"*

He spoke of loving *"without limits,* as our Heavenly Father loves." He advised, like so many of the Saints did, to learn from the Cross. "How much do you love me?" they asked Jesus. *He* opened His Arms on the Cross and answered, 'This much!' Maybe we cannot love, as Jesus did on the Cross. But maybe, *our* Cross is obeying someone we do not respect or even like.

You can see by his letter to his brother, how far along the path he was, to the day he would glorify the Lord and His Mother. He was only twenty-five years old, yet he was already a well-balanced priest, pointing *everything* to man's final triumph: God! This flowed through all his writings. But when he wrote of the Blessed Mother, he wrote with the sincere love of a son for his Mother, "of a knight for his Queen!"

He had a very special teaching about making the *Sign of the Holy Cross*:

"Remind yourself of obedience, each time that you make the Sign of the Holy Cross.

"In pronouncing the words, 'in the name of the Father,' remember that you intend to consecrate your judgment to the Heavenly Father.

"At the words, 'of the Son,' you will consecrate your will and heart to Jesus.

"At the words, 'of the Holy Spirit, you will consecrate your shoulders to bear the burden for the glory of God for the good of the order and of the Church and for the salvation of souls.

"In joining your hands and pronouncing the word, 'Amen,' you will remember to love your neighbor supernaturally in thought, word and actions.

"If you have worked in this way, you will find Heaven; otherwise, hell will be reserved for you.

"Life is short. Even sufferings are brief.

"Heaven, Heaven, Heaven!

"Courage!

"Take up your cross and follow Jesus."

Father Ignudi, his spiritual director, said, "Never in my life have I met anyone who loved the Madonna more than Father Maxmilian. He was a true son of Mary." The night before the Feast of the Immaculata, Maxmilian and Father Ignudi were returning from the Basilica, when they met four young rowdies. They still had on their work clothes, probably had stopped at the local bar for some *socializing*; they were blaspheming against the Mother of God, Mary most Holy. All of a sudden Father Ignudi missed Father Maxmilian; he was beside the young men, asking them why they were using such foul and disrespectful language against His and their Mother. He could not contain himself and at the end, he wept so passionately and pitifully, they apologized, saying at first, it was just a bad habit; but seeing how deeply they had hurt him, begged his forgiveness.

A Militia under the Banner of the Immaculata!

He came away from Rome with *Three Loves*. His seven years there, had nurtured and rekindled his love in: the Eucharist, the Body of Christ; the Madonna, the Mother of Christ; and the Pope, the Vicar of Christ.

In defense of the Pope, he founded a movement of prayer and *evangelism* under the Mantle of Mary the *Immaculata*. At first, it appeared he was called to form a *Militia* in Poland to fight the oppression of the Russians. But he quickly saw the need to include the whole world!

In Rome, he became aware of anti-Catholic propaganda that was spreading like a plague, with the Masons at the forefront. With their power and unlimited resources, they were a real threat. Here, in Rome, the heart of Christianity and the seat of the Vicar of Christ, our own backyard!

The onslaught was directed by the government, itself. It began with an attack against the Marian Sanctuary of our Lady of Pompei and then it went, *full steam ahead*, after our Popes, beginning with Pius IX and on to Benedict XV. Father Maxmilian did not ignore these as: merely rumblings, as a result of political and economic crisis, history repeating itself, but sure to pass over. To him, and rightly so, it was a clear indicator of a conspiracy against Christ and His Church.

He inherited his love of Mary Immaculate from the Order of Francis, itself. Unlike other Franciscans committed to reform, he did not desire to modify or improve, but to *renew* the Treasures we already had in the Catholic Church. Like St. Francis before him, he felt his calling was not within the Friary walls, but that he was called to bring Christ to *all* people, of all *kinds*, to all parts of the *world*. Was this *Militia*, he was talking of, possibly starting a *gentle revolution*?

For seven centuries, the Church was fighting for the world to accept that which already was: Mother Mary's Immaculate Conception. Pope Pius IX had declared the dogma of the Immaculate Conception, on December the 8th, 1854[4]. No wonder the government's attack on *him*, he had

---

[4]In Lourdes, our Lady appeared to St. Bernadette, in 1858, and declared Herself, the Immaculate Conception.

defended Mary; get him! So, the target was really Mary, the Virgin who would crush his head. Well, if the *devil* had an army, we, the faithful, could afford to do no less.

As the seed, planted inside Maxmilian, started to grow and crowd out all his other thoughts, he began to share with some of his closest companions, his ideal, an Army to defend the Immaculata, Her Son and His Church! The organization of the *enemy's* army appalled him. He complained, while we are limiting ourselves to passively praying, the enemy's forces are so active they are gaining the upper hand. He said, the Madonna does not need us, but she wants to use us to make the victories that much more *powerful* coming from those the world despises, the little people!

"If She finds faithful servants, docile to her command, She will win new victories, greater than those we can ever imagine." With this in mind, the friars placed themselves into the hands of Mary, as *docile instruments*, armed by the Miraculous Medal. Acting within the law, following the Gospel, speaking through a Marian Press, combining prayer with action and by being a *living example* of all, they would *defend* and *evangelize*. When Father Kolbe spoke of his vision, he spoke as if it had already begun.

But, when the Friars sang, "I will go to see Her one day," Father Kolbe's face glowed with the sweetness and innocence of a trusting, loving, *child* for his Mother. For awhile, he could be a child again; he would ask his companions to sing it over and over again. But this was not the time for children. Dreamer of dreams, Apostle and Zealot, it was *Catholic* Camelot, and he was to be Her Knight of the Immaculata!

No longer a dream -Knights of the Immaculata, a reality!

When Father Maxmilian had an idea, he put everything behind it, his mind, his heart, every ounce of his strength, and he was off and running with everyone trying to keep up with him. This man, who was *seriously* sick most of his life, had the *might* of an army and the determination of a General.

The more we read, it becomes more and more obvious, Mary was not only the inspiration of his work, she was the Authoress! Like the great Mother she is, she prepared his work for him and helped him to begin. She never left his side; with Her he would move mountains and men's hearts.

One day, at daybreak, all the student friars were gathered in the Chapel for common prayer. Father Maxmilian was there, too. From his appearance, one would never have suspected, this was to be one of the most important days of his life.

Father Rector read some meditations. It was the seventy-fifth anniversary of the famous victory of the Immaculata: the Blessed Mother had appeared to the *Hebrew* Alphonse Ratisbonne, in the church of S. Andrea delle Frate in Rome, and he was *converted* to Her Son and His Church through Her. As Ratisbonne was wearing the Miraculous Medal when this conversion came about, it brought about increased devotion to Mary through the wearing of Her Medal.

It was only fitting then, that on this very day, Father Maxmilian would not only be inspired to *found* the Militia Immaculata, but would choose the Miraculous Medal as the shield and insignia of its knights. The same Immaculate Mary who had appeared to St. Catherine Labouré and to Ratisbonne, was now you can be sure, here with Father Maxmilian leading the way.

A *Foundation*, which would grow to hundreds of friars under one roof, was started by one man and six friars from the college. They shared a dream, and the Mother of God made it a reality. Nine months after that earth-shaking day in January of 1917, seven friars, Father Maxmilian Kolbe and his six knights knelt before the Immaculata's Altar and consecrated themselves to Mary. *The Militia Immaculata was officially founded!*

It was the night before the Feast Day of St. Margaret Mary Alacoque[5]. Here, we see the Hand of Her *Son*. Was this His way of saying: "Through My Mother's Immaculate Heart, you will be able to sooth this Wounded Heart of Mine?" Was this our Lord saying: His Heart and His mother's Heart are one; when you hurt One, you hurt the Other; when you know One, you know the Other? There are no coincidences only Holy Design! Never overly impressed with himself, Father Maxmilian humbly used a scrap, an eighth of a piece of paper, to set up this Apostolate that would touch millions of lives, some day.

Aims and Commitments of the Militia Immaculata

What was Father Maxmilian's dream? He said:

"It is a movement that must draw the masses, snatch them away from Satan. Only among these souls, already conquered for the Immaculata, can some be formed to the highest, even heroic abandonment for the cause of spreading the Kingdom of God through the Immaculata."

There were *three* degrees of commitment to the *Militia*, based on the talents and zeal of the knight:

First degree: "*Anyone may consecrate himself individually to the Immaculata and strive to carry out privately the end of the Militia according to his own possibilities and prudence.*"

---

[5]St. Margaret Mary Alacoque - Our Lord appeared to her, and showed her His Heart. He said, "My enemies placed a crown around My Head, My friends around My Heart."

Second Degree: adhering to "particular bylaws and programs binding together in a union of strength the members who want to carry out the end more speedily."

Third Degree: "Consecration to the Immaculata made without limits. Thus She can do with us everything She wants and as She wants. We are entirely Hers and She is ours. We do everything with Her help; we live and work under Her protection. When it concerns Her cause, there does not exist any 'but!'...We always obey, even if She orders us to go to Moscow, to Spain, or to Mexico.[6]"

"Our victory will be the salvation of souls."

Problems face the little Apostolate

They're official! They're so excited! Now, they can begin! *Wrong*! Father Maxmilian and the little band had to wait for permission from their superiors! There was what seemed an endless delay! It was not caused by problems resulting from World War I and its call to arms of many of the students, but by the superiors' decision to postpone, rather than outright *forbid* them to begin the work and the Apostolate. And Father said, "*Yes*!"

It wasn't until two of the original seven *died* that they received the blessing and sanction of the Pope and their superiors. Father Maxmilian always gave credit to these two friars who had preceded them to Heaven. From the moment they received permission, the number of *knights* began to multiply.

Three years passed. January 2, 1922, the Apostolate was given *formal* approval by the Pope. On April the 23rd, 1927, His Holiness Pius XI elevated the *Militia Immaculata* to the dignity of "*primary pius union*." With this they could

---

[6]At this time, priests were being tortured and killed in Mexico. Read chapter on Bl. Miguel Pro.

not only admit recruits under their own constitution, but they would be able to open other houses or centers.

Their magazine, *The Knight of the Immaculata* was a part of the seven knights, right from the very beginning. They knew, the way, Mary was calling them to make Her name known, was through *communication*, and what better media, of its time, than a magazine. The printed word (propaganda) had spread such hate and destruction; *they* would use it for the Good News of Jesus through Immaculate Mary.

When one battle was won, another began. Father Maxmilian always looked upon them as part of winning the war for Mary! Tuberculosis was the form, the *enemy* would use to knock Father Maxmilian on his back. He was in and out of hospitals and sanitariums for most of the years of his Apostolate. But when a work is of the *Lord's*, especially through His Mother, it goes on. Some of the greatest strides were made when Father Maxmilian obediently *rested*.

It's not that he didn't try to keep going on! One time, the index finger of his right hand became *gangrenous* and the decision was made to amputate! He would not be able to fulfill his duties and privileges as a priest (except by special dispensation), if this were to happen. Father Maxmilian went to his Mother, Our Lady of Lourdes; he poured some drops of water taken from Her grotto, on his finger. He believed. She answered that belief. Within days, there was no need of an operation.

He was only twenty-six years of age when he made himself as close to Christ on the Cross as he could, totally abandoning himself to the Father, dying to his own will, offering all he desired to his Lord through the Hands of his Mother Mary! He said,

"In regard to the Militia, we are in the Hands of the Immaculata." The Immaculata can do with us what She wants

and as She pleases, because I am Her property and completely at Her disposal." Yes!

He never really stopped working for his Lady. Even in the hospital, he would walk through the wards, teaching Catholics and non-Catholics, alike. He would engage them first in challenging conversations. Slowly his words, the seeds he had been persistently planting would start to bloom, and *conversions* came about. No one was safe from him, including many of the *intellectuals* who were patients. They all fell under the spell of this knight and his Queen.

He baptized a Jewish student who was at the point of death. His mother and brothers didn't appreciate that, when they arrived later, furious with him for what he had done; but it was too late! *His* Jewish Mother, the Immaculata, had intervened as She had done at the wedding feast at Cana, and Her son, Maxmilian had given this Jewish boy, *new life.*

One of the encounters he had in the sanitarium, was with an intellectual; every time he met him in the hall, Father would ask him to go confession. Always it was the same, "Not now, maybe later. I have no time. I beg your pardon, Father, I have to rush to the station." And always, Father, like the persistent woman in the Bible, would come back with: *"Would you like to go to confession?"* One day, before the intellectual could rush away, Father said, *"Then at least, accept this Miraculous Medal."* The man politely conceded, and accepted the Medal, not wanting to hurt Father's feelings. As the man rushed off to the station, Father Maxmilian went down on his knees and implored his Immaculata for the conversion of this obstinate, but precious son of Hers. To quote from his Beatification:

"A moment later, a knock was heard. Still standing on the threshold, the same gentleman who had been in such a hurry exclaimed: 'Father, please hear my confession!'"

I find myself smiling a great deal writing about Father Kolbe. He reminds me of the many men, I have met, with my husband in front, who blind you with the love they have, unashamedly, for the Immaculate Mother of Jesus.

The first issue of The Knight of the Immaculata magazine

Toward the end of April, 1921, Father Maxmilian was released from the sanitarium. By November, he had recovered sufficiently to return to Krakow and the knights. He began working *immediately* toward the work Mary had laid out for them. Maybe it was because of his ill health and frequent interments in the hospital; in any event, Father Maxmilian worked *always*, with an urgency, as if his life here on earth would be short, and he had to make the most of what little time he had.

January of 1922, our priest started up his first publication of *The Knights of the Immaculata*. With this magazine, he felt he could get the message of Mary into the homes, into the place where the enemy had been striking, with radio, newspapers, books, magazines and other means. As the home is the *primary* source of teaching, he knew he had to strike a blow for Jesus and Mary *there*.

The little Apostolate immediately had money problems, too much to do with too little finances. The Superiors had given permission, at first. It was a worthwhile cause and they could see the wide-spread good that could be accomplished. But when they became aware of the financial problems that threatened Father Kolbe, they immediately flashed the *stop* sign. If he got in trouble, they would be on the line with him.

Father Maxmilian got on his knees and begged, "*Father Provincial, just give me the permission; I'll find the money.*" What could they do! They said "Yes."

Father Kolbe was committed to publish this magazine and to do whatever it took to do it. It appeared the only way would be to *beg*! He later shared how difficult this was for him. (Author's note: It's funny, Bob was saying, the other day, we never had a problem begging for *any* other charities, but when it comes to our Ministry, it's so difficult.)

He went to a stationery store, one day, with the express purpose of begging for the Apostolate. He ended up *buying*, instead of begging, just picking up some small item to avoid humiliation. Feeling remorse at having let his Lady down, he went into a second store. There, without uttering a sound, disoriented, he landed on the street, completely unaware of how he got there.

The debts still owed on his very *first* publication were way beyond his capability to pay. He made an appeal for donations to continue his work; they were not fast coming in. Just when it looked as if his *first* publication was to be his *last*, a priest made a generous donation. That was followed by other priests responding with contributions. With their affirming generosity, Father Maxmilian was able to cover *half* the cost. Now where was he to get the rest? Back he went on his knees! His Lady would not let him down! After all, it was Her idea, Her Militia, Her magazine; he was only Her poor instrument. (Author's Note: Upon investigating St. Anthony's bones, by the size of his knee bones they could tell he had spent a lot of time kneeling. As we journey through this great Saint's life, we know someday in Heaven, we will discover how large St. Maxmilian's knees are.)

After he finished praying, he was about to leave when he spotted an envelope on the Altar. Since it was not something that belonged on the Altar, he ascended to remove it. What did he see? Written on the envelope was: *"For You, Immaculate Mother."* He opened it; out spilled, the *exact* money he needed to cover the outstanding bill for the first publication. His Lady had come through! Dropping back down on his knees, he burst into tears. We know they were tears of *gratitude*, but I wonder, if not like with us, they were not also of *sorrow* for doubting, even for a moment, She would come through.

Impressed and frankly a little overcome by what he told them, his Superiors matched the amount that was in the envelope and gave it to Father Maxmilian. It covered *exactly* what was due on his debt; not a penny more; not a penny less. Our Lady is very prudent, asking Her Son only for what we *need*.

Criticism is deadly, but Father Maxmilian refused to die

Father Maxmilian had no training in publishing a magazine. His noble efforts, what with little money and less resources, were brutally criticized. Without his *Boss* in charge, his problems would have been unsurmountable. One priest, who just happened to be censor of Krakow, when he read their first issue, said the future of *The Knights of the Immaculata* was at *best* hopeless. This same priest would retract this statement, twelve years later.

During the first year, they had to change printers five times. Everything was against them. When there were not strikes holding up delivery, there was some other calamity. The price kept going up, but not the quality. Father Maxmilian turned to the Army for help. The delivery, the quality, *everything* was going smoothly when they had to change again; Father would not compromise; how could a moral publication come out of an immoral atmosphere.

As we like to say, Father Maxmilian had a *thought*! He would open their own print shop, right there in the Friary! No money and now, he wants to open his own printing facility? Sounds like a powerful woman we love, Mother Angelica, doesn't it.

But Jesus and His Mother have their ways. Naturally, it starts with a negative. Father Maxmilian and his Fathers were entertaining a certain priest, one night. Their guest lit into them, cutting their efforts to pieces. He even went so far as to sarcastically poke fun, calling their chance at winning and keeping any souls for the Immaculata *feeble* and inept. Father Maxmilian, like Jesus before him, said nothing in his defense. He just hung his head. How hurt he must have been! Was he, at last, discouraged? After all, this was a fellow priest, someone he respected, someone who would someday become Minister Provincial of the American Province of St. Anthony!

As if the Holy Spirit *suddenly* had gotten a hold of his tongue, this same priest, who had been attacking, began to *defend* them and their publication. He said, people, like himself, should *help* instead of looking for areas in their publication to find fault and error. He went on to pledging not only his support, but to reaching out to others to do likewise. He backed that vote of confidence with a check for one hundred dollars. In those days, that was a small fortune.

The publication flourished, always because of an eleventh hour God responding to His Mother. The amount of copies grew, and somehow the resources always came in, just in time.

The Knight of the Immaculate goes on without Father Kolbe

Hell will not prevail against His Church, nor against the *Militia* our Lady had chosen for Her Son to fulfill His Promise. Satan must have been very frustrated. He didn't have any *new* ideas. Strike down Father Maxmilian with Tuberculosis, *again*! Only now, the enemy worked on a body terribly weakened by subsequent attacks; the damage would be more serious and the recuperation longer, if at all.

And so, now with everything on the move, with greater acceptance requiring greater involvement and headship, Father Maxmilian is faced with abandoning all they had built up. All the suffering and labor had been for nothing. There was no other course; he had to *obey* his doctors; he had to leave. No General at the head of this Militia, it would collapse. Not only did it *not* buckle under, their circulation *doubled* and with it, the *work* of the Militia Immaculata.

When we looked for a word, which gave Father Maxmilian the strength to carry on His Lady's plan, it has to be *obedience*. He was always obedient, even when I am sure he wanted to say *"no."* Because of this, our Lord and Lady were able to step in and make not only what Father Maxmilian had envisioned come true, but the *impossible*!

He considered acts of obedience and abandonment the most powerful means to defeat Satan. Father Maxmilian *knew*: no man, not even the most talented, strongest leader could bring about victory against the merciless bombarding of the Enemy. Accepting this, he turned it over to the Lady, the Virgin Who would crush the serpent's head. Our Lady did so well, that within five years, the circulation would grow to *100,000* copies every month.

Father Maxmilian never sacrificed his commitment to Jesus, His Immaculate Mother and to Father Francis. They now had *their own machines*! The friars had a plan. They could make money taking in outside work, other than their own publication. Father Maxmilian came down *hard*:

"In such a way, the means becomes the end, and the end the means; while reasoning in this way, no thought is given to future development.

"The souls go to ruin, the diabolical press works feverishly to sow disbelief and immorality, and we reap profit from machines.

"It is then evident that the curse of St. Francis should fall on this work which would secure a quiet livelihood for the religious. It would then be a blessing from Heaven that everything would be destroyed..."

The Militia Immaculata never took on any other work.

City of the Immaculate - Niepokalanow

Circulation of *The Knight of the Immaculata* zoomed to *60,000*. Father Maxmilian needed new and larger printing facilities. Through a priest, with whom he had shared his needs and vision, he made the acquaintance of a Mr. Srzednicki. This man arranged a meeting with a prince, who owned some land near Warsaw. Its location and generous acreage were perfect!   When the prince heard Father Maxmilian speak of the Apostolate, he agreed *verbally* to the Militia's use of his land.

Father Maxmilian immediately placed a statue of the *Immaculata* on the land, *believing* She would take care of everything. *She* would intercede with his Superiors, convince them and the other friars to allow this to come to pass.

Although not all the Superiors were in agreement, it was approved.   There were only two items they had to vote on: *first*-the Militia Immaculata's *need* of this center, and *second*: the possibility of strings attached to the giving of this donation.   They agreed on the first item; there was most definitely a need. But they were equally adamant, as well, on the second: there was to be *no* special considerations shown the prince for this property. No strings or no deal.

This didn't seem like a problem...*except*, at the last minute, the prince asked that Masses be said for him in exchange for the gift. The Superiors refused! The prince stormed, if they could not do this for him, in light of his generosity, well they could keep their Masses and he would keep his land!

He demanded Father Maxmilian *remove* the Statue of Mother Mary from his land, at once. Father insisted the statue *remain* as a sign, the Madonna had made a promise and had not kept it. When Father spoke, suddenly, the prince did not see a founder, a priest who had made great strides with his work, he saw a child with faith in *his* Mother, and this Mother, he loved and trusted, had let him down. But Father Maxmilian was careful to defend Her, emphasizing it was the *first* time.

This love and trust, this child-knight had for his Queen-Mother, so touched the prince; he gave in and the land was theirs. In his testimony, the prince said: "His humility and childlike simplicity attracted me. If ever there was a man who was not proud, it was Father Maxmilian."

Father Maxmilian's superiors accepted the land and ordered the transfer of the printing facility to what was to be: their *City of the Immaculata Niepokalanow*. Father and his friars, together with their publishing Apostolate, left for their *City*, October of 1927. When they began, they'd made it with one small suitcase; now, five short years later, they needed eight *railroad cars* to carry all the equipment.

The new Friary, which became known as the *Factory of the Immaculata*, opened with twenty friars: two priests and eighteen brothers. They chopped their way through the dense forest, using the wood it yielded, to build: a House for their Lord-their Chapel, dormitories for them to sleep in, huts for their equipment, workrooms, and offices. The days were long and the work endless. The Polish winter came too soon. The days were not only colder, but shorter, and so they worked *harder*. Because they were of one mind, one heart and one vision, the struggling and the suffering only made them stronger and more determined. They sweat together, they cried and laughed together, they were brothers, they became *community*!

It had to be a difficult walk, seeing Father Maxmilian so ill, working beside them until hemorrhaging so badly, he was forced to stop. A betting man would not have given them a chance. Everything was against them. But believing in that *God* Who can do the impossible; knowing through Him, it only takes *longer*, they went on. You see, they had the same Lady, the same Mother, Jesus had left to the Apostles, knowing they would need Her.

Build a Seminary

When their Provincial came to visit them, it was obvious, to him, they could not handle all the work. Teasing, he told Father Maxmilian he'd have to build a seminary so he would have more priests and brothers to serve in the *Militia*. Did he not know Father would consider this, a signal from his Lady? Well, if his Queen wants it, Her knight will do it. Father Maxmilian and his band of friars began building a seminary. They had taken him seriously! The Provincial was upset! His anger soon turned into resignation. He loved the City of the Immaculata and its knights; it was difficult to stay upset with them, but he would worry!

They announced, they had permission from their Provincial and they would be opening a Seminary. Then, the Provincial changed his mind*! Too late*! They had made the announcement in *The Knight of the Immaculata*, and it had no only been printed but distributed! *"If it is of God..."* Letters poured in; young and old, men from all walks of life, wanted to come and give their lives. The response was *enormous*! They continued building the seminary.

Through faith, and the work behind that faith, building after building was added. The prince gave them more and more land. The friars grew from the original 20 who had first come to the forest to almost 800! The two priests had grown to thirteen! Each brother specialized in some part of the Apostolate. *Niepokalanow*, as City of the Immaculata was called, had the largest religious community in the world.

Father Maxmilian never wanted any personal reward or wealth for himself and his friars; like Father Francis, he knew it would destroy them. Therefore, Father Maxmilian made sure there were always new places to build and new places to spend money, even before it came in.

During the first five years, they added a college, a novitiate, a friary for professed Franciscans, a hospital with

100 beds, a plant which furnished them all their electricity and even, a fire department. Communication was on the move; they added a radio station! The work was to go world-wide; they needed and built an airport!

But with all this building of the Church with bricks, stone and cement, Father and his knights never forgot *Who* the Church was! As Father Maxmilian *loved* his Mother Mary, he *adored* his Brother Jesus, especially in the *Holy Eucharist*. At *Niepokalanow*, the Eucharist was the Center of their life and Apostolate. Father and the friars would interrupt their work and sleep, to take turns adoring the Lord in the Holy Eucharist. The more they adored Her Son, the more the Lord's Mother fought for them, and they grew!

The circulation of *The Knights of the Immaculata* swelled to a million copies per issue. Added to this, were nine different publications, all serving Mother Church in a different area, filling the needs of all the parts of the Mystical Body of Christ. It was exciting!

Down the roller coaster we plunge. With success, comes envy! *The City of the Immaculata* became a battlefield. Their magazine, *The Knights of the Immaculata* came under attack. It became the *life-work* of good people finding fault for the *sake* of finding fault; anything to discredit them! One day, a canon visited them. With more than a little sarcasm, he questioned Father Maxmilian, "What would St. Francis say if he were still living, seeing these expensive machines?" Father Maxmilian replied,

> *"He would roll up his sleeves and, speeding up the machines as much as possible, he would work like these good brothers to diffuse the glory of God and Immaculata with the most modern means."*

No matter what he said, he would no sooner convince one, than he would become the target of another. *They questioned his motives*! They sharply condemned what they called, the *rigorous* spirituality of his friars. Father and his knights were subjected to assaults of every kind. Nothing could satisfy the jealousy brought about by the *City's* success. But as our Lord allows us these crosses, the Immaculata always comes to the rescue. And so, She did. With Her mantle over them and with the loving patience of their founder, the faithful knights not only survived, they won the war!

Go out to all the World

"The knights of the Immaculata must have missions! In spite of all the differences, we must have faith in the Immaculata. For this purpose, She will send us many vocations." Prophecy?

Father Maxmilian set his sites on the Far-East. God, Father Maxmilian and some Japanese students were on a train, one day. This is when the Lord decided to plant a desire in his heart to go to Japan! Although the students were friendly and polite, Father Maxmilian was sad; they didn't know Jesus and his Gospel. He saw the need and answered that need: establish a *City of the Immaculata*, in Japan!

By this time, his superiors were surprised at little, Father Maxmilian said or did. But when he sought their approval to open a second *City*, in the *Far-East*, this had to top all the other unorthodox propositions he'd ever made. Needless to say, he received permission to go to China and Japan.

In February of 1930, Father Maxmilian, with four brother friars, left their *City of the Immaculata* in Poland. He said good-by to no one, not to the priests and brothers in the Friary, not to his own brother, nor even his mother. He later wrote, asking for her forgiveness and understanding. He said, he loved her so, he could not bear to say good-by.

The little group travelled through Europe to France and the port of Marseille. They stopped to pray to the Saint of the Missions, St. Therese of Lisieux. They also pilgrimaged to Lourdes, to say thank you to their Mama Mary for past favors, and I am sure, to ask Her to guide and protect them as they set out to bring Her and Her Son to a *pagan* people.

As they stopped at different ports, Father Maxmilian looked around, every one of them, a prospect for another *City of the Immaculata*, where Jesus and Mary would become known and triumph.

They arrived in Nagasaki, Japan, toward the end of April in 1930, wearied and a little disappointed. Things had not gone as they had hoped in Shanghai. Although enthusiastically received, it was obvious God was not opening the door, at this time. They hadn't given up, though; they left two friars there with the hope of setting up a center, in the future.

The threesome went to the Cathedral of Nagasaki. There in the center of the square, was a statue of Immaculate Mary. She was on a pedestal with hundreds of the most beautiful, exotic flowers they had ever seen, surrounding her. Her arms were outstretched. It was as if Mary was greeting them: "I've been waiting. I thought you'd never get here." Taking this as a sign She was behind them and this mission, Father prophesied:

"If we have found her, it is a sign that all will go well."

Father Maxmilian went to the bishop. The bishop, pleased with Father's plans to set up a Japanese *City of the Immaculata*, pledged his support, immediately. There was only one provision; in exchange, Father would teach philosophy and theology in the Nagasaki seminary. Although this meant an extra physical burden on Father Maxmilian, he quickly agreed, on *condition he* could publish his magazine here in Nagasaki. If the bishop had ever thought his proposal through, I'm sure he would have suggested some psychiatric care for Father Maxmilian.

But the bishop hadn't, and the knights took their first giant step toward their Japanese *City of the Immaculata*! (Author's note: We say, in the Ministry, if this is not for our Lord, take us away; we're hopelessly mad.) It's kind of fun to look at these three friars. Without knowing a word of Japanese, not to read or write, to speak or even to understand, they proposed to publish an issue of the Immaculata in *Japanese*!

Father Maxmilian and his two friars began working on their publication within a few days! Leaving nothing untried, depending solely on his Immaculata, the impossible was published and distributed in one month!

His job, teaching at the seminary, had not drained him, rather it became a help. The big problem had been: how would he produce articles in Japanese. Through his job at the seminary, he found the solution. He wrote in *Latin*, and some of his students translated it into *Japanese*. The Language problem was no more!

He took the finished product to a printer to be typeset and printed. One month in Nagasaki, his first magazine in a Japanese print shop, he has not seen the finished issue, yet, and Father went out to buy his first *printing press* and 145,000 characters of Japanese type.

He had arrived the end of April. His first issue had just come out, and Father Maxmilian had to leave to go back to Poland. He had promised, before leaving Europe, he would return for this important Provincial Chapter.

August 13, 1930, Father was on his way *back* to Japan. He had received the unanimous approval, of his building the Japanese *City of God*, from the Chapter. It was official. He had the proper paperwork. Full steam ahead! His joy was short-lived.

He had received disconcerting news; their mission in Nagasaki was on the verge of closing; the publication of *The Knight of the Immaculata* had been suspended for a month.

When he had left hurriedly, they judged Father Maxmilian had given up on the project. All the support he'd had from the Japanese priests and seminarians, had been withdrawn.

As he came down the gang plank, he was greeted by two very relieved friars who were not trying to hide how happy they were to see their founder. *He would re-establish order to the Apostolate.* And, he did! He brought two more friars, who would help out, while they learned Japanese.

No sooner, had he resolved matters, new problems came to the surface. The typesetters did everything possible to make life *impossible.* The Nagasaki Printers were determined this magazine would fail and the typesetters were in collusion. All right, the knights would typeset the issue themselves! This was not a simple task. The thousands of characters were confusing. But, in November, the first publication ever done *completely* by members of the *white race*, was on the streets.

Another hurt for Father Maxmilian to suffer: just as things started to go well, two of his friars left. He was back to two, like when he had begun! But, not for long! Their courage and true Franciscan *living* of the Gospel, attracted recruits. They came, Christian and non-Christian Japanese, alike. Vocations started to flourish as the Japanese became more and more aware of their Apostolate. Their community grew from five to *twenty-four*, in a period of four short years. In another two years, *twenty* were studying for the *Franciscan priesthood*!

They called their second *City*, "*The Garden of Mary Immaculate*," and garden, it was. It bloomed; it produced rich fruit; vocations grew; devotion to Jesus through the Immaculata spread throughout Nagasaki. (Was it Jesus or Mary Who stepped in the way of the atomic bomb, in 1945, sparing the Garden and the Franciscans, there? These Franciscans accepted many of the countless orphaned children, who were running through the streets, into their

Garden. They turned it into an orphanage, and they were soon able to care for close to a *thousand* children.)

Father Maxmilian must return to Poland

Father Maxmilian was called back to Europe to attend a Provincial Chapter. He boarded an Italian ship and left Japan on May the 26th, 1936. He landed in Italy; his short stay there included a pilgrimage to the Holy House of Nazareth in Loreto.

What had the Mother of God said to him, in the Holy House? No one knows; but what we do know is, when he arrived in Poland, Father Maxmilian proposed to the Provincial Chapter, the consecration of the entire Order to the *Immaculata*. It was not only received wholeheartedly, they decreed it be renewed each year on the Feast of the Immaculate Conception.

It was 1936. Most people were calling Hitler a *Maniac*, who no one would or should take seriously. Could it be, Mother Mary had called Her son Maxmilian to Italy to the House where She had said "Yes," to strengthen Maxmilian and the Franciscans for the horror and holocaust that was to come?

He was so happy! Their magazine in Japan was doing well. Their Japanese *City*, "*The Garden of Mary Immaculate*," was bearing fruit. He had come home with hope of opening a third *City*, in India! He knew he would get their approval; the success in Japan was testimony it could and would work.

It was good to be back. His *Niepokalanow* was beautiful. The knights were doing well without him. Everything was going well...and then, the Provincial Chapter elected him Guardian of The City of the Immaculata, here in *Poland*! The hot, humid climate of Japan had played havoc with his health. His tuberculosis had returned. He was hemorrhaging so badly the loss of blood had dangerously weakened him. He was ordered confined to his bed, until he regained his strength.

Was he disappointed? Not that anyone would notice. He accepted and obeyed, with a full heart and will. The friars at The *City*, in Poland, were overjoyed. They said, it was not that their other superiors had not been outstanding *religious*, they were; but they were not Father Maxmilian! They'd missed him!

The Golden Age of Niepokalanow[7]

During this time, Niepokalanow received a *crown of distinction* in recognition of its accomplishments. He was content, but he never forgot his *Garden of Mary Immaculate*, in Japan. As he shared with the friars at Niepokalanow, the custom of greeting one another with "Maria," that had begun at their sister *City* in Japan, it was to him, like being there, too. He never forgot one of his sons. Miles could not separate them from him.

Father Maxmilian personally directed each of the friars. There was love that passed from Father Maxmilian to his *sons*; they said: "Everywhere he passed, he sowed peace, harmony, reciprocal love; he dispelled doubts, infused courage."

They loved calling him, "Father." He loved hearing them call him *Father*. And, although he was only forty-two years old, he was their father. He would always tell them:

"I am your father, even more so than your earthly father from whom you have received your physical life. Through me, you have received a spiritual life, and this is a divine life; through me, you have received your religious vocation, which is more than physical life.

To this day, those who knew him, speak of the incredible capacity he had to love and parent. One night, after dinner, he spoke to his friars:

---

[7]written by one of his Polish biographers, Morcinek.

"My dear sons, if only you knew how happy I am. My heart is overflowing with happiness and peace...My dear sons, love the Immaculata. Love Her and She will make you happy. Trust Her without limits."

He looked at each one of them, as if to imprint them on his mind and heart. He paused and went on:

"I have something to tell you...The reason I am very happy and filled with joy is that I have been given an assurance of Heaven."

They tried to get more out of him. He hesitated. It was Mount Tabor, again. Jesus was speaking to Peter, James and John. Father was preparing *them* for what he already knew was ahead, his *death*. His voice shook, as he spoke:

"I have revealed this secret to you to strengthen your courage and spiritual energies for the difficulties ahead. There will be trials, temptations and discouragement. The memory of tonight will strengthen you and help you to persevere in your religious life. It will strengthen you for the sacrifice Mary will ask of you."

He begged them to tell no one of this, until after he died. He said he would never have told them of Mary's promise to him, except the time was growing near, when they would all go through a terrible trial.

Was it that his Mary had shown him the whole picture, that there would be rebirth of a people that would rise from his ashes? At another time, when he had been speaking to a large audience he declared, *no, he prophesied*:

"We do not believe the day to be far off, or a mere dream, when the statue of the Immaculata will be enthroned by her Knights in the very heart of Moscow."

The Lady's Knight from Heaven, you can be sure, was there when the church bells began to peel in Moscow, in December of 1989. He was there carrying a statue of Immaculate Mary. And you can bet on it; he sang,

"Immaculate Mary" with them, as Her children welcomed
Mama home, and with Her, Jesus!

Hitler invades Poland

On September the 1st, in the year of infamy, 1939,
without even a declaration of war, Hitler's ruthless Army
invaded Poland. The Poles didn't have a chance. England
had not come to their aid. No one had. They stood alone.
The Poles were brave, but these *Davids* could not kill the
giant *Goliaths* that came rumbling through, mowing down
everything and everyone who still dared to be on the once
quiet streets.

Their Provincial had briefed the friars on what to do in
the event of invasion. On September 5th, Father Maxmilian
passed on these orders to his Knights: they were to evacuate
and flee to Friaries where they would not be in danger of
being captured by the Germans; or if it were safer, to return
to their families. Father Maxmilian embraced the friars who
were leaving. Tearfully, they held on to their dear *Father*,
not wanting to let go. And he, with his father's love, blessed
each of his sons as he said his final *farewell* to them:

"Good-by, my dear sons, I will not survive this war!"

Most of his sons, safely gone, Father Maxmilian rushed
to Warsaw to ask his Provincial what he was *personally* to do.
Although Father did not seemed alarmed or anxious, those
present later testified, it was apparent he would have
preferred to go to a safer place. *He didn't want to die!* He
loved his *Niepokalanow.* He loved life! The Provincial, with
the prodding of the superior of the Warsaw Priory, ordered
Father Maxmilian to *stay* at *The City of the Immaculata.*

It was a death sentence! The *City* was right in the path
of the advancing German Army. They were sure to take
over the Niepokalanow. He said "*Yes!*" And with him, fifty
brothers and five priests, stayed. If he was to remain, then
they would remain with him, no matter the danger. As each

hour made its slow journey into night, the commitment they had made became more and more difficult. They spent every day from September 8th through the 19th, terrorized and crippled by fear! All that is, but Father Maxmilian. Each day, during their meditations, he'd try to strengthen them, gentling reminding them: that day could be the last day of their lives and they were to be prepared to die a *holy* death.

Father Maxmilian would go out to console his countryman, outside of the *City*, those who were returning from the front as well as those that had been left behind. When Polish soldiers were too exhausted or wounded to go on, he took them into the *Niepokalanow*. He even gave refuge to the Jews who had been against the *City* being in their midst, only a few months before. Here was truly Christ in their midst, with his charity and unconditional love.

German soldiers reach Niepokalanow!

It was the middle of September, and it was Father Maxmilian's turn. The soldiers rushed from building to building, destroying everything they could get their hands on, furniture, tools, nothing was spared, that is nothing but the machinery. They had plans for it; they would send it *intact* to Germany!

Did they remember something from their mother's knee, they needed to forget? They ripped the crucifixes off the walls and flung them on the floor. They stomped on them with their heavy boots, as if to crush the *Christ* on them..."*Come down from the Cross!*" They took extra pains smashing into dust, statues of the *Immaculata*, as if She were *there*, reminding them of the new Calvary they were creating.

Father stood helplessly by, and saw them mercilessly tear down everything they had built. In a matter of days they had shattered a dream that twelve years of sacrificing had made a reality. He held on, repeating over and over again:

"The Immaculata has given all. She has taken all away. She knows how things are."

A few days before the Nazis invaded Poland, Father Maxmilian had gathered his Knights, together. He knew what his end would be. He had no illusions how he would be treated by the Nazis. In his press and on his radio station, he had condemned both Nazism and Communism. He had tried to warn the *dangerously complacent*: these two philosophies were godless and as such, represented an evil which would spread inhuman and diabolical suffering, unlike anything the world had ever known.

Trying to prepare them, he spoke of the three stages of his life:

In the *First Stage:* his life had been *preparing* for his apostolate;

In the *Second Stage*: his life *became* his apostolate;

In the *Third Stage*: what was about to happen, his life was to be one of *suffering.*

"I would like to suffer and die in a knightly manner, even to the shedding of the last drop of my blood, to hasten the day of gaining the whole world for the Immaculate Mother of God."

The Nazis would soon accommodate him. On September the 19th the soldiers came and ordered all the *religious* into the town square. They crammed all but two of them into trucks. They would be allowed to stay behind to care for the wounded soldiers. Father Maxmilian had the choice of staying behind with one of the brothers, but he joined his brother knights, instead.

They were transported, jammed in with livestock, to a concentration camp in Germany. It was not one of the camps known for extreme cruelty, but it ranked up there. The cold and hunger would have gotten them, but, as they reported: there was always Father Maxmilian there to encourage them. He was *living* the words he'd said to the friars when they departed from the City:

"*Niepokalanow is not only this place, these premises, these machines. Niepokalanow is wherever one of its members dwells. Niepokalanow must be in your souls, in your hearts.*"

And so, they made a statue of the Immaculata out of clay and they had their *City of the Immaculata*, their Niepokalanow!

Father Maxmilian never lost trust the Immaculata would free them. One of the brothers, later confessed, he would become upset and angry every time Father would say,

"*The Immaculata will drive us out of camp.*"

But she did! In November, they were transferred to a camp in Poland, thanks to a *Catholic* officer who'd replaced the one they'd had.

Conditions were better at the new camp in Poland, better than they'd been in the camp in Germany. It seemed the Germans were going to let up, a little. They even allowed the religious to celebrate the Feast of the Immaculate Conception. After three months, without the Holy Eucharist, Father and his fellow Franciscans received Holy Communion! The camp commander had given permission to a priest from a nearby town to bring the Eucharist to them. That afternoon, without explanation, an order was given: they were to be *released* from the camp and were to return to their homes.

We are back, Niepokalanow!

Germany had swept Poland in less than one month. That momentarily satisfying her, she generously split with her ally Russia, what wasn't hers in the first place. Germany took the western and central parts, and Russia took the rest. To the foolish, it looked as if this greedy monster had had its fill.

The band of Franciscans, with Father Maxmilian in front, trudged lightheartedly toward home, to their Niepokalanow. They used whatever means of transportation that presented itself. Nothing discouraged them; nothing mattered except that they were on their way to their Immaculata.

At the entrance of the *City*, there was no Immaculata to greet them. They found a small statue of the Immaculata on a pile of debris and making a make-shift pillar, they raised Her high. But, before doing this or anything else, they repaired the Chapel and returned the Blessed Sacrament to His home. This they did on their first day home.

All in place, that was *really* important, they began to repair and rebuild their Niepokalanow. Their beautiful *City* had been ransacked, almost flattened. What the Germans hadn't destroyed, they carried away, and what they couldn't carry, they destroyed. The sons of the Immaculata looked around, retrieved what scraps they could and began to mold them into: a garage, a repair shop for watches, a carpentry shop, machine shops and even a cheese factory. These were the immediate needs of the people of the area, so first things first, these were those they met.

The brothers kept returning, until they numbered 300. Those who didn't, *couldn't*, as there was a price on their heads. They had been, for the most part, editors of the magazines and because of this a prime target of the dreaded Gestapo. The Nazi philosophy was, control the mind and you control the people. They got rid of all the professors, writers, editors, everyone who could remind the Poles of who they really were - a proud and free people.

Through the intervention of the Polish Red Cross, Niepokalanow was turned into a *hospital*. Father Maxmilian insisted that no one be turned away, that all be received, that all be treated *equally*. Niepokalanow would be available, not only to the wounded, but to those who were considered undesirables: dissidents, people expelled from parts of Poland, *Jews*.

It was 1940; the number, they were caring for, grew to as many as 2000 of the expelled, and close to 1500 Jews. The Gestapo was not very happy with their *tenants*; consequently they kept a close eye on the Franciscans. Brothers were working in the infirmary caring for the *physical* wounds, and the priests for their spiritual, acting as *chaplains* to the Catholics and *brothers* to the Jews. Because of their true Franciscan spirit, many conversions came about.

A former rabbi from the Synagogue of Rome, told it best: "If I knew how to write a book on Father Kolbe - I am not worthy of so much, otherwise Providence would have given me the capability of doing so - I would entitle it: *'Father Maxmilian Mary Kolbe who died for love.'*"

Their charity was universal, even including German soldiers. When Father Maxmilian heard one of the non-commissioned officers was ill, he went to visit him and gave him and other soldiers the Miraculous Medal. His love and concern for them, really touched them! How could he care for them, after they had been responsible for so much pain!

With the steady flow of religious, returning, the number grew to 349! Whereas perpetual adoration of the Blessed Sacrament had begun immediately, other religious practices were *slowly* returning, but return they did. Formation had started up again, and new applicants were becoming new *friars*. Father was able to resume communication with his friars in Japan.

Life was getting back to before *all hell had broken loose*. It looked like it was time to resume publishing *The Knights of the Immaculata*, not only in Polish but in *German*, for the soldiers stationed in Poland. Father Maxmilian made many trips to Warsaw, seeking permission to start up again. By some miracle, he was able to convince an official of the German Propaganda office, there. He sent *his* approval to Krakow, and the *wheels* of that office were put into motion, and the magazine was on its way!

They were allowed to start up again! They worked night and day. On *December the 8th*, Feast of the Immaculate Conception, their Lady gave the world Father Maxmilian Mary Kolbe's last will and testament- their last issue of The Knights of the Immaculata was printed!

He wrote:

"December 8, is drawing near, the Feast of the Immaculate Conception.

"Let those who can, go to confession. For those to whom this is impossible, because circumstances do not permit it, let them wash their souls with perfect contrition-the sorrow of the loving child who thinks not so much of the punishment and the reward, as of asking forgiveness of the father and mother whom he has displeased."

The Journey to Life, Death and Resurrection

It was the year 1940. Father Maxmilian had been preparing them for the time when he would leave for his final walk to *Calvary*. When he wrote and published his *Knight* he knew his arrest would be any day. Loyal Poles who were working inside the Gestapo offices, kept warning him to leave Niepokalanow, but he wouldn't!

The Gestapo had noticed his many gifts. *Why not use them for the Third Reich! He could influence the stubborn Poles to cooperate, especially through his press. How to go about this?* They told Father Maxmilian that the High Command had heard of him and were pleased with him. They would be even more appreciative (with all the privileges that would bring), if he would apply for German *citizenship*. It was obvious, with his name, he had German blood.

No one knows of the temptations Satan might have put into Father's mind and heart. *He could continue his work. His sons needed him. He certainly could do more alive than*

Above. **Nazi soldier *smiles*, as he escorts Father Kolbe and his fellow
Knights to prison, the first step in their cruel Way of the Cross.**
Below: ***City of the Immaculata Niepokalanow***

dead! If he had accepted their offer, how different things might have been. What a price to pay for life on earth, even doing *good things*, if the end result is the loss of your soul and the souls of others. His love for his Mother in Heaven was sacred. He could not see himself betraying Her, and doing less than Her Son Jesus, saving his own life at the cost of his Poland. And so, he said: *"No!"* Father Maxmilian had *lived*, a son of Poland, and he would *die* a son of Poland.

February 17th, 1941, at 9:45 in the morning, they came to arrest him. Two cars pulled up and entered the Niepokalanow. Five Gestapo officials got out, four with uniforms and one in plainclothes. As they approached the house of the religious, a brother phoned Father Maxmilian, who was in his room. Father had been expecting this moment, but when he answered the phone, the brother said, his voice *trembled* with his "yes." But only for a moment; regaining his composure, he said:

"All right, my son." Then he gave him *their* greeting, *"Mary,"* for the last time.

The night before, he had said:

"What indescribable happiness! What a great grace it is to be able to seal one's ideal with one's life."

Was brother thinking of this, as the Gestapo called out Maxmilian's name and that of five other priests. Satan was not finished tormenting him. Isn't that a German name, the Gestapo asked? Once again, Father Maxmilian proclaimed:

"Perhaps some of my grandparents may have come from Germany, but I was born in Poland and therefore I am Polish."

Father and the other five priests were taken to Warsaw and kept in prison. Now, the Gestapo had a problem. Father Maxmilian was not one of the thousands of unknown priests who would be arrested and killed. He was known worldwide and highly acclaimed. They would have the whole church down on them, unless they could provide some kind of justification for their action.

And the Church came; his Provincial as well as a nun, who worked for the Gestapo, came, putting their necks on the block. Nothing would dissuade the authorities. They used a trumped-up charge signed by a former brother, who had been expelled by Father Maxmilian because of some wrongdoing, while at Niepokalanow. In highly legalistic terminology, it alluded to a plot supposedly hatched by Father Maxmilian against the Germans occupying Poland. Anyone, who knew Father, would call this *impossible*! But the Gestapo said, since the papers were signed, nothing could be done.

The brother later testified, he didn't understand what was in the papers. Not knowing the German language, trusting it said what they said it did, he signed. So, they condemned an innocent man with a *forgery*.

As the days passed into weeks, in prison, Father Maxmilian spoke repeatedly of dying a martyr's death for the Faith. One of the brothers in the prison objected, complaining, "You, Father, speak of martyrdom for the Faith, while there are *many*[8] people who are in concentration camps perishing; this is not for the Faith but for the country."

Father's answer, wisely and prophetically was:

"*Son, I tell you that if it is thus, the martyrdom is certainly for the Faith*".

All wars are religious wars. The war is *always*, not between countries or people, but between God and Satan. And certainly, this war, with its inhumanity against God's children was not political to *Him*. Ask parents whose sons or daughters died, if it was political. They'll tell you, it was *personal*. So, when anyone of us is hurt, God is hurt and so is His Faith.

---

[8]meaning many who were not Catholic.

Auschwitz - Roll Call of Hell

On May the 28th, 1941, Father Maxmilian, although suffering seriously from tuberculosis, was transported along with 320 other prisoners, to *Auschwitz*. He was treated no better because he was a *religious*. Rather, they were harsher on the *religious*, taking some kind of delight, determining how much torture they could take before cracking.

Father Maxmilian was given a number, 16670; he was assigned to block 17. The guards pushed, kicked and beat Father when he was too ill to walk. He struggled, as he tried to haul the wheel barrels full of gravel, they needed to build the crematorium walls. Oh, they were not past using prisoners to build their own means of torture or death.

No matter how they brutalized him, how they tried to humiliate him, they could not force Father into hating them. He had so much love in his eyes, they made him lower his eyes so they wouldn't have to look into them.

Auschwitz or *the Death Camp*, as it was more commonly called, was originally to be for the extermination of *Jews*. Then, the Third Reich added to their martyred number: the Danish, French, Greek, Spanish, Flemish, Yugoslavian, German, Norwegian, Russian, Rumanian, Hungarian and Italian undesirables, whose only crime was they were leaders or intellectuals.

Although its horror was not singularly its own, it had the reputation of being the most efficient of all the concentration camps, building up to a record of *exterminating* 3500 enemies of the state in 24 hours. They became so good at their job, the sign above the entrance gate reading "*Work makes one free*," they were capable of killing prisoners on arrival. Many they did; others they saved for slave labor; others they had *fun* with: their action-to degrade, to see how low they could make a human stoop with enough torture.

I think, the saddest testimony I ever heard was from a survivor of the concentration camps. He told-how parents

would have their children go before them, into the *showers*
(the Nazis jokingly called the gas chambers), so they would
not be frightened, the parents reassuring them, it was all
right, they would be following.

A fellow prisoner testified that nothing they did to
"Father Maxmilian could break his spirit. He would lift up
the other victims, repeating:

*"No, No, these Nazis will not kill our souls, since we
prisoners distinguish ourselves quite definitely from our
tormentors; they will not be able to deprive us of the
dignity of our Catholic belief. We will not give up. And
when we die, then we die pure and peaceful, resigned to
God in our hearts."*

He infuriated the Nazis as he worked to keep the Poles
and the European Jews from being reduced into groveling
animals, turning on each other. To punish him, the guards
would save the most demeaning work for him. At one time,
they even set their vicious dogs on him.

They used Father to carry corpses to the crematorium.
A former prisoner testified: one time, when he (the prisoner)
was asked to carry a young man's horribly ravaged body, his
ripped open stomach, evidence of just part of the torture
he'd suffered before dying, he was so repulsed by the sight,
he did not have the strength or the stomach to lift him. Then
he heard a gentle voice, hardly above a whisper: *"Let us take
him."* As they carried the young man to the crematorium,
he could hear the prisoner helping him, *"Holy Mary, pray for
us."* Father Maxmilian was calling to his Mother, and as She
did with Her Son Jesus as He carried His Cross, Her eyes
sustained him.

One day, Father fell under the weight of the wood he
was carrying. Face down, in the mud, unable to get up, the
picture I see before me is, again, the one of Jesus on the way
of the Cross, when He fell the third time. Was that the
picture before Father Maxmilian? Was that how he was able

to get up? With his last ounce of strength, each day, he carried his sufferings, taking on the sins of *his* jailers upon his wounded body, as his Jesus before him. He said over and over again:

"For Jesus Christ, I am prepared to suffer still more."

But soon, they beat his weary, broken body to such a point of breaking, he landed, more dead than alive, in a hospital. His tuberculosis got so bad, he was, again, like Jesus before him, dying of asphyxiation, unable to breath. They determined he had *pneumonia.*

His face had begun to show the scars of his mistreatment, and his voice, betrayed by the dryness from too much heat and too little water, was robbing him of his speech. But yet, a fellow priest testified, he was an inspiration to everyone. He was never too weary, too tired, too broken, too sick to hear confessions.

He was happy to be in the hospital because so many there needed a priest. One of the prisoners had somehow gained the trust of the guards and they would let him out. He would return, hiding food under his clothes, which he shared with the other prisoners.

One day, he sneaked in some hosts. *Now, it was immediate execution, if a priest was caught celebrating Holy Mass. Even those men, who had become monsters, knew the Power of Jesus.* Father took the hosts, said the words of consecration and he brought Jesus in the Holy Eucharist, the Bread of Life, to his fellow patients. He celebrated Holy Mass not once but twice. At times, he took what little bread he had and consecrated it, distributing the Lord to all. But, he never would accept any of the other prisoners rations, saying *"You need them. You must live."* Father Maxmilian, priest!

A prisoner escaped! The shrill sound of the alarm pierced the still, dark night. The prisoners lay frozen, praying they would not be part of those chosen to be executed. According to the barbaric law of the camp, when an inmate escaped, *ten* men from his cell were chosen to starve to death, in the underground bunker. They rounded up all the prisoners and had them stand at attention, for three hours, in the prison yard. Then, they marched them in to have their meager supper, all that is but the men of *block 14*! Instead, they were forced to helplessly look by, as their rations were dumped into the canal.

The next day, they were lined up in the scorching sun, as the rest of the prisoners went off to work. They were given nothing to drink or eat. Their condition became so unbearable, many of them collapsed and not even the guards' brutal beatings could arouse them. They just dumped them, one on top of another, in a heap.

As night approached, the rest of the prisoners came back. They, too, were lined up, facing those of *block 14*, so they could witness what happens when someone escapes. They stood there, helpless to ease the fear they saw in their fellow inmates eyes, as they stared across at them...And then, the dreaded announcement: "Since the fugitive has not been found, ten of you are condemned to death." The commander Fritsch took delight as he passed back and forth, before the prisoners of *block 14.* He could read their minds, *Oh God, don't let it be me.*

"Good-by, friends; we will meet again where there is justice," was joined by another sobbing, "Long live Poland!" "Good-by! Good-by, my dear wife; good-by, my dear children, already orphans of your father," cried out Sergeant Francis Gajowniczek.

A prisoner from *block 14* stepped out of the lineup. It was Father Maxmilian! He had been assigned to block 14, had endured all the torture and was still standing. He walked slowly and calmly toward the commandant. He stopped in front of Fritsch. The sight was blinding! There was a hush that went through the men lined up. No one, in

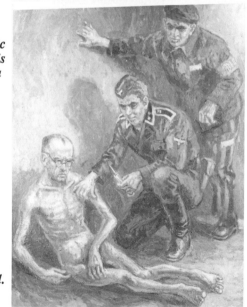

Above:
"I am a Polish Catholic priest; I want to take his place because he has a wife and children..."

Right:
*He saw
Father Maxmilian,
a prayer on his lips,
love and forgiveness
in his eyes,
hold out his left arm
to the killers,
to be injected
with the poisonous acid.*

the history of the camp, had ever done anything like this before.

They stared; they tried to take their eyes away, but they couldn't or wouldn't. Suddenly they were not afraid of this man who reduced men to animals; he no longer posed a threat. The man before him, chest caved in, little more than hanging flesh on thin bones, had the upper hand. The commander was stunned, frozen. Was he afraid at what or who it was, he saw? Did he remember from a thousand lifetimes ago, his mother telling him about the Savior who gave His life for him?

Here was a man who had traded his God in for a lie and he looked frightened. Facing him, was one who death could have no victory over, one who dared to love *Him* with all his heart, mind and soul, totally abandoning himself to Him. He had loved others through *Him*, in *Him*, with *Him*, even this monster in front of him. This one who so exemplified the *Sacrificial Lamb* who died, forgiving them, saying "They know not what they do," frightened him!

The commander found his voice; regaining his composure, he barked, "What does this Polish pig want?"

Father Maxmilian, pointing toward Sergeant Francis Gajowniczek, answered:

"*I am a Polish Catholic priest; I am old; I want to take his place because he has a wife and children...*"

Father Maxmilian was 47 years old!

The underground bunker, *block 13*, was a *chamber of horror*. It was closed in by a wall twenty-one feet high; prisoners were to have no communication from the outside. Upon entering, inmates knew they would only leave as corpses, on their way to the crematorium. Only a few Poles came in any kind of contact with the bunker, those who the Nazis needed, to carry out bodies and etc. This is how we have any idea of what went on.

They led Father and the other nine to *bunker 13*. They stripped them of all their clothing and left them, sneering, "We will dry you up like tulips!" A Pole later testified: when they went down to the bunkers, it sounded as if the angels were accompanying the prisoners singing hymns to Jesus and Mary; instead of curses, the Rosary and Litanies of prayers resounded through the dungeons, petitioning God for mercy in what He *would* give them and thanking Him for what He *had* given them. The other bunkers, having joined the little priest in *bunker 13* were heard echoing his love song to Mary and Her Son Jesus. They were so immersed in their praise and worship, they often did not hear the guards until they shouted at them to be quiet!

When the door opened, the prisoners pitifully begged for some water and bread. Those who were strong enough to make it over to the door were kicked in the stomach, and when they fell, if they did not die, they were shot right there. Conditions got so bad, the prisoners drank their own urine (as was evidenced by the empty and dry pails that had been left for them to relieve themselves).

Father encouraged the other innocent prisoners not to give up hope, to pray that the escaped prisoner would be found and they would be freed. For himself, he asked nothing. He even got to the guards, who came in each day to check up on the prisoners. They had never experienced such love and compassion. For some, it was more than they could handle; was he showing them what man could be like, according to God's plan? They called him a real gentleman.

Father Maxmilian lived longer than the rest, consoling them and praying with them until they mercifully gave up their last breath. Two weeks passed; prisoners died one after the other. At the end of the third week, there were four left; Father Maxmilian was one of them! So, needing the bunker for more prisoners, they called in the director of the hall of the sick, the infamous and wicked Boch. He lifted the arms of the prisoners left. As they looked up at him, helplessly, he injected them with poisonous *acid*.

One of the Poles testified he had been with the Nazi officers in the block. He saw Father Maxmilian, a prayer on his lips, love and forgiveness in his eyes, hold out his left arm to the killers. He said he couldn't stand it anymore and he (the Pole) left, with the pretense he had work to do. When he returned, he found Father Maxmilian sitting, his body leaning against the wall, his beautiful eyes open, and his head bent to the left side. He did not look as if he had died a horrible death. He was radiant, he looked serene as if he had fallen asleep or was just dreaming with his eyes open. He was beautiful! When You died, Jesus, You died that all man could live, once and for all. Now, another son was called to give up his life that *a* man could live and that son, Your brother Father Maxmilian Mary Kolbe said "yes!"

Father Maxmilian died on the vigil of the Feast of the Assumption of our and his Lady into Heaven. What the world, with the world's eyes, saw was an emaciated body brutally tortured, wasted away, desecrated by his forced nakedness-more bones than flesh. But witnesses testified when they saw him, he was shrouded in a flood of light, almost transfigured. He looked as if he were in ecstasy. Had Jesus and Mary come to accompany him home?

It was Friday, August the 15th, men came for his body and placed it in a box. It was taken to the ovens. They had been burning for him, day and night, as they had for others. There was a silence that screamed through the camp. Love had been there. Compassion had lived in their midst. Hope had battled fear. God had been present among the godless. *He*, through His priest, had entered this holocaust, had brought the dead to new life, and it would never be the same!

Survivors of Auschwitz testified that the camp became a better place; its hell had lost its sting. Was it because perhaps, through this priest they were no longer prisoners of godless men, but willing slaves of Jesus and Mary?

"I would like my ashes to be scattered to the four winds," a prayer he had often said, was on this day, the day celebrating the Feast of Her Assumption into Heaven, *answered* by the Lady he had always loved, his Mama, his Queen, his Niepokalanow.

But his desire *"to decrease while Christ increase"* was *not* to be granted by his Father in Heaven. He would not disappear *"without a trace."* On the vigil Feast of the Assumption, 1941, a man died, a Pole, a Catholic priest and a son of Mary.

His story needed to be told. In this world, where man sometimes sinks to a level beneath the animals, he was given dominion over, we need a Father Maxmilian Mary Kolbe, true son of Francis. We are in the time of Francis. We are in the time of Maxmilian Mary Kolbe. We are in the time of Mary. We are in the time of Pope John Paul II.

We may be in the time of new martyrs. A modern day *dry martyr,*[9] Pope John Paul II, another Pole, on October 10th, 1982, raised a knight of Mary to sainthood, and in Heaven, Mary said *"This day, son, you have lived your motto 'Totus Tuus' (all yours, Mary)"* Thank you!

---

[9]see chapter on Bishop Sheen

Right:
The Forgione family lived in the poorest section of Pietrelcina. Francesco was poor, but by his own testimony, he never lacked for anything.
(Street in Pietrelcina)

Left:
A huge man dressed like a priest, would block the entrance to his house, when he came home from school. Then a young boy, whom he didn't know, walked up to the priest, made the sign of the cross, and the priest disappeared.
(Entrance to his home)

Padre Pio

"I will do much more after my death."

God is so good! He knows our needs before we do. Who realized at the turn of the century how the beliefs and traditions of our faith would be under so much attack for the next ninety years. Who suspected that we would need so desperately, *a role model,* someone we could point to, and tell the world, *"Ecce Homo,* behold the man! He affirms our faith. The Eucharist and the Word, Our Lady, the Angels, our heritage in our brothers and sisters, the Saints, are truly rich gifts from Our Lord Jesus." We are strengthened by the powerful men and women the Lord sends to help us in times of crisis, when we judge that everything, we have ever held dear in our Church, is falling apart around us. Padre Pio of Pietrelcina is one of those men.

There are literally thousands of stories of Padre Pio, with regard to the many spiritual gifts he received. Many of these have been documented, while others have been woven out of a sincere love people have had for him. We will share some of the documented miraculous occurrences with you, and there are many, because they form a part of who this man was and is.

If Mother Church chooses to raise him to the Communion of Saints, the qualities of sanctity in Padre Pio will not be solely because he bore the stigmata[1] for 50 years

---

[1]Stigmata - from the Greek, meaning "marks". This refers to the wounds, scars or abrasions that appear on the skin of people, corresponding to the five wounds of Jesus, in the hands, the feet and the side.

of his life, that he had the gift of bi-location[2], the fragrance of Heaven[3], or the many miracles attributed to him during his lifetime. The proclamation of his sainthood will come from the extraordinary spirituality he showed during his ministry, his enormous love for Our Lord Jesus in the Eucharist, his devotion to Mary and the Rosary, his willingness to take on the sins of the world during his eighteen-hour days in the confessional, his inspired writings, his spiritual counselling, his obedience to his superiors, most especially His Holiness, the Pope, and possibly more than anything, his lifelong commitment to his Sacrament, his priesthood. In short, his loyalty to the *Body of Christ, the Mother of Christ, through the Vicar of Christ.*

Writing about this powerful man in the Church, may be the most difficult task we have undertaken. We want to present to you the whole man, the man who has touched us, the man whom we love. The Cause for Padre Pio's Beatification has been opened. It's very important that none of us, out of some misdirected sense of love for Padre Pio, say or do anything that would prejudice his cause in any way.

We know that nothing is coincidental with the Lord. At best, occurrences that appear to be coincidental, can be termed "*Holy Coincidence.*" And so we know in advance that it was God's plan that Francesco Forgione, the future Padre Pio, be born so close to the Castle Gate of Pietrelcina. Also, in the same vicinity were the ruins of an ancient feudal church in honor of St. Michael the Archangel. He would need the protection of St. Michael and the Angels throughout his life. Very close to the place where Francesco

---

[2]Bilocation is the actual presence of one finite person in two places at the same time. Padre Pio was known to have been seen in various parts of the world, including St. Peter's Basilica, although he never left San Giovanni Rotondo.

[3]A heavenly fragrance, unique and identifiable, which, in Padre Pio's case, exuded from his open wounds.

was born is the Church of Santa Maria degli Angeli[4] (Our Lady of the Angels), where he was baptized, also not coincidentally. Santa Maria degli Angeli in Assisi, is the home of the Portiuncola, the first church of St. Francis, after whom Padre Pio was named, and whose way of life he would embrace.

So you can see, right off the bat, how the Lord was working in Padre Pio's life from before he was born. We really believe the Lord has had a plan for all of us from the beginning of time. Our job is to say "*Yes*" to His plan. Researching the lives of the powerful men and women in our Church has been such a gift to us, in that we can see clearly, how the Lord has orchestrated the lives of those who have said "*Yes!*" Undoubtedly, the enemy will attack, very often, from the most unsuspecting sources. Time and again, those we believe to be our best friends and allies, will unwittingly do the devil's work. But if we have our eyes on the Cross, if we are willing to pick up our Cross daily, the Lord takes care of us. We believe Padre Pio was a man who carried his Cross, and the Crosses of many, all his life.

The Forgione family lived in the poorest section of Pietrelcina. Francesco was poor, but by his own testimony, he never lacked for anything. Values were much different in those days. A child considered himself well off if he had the *basics* in life. Francesco came from a good family. His father, Grazio, and his mother Maria Guiseppa, were hard working farmers. Their children's well being was number one in their priorities. They were able to provide for their family's needs, but not much more. There were no frills. Francesco grew up a very sensitive, very spiritual boy. It was as if he knew from earliest childhood, the road the Lord had for him to follow. He would always follow that road.

---

[4]Later restored and named St. Anne

His mother, Guiseppa, claimed that Francesco was a good boy, who never gave her any trouble. Naturally, she'd say that. She was a mother. Padre Pio, on the other hand, had a few comments to make about little Francesco Forgione. While he admitted that he was never spanked, he recalled his mother running after him, calling out, *"Come here, you shameless boy!"* When asked why she did this, the famous grin, and little twinkle came into his eye. *"Little incidents with my sister."*[5] That one sentence affirms that, while he was specially chosen, he was a normal boy!

His world was the little church of Our Lady of the Angels. It might as well have been his home. All the important events in his early life, took place in that church. In addition to being baptized there, receiving his First Holy Communion, and Confirmation there, he went into ecstasy in that church, and had an apparition of the Sacred Heart of Jesus at age five, there. *"Our Lord Jesus appeared to Francesco, and beckoned him to come to the main altar*[6]*."* He placed His hand on Francesco's head. The course of his life, and his vocation were sealed. He offered himself as victim at that early age.

Age five was an important time for Francesco, a turning point, so to speak. He began to have apparitions of Our Lady, which continued all his life. It was also then that demons began to torture him. There's an elm tree on the Piana Romana (Roman Plain), which has been picked clean by over-enthusiastic pilgrims since Padre Pio lived there. Francesco used to sit under that tree to take advantage of the shade during the hot summer days. He went through harsh battles with demons at that place. Friends and neighbors testified, they could see him under the tree,

---

[5]Alessandro da Ripabottoni, Padre Pio of Pietrelcina, Everyone's Cyrenean, Pg. 20

[6]Statement made by Padre Benedetto da San Marco in Lamis, Padre Pio's spiritual director

fighting with some invisible force. It looked like he was defending himself against a swarm of bees. These battles continued on and off until his final days.

In the slang of today, Padre Pio used to hang out at church as a child. He went there to pray. He stayed hours after Mass. He worked out an arrangement with the sacristan to lock him in the church at times, so he could adore the Lord in the Eucharist. His parish priest was Don Salvatore Pannullo, whom he affectionately referred to as Zi' Tore (Uncle Tore or Salvatore). Zi' Tore recalled the future Padre Pio as having told him at age *five*, he wanted to become a priest. The priest could see special attributes in Francesco Forgione. Others saw the same traits, but could not distinguish their meaning. He had to be categorized; the world insists on putting everybody into a box. Qualities that his friends and neighbors categorized as "shy," "different," "quiet," Don Salvatore saw as the signs of deep spirituality.

Francesco had a hunger to learn. But there were no schools for him to attend. Two men of the town, farmers, volunteered to teach the children of the area. Their major qualifications were that they could read and write. But that, coupled with their sincere desire to help the children, started a school. The children went to class at night, because they had to work during the day. Francesco tended sheep for his father and mother. He studied during that time. His friends tried to get him to play with them, but he kept to his books.

When he did play with his friends, he drew the line at swearing. He used to run away from boys, when they began to curse. But although he was willing to play, it was not one of his priorities. His preference was to spend time in church, praying, and if the church was closed, sitting on the rocks outside, also praying.

Francesco knew what a sacrifice it was for his family to sponsor him in school. At the beginning, when he was being taught by the farmers, there was little cost to his father, little financial cost, that is. Grazio had to allow Francesco to take time off from helping with the sheep, to study. But when it became obvious that Francesco had advanced far beyond his volunteer teacher's ability to teach, when he told his family that he was serious about becoming a religious, after St. Francis, they knew they had to make much *greater* sacrifices.

It was at this time that Grazio left his family, and came to the United States, to Jamaica, Long Island, New York. There was no way, he could support his son's education on the meager earnings he made from the land in Italy.

And so Grazio kissed his wife good-by, gave instructions to his children, who were now in charge, and traveled the six thousand miles it would take to bring him where there was enough money. He worked hard in New York, and sent as much money home as was possible. You know, the more we read about Grazio, we come to realize that Padre Pio had a saintly father as an example all his life. Although he did not attend Mass as regularly as he should have, and profanities flew from his mouth when he was angry, he was truly a man of God, completely selfless, focused on his family.

We, the mothers and fathers, *are the priest-makers*. Last year, in one of our talks, Penny pointed her finger at a large audience in a Texas town.

"Don't be blaming the priests for lack of vocations. They come from us, the family. Sure, we all want grandchildren, for our name and heritage to go on. But are you aware that though the priest gives back to God, the gift of having children by his vow of celibacy, he is given the gift of eternal life through his consecrated hands? When we Catholics become truly aware of the gifts of the priesthood, our seminaries will be filled to overflowing. But you're the ones who have to make it happen!"

We believe that Grazio and Guiseppa Forgione were given this word of knowledge. Though they were simple folk, the Lord gave them the wisdom to see the path their son had to take, and they did everything in their power to make it happen, at enormous sacrifice in their own lives.

Padre Pio always walked the narrow line, never allowing himself the luxury of anything that could jeopardize his relationship with Jesus. His parents brought him to the school of Don Domenico Tizzani, a former priest, who had left his vocation to marry. Although it was a bad choice from the outset, Don Tizzani had the only real school for miles around. So Francesco went there for three years.

It was a battle from the beginning. Francesco felt a natural antagonism for this man, which reflected in the fact that he did not advance as rapidly as he should have, much to the chagrin of the teacher, and Guiseppa. The teacher complained to her. She got on Francesco, berating him for not making the most of this opportunity. After all, his father had to leave the family and go to America, just so he could have this education. Francesco cried from the depths of his heart, "*The problem is he's been a bad priest!*"

Guiseppa backed off immediately. At about that time, we believe, some Angels whispered into Grazio's heart in New York. "*If Francesco wants to be a friar, what logic is there in sending him to an ex-priest for his education?*" He wrote to his wife, "Stop sending Francesco to Don Domenico's school and look for a better teacher."

The Lord led Guiseppa to a Signor Caccavo, under whose tutelage, Francesco advanced in leaps and bounds. Signor Caccavo recalled that Francesco had told him once, a huge man dressed like a priest, would block the entrance to his house, when he came home from school. Then a young boy, whom he didn't know, walked up to the *priest*, made the sign of the cross, and the *priest* disappeared.

The Seminary

By the time Francesco was fifteen years old, he was advanced enough in his studies to enter a friary. He had decided, years before, that he would be a Capuchin. He had to wait some months before entering. His uncle Pellegrino pointed out other religious orders to him. Francesco shook his head, "*No, they don't wear beards.*" This may be the logic of the young, but the Lord had a reason for wanting Francesco to follow in the footsteps of his namesake, who was to become his Spiritual Father. And if an attraction to beards would do the trick, so be it.

Finally, he received permission to enter the Capuchin friary at Morcone in January 1903. The few days before his entry into the seminary, were days of visions from the Lord, to prepare him for the battle that lay ahead for him. Jesus was allowing Francesco to see the battle plan, the treacherous enemy, the obstacles, the impossible odds. It was as if He had laid out the conflicts Padre Pio would experience all his life, and how, with the help of his Guardian Angels, and Jesus at his side, he would *overcome* the enemy.

In this vision, Jesus acted as Francesco's guide. He led him onto an immense battlefield. On one side were radiant looking men dressed in white. On the other, hideous creatures dressed in somber, dark, gloomy colors. Jesus pointed to a towering monster, bigger than anything Francesco had ever seen. It was a terrifying sight. Jesus told the young Francesco, he had to do battle with the creature. Francesco's knees began to shake. He pleaded with the Lord not to ask him do it. There was no way he could be victorious over such a grotesque beast.

Jesus repeated His request to Francesco, but said He would be at his side. Francesco did as he was told. He went into a ferocious combat. The pain inflicted on him was excruciating. But he was triumphant. The monster fled, as did all his repulsive followers, screaming at the tops of their voices, making inhuman sounds.

Jesus told Francesco, he would have to do battle with this demon again, and throughout his life. But Jesus would always be with him, to protect him, and help him. *"Fear not, I will be with you always, until the end of the world."*[7]

This *particular* vision petrified Padre Pio for the next twenty years. In reflecting on it, the thirty-five year old Padre Pio shuddered as he spoke of the experience. Just think of how the fifteen-year old Francesco felt after he went through it. Jesus was giving Francesco a physical sign of the enemies that *all* of us have to battle, all our lives.

Today, we're told that there is no devil, no Satan, no Lucifer. He doesn't exist. He's just a mirage that religious leaders have cooked up over the centuries, to control our behavior patterns, to force us to act according to their prudish standards. What is happening, people, is that we're being lulled into a *euphoric* state. The *intelligentsia* of the world are trying to play mind games on us. If we're not aware of the enemy (*the devil*), or we don't believe he exists, why bother keeping our defenses up to do battle with him?

And so it was with the future Padre Pio. The Lord knew the road he would travel, to bring His children to the Kingdom. He knew the obstacles, the future stigmatist would have to overcome, the enemy that would attack him throughout his life, and the strength of that foe. He showed Francesco the worst, so that he would never underestimate what he was to be up against, or let his guard down.

But as a balance, perhaps, the night before he entered the friary, he was given a vision of Our Lord Jesus, and His beautiful Mother, Mary. In this vision, Jesus put His hand on Francesco's shoulder, as He had when Francesco was five years old. Jesus gave him the courage to go on. Mary, for her part, spoke to him gently, tenderly, motherly, burrowing through to his soul with her beautiful gaze.

---

[7]Mt 28:20

Francesco took the religious name of Fra Pio. It was a never-ending challenge for him to go through his training. He kept being pulled back to the land of his birth, Pietrelcina. How he managed to go through six years of training, was a miracle in itself. He suffered bouts of illness all that time.

He was constantly under attack by *messengers* of the devil. The assaults took on every form possible. There were physical abuses that went on during the night, which would leave him in a pool of perspiration and exhaustion in the morning. There were onslaughts against his *purity*. Naked women manifested themselves before him in all forms of lewd behavior. But these were the obvious. Another, more deadly form of attack came in the form of demons disguised as spiritual directors, respected confessors, even as Jesus and Mary. They tortured him through the night, criticizing him, admonishing him for not being good enough, not holy enough, not studious enough.

In addition, he, like his father in faith, St. Francis, practiced mortification. The Capuchin fraternity was a far more austere branch of the Franciscan Order, actually much closer to the original rule of St. Francis. Fasting and penance were a normal practice of the fraternity. Fra Pio embraced all forms of self-deprivation. He ate very little, under normal circumstances. At one time, he lived on nothing but the Sacred Body of Our Lord Jesus in the Eucharist, for twenty days. He was physically weak, and undernourished. Yet, he went through his studies so excitedly, so happy. It was the best time of his life.

"I am happier than ever when I am suffering, and if I would listen to the promptings of my heart, I would ask Jesus to give me all the sufferings of men."

He threw himself into his life at the seminary. It was the place, he was destined to be all his life. Everything he had ever experienced was in anticipation for this time. He prayed; he studied; he cried over the Passion of His Lord Jesus. He maintained silence most of the time. Others who had entered the fraternity before him, marveled at how he embraced the religious life. He attracted them to himself by his meticulous attention to the rules. After a year, he *officially* proclaimed the vows of Chastity, Poverty and Obedience; but he had always practiced these virtues.

In 1905, only two years after he entered the Seminary, Fra Pio experienced bi-location for the first time. He was in the choir of the friary of Sant Elia a Pianisi on a cold January night. It was around 11 p.m. He was praying with another Friar. All of a sudden, he found himself far away, in a very elegant house, where a father was dying at the same time as his child was being born.

Our Lady appeared to Fra Pio. She told him, "*I am entrusting this creature to your care; it is a precious stone in an unpolished state. Work on it; polish it; make it as shiny as possible, as one day I want to adorn myself with it...*"

He replied, "*How will this be possible if I am still a poor student, and don't even know if I will have the good fortune of becoming a priest? And even if I do become a priest, how will I be able to think of this baby girl, being so far from here?*"

Our Lady said, "*Do not doubt. It will be she who will come to you, but beforehand you will meet her in Saint Peter's* (Basilica)." Then he found himself back in the choir where he had been praying.

The girl, Giovanna, was born in Udine, way up at the northern part of Italy, on the evening of January 18. The mother insisted she had seen a Capuchin Friar leave the house. The father died that night. The mother and daughter moved to Rome.

Eighteen years later, in 1922, Giovanna went to St. Peter's Basilica late one day. She was troubled; she wanted to confess, and get some spiritual counselling. There were no confessors available, as it was late, and they were about to close the Basilica.   She looked around her; she saw a Capuchin friar walk into a confessional and close the door. She went over to the confessional, and began to tell her problems to the priest.

In short order, he had given her peace of mind and spirit, and absolved her of her sins. She got up, and wanted to thank him by kissing his hand. *There was no one there!* A custodian came by to ask her to leave. She explained what had happened.   The man opened the door of the confessional, and showed her the empty chair.   "But Signorina, there's no one here."

A year later, this same girl went to San Giovanni Rotondo, with a relative and some friends.   The corridor, through which Padre Pio walked to his cell, was jam packed with pilgrims. He saw this girl in the first row. He pointed to her. "*I know you. You were born on the day your father died.*" With that, he blessed her.

She was completely taken back by his statement. How did he know her? How did he know about her father? She had to speak to him. She waited on the long line the next day, to go to confession to Padre Pio. When she entered the confessional, he said to her, "*My daughter, you have finally come! I have waited so many years for you.*"

She pleaded with him, "Padre, I do not know you. This is the first time I've come to San Giovanni Rotondo. Perhaps you have made a mistake; perhaps you have mistaken me for some other girl."

"*No, I am not mistaken*" he replied. "*You already know me; you came to me last year in Saint Peter's Basilica.*"

Then Padre Pio explained how he had bi-located to her home the day she was born and her father died. He shared the apparition of Mary, and the command she had given him, about the child.

She became his spiritual daughter. She accepted his advice, married, raised a strong Catholic family, and returned to San Giovanni Rotondo often, for counselling from Padre Pio. One day, she felt him calling in her heart. She rushed to San Giovanni Rotondo. When he heard her confession, he told her, it would be the last time she would see him, *"because I must leave."* Four days later, he was dead.

Return to Pietrelcina

In 1909, he was ordained Deacon of the Church, in anticipation of his ordination to the priesthood the next year. He became extremely ill. He had to return home to Pietrelcina. This was to be the strangest seven years of his life. Each time he would return to one of the friaries, he became deathly ill. He never lasted more than a few months. Then he would have to go home. The day after he arrived home, he would be in perfect health.

He and his superiors were bewildered. No one could understand why the Lord kept bringing him back to Pietrelcina. To this day, it has never been clearly explained what the Lord's plan was during that time. The closest anyone ever came to an answer was, when Padre Agostino of San Marco in Lamis asked the question some years later. Padre Pio stated, *"I can't tell you the reason the Lord wanted me back in Pietrelcina, Father. I would lack charity."* Nobody ever pursued the subject again.

Was God testing Padre Pio? Was He testing his superiors? Was He testing the entire Capuchin Fraternity? It got that bad. It was like a battle of wills. The provincial insisted that he wanted Padre Pio back in the friary, any friary. He reasoned that if the Lord were not going to heal Padre Pio from his illness at home, at least he should die with his fraternity.

Despite all of this trial, Fra Pio was able to continue his studies with a local priest, and was finally accepted into the priesthood in 1910. This was the happiest moment of his life. But his joy was short-lived. After his ordination in the Cathedral of Benevento, his Superiors assumed that he would be able to return to his fraternity. He was ordered back to a particular friary. He always went obediently, but within a short time, he had to return home again.

At one point, in 1908, early on in his training, his Provincial became so frustrated by this never-ending illness, that he asked his Father General for permission to have Padre Pio separated from the Capuchin Order. *And it was granted!* Padre Pio was devastated. He would rather die than be separated from the Capuchin fraternity. He begged Jesus to take him to heaven, rather than separate him from the Order of St. Francis. But the Lord had different plans. He wanted his servant very much alive.

There was a friary which had never been recommended by his Provincial, hidden away in a little mountain village, called San Giovanni Rotondo. In February of 1916, the Provincial, Padre Benedetto, ordered Padre Pio to meet him at the train station in Benevento. He was afraid to go into Pietrelcina, and physically take the favorite son away from his flock. When Padre Pio met Padre Benedetto, they traveled to Foggia, to St. Anne's Friary there. Padre Benedetto vowed that Padre Pio would stay there, "*until death, if necessary.*"

It's so exciting to see the Lord's plan in action. You can actually visualize Jesus moving His "yes" people from place to place, so that He can accomplish Step 2 or Step 3 of His plan. Padre Pio stayed at St. Anne's Friary for seven months, longer than he had ever stayed at any friary since 1909. His condition became steadily worse. No one was sure whether he would live or die. The Provincial, Padre Benedetto, who really felt he was doing the Lord's Will by insisting that Padre Pio stay in a friary, was now having second thoughts. He didn't want to be responsible for the death of one of his Friars, and yet....

Then, according to the Lord's timetable, Padre Paolino, the superior of the small friary at San Giovanni Rotondo, came to St. Anne's Friary to preach a novena. Upon seeing the emaciated figure of the young Padre Pio, he invited him to spend a few days at San Giovanni Rotondo, where the mountain air would do him good. Padre Pio accepted, and shortly thereafter, he went to the high mountain friary. Once there, his breathing became better; his head was clear. He was home. The Lord's plan had been accomplished. He asked permission to be permanently assigned there; he got it. Everyone was happy.

However, for those of you who have visited San Giovanni Rotondo, and the marvelous complex that is there today, don't think that's what Padre Pio walked into. All of that is A.P.P. (after Padre Pio). When he first went there, the friary of Our Lady of Grace was way at the very end of the town. There was just a dirt path leading from the center of town to the Church, for those few people who wanted to venture out that far to attend Mass. The little friary was the victim of earthquakes, and abandonment on two occasions, when the ruling governments actually threw the Franciscans out. But they kept coming back, and in 1907, just nine years *before* Padre Pio went there, they returned for good.

The Stigmata

Padre Pio began to receive what he termed "*red patches, about the size of a cent, and accompanied by acute pain.*" This is from a letter he sent Padre Benedetto on the Birthday of Mary, September 8, 1911. He went on to say, "*The pain was much more acute in the left hand and it still persists. I also feel some pain in the soles of my feet.*" He told his superior that this had been happening, on and off, for almost a year. So from the time of Padre Pio's ordination, at twenty three years old, he began to feel in his body, the wounds of the Passion of Christ. The physical signs disappeared, but the pain continued.

As if in anticipation of the gift he was to be given very shortly, the Lord granted Padre Pio a very special favor, one that would give him joy and pain all his life. On August 5, 1918, he received the gift of transverberation of the heart. Padre Pio wrote of this experience,

"While I was hearing the confessions of our boys on the evening of the 5th (August), I was suddenly filled with extreme terror at the sight of a celestial being whom I saw with my mind's eye. He held a kind of weapon in his hand, similar to a steel sword with a sharp, flaming point. At the very instant I saw all this, I saw the person hurl the weapon into my soul with all his might. It was all done in a split second. I was hardly able to cry out and felt as if I were dying. I cannot tell you how much I suffered during this period of anguish. Even my insides were torn and ruptured by that weapon, everything lashed by fire and steel. From that day on, I was wounded to death. In the depths of my soul, I feel an open wound which causes me to suffer continual agony."

The only other person that we know of, who has experienced the transverberation of the heart, was St. Teresa of Avila. She described her experience as follows:

"She (St. Teresa of Avila) *saw an Angel to the left of her. He was small and very beautiful. He was so illuminated he had to be one of the very highest of the Angels, the Cherubim. He had a long golden dart in his hand, with what appeared to be fire at the end of it. She said he thrust it into her heart several times, piercing her down to her innermost organs, leaving her burning with a great love for God.*[8]*"*

As you can see from their writings, their reactions to the transverberation of the heart were different.   Teresa

---

[8]Saints and Other Powerful Women in the Church, Bob and Penny Lord, Journeys of Faith, 1989 - Pg 178

experienced such a feeling of love, which stayed with her all her life. Padre Pio, on the other hand, continued to record his suffering. However, although Teresa stressed the ecstatic nature of her gift, she also mentioned the pain, but even in expressing her pain, she lapsed back into *ecstasy*. She wrote,

"Even though it is a spiritual pain and not physical, the body participates in the pain, in fact a lot......In this state I was beside myself. I did not wish to see or speak to anyone, except to remain alone with my suffering, which seemed the greatest joy that could exist in creation."

In a letter to Padre Benedetto, on September 5, 1918, Padre Pio talked more about the suffering and anger he was enduring.

"I see myself submerged in an ocean of fire! The wound which has been reopened bleeds incessantly. This alone is enough to make me die a thousand times.

.....The excessive pain of this open wound makes me angry against my will, drives me crazy and makes me delirious. I am powerless in face of it."

This letter was written 13 days *before* he received the stigmata. He was referring to the transverberation of the heart. We believe we have each been given gifts in accordance with our walk with the Lord. For Padre Pio, the transverberation of the heart may well have been to prepare him for the stigmata, which he was to receive shortly after. It may also have been given to him as a source of strength and joy, that would offset the physical pain and agony which the Lord wanted to use for His glory. We say this because of a letter he wrote on January 12, 1919.

"Because of the exultation of possessing Him in me, I cannot refrain from saying with the most holy Virgin, 'My spirit rejoices in God my Savior.' Possessing Him within me, I am impelled to say with the spouse of the Sacred Song, 'I found Him whom my soul loves; I held Him and would not let Him go.'"

Left:
Crucifix in the choir, where Padre Pio prayed on September 20, 1918. *"The vision disappeared and I became aware that my hands, feet and side were dripping blood."*

Right:
"In the midst of this torment I find the strength to utter a painful fiat! Oh, how sweet and yet how bitter is this `May Thy will be done!' It cuts and heals; it wounds and cures, it deals death and at the same time gives life! O sweet torments, why are you so unbearable and so lovable simultaneously?"
Padre Pio, 1918

Padre Pio experienced the bitter-sweet love of Jesus. The bitter pain of his physical wounds was mixed with, and overpowered by the sweet, spiritual ecstasy he tasted by containing his Lord within his heart. Jesus never gives us more than we can handle, and showers us with more grace than we can ever use. As Jesus was born to die for our sins, so we believe Padre Pio was born to share in the Passion of Our Lord for our salvation.

September 20, 1918 was a turning point in the life of Padre Pio. While he had gathered a small following, because of his intense spirituality, and great wisdom, he would truly be the *Crucified Christ* after this day. He described the events of the day himself.

"On the morning of the 20th of last month, in the choir, after I had celebrated Mass, I yielded to a drowsiness similar to a sweet sleep. All the internal and external senses and even the very faculties of my soul were immersed in indescribable stillness. Absolute silence surrounded and invaded me. I was suddenly filled with great peace and abandonment which effaced everything else and caused a lull in the turmoil. All of this happened in a flash.

While this was taking place, I saw before me a mysterious person, similar to the one I had seen on the evening of 5 August. The only difference was that his hands and feet and side were dripping blood. The sight terrified me, and what I felt at that moment is indescribable. I thought I should die and really should have died if the Lord had not intervened and strengthened my heart, which was about to burst out of my chest.

The vision disappeared and I became aware that my hands, feet and side were dripping blood. Imagine the agony I experienced and continue to experience almost every day."

This visible sign of the Lord's Passion, which had been with him invisibly for eight years, became an immediate cause of panic in the young Capuchin. He didn't know what to do. He couldn't let anyone know what had happened. He didn't quite know himself. Perhaps it would go away. If he could just be away from people for a while, but how? As he wrote in the same letter, in which he described his receiving the stigmata, it was a source of embarrassment to him. Again, we come to the bitter-sweet, agony-ecstasy aspect of the stigmata. As with the transverberation of the heart, he wanted it and didn't want it. Physically, he couldn't stand the pain; yet spiritually, he felt himself lifted to the heights of ecstasy by the experience. It was truly a paradox.

When word got out of his stigmata, as it had to, his superior contacted Padre Benedetto, the Provincial. He asked him to come to San Giovanni Rotondo immediately, to witness for himself what had happened. He refused to come. He waited for Padre Pio to give him details of what had happened. Although Padre Pio wrote to the Provincial in between that time, it took over a month before he told him about the occurrences of September 20. He explained, he was too mortified by the situation.

Padre Benedetto was intent on drawing out from Padre Pio, his true feelings about having received the stigmata. It was understandable that he felt unworthy. Padre Benedetto had no problem with that. But Padre Pio used words like "monstrousness", "revolting, hate," and "detest" in referring to himself. Padre Benedetto wouldn't accept that. He felt the need to force Padre Pio to look squarely at his gift, and accept it, no, *embrace* it.

In a letter of November 16, 1918, the Provincial told Padre Pio,

"You are able to tell me all about the pain of love, and you will never tire of relating this, yet you are often, indeed almost invariably silent as regards painful love and love of

suffering, with all the love they produce and the loving expressions of tenderness which you enjoy and over which you weep.

When you make up your mind to tell me positively and distinctly about the sweetness of love, then I'll answer at once, point by point, your lamentations about what you are suffering."

It was in response to this that Padre Pio forced himself to come to terms, reluctantly perhaps, with the fact that he had been specially chosen. He answered his superior,

"In the midst of such torment which is lovable and painful at the same time, two conflicting feelings are present; one which would like to cast off the pain and the other which desires it. The mere thought of having to live for any length of time without this acute yet delightful torment terrifies me, appalls me and causes me to suffer agonies.

In the midst of this torment I find the strength to utter a painful fiat! Oh, how sweet and yet how bitter is this "May Thy will be done!" It cuts and heals; it wounds and cures, it deals death and at the same time gives life! O sweet torments, why are you so unbearable and so lovable simultaneously?"

The contrast in attitude between this letter and the one he had written his Provincial previously, is like night and day. Padre Benedetto actually forced Padre Pio to free himself of a self-inflicted guilt. As you read this letter, you can feel that he has lifted hundreds of pounds of guilt from Padre Pio's shoulders.

We want to take a minute out to talk about Padre Benedetto, a man surely sent by God, to walk Padre Pio through some of the most difficult times he suffered at the beginning of his ministry. In reading through the letters of Padre Pio, where most of this information comes from, we see in Padre Benedetto, a man who was gentle when he could be, rigid when he had to be, but always a loving father. He was given a most challenging task in being Padre Pio's provincial during his difficult years in Pietrelcina, and the first few years after he received the stigmata.

From these writings back and forth, between Padre Benedetto and Padre Pio, and trying to read in-between the lines, we can sense the frustration of Padre Benedetto. At times, it looked like he was throwing in the towel. But the Lord gave him patience when he didn't want to be patient anymore. He gave him just the right words to say at just the right times. It's much easier for us to look back in hindsight, and recognize Padre Pio's special gifts, his role as a suffering servant of Christ, through his fifty years of wounds. But the day-by-day living of that, must have been extremely difficult for Padre Benedetto. Padre Pio was aware of the frustration his superior was experiencing. In some of his letters, he would plead *"Don't give up on me, Father."*

The word spread to all the world

Padre Pio was tested all his life, but never so much as during the years immediately following his receiving the stigmata. Truly it was a gift from the Lord, but a hard gift to live with. Nobody really knew what to do with him at first. They tried to keep the knowledge of it a secret from the outside world. That didn't last very long. Within a few months, word had spread all over the southern part of Italy. Pilgrims came to the quiet little village of San Giovanni Rotondo from all over the area, to see, to be prayed over, to be healed by the priest with the wounds of Jesus. Mingled with the faithful were the curiosity seekers, the skeptics, the anti-clerics, and the fanatics. All of them converged on the peaceful little town. It was mass chaos. There were not enough facilities to handle the large crowds. There were not enough hotels, restaurants, restrooms, or police to control the crush of humanity that overtook San Giovanni Rotondo.

All of this activity was directed at one man. The church and grounds swarmed with people, trying to touch him, grab a piece of his tunic, see his wounds, have him pray over them. His superiors became concerned about the situation, as did the police and townspeople. But nobody knew quite how to handle it. The superior of the friary, under the direction of Padre Benedetto, forbid his Friars from mentioning the happenings at San Giovanni Rotondo, with regard to Padre Pio, to anyone. But the news leaked out.

Correspondents from secular newspapers all over Italy, began to show their faces in the little town. They were so smooth. They had ways of making casual conversation with the Friars, gaining their confidence, so that the Friars wound up giving them all the information they needed to put together a juicy story for their newspaper. The Catholic press respected the Provincial's request to keep the stigmata of Padre Pio quiet, but what good was that, when the secular papers, with far more readership, took enough half truths to make convincing stories about Padre Pio.

Padre Benedetto came down hard on the superior of the friary, and the Friars. In June of 1919, he chastised all of them, and made some firm rules.

"You may be confidential with lay-people, but always be wary of indiscretion. Use whatever diligence is necessary to see that divine things are not brought into the piazza, nor used as grazing grounds for newspapers, especially those profane ones.

....From now on I forbid 'sub gravi'[9] the communication to anybody and for any motive whatsoever, the intimate news of deeds or happenings which have already occurred or will occur."

However, it was too late. The news began a chain of events, like a nuclear reaction, which has never subsided.

---

[9]Sub Gravi - Under severe penalty

Now, instead of throngs from the southern region of Italy coming down to San Giovanni Rotondo, people from all over Europe, then the Americas, flocked to see Padre Pio.

At about the same time as this was happening, the medical examinations began. The ecclesiastical authorities wanted scientific explanations for what had happened to Padre Pio. To this end, they enlisted the aid of three doctors. First, there was Doctor Bignami, head physician of a hospital in Barletta. Then, almost on the heels of Professor Bignami, Dr. Romanelli, a very respected, and well-credentialed professor of medical pathology at the University of Rome, came to examine Padre Pio. The last doctor was Professor Giorgio Festa. He dedicated the greater part of his medical career, studying, researching, and writing on the stigmata.

Of the three, possibly the most famous was Dr. Romanelli, from Rome. After his investigation, he came to the conclusion that the wounds were the product of auto-suggestion and the application of a strong chemical, such as iodine. But bottom line, they were not caused by supernatural causes.

Professor Bignami and Dr. Festa came down on him like a ton of bricks. Working together, they disproved beyond a shadow of a doubt, his findings, and through intensive investigation, offered proof that there were many aspects of Padre Pio's wounds which were unexplainable by human or scientific terms. They used words like phenomenon, enigma, and paradox. We use words like *miracle*, and *Gift of God*. But people believe what people want to believe. There were many, the majority of people, for that matter, who believed the Lord had come to bless His people, through this servant. There were others, not that many, but with perhaps bigger mouths, who claimed it was a hoax, a fraud, perpetrated by the Church at a time when her children were turning their back on their age old beliefs, and embracing the new, more powerful words of *Il Duce* and the *Fascisti*, who were gaining power and popularity after a devastating and crippling World War I.

The Padre Pio Question

As sides were taken in the secular community, camps were set up in the religious fraternity as well. We're all human, and subject to the frailties of our legacy from Adam in the Garden of Eden. Many of those opposed to Padre Pio, sincerely thought they were following the voice of the Holy Spirit in their judgments against him. But the *fruits* were so strong. Bishops and Cardinals asked for his prayers. One Bishop, Alberto Costa, wrote of Padre Pio,

"'By their fruits, you shall know them.' Innumerable souls return to God; reawakenings in the faith, change of habits, frequent reception of the Sacraments especially on the part of men who had been away from them for many years... These and other facts, too numerous to list here, formed the impression which increased my desire to return to this house which is hallowed by the perfume of the exceptional virtue of the young religious."

Padre Pio had a friend in Pope Benedict XV. He considered Padre Pio as *"one of those truly extraordinary men whom God sends on earth every now and then to convert sinners."* He defended Padre Pio against attacks by members in the Vatican, who openly criticized the Capuchin stigmatist, and cast doubts about the veracity of his gift. But the Lord didn't choose to make Padre Pio's life easy. He was to be a victim. He had said *"yes"* to that, and the Lord was holding him to his commitment. Pope Benedict XV died suddenly on January 22, 1922.

Six months later, the Holy Office made a decision, with regard to Padre Pio:

He was not allowed to say Mass for the people, but privately.

He was not allowed to have Padre Benedetto as his spiritual director.

He was not allowed to correspond with him in any way.

He was not allowed to correspond with any of his followers, asking for spiritual direction.

He was to *leave* San Giovanni Rotondo, for somewhere far away from his province, perhaps Northern Italy.

His superior, Padre Paolino, was replaced by Padre Ignazio in September, 1922. *His* was a thankless job. On the one hand, he had to comply with the demands of the Holy Office, especially where it concerned moving Padre Pio out of San Giovanni Rotondo. On the other hand, he was under suspicion from the townspeople as being sort of a *hatchet man*, brought in to resolve the Padre Pio problem. The Friars may have also manifested some resentment for this newcomer, who was taking the place of their beloved superior. In his own words,

"I was in San Giovanni Rotondo from the 7th to the 11th of September. For the record, I report my less than warm welcome, received on the evening of my arrival.

....when I arrived, I was surrounded by all these people and every effort was needed to calm them. Despite all my assurances and that of others (that Padre Pio would not be sent away), the friary was guarded during the night. We never deluded ourselves with regard to (the danger) moving Padre Pio from San Giovanni Rotondo, but this episode might serve to persuade anyone who doesn't know (those people) well."

We're always amazed when we find Italians who cannot read other Italians. I'm not Italian; my wife is. Actually, she's Sicilian. But *I would know*, and could predict the passion that would be forthcoming from the local people of the little village. I'm sure the new Provincial of the Capuchins (Padre Benedetto was relieved of his post as Provincial in July 1919) was aware of the sentiment of the local people for Padre Pio, and how volatile the situation was there. Did the officials at the Holy Office in Rome, who were most likely Italians too, underestimate the devotion the people of San Giovanni Rotondo had for Padre Pio? Actually, the situation proved far worse than I would have predicted, when the locals learned of the plan to remove Padre Pio from their midst. To put it bluntly, all hell broke loose.

Rumors flew wildly throughout the town. While they may not have been on the mark, the essence of them was correct. Padre Pio was going to be sent away. One day at Mass, a young man approached Padre Pio with a pistol, and threatened to shoot him. His reasoning was sound enough. He shouted, *"we would prefer him to remain in San Giovanni Rotondo dead, than that he abandon them."* While no one condoned that extreme, the feeling was pretty well on target.

This was followed by a mass protest, sponsored and spearheaded by the mayor of the town. He presented the friary with a list of fifty pages of signatures against removing Padre Pio from San Giovanni Rotondo. In it, he stated,

"....his (Padre Pio) removal would give way to serious and grave inconveniences, as the people have decided to obstruct, with every means, the transferal.

I hand over, from now, all responsibility for the unpleasant consequences and for the disturbance of public order which will be inevitably brought on by the said action."

It became a contest of wills, who would give in first, the people, or the powers that be. We're sure the authorities in Rome thought, Padre Pio and his followers in the friary were provoking the people. The truth of it is, they were not. The one person who stayed as far away from the front lines as possible was Padre Pio. The Friars, even the harried superior, were afraid to make a move, for fear the keg of dynamite which was building up in the town, would be ignited and explode.

An example of this came about when orders came down that Padre Pio would not celebrate Mass for the people of the village. The day was the 25th of June, 1923. Padre Pio, in obedience, celebrated Mass privately in the friary chapel. What followed was recorded by his Superior, Padre Ignazio, to his Provincial;

"The people....regard this decision as offensive and almost as a punishment inflicted on him. And convinced that this was only the first of many other more serious orders, they held a meeting in the piazza, and it was decided that they wouldn't leave it at all until the repeal of the said order was obtained.

A mass of people, about 3,000,....climbed to the friary asking for assurances with regard to Padre Pio's transferal and his celebrating Mass in public. The mayor and other authorities of the village came to the friary to persuade me to suspend the execution of the orders, so I, in order to avoid further grave inconveniences, thought it better to agree to the request, allowing Padre Pio to celebrate in public once again."

In the meantime, the mayor of San Giovanni Rotondo contacted the Prefect in Foggia, who contacted the Provincial of the Capuchins. He strongly suggested, they not press the issue of Padre Pio's celebrating Mass privately, in order to avoid any further disturbance of public order. The Capuchins backed down in an effort to maintain peace.

But with all of this, *they still went ahead with the plans to move Padre Pio from San Giovanni Rotondo!* We have to wonder about their strategy. If the above outbreak didn't convince them that the people were serious, and possibly on the verge of violence, what was it going to take? But they forged on with what they hoped, would have been the final resolution of the Padre Pio question. On July 30, just a month after the last incident, orders came down for Padre Pio's transfer to Ancona, way up north, near the area of the Holy House of Loreto.

The officials in Ancona were not happy about Padre Pio's presence in their peaceful little province. They thought it more prudent to hide him out in an extremely rural area, Cingoli. While their reasoning may have had merit, what could have been more remote than the little village of San Giovanni Rotondo? How long would it take for word to get out that Padre Pio was in Cingoli? Still, they went ahead with their plans.

The Provincial of Ancona made a statement, which proved to be very wise. He asked the question, "*The friary of San Giovanni Rotondo is surrounded day and night by devout and interested people who do not want Padre Pio to be moved. Will those Friars succeed in sending him off?*"

Although the superiors in Foggia reassured him that there was no problem, that Padre Pio would leave San Giovanni Rotondo without incident, they really had no reason for such confidence. The tension escalated. Armed guards from the town were posted at the friary on a twenty four hour basis. Fascists came by with clubs, and, as an act of love, we're sure, threatened to club Padre Pio and the superior to death, if they tried to move him. Neither Padre Pio nor his superior were too thrilled about this idea. An alert was given that if there was any strange movement of men or cars at the friary, day or night, to sound the alarm, and the whole town would converge on the friary, with guns. The situation was impossible.

But Rome was a *civilized* city, some 352 kilometers (228 miles) away from San Giovanni Rotondo. The higher ups in Rome could not imagine the situation was actually as bad as the reports indicated. Predicaments like this don't happen in civilized Rome. Someone was creating a *giant fantasía*. But General Emilio de Bono, head of the Police in Rome, had the wisdom to send one of his officers, a Carmello Carmilleri, to San Giovanni Rotondo, to assess the situation, and if possible, to get Padre Pio out. He spent some time there, where he became completely captivated by Padre Pio. But on his return to Rome, his candid appraisal of the dilemma was that Padre Pio could not be removed from the friary at San Giovanni Rotondo without *"forceful action....with the certainty of spilling blood."*

So convinced was General de Bono of the senselessness of making such a move at that time, he used all his influence to persuade the Father General to cancel the order of transferal. The entire situation ended with a statement by the Father General, *"for the present, Padre Pio's transferal can be forgotten."* It was over, but *never forgotten.*

The Obedience of a priest

How did Padre Pio react to all of this? We've been so busy giving the viewpoint of the people of the town, and that of his superiors from San Giovanni Rotondo, all the way to Rome, we never thought about Padre Pio. Which is, I'm sure, exactly what happened in 1923. Everybody was fighting over or about Padre Pio, but nobody was really concerned about what it was doing to him, or how he was being affected by all the *insanity* he saw about him.

If we were to use one word to describe Padre Pio's attitude during this time, and most likely, all his life, it would be **obedience**. He was an obedient priest. Padre Luigi D'Avellino brought the order to Padre Pio that he was to leave the friary at San Giovanni Rotondo. He wrote of Padre Pio's response to the order. "I showed it (the order) to him, and read it, ordering him to place himself in my care, to be handed over to the Provincial of Marche (Ancona). Padre Pio bowed his head, and with his arms folded, answered me, *'I am at your disposal; let's go immediately. When I am with the Superior, I am with God.'*

Then I said, 'But would you come with me immediately? It is late at night; where would we go?'

He answered me, *'I don't know; I will come with you when and where your paternity wishes.*"

Two weeks later, Padre Pio wrote to this same priest,

"I believe there is no need to tell you, thank God, that I am ready to obey any order whatsoever which is conveyed to me by my Superiors. Their voice is the voice of God for me, to which I want to be faithful 'till death. With His help, I will obey whatever command, however painful, which I can succeed in obeying in my misery."

He tried to dissuade the mayor of San Giovanni Rotondo from blockading the friary. He was concerned about what might happen. He wrote to Mayor Morcaldi,

"The events of these days have profoundly moved me, and they worry me intensely, as they make me fear that I could, involuntarily, be the cause of these sad events for this my very dear village.

....But if, as you have advised me, my transferal has been decided upon, I beg you to make every effort so that the will of the Superiors, which is the will of God which I blindly obey, be carried out."

There is a priceless story that highlights Padre Pio's fixation for obedience. It was told by the doctor involved, Dr. Festa, one of the first doctors to examine his stigmata. Towards the end of September, 1925, Dr. Festa came to San Giovanni Rotondo again. Padre Pio was having a lot of pain; he asked Dr. Festa to examine him. Dr. Festa determined that he had a hernia, and an operation was necessary. There were many feast days coming up, that of St. Michael, September 29, and St. Francis of Assisi, October 4th, and so they decided to wait until the day after the big Feast of Father Francis for the operation.

A special room in the friary was painted white. Dr. Festa and a local doctor, Angelo Merla, prepared for the operation. Padre Pio followed his normal custom of getting up at 3:30 a.m., and preparing for Mass. He celebrated the Mass at 6 a.m. He gave thanks, heard confessions, and then about 10 a.m., walked over to the makeshift operating room. He told them he would not take anesthetic. Both doctors gasped. A hernia operation was a long and painful one. How could he possibly endure it without anesthetic? Padre Pio looked at Dr. Festa. *"Can you honestly tell me that when you have me under the chloroform, you will not examine my wounds again?"* He could tell from the expression on Dr. Festa's face that he would indeed, look at the stigmata again. Padre Pio was under obedience not to show his wounds to anyone. There's no question in our minds but that he would have been given permission by his superiors to let Dr. Festa see his wounds, because of the extenuating circumstances. But he didn't ask. So he could not of his own volition, allow the doctors to give him anesthesia.

There's a P.S. to this story, however. After two hours of agony, during which the hernia operation took place, Padre Pio collapsed out of agony. Don't you think Dr. Festa gave in to his temptation to look at the wounds again? He surely did. They were the same as he had remembered them when he had examined Padre Pio five years before, with one exception. When the doctor investigated the wound under Padre Pio's heart, the scabs had fallen off; the wounds appeared fresh, but there was a *luminous radiation* all along the borders, which he had not seen before.

I have always had a problem with Dr. Festa, each time I read that account. But the point here is not Dr. Festa, or his trustworthiness, but Padre Pio, and his obedience, under the worst possible circumstances.

Most of us think of Padre Pio as an old man, the way we see him depicted in most photographs. But when all of this was taking place, he was in his early to mid-forties. He was a very young man. What wisdom, what discernment, what humility he showed. It's really in keeping with the way he lived his entire life, but I think we have to stop and consider how he held on to these values, in the face of such temptation. Let's keep in mind that he had become very famous, whether he liked it or not, and it's obvious that he disliked any attention. But how easily it could have gone to his head. People were clamoring for him, to touch them, to pray over them. Did he ever feel a tinge of pride, or vanity? To the contrary, he felt embarrassed to be such a center of attention. He tried to hide his gift of the stigmata, not because he was ashamed of it, but because he didn't want to be singled out as anyone special. His focus was on the Cross; he wanted everybody to focus on the Cross.

As we go along, we have to stop at times to point out why *we believe* this man was such a special gift from God, why the stigmata was just a way for the Lord to attract us to him, so that we could go beyond him to Jesus. From all that we've ever read of Padre Pio, from interviews we've had with people who knew him personally, we've never heard that he focused on self, the I, the ego. His focus was always on Our Lord Jesus and His Mother Mary.

The Battle Continues

In the early months of 1931, the Holy Office started up the plan again to remove Padre Pio from San Giovanni Rotondo. A guardian was appointed from Milan, who would be in charge of San Giovanni Rotondo. There was a strong network of information being filtered to the townspeople, causing *near-rioting* again. They had much more courage this time than in 1923. At one point, when a *foreign*[10] friar was staying at the friary, whom they believed to be the new Guardian, they battered down the doors of the friary, demanding he leave San Giovanni and never return.

---

[10]Foreign - in the context that he was not of the Province of Foggia

They didn't believe the superior when he told them the Friar was just a visiting priest, on his way to another friary. Even when Padre Pio came out of his cell to convince them, there was nothing wrong, that he was in no danger of being removed, they didn't believe *him*. And so it began all over again.

The upshot of all this came crashing down on Padre Pio in an order from Rome, written on May 23, which was received in San Giovanni Rotondo on June 9th. In it, all of Padre Pio's priestly powers were taken away from him, with the exception of celebrating Mass, which had to be done privately. He could not hear confessions; he could not give any spiritual direction. He was virtually a prisoner of the friary. This went on for two years. Padre Pio's surface reaction was one of docile obedience. Very few people were allowed to get inside Padre Pio, to share the agony he suffered. One who did was Padre Agostino, one of his Spiritual Directors. He wrote in his diary,

"I found Padre Pio very low. As soon as we were in his cell together, he started to cry. I was deeply moved, but I was able to check my emotion, and I let him cry for a few minutes. Then we talked. The beloved Padre Pio told me that he felt this unexpected trial very deeply."[11]

Tensions ran rampant in the little town. But Padre Pio distanced himself from them as much as possible. He went through his daily routine peacefully, obediently, although his heart was breaking. All that he was, all that he did, being a priest, was taken away from him. And he had to say *yes*.

Just recently, we had the pleasure to watch a videotape on Psychology and the Spiritual Life, given by a Capuchin from New York. In his talk, he stated that the most difficult vow for a religious to live up to was *Obedience*. He was not

---

[11]Acts of the First Congress of studies on Padre Pio's Spirituality
May 1-6, 1972

referring to Padre Pio. He had no idea we were at this point in our book. He doesn't even know us. He talked about "Perfect Joy," according to St. Francis. *"Perfect joy,"* he said, *"is when your best efforts are misunderstood. Perfect joy is when you do good, and they punish you."* Padre Pio learned perfect joy the way St. Francis did.

But God is in charge. God is *always* in charge. We know He didn't cause this tragedy in the life of Padre Pio. He allowed it for a time, perhaps so the people would not take Padre Pio for granted. Perhaps it was so Padre Pio would not take his gifts for granted, or ever get the idea he had anything to do with them. Maybe the Lord just wanted Padre Pio to be aware that his entire life would be a series of crises, and that he had to be ready for them. Whatever the reason, the Lord decided when it was enough. On July 16, 1933, Padre Pio was given the right to celebrate Mass for the *people*. This was followed by permission to hear men's *confessions*, and pretty soon, he was performing *all his priestly duties* for the people. That trial was over.

There were undercurrents all the time in Padre Pio's life, but every few years, they erupted into giant conflicts. He was always being accused of something. Usually, anonymous letters, or rumors in the press began the ball rolling. The pressure would build. Sides were taken; war was waged; inevitably the Lord would be victorious. But they always caused so much distraction and frustration. It was as if the evil one used these diversions, to try to keep Padre Pio away from his main work, which was saving souls.

While Padre Pio encountered animosity from many in high places in Rome, he was always supported and admired by the Popes. For his part, he expressed complete loyalty to the Pope, no matter what. He said many times, *"I would give my life a thousand times for the Pope and for the Church."* Pope Benedict XV was the head of our Church when Padre Pio received the stigmata. He was a source of Padre Pio's defense in Rome. On one occasion, when a bishop criticized Padre Pio, this same Pope suggested the bishop go to San Giovanni Rotondo, get to know Padre Pio, and ask his pardon for the things he had said.

Pope Pius XI was the ruling pontiff when Padre Pio went through his worst struggles with the Holy Office in Rome. The Pope said he was never against Padre Pio, but that he had been given misinformation about him.

Pope Pius XII was one of Padre Pio's greatest admirers. He could see the spirituality of this man who bore the wounds of Christ. Towards the end of Pope Pius XII's life, Padre Pio told a Professor Medi, *"Tell the Pope that I give my life for him."* When the professor repeated it to Pope Pius XII, he smiled and said, "No, Professor. Thank Padre Pio. I am very tired," as if to indicate he was ready to go to Heaven. After the death of Pope Pius XII, Padre Pio said he saw him in glory.

Vatican II was a time of trial for Padre Pio, because of adversaries within the Vatican. While it was an opportunity for many Bishops to visit him in San Giovanni Rotondo, a goodly portion had to come incognito, so as not to incur the wrath of the powers that were in Rome.

Pope Paul VI was a prominent supporter of Padre Pio's. After his election as Pope, many of the attacks that had been leveled at Padre Pio from within the Vatican, ceased. He wrote a beautiful letter of consolation, the closest to an apology, for what had been heaped on Padre Pio.

A True Franciscan

Padre Pio was as Franciscan as you can get, following in the footsteps of St. Francis. His life was a continuing effort to feed the hungry, take care of the sick, heal the body as well as the soul. There's a Franciscan foundation in San Francisco, called St. Anthony's Dining Room. Their focus is to feed the hungry, and provide for the homeless, *with dignity.* The keyword here is *with dignity.* We have to believe that the founder, Fr. Alfred Boeddeker, OFM, got his inspiration from Padre Pio. Or that both of them got it from St. Francis, who got it from Jesus. In any event, from his earliest days at San Giovanni Rotondo, Padre Pio grieved for the poor sick, who had no medical facilities to care for them. The nearest hospital was in Foggia, some 41 kilometers (27 miles) away, and it was overcrowded at best. As early as 1925, he was instrumental in having a meager dispensary set up in the town, but it was destroyed by the earthquake of 1938. Padre Pio continued to talk to anyone who would listen, about the need for some form of medical help there on the mountain.

In our lifetime, we have found that all great works of God begin with a small group of two or three, over a kitchen table, or in a living room. Marriage Encounter was born in the kitchen of a couple's home, with a priest, Fr. Chuck Gallagher, and two couples. In the case of the *Home for the Relief of Suffering*, it was conceived in Padre Pio's cell in 1940, with two other people. Work on it began immediately, but World War II quickly put a stop to it, until 1946, when the work resumed again.

There were guidelines, rules that Padre Pio insisted on, which were so Franciscan. All the money for the Home had to be in the form of donations, and none of it could be solicited. That in itself was a tall order, but the Lord was up to it. The only single major donation came through Fiorello La Guardia, former Mayor of New York City, in his role as administrator of UNRRA, (United Nations Relief and Rehabilitation Administration). There was only one hitch. His honor wanted the hospital to be named after him. Padre Pio had already decided on a name, but to accommodate the former mayor, a plaque was put on an outside wall, naming it the Fiorello La Guardia Clinic. But with that exception, all the rest of the money needed for the initial building came from donations. Much of it came from Americans, G.I.'s who were stationed in Foggia. Padre Pio always had a heartfelt love for Americans, not only because of their donations to the hospital, but for the help his father had received when he was in Jamaica, New York.

The need for money was an ongoing problem, or should we say, *is* an ongoing problem. The demand for funds continues to this day. So during the building process, Padre Pio would not give too much importance to the fact that they were always broke. In this, he reminds us of another Franciscan who lives on the edge financially, our Mother Angelica. She has a Home for the Relief of Suffering, too. It's Eternal Word Television Network, and the suffering she relieves is that of the soul.

There was also a logistics and material problem. The roads up and down the mountain were poor. There was a need for tonnage of concrete to build this hospital. There was really nowhere to get the material from, except the mountain. So that's what they did. They used the gift God gave them of the material at hand. All they had to do was build factories to process it, and they were in business. The craftsmen came, and many of them stayed. You see the Lord's hand in everything here. He built a city on this mountain.

The Home for the Relief of Suffering was officially opened on May 5, 1956, with 300 beds, and all the most updated equipment. There were over 15,000 people on hand for the inauguration. Pope Pius XII sent his Apostolic Blessing, with a statement read by the Capuchin Superior General. In it, he highlighted the work as being truly "*a work inspired by a profound sense of charity,*" in the spirit of the Gospel and St. Francis.

Within a few days, the beds began to fill up. Everyone was joyous at the work that was being done. Everyone that is, except Padre Pio. He was looking towards the future, to the day when someone would tell him there was no more room, and they had to turn people away. The day he feared came within a *year*. The hospital administrators reported to him, "Padre, the hospital is full; we cannot admit anyone else." As a stopgap measure, he told them to put extra beds wherever they could, in the library, in the offices, in the hallways. "...*but do not say no to the sick.*" On the second anniversary of the opening of the Casa, Padre Pio detonated the dynamite to begin the addition of more rooms, the first addition to the Casa. The Casa can accommodate 1,200 beds at present (the last part is under construction at this time).

Padre Pio never wanted it to be called a hospital. "*Hospitals are for sick people*," he would say. He felt they were too sterile, too impersonal. He insisted on the dignity of the suffering. He called it *Casa Sollievo della Sofrenza*, Home for the Relief of Suffering. Even the name had to glorify God. He insisted that those who could pay, should pay. But no one should be refused because they could not pay. Now, to the logical mind, especially here in the United States, where hospital rooms are going for $700 per day, this is no way to run a hospital. And even though there were some really tight times, when they didn't know if they could continue, and even though they are always desperately in need of money, they are never *desperate*. The Chairman of the Board, Our Lord *Jesus*, provides for their needs. He doesn't give them a lot. They can't afford to spend a cent unwisely, but He does take care of them.

Padre Pio in the Confessional

Padre Pio spent his whole life living the Gospel. He took his vows as a Franciscan and a priest *seriously*. The Lord gave him the stigmata to attract people to him, and come to San Giovanni Rotondo. But once there, it was the *wisdom* of the man, the *love* for his brothers, the preoccupation with their *salvation*, that kept them there, and compelled them to return. He heard confessions for as much as *sixteen* hours a day. We're told he took the burden of men's sins on his shoulders, to the point that he had to drag himself out of the confessional at the end of the day.

Confession has never been a popular Sacrament. We go to the Sacrament of Reconciliation on Saturday night, to find the church just about empty. Our dear priest gets all his spiritual reading done in the Confessional, waiting for someone to show up. Yet, in San Giovanni Rotondo, the crowds were so enormous, they had to start a numbering system to go to confession to Padre Pio. And it was not an hour's wait, or two hours. At times, it was a *ten day wait* for Padre Pio to hear your confession.

We're told that very often, after a penitent waited however long for Padre Pio to hear their confessions, and finally entered the confessional, *he threw them out!* Can you picture waiting ten days, only to be thrown out? But he knew *exactly* what he was doing. He took chances, for sure. But the Lord had given him an insight that what he did, had to be done. Sometimes the penitent would just get back on the line, and by the time he reached Padre Pio a second time, he was in the proper spiritual state to confess his sins. There were other times when it took two years for a penitent to return. Then, when he or she would reach the confessional, Padre Pio would exclaim joyously, "*Finally! I've waited two years for you to come back.*" or "*Testa dura (hardhead), why did you wait so long?*"

Padre Pio's reputation for throwing people out of the confessional spread rapidly. A fellow priest once confided to Padre Pio that he, too, began this practice. Padre Pio reprimanded him severely. "*Don't ever throw anyone out of the confessional!*" From this, we have to presume that, while he took a calculated risk, he knew his penitent pretty well. Of course, this was not due to a worldly knowledge of human

Right:
**Padre Pio
hearing the
women's
confessions**

They had to start a numbering system to go to confession to Padre Pio. At times, it was a ten day wait for Padre Pio to hear your confession.

Left:
**Padre Pio received the
Transverberation
of the Heart
on August 5, 1918.**

"I was suddenly filled with extreme terror at the sight of a celestial being whom I saw with my mind's eye. He held a kind of weapon in his hand, similar to a steel sword with a sharp, flaming point. At the very instant I saw all this, I saw the person hurl the weapon into my soul with all his might."

nature. As Jesus said to Peter, "*No man has told you this.*" Padre Pio always felt the guidance of the Holy Spirit, but especially in the confessional.

He was said to be a gruff, irritable man. We used to think it was due to the fifty years of excruciating pain he endured, suffering the wounds of the stigmata. But the more we study him, and speak to those who knew and loved him, we have to say he was a *pezzo di pane* (a piece of bread). He didn't have a mean bone in his body. Very often, he used his abruptness to accomplish a goal, like getting through a crowd. Remember, he was always surrounded by people, the minute he made an appearance. Oftentimes, after having shouted at a group of pilgrims to let him through, he would smile and tell the Friars in his company, "*I'm not angry with them.*" Other times, he would use his surly tone to snap people into the realization that their sins were destroying them. But behind the harsh exterior was a heart filled with love for all. On the occasion of his fiftieth anniversary as a priest, he said, "*The only thing I desire is to love, to suffer another fifty years for my brothers, to burn for everyone with you, Lord, with you on the Cross.*"

Padre Pio and the Eucharist

Padre Pio was truly a servant of God. He had a lifelong love affair with Our Lord Jesus in the Eucharist. To him, the Eucharist was the center of all spiritual benefits. It was the life breath of the soul. We believe the Lord gave him an insight as to the power and the magnitude of the Eucharist, from a very early age. As a young man, before he entered the priesthood, he spent hours in the church, adoring Jesus in the Blessed Sacrament. After his ordination, he took a long time for the Consecration of the Mass, to the point where parishioners complained about all the time he spent, in ecstasy, before the bread and wine as they became the Body and Blood of Our Lord Jesus. He had to control himself, to break out of his ecstasy, and force himself back to the Mass, at the orders of his superiors.

He began his preparations for Mass hours before the Mass began. He would constantly ask his fellow Friars what time it was. He always thought it was time to begin Mass, even though it might have been two hours early. When it came to celebrating the Eucharist, he was like a young race-horse, chomping at the bit, waiting impatiently to get out of the starting gate.

We read an eyewitness account in *the Voice of Padre Pio*[12], about Padre Pio and the celebration of the Mass.

"But as he started vesting for Mass, his body began to bend forward. As he slowly approached the altar, his body stooped over more and more as if he was being crushed under a heavy cross beam on his shoulders; his gait dragged, his face took on the sorrow of his Lord and Savior. As the mystery of the Sacrifice of the Mass unfolded, Padre Pio reached the pinnacle of suffering at the moment of Elevation of the Host in Consecration.

To quote a witness, 'In his eyes I read the expression of a mother who assists at the agony of her son on the scaffold, who sees him expire and who, choked with suffering, silently receives the bloodless body in her arms, able only to give slight caresses.'

He cried during the Mass. It was not weeping so much as it was deep, involuntary sobbing. He cried from the depths of his soul. When he beat his breast during the Confiteor, it was as if he was accusing himself of all the sins committed by man."

Giant tears cascaded from his closed eyes onto his beard. He took everything that was happening during that time so seriously. *"Padre Pio's Mass put him into the drama of Calvary. For him it was reliving daily the pain which had*

---

[12]Fra Modestino - Voice of Padre Pio - Vol XIX, Summer 1989

wounded him in soul and body that morning of 20 September 1918. The Mass was his daily restigmatization."[13]

Padre Pio and Mary

We can track Padre Pio's love and relationship with Mary, the Mother of God, back to age 5. It continued all his life. He mentioned at various times in his life that he received apparitions from Mary on a regular basis. He derived a great deal of his strength from these apparitions, especially when he suffered the onslaught of demons, and grotesque monsters, sent from hell to torture him.

We would like to share a few excerpts from a homily he preached on the Feast of the Assumption.

"We Catholics, who do homage to this most gentle and kind mother cannot do less than exult with joy on this holy day in memory of her greatest triumph, her Assumption into Heaven and Coronation as Queen of all the Angels and Saints....

After Jesus Christ ascended into Heaven, Mary longed with an ever growing desire to be reunited with Him. And oh! with what ardent sighs and pitiful weeping did she supplicate Him to call her to Him. Without her divine Son, she was in a most painful exile....But finally the hour she so desired came, and she heard the voice of her desires calling her from above....

Now, who can adequately describe the triumphant entrance of Mary into Heaven?....St. Anselm says that Our Savior wished to ascend into Heaven before His Mother so as not only to prepare a throne worthy of her but also so as to make her entrance more glorious and triumphant by being able to meet her Himself with all the Angels and Holy Souls of Paradise."

Very seldom was Padre Pio ever seen without the Rosary in his hand, beads slipping through his fingers, his lips

---

[13]Fernando of Riese Pio X - Voice of Padre Pio, Vol XX, No 1, 1990

moving silently, as he prayed the mysteries. He had such a *special* relationship with Mary. She was his Mother, his Friend, and his Queen. Some of his writings about Mary projected his undying love for her.

"This most tender mother, in her great knowledge, mercy and goodness, has desired to punish me in a very high way by pouring into my heart so many graces....."

"My poor little mother. How much she loves me. I realized it again at the beginning of this beautiful month. With how much care she accompanied me to the altar this morning! It seemed to me that she didn't have anything else to think of but me alone."

"The strength of Satan, who is fighting me, is terrible, but God be praised, because He has put the problem of my health and a victorious outcome into the hands of our heavenly Mother. Protected and guided by such a tender Mother, I will keep on fighting as long as God wishes."

One of his followers wrote about Padre Pio and Mary, "When he spoke about his heavenly Mother, as he called her, he could hardly contain his emotion. When he recited *"the Visit"* (prayer) to the Most Holy Mary, he often could not keep back the tears and the emotion in the tone of his voice. And sometimes he was seized by such violent sobbing that he could not continue the recitation of the prayer."[14]

A normal reaction to this would be, that's a bit much, even for someone who professed that kind of love for Mary. But one thing we must keep in mind is that Padre Pio had the privilege of *seeing* Mary all his life. That is a gift that is beyond our human comprehension. We have read the attempted verbalizations of those who have seen Mary. We have asked the question of Vicka, one of the visionaries in Medjugorje, *"What is it like to be in the presence of Our Lady?"* Her only reply was, *"There are no words."* Why *wouldn't*

---

[14]Voice of Padre Pio No. 6 - 1971

anyone be overcome with emotion, when an actual image of the most beautiful woman in the history of creation, comes before you every time you hear the name? *I have often said I would get a heart attack and die if Mary ever appeared to me.* That will give you just a teeny idea of what Padre Pio may have experienced with his Lady.

Padre Pio points to two helping hands for the world, that of the *Church* and that of the *Blessed Mother.*

The Final Days

For Padre Pio, his last year, 1968, was one of the most difficult, physically. For many years, he had been partially disabled, due to the stigmata, and also to his own health problems, which had plagued him from childhood. In 1965, when the Mass went to the vernacular from Latin, as a result of Vatican II, Padre Pio received permission to continue using Latin. This was not because he disapproved of the Vatican II findings, but because at his advanced age, it would be next to impossible for him to re-learn the Mass. In the early days in 1967, he received permission to sit during the Mass, and have physical assistance during the Consecration of the Mass.

We have to remember that Padre Pio celebrated his 81st birthday in May, 1968. For a normal man reaching this age, the body would be in the process of falling apart. But this is Padre Pio we're talking about, the crucified Christ for fifty eight years of his life. Early in 1967, he had developed asthma. His physical condition just went downhill from there. During his last few months on earth, his wounds began to dry up. They literally stopped gushing the way they had for the better part of fifty years. The wounds in his side became smaller; those in his hands and feet ebbed a mixture of blood and liquid.

He alluded to his death on several occasions. As early as 1959, when the new church was being built, a woman asked him if he thought it to be an omen of his death. He said, "*No. I'll die when they bless the crypt.*" This turned out to be a prophecy.

In the eyes of the world, the final days of Padre Pio were a complete contradiction. As he got older, and more tired, he became that much more popular. Pilgrims thronged to see Padre Pio. The Lord chose to take Padre Pio on the weekend of the 50th anniversary of his receiving the stigmata. In retrospect, it was possible the Lord wanted as many of his spiritual children as possible to be there for the end. And so it was. Many celebrations were planned for that weekend. The blessing of the crypt, the Way of the Cross, and the official recognition of the Padre Pio Prayer Groups by the Vatican, all were to take place during those three days.

He struggled through the day of his anniversary, Friday, September 20. He celebrated Mass at 5:00 a.m., and took part in the Rosary and Benediction. There was a crush of people at all times. As much as the Friars tried to protect him from the crowds, the lack of air may have caused an asthma attack. But it was not severe.

Saturday, September 21 was worse. He was not able to celebrate Mass. He snapped back, as was his way, and went on to take part in the Rosary and Benediction. But that was it for that day. He stayed by himself for the most part, for the rest of the day.

Sunday, September 22. *The spirit is willing, but the flesh is weak.* His body was fighting his spirit. He felt too sick to celebrate the Mass. But he knew the church would be filled to overflowing. He could see the disappointment on the face of Padre Carmelo. Always obedient to his superior, he gathered all the strength he had, most likely prayed to the Angels for support, and celebrated Mass. He even *sang* the Mass. Towards the end, he collapsed, and was grabbed by

Above: *Padre Pio during the Consecration of the Mass*

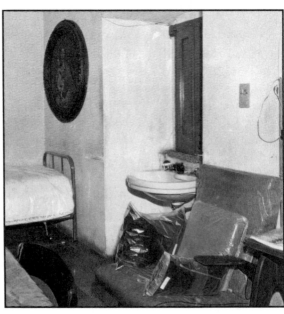

Left:
The cell where Padre Pio lived; window (above the sink) from which he blessed the crowd, and the chair on which he died.

the brothers. He recovered momentarily, and continued to bless the crowd.

He struggled through the rest of the morning. After his usual thanksgiving, he wanted to hear confessions. He started out, but had to return to his room. Then, a few hours later, he insisted he go down to hear the men's confessions. Fortunately, there were not many people in the church, as they didn't think he'd be able to hear confessions. So he was not too tired out from that. He did, however, miss most of the festivities that Sunday, all held in his honor.

He went out once to bless the crowds from the choir window. It was obvious to all who saw him that he was sinking fast. But he fought his body this day, as he had fought it all his life. He would not stay in bed. He got up, sat on a chair; walked over to the veranda; went back to his bed. He was restless throughout the day. At 4:30 p.m., he took part in the Benediction of the Blessed Sacrament.

He spent the evening by himself, with a Friar in close attendance, but not with him in the room. He began calling out over the intercom, beginning at 9 p.m. Padre Pellegrino was summoned.

Padre Pio kept asking what time it was. Four or five times within the next three hours, he asked the same question again. Each time, Padre Pellegrino came in, and told him the time. Padre Pio appeared quite disturbed. His eyes were red; he was crying. After midnight, Padre Pio called him again. His hands were shaking. This was the first time that he gave any indication that he was getting ready to leave this world. He asked Padre Pellegrino if he had celebrated Mass yet. The Friar responded it was much too early. Padre Pio said, *"Well, this morning you will offer it for me."*

He asked to go to confession. After it was over, he said, *My son, if the Lord calls me today, ask my brethren to forgive me for all the trouble I have caused them, and ask my brethren and my spiritual children to pray for my soul."*

At or about 1:30 a.m., Padre Pio asked to change from his pajamas into his Franciscan habit. The Friar, Padre Pellegrino stayed with him. He became fearful for Padre Pio. He was slipping quickly. Padre Pellegrino wanted to go for help. Padre Pio told him not to call for anyone. The younger man knew he had to get aid. He ran out of the room, and went to Brother Bill Martin's (Fr. Joseph Pio) room. Brother Bill came back with him, and after looking at Padre Pio's condition, the doctor was called.

The doctor arrived in very short order, and began working on Padre Pio. But the Lord had decided it was enough now; *come home, My son.* At 2:30 a.m., on 23 September, 1968, Padre Pio of Pietrelcina, loyal son of the Father, and the Church, left this earth. His final words were "Jesus, Mary."

For many, this, the death of their friend and mentor, Padre Pio, seemed like the end of the world. There were fears that all the work he had begun in San Giovanni Rotondo, and around the world, for that matter, would come to a crashing end. But as we read in Acts 5: 38-39,

"If their purpose or activity is human in its origins, it will destroy itself. If, on the other hand, it comes from God, you will not be able to destroy them without fighting God Himself." We believe the proof is in the fruits.

Today, when one goes on pilgrimage to San Giovanni Rotondo, for as far as the eye can see, there are tributes in brick and mortar to the dreams of Padre Pio. There is a Spastic Center for Children, a Convent for the Poor Clares, a Home for retired priests, not just Capuchins, but priests.

We are always delighted when we see the end of God's rainbow, how He works to accomplish what He wants. One of the big questions we would have had, if we had looked at San Giovanni Rotondo in 1917, when the Lord let it be known in blood and ink, that this is where He wanted Padre

Pio, would be *why here?* How could He accomplish great healings, great conversions, through this simple little man, in such a desolate place? But then we are reminded of the words of the Gospel, *"Can anything good come out of Nazareth?"* Could it be that the Lord had all of what we see today in San Giovanni Rotondo in His mind's eye from before the beginning of time, and all He needed was the Yes of this extremely humble Friar? We believe so. The Lord picked the spot, the mountain, with all its resources, the area of the country, and the man. Perhaps He even gave Padre Pio the gift of the stigmata, so that he would develop such a following. Then, when the time was right, He used all of it for His glory.

We really maintain that's how God works, how He has always worked. With that notion in mind, trace the life of Padre Pio from its very beginnings to its very end. It all falls into place. One would have the tendency of smacking his head, and saying, "Of course. Why didn't I think of it before? It all makes so much sense."

To many of Padre Pio's adversaries, he was a throwback to the Middle Ages. Everything that he represented was pulling us back to where we came from, rather than bringing us into the modern age of Science and Technology, this Twentieth Century. Perhaps that's true. Very possibly, we've high-teched ourselves right out of the Kingdom. Padre Pio represented *back to basics*, to those values which made our Church and our world, grand. He fought all his life to preserve the beliefs of Our Lord Jesus, the Apostles, and the early Fathers of the Church.

Could Padre Pio see into the future? Was he aware of what the world was becoming during his lifetime, and would deteriorate into after his death? Did he sacrifice his 81 years of life, being physically as well as spiritually tortured by the fallen angels of Satan, so that the common man, the simple believer, would have something to hold onto? Did he allow himself to be a crucified Christ to give us strength?

We'll probably never know the extent of sacrifice that Padre Pio made for us during our lifetime. We may not even understand it in what time is left of this world of ours. Perhaps he was a modern-day Don Quixote, the Man of La Mancha, who wanted nothing more than to save the world, and was willing to sacrifice himself in the process. Doesn't that sound a lot like Jesus? We believe the Lord gave Padre Pio the *impossible* dream, that Padre Pio *held onto* that dream, *fought* for that dream, and *died* for that dream. Did he live in vain? Were his 81 years of agony for nothing? *That, my brothers and sisters, depends entirely on us.*

✝

Prayer before the Crucifix where Padre Pio received the
Stigmata

You call Me the Way	but you don't follow Me.
You call Me the Light	but you don't see Me.
You call Me the Teacher	but you don't listen to Me.
You call Me the Lord	but you don't serve Me.
You call Me the Truth	but you don't believe in Me.

Don't be surprised if one day, I don't know you!

✝

Photo Credits
Courtesy of Voice of Padre Pio
Excerpts and quotations from
Padre Pio Letters Vol. 1
Padre Pio of Pietrelcina, Spirituality Series 1
Everybody's Cyrenean
Pio of Pietrelcina, Infancy and Adolescence

Archbishop Fulton J. Sheen

Prophet, Priest, a man for all Seasons

We could not think of writing a book about Saints and Powerful Men who have changed the course of our lives and not include *Archbishop Fulton J. Sheen*. I must admit I never watched Fulton J. Sheen on television, nor was I influenced by him while he was *alive*. But, as we began to discover our Catholic Faith as *adults*, his words, and his living out of those words, became a strong part of our journey of faith toward *new life* in the Lord.

Unto us a Prophet is born

It was 1895, in the month of Mary; one century was ending and another beginning; and with its beginning, was the need of a voice in the desert, crying out, proclaiming the Word of God. Fulton J. Sheen was to be that *voice*. The prophet, whose words and voice would ring out for all time and place, was born above the family's *hardware store* in El Paso, Illinois.

Fulton J. Sheen was brought up on the need of putting in a good day's work. It was not the hard work he minded; it was that the *hard work* was done on a *farm*. Out of necessity, his family had moved to a farm (after a fire had destroyed their store). Whereas his brothers loved to work on the farm, *Fulton suffered it*. A neighbor once told his father, he (Fulton J. Sheen) would never amount to much; his head was always in a book.

His early years on the farm ended, when the family moved to Peoria to be near a fine parochial school for their children. Although not well-educated themselves, his parents instilled the need and love of higher learning in their children.

The making of a Priest

When Bishop Sheen wrote of his life, he wrote as a priest, "*a man with a body of soft clay, to be stretched out on a cross of fire (in order to remain a pure treasure).*" Speaking of God choosing him for the priesthood, when there were thousands he (Sheen) knew more deserving, he humbly said, "*God's love is blind.*" He wrote, "*God purposely chose weak instruments so it would be clear that the work was not being done by the clay but by the Potter.*"

The molding of the clay, as Bishop Sheen liked to refer to his life, was done by great sacrifice on the part of his parents. Very often, they denied themselves even the smallest comforts so their children would be well dressed and cared for. His family was a holy family; they said *Grace* before and after each meal. Respecting each other and the *solemnity* of their meal together, the men of the family always came to the table wearing jackets. They prayed the Rosary together as a family in the evening. Each week, they entertained priests from the Cathedral. The children were either surrounded by the strong affirming influence of holy priests, their immediate holy family, or close cousins from the country who would visit them.

One day, while serving as Altar boy to Bishop Spaulding, he dropped a glass cruet on the marble floor of the Cathedral. *You'd think the incident would have lost its sting to the Archbishop recounting it, with 60 years as a priest behind him. But, in his autobiography Bishop Sheen shares, no atomic explosion could equal the deafening sound of that cruet falling, in a Cathedral, in front of a Bishop*! When the Mass was over, Bishop Spaulding called the stunned boy to him and asked Fulton where he planned to go to school, when he was *big*. Being all of eight years *young*, Fulton thought the

Bishop meant *High School big*, and so he answered, *Spaulding Institute* (named after the Bishop). The Bishop told the boy to go home and tell his mother he was to go to *The University of Louvain*; he also prophesied that some day *he would be just like him*. Fulton J. Sheen forgot the Bishop's words until two years after he was ordained to the priesthood, when he entered Louvain University.

Archbishop Sheen said he could never remember a time he did not want to be a priest. He attributed as major contributions to his becoming a priest: *first*, as a child, being an Altar boy in the Cathedral; *second*, growing up, the example of the Holy priests who visited his family; and *third*, daily recitation of the Rosary. The only doubt he had was his *unworthiness*, but that doubt was strong enough to drive out and drown out the *Voice* that persisted, that same Voice that called to Samuel. But here, we have another strong message that goes out to the whole world, that God chooses you; you do not choose God. And when He wants you, you can run but you cannot escape. The Persistent Lover is that *Whisper* in your heart, that *Wind* at your back, and Fulton J. Sheens of the world, you are on your way to becoming priests.

*"If society calls, I can stop service (*serving*); if Christ calls, I am a servant forever."* By the grace of God, On Saturday, September 20, 1919,[1] Fulton J. Sheen *became* Father Fulton J. Sheen.

Immediately after ordination, he went to Catholic University in Washington. After studying philosophy for two years, he shared his concern with his professor; he would not have the education necessary to merit the degree, *Doctor of Philosophy*. The professor asked him, "What would you wish from education?" He replied, "...*two things - first, what the modern world is thinking about; second, how to answer the*

---

[1] A year to the day after Padre Pio received the Stigmata.

errors of modern philosophy in the light of the philosophy of St. Thomas (Aquinas)."

His professor's answer, "You won't get it here, but you will get it at the University of Louvain in Belgium," was to fulfill part of Bishop Spaulding's prophecy; Father Sheen was on his way. Not only did he receive a Doctorate at the University of Louvain, but graduated, receiving the most coveted award that can be given, *"Very Highest Distinction."* He received, as well, two offers to teach; *one*, in London and the *other* at Columbia University. When he wrote to his bishop asking which he should accept, the bishop replied, *"Come home!"*

He returned home from Europe. All the education and honors behind him, *home* became a parish in that part of the city called the "lower end." All the well-to-do parishioners had fled the little church, he was sent to, but it soon became crowded as these same people came back to hear the young priest preach. The pastors from the other parishes forbade their parishioners to go; they ordered, "Stay in your own parish."

As Father Sheen's preaching became well known, even the newspapers started to question, "Why has this priest with so much talent and obvious education been hidden away here?" Finally, one day, the Bishop called in Father Sheen and told him, he was keeping the promise he had made three years ago to Bishop Shahan, and was sending him to be on the faculty of Catholic University. When Father Sheen asked why he hadn't sent him in the first place, the bishop answered he wanted to see if he would *obey*.

Looking back over his years of studying vocations, he found that, in his case and in those of many others, they *thought* they had a vocation because they wanted to *"work among the poor"* or *"defend the political rights of prisoners "* or *"bring a religious mission to the political-minded in South America."* He discovered *"no true vocation starts with 'what I* want' or with 'a work I would like to do,' but with God." As the Lord pruned away at any ego he might hold on to, he *lived* the reality of his ongoing "*yes*" to the Lord, his words,

"*If we are called by God, we may be sent to a work we do not like, and obedience is better than sacrifice.*"

Bishop Sheen was convinced that those who believe "*vocation*" is to be identified with the *world*, have completely forgotten Christ Who warned, "I have taken you out of this world."

He spoke of the priesthood as the finest *fraternity* in the world. "*No introduction is necessary to another priest; nothing to live up to, nothing to live down. No introduction is necessary; Christ has already introduced them to one another.*"

He spoke lovingly and compassionately of his brother priests, as he called them *sons* of Mary and *ambassadors* of Christ. But he also spoke sadly of the world and its lies, that was infiltrating and decaying the priesthood.

"*In the late sixties, many seminaries began to put less emphasis on the doctrinal and spiritual, and more on the sociological and even the political. Not only in this country but throughout the world there began a fission between the priesthood and the victimhood of Christ;... victimhood was sometimes interpreted solely in terms of service to the world rather than also bearing the guilt and sin and poverty of the world in the Name of Jesus.*"

Bishop Sheen was not speaking out against the changes that came about authoritatively and authentically, through Vatican Council II; rather he was coming out against *secularism* that was trying to discredit the Gospel, which centered on the message and its *Messenger*. He could see the emphasis shifting from dependence on the "*Potter*" (God) to the "*clay*" (man); he could not remain silent and so, like Jesus before him, he was persecuted, rejected and crucified.

Although he spoke out strongly against the ills, never get the idea he was giving up on the priesthood. His greatest delight was giving Retreats to his fellow-priests. *He loved them*! He emphasized, over and over again, the Eucharist and Mother Mary, the two Strengths, he held on to during that dark night of the soul, when in the stillness of his aloneness, he cried out. As he lectured, his eyes and heart scanning the auditorium, he could tell *who* would leave the priesthood, by the reaction a priest would have when he mentioned the Eucharist or Mother Mary. He *knew* and prayed, but the answer was always the same.

He took seriously, the *honor* given to the priesthood by the laity, of seeing *Christ on earth* in them. He felt this most deeply as he joined Christ during the Mass, as priest-victim, with the Spotless Host being raised in sacrifice to the Father. For Bishop Sheen, as he ascended the Altar to celebrate the Holy Sacrifice of the Mass, *this* Mass was his *first* one; *this* Mass was his *last* one; *this* Mass was his *only* one.

When he spoke to anyone, Catholic or non-Catholic, he spoke as *Christ*, with concern for their soul. When a well-known Communist was questioned as to why he converted to the Catholic Church, he replied, "He (Bishop Sheen) was the first person who ever said he was concerned with the salvation of my *soul*."

Fulton J. Sheen - teacher

Teaching, Fulton J. Sheen's one true love, was *surpassed* only by his priesthood. His teaching career began in England, at the seminary of the Westminster Archdiocese, St. Edward's College. Sheen loved to poke fun at himself. One day, a student called him an extraordinary lecturer. When he asked the student what he said that deserved this compliment, he responded, "I don't know." Fulton J. Sheen learned early in his career that sometimes when you are *confusing*, you are most often mistaken for being *learned*.

Father Sheen was appointed to the School of Theology, at Catholic University in Washington, by Bishop Shahan.

One day, when all the professors were asked to give their opinion on Bishop Shahan's proposal of how to increase the number of students in the graduate program of Theology, Father Sheen, being the youngest on the board, was called on last. Although all the others had agreed with the bishop, Father Sheen could not. The Bishop stood up and shouted, "If I cannot get professors to agree with me, I'll get professors who will." And he left the room. With the other professors' look of, *Well you really cooked your goose*, coupled with no further word from the bishop, the next few weeks were, to Father Sheen, the longest of his life. But they were not to be the last of such suffering on the cross.

Finally, the bishop called him into his office. He told him to kneel and said, *"Young man, this university has not received into its ranks in recent years anyone who is destined to shed more light and luster than yourself. God bless you."*

The twenty-plus years he spent teaching and lecturing, at the university, were filled with loneliness and pain. He was misunderstood and often victimized. A situation arose where the professors of the School of Theology signed a petition against the rector of the university, all that is but Father Sheen. He pleaded with the other professors to allow the rector to *face* his accusers. Because of his stand, he suffered *retaliation*; a sign appeared on the bulletin board: *"All the classes of Dr. Fulton J. Sheen have been suspended in the School of Theology."* Knowing the reason for the suspension, was that Father Sheen had refused to sign the petition against him, the rector transferred him to the school of Philosophy where he taught for more than twenty years.

Some time after the incident at the University, the following summer to be exact, Father Sheen had dinner with Cardinal Pacelli, then Secretary of State, (who later became Pope Pius XII). The next morning, the Cardinal called him into his office and asked him about the *problem* at the University. Father Sheen replied he would rather *not* discuss

Left:
Fulton J. Sheen,
Prophet,
Priest,
a man for all
Seasons.
Archbishop Sheen
said he could
never remember
a time
he did not want
to be a priest.

Right:
Archbishop Sheen
with Pope Pius XII
in 1969
When Pope Pius XII was
a Cardinal, he met with
Archbishop Sheen and
asked him about a
"problem" at the
Catholic University.
Father Sheen thought it
best not to discuss it, and
later was falsely accused
of speaking against the
rector. Father Sheen was
never allowed to defend
himself.

the issue. The Cardinal left it at that and then proceeded, for the next hour, to discuss the situation which was weighing *heavily* on his heart, the danger of Hitler and Nazism.

Father Sheen left the Cardinal's office. Who was waiting to speak to the Cardinal, but the *rector* of Catholic University. He inquired of one of the Cardinal's attendants the name of the person who had been in with the Cardinal for such a long time. He was told it was Fulton J. Sheen. So later, when the rector was *transferred* to another university and Fulton J. Sheen's name was proposed for rector of Catholic University, it was vehemently rejected. A story had circulated accusing Fulton J. Sheen of speaking against the rector to the Cardinal. Never allowed to defend himself, condemned and ostracized, that was only one incident in the *long years* he spent in Catholic University.

Fulton J. Sheen - lecturer, armed for battle

He tried to live the advice, Cardinal Mercier gave him, when he had completed his studies at Louvain University,

> "*Always keep current; know what the modern world is thinking about; read its literature; observe its architecture and art; hear its music and its theater; and then plunge deeply into the wisdom of St. Thomas (Aquinas) and you will be able to refute its errors.*"

We have such a heritage, a treasury of *knowledge*, passed on to us by those *faithful* to the authoritive teaching of the Church! We only have to look around us; everything we have held dear is being disputed and destroyed by the *media*. Thank God, we have the *living* Truth of Christ through His Church, that unchanging *hope* and true *wisdom* of 2000 years, not denying but affirming what we have been taught and have believed in *faith* and *obedience*.

When lecturing, Bishop Sheen *never* talked down to his audience. He carefully prepared his text and never used notes. He loved young students, often ignoring their sometimes abusive language and remarks, patiently waiting like Jesus, for them to play out the role they thought they were required to play.   One time, when he was met at the airport, he was advised, the students had just burned down two buildings.   "You can cancel the lecture as we cannot offer you any protection," he was told. Forgetting the talk he had originally come to give, Bishop Sheen spoke for an hour and a half on *chastity*. At the end, the students stood and cheered for him; they came up to the platform to speak to him and ask questions.   Bishop Sheen saw the enormous potential in the young; their needs were important to him and he addressed them, very often by challenging them to be *one* with the Lord in a truly radical way - *through the Cross.*

Toward the end of his life he spoke longingly of being able to continue giving Retreats, especially to his brother priests. He shared, more than a little regretfully, he didn't know how much time he had left to give Retreats, but he prayed the Lord would allow him to *return* to do more. As we study Bishop Sheen's writings and the truths he taught and defended; as we encounter the many thousands who still read and listen to his wisdom, his prayers are being answered.

He has returned! Through his tapes, the Treasures of the Faith that boomed forth over radio and television are still resounding throughout the Church. Only now they are *hauntingly* breaking through, attacking our comfort and the compromises we make of our Faith; and we can no longer be lukewarm.   The ageless teaching of the Magisterium, he handed down at his Retreats, his calling of his fellow priests to the Love, they had been chosen for, is as alive as Jesus, our King and His promise to His Church.

Dear prophet, the gifts so wisely bestowed on you by the Lord are ricocheting against the walls of our churches and our hearts, echoing your words, "*What have they done with my Lord?*" As we search in some of our churches for the

Tabernacle and the Crucified Christ on the Cross, Bishop Sheen, your voice *thunders*, shattering the apathy of our commitment to our Lord. You are still doing battle, like St. John the Baptist before you. You have diminished in that we can no longer see *you*, but through your faithfulness, through your words that live after you, Christ has increased and we want to follow *Him*.

Bishop Sheen and the electronic age

Born into what he called the *electronic age,* Bishop Sheen said, while "*the radio is like the Old Testament, for it is the hearing of the Word without the seeing; television is like the New Testament, for the Word is seen as it becomes flesh and dwells among us.*"

He began in *radio* in 1928, having been invited by the Paulist Fathers of New York to give a series of sermons in the church, which would be broadcast by the then very popular station WLWL. The spacious church was overflowing with the faithful who came to listen. He got off to a slow start, the words coming slowly and laboriously. The pastor of the church, embarrassed, asked himself *why* he said yes to Bishop Sheen using his church. Bishop Sheen was to broadcast from that pulpit for many years.

The Bishops asked Fulton J. Sheen to be the first one to appear on national radio representing the Catholic Church. Catholics, Protestants and Jews had been asked to choose representatives. There were many preachers requesting to speak who would then use the radio as a platform to spread hatred and division, condemning their enemies and opposition. By allowing the heads of the main expressions to pick their preachers, the broadcasters felt there could be some *control on decency and charity.*

When Bishop Sheen broadcast at the same time as "Amos and Andy[2]," a very popular comedy team of that day, he received vocal opposition from the most unlikely quarter, the *Catholic press* in Milwaukee and Oklahoma City. The theme he had chosen was *"a popular presentation of Christian doctrine on the existence of God, the divinity of Christ, the Church and the spiritual life."* They demanded he be taken off the air and replaced by two men who could *imitate* Amos and Andy and teach religion. Bishop Sheen later wrote, *"Thus the tendency to imitate whatever was popular became a pervading spirit among some churchmen throughout the years."*

Consecrated Bishop on June 11, 1951, the rainbow of our Lord Jesus would now be *seen* as Bishop Sheen's horizon broadened from radio to *television*, in that same year. Although the fee was $26,000 a night, Bishop Sheen never took a penny; it all went to the Society for the Propagation of the Faith, as by this time he was dedicated to the Mission Church in Africa, Asia and other parts of the world. Gifts were spontaneously sent which eventually brought millions of dollars to the four corners of the earth to build *hospitals* and *schools* as well as bring the Word of Jesus Christ through His Church. He *touched* his viewing audience; his office counted an average of fifteen to twenty-five thousand letters per day.

He appeared on television as who he was, *a Bishop*. He wore a black cassock and was so very handsome in his purple cloak. He spoke Church; he looked Church, and he gave us, *the Church*, a strong sense of belonging to the ages. There was never any rehearsal for his television show. Archbishop Sheen never used notes of any kind. He would spend *thirty* hours preparing enough material for an *hour*

---

[2] *Amos and Andy-black face* situation comedy revolving around two entrepreneurs played almost uninterruptedly 5 times a week 7 P.M. each evening from 1929-1943. (American Folklore and Legend, Readers Digest 1978)

Above:
Life is Worth Living:
not only a
successful
long-run
TV series for
Archbishop Sheen,
but his own
vibrant philosophy
on life.

Right:
***Archbishop Sheen
with Ed Sullivan,
TV show host in
the '60's.
Sheen held Christ
up to the world,
to see.***

program. So he would never have to end abruptly, the only prompter he used was a clock positioned where he could see it; his time was limited to twenty-seven minutes and twenty seconds.

When asked how to prepare sermons, he spoke through his own experiences, *"All my sermons are prepared in the presence of the Blessed Sacrament."* He wrote that Pope John Paul II always keeps a small desk or writing pad next to him, whenever he goes before the Blessed Sacrament. Bishop Sheen said he, too, has done this all his life, and *"he was sure the Pope did it for the same reason as he had, believing the lover always works better when the Beloved is with him."*

He further wrote that, as the Holy Spirit presided at the Incarnation, so He is truly here in the *Presence* of the Blessed Sacrament; he is lighting our way, opening us to His Word and direction, as we come face to Face with our God.

He wrote there are three kinds of sermons: what is *written*; what is *delivered*; and what you *wish* you had said. He always would deliver the sermon to the Lord (before the Blessed Sacrament) so He could tell him what to keep in and what to discard, enabling him *"to discover not only its weaknesses but its possibilities."*

Bishop Sheen sadly shared how the mood of the country changed during his fifty years of involvement in *"the electronic media."* When he first began on radio, the mood of the country was *Christian*. Therefore a Catholic Hour presenting Christian doctrine was a popular approach. And although he did have his fair share of *hate mail* from people who were bigoted against Catholics and the Church, they were few and far between. Bishop Sheen, trying to emulate his Lord Jesus and His unconditional Love, could always find *something* to smile about, even in one of *those* letters, and *something to love* in the writers of *those* letters.

Bishop Sheen said that in any period of the Church's life in America there has always been a responsive audience.

"The audience is always there, the opportunities ever present. There is need to take hold of tortured souls like Peter, Agnostics like Thomas and Mystics like John and lead them to tears, to their knees or to rest on His Sacred Heart."

He spoke of the *urgency* of studying and reading, that books are outstanding friends; they always have something worthwhile to *teach* us every time we pick them up.

Bishop Sheen had a *delicious* sense of humor. You cannot read his autobiography without smiling, at times laughing out loud and then caught off guard, crying. He read many books, he said, but that they were all in relationship to his calling to serve God's people as a priest. He never read *novels.* He would read book reviews and summaries of novels, so he would be aware of the trends of the time through reading them.

One day, he was giving instructions to Jo Mielzner, the famous theatrical artist. Jo told Bishop Sheen that Humphrey Bogart had just dropped in. He shared that when he suggested to Bogart, he might care to remain or go into another room, Bogart replied, "Why should I listen to any priest? I know more about the Catholic Church than any priest."

Pretending not to know of the conversation, Bishop Sheen joined Bogart and others in the next room; the subject under discussion was "novels." Bishop Sheen admitted he knew nothing about the novels they were discussing. He added, *"Whether this was inherited from my father, I do not know, for he never read novels."* Humphrey Bogart who had been boasting of his extensive knowledge of the Catholic Church, inquired, "Was your father a priest too?"

It's really very funny in one way, but oh so sad in another because so very often people learn what they believe is the *Catholic Faith* from people who do not *know* it all.

Bishop Sheen speaks out on Communism

Bishop Sheen not only studied the teachings of the Fathers of our Faith, but the enemies of the Church and mankind, like Marx for example. If he was to defend his Church (and defend he did), he had to know what the *enemy* was teaching.

Communism started to grow in popularity, after the Soviets became our allies in World War II. Bishop Sheen felt the need to know more about it. As a philosopher, he had been trained "*in the philosophy of St. Thomas Aquinas which is complete and total in that it embraces God, man and society.*" He wrote, "*Communism also has a complete philosophy.*" "*But*" he further stated, "*if one starts with a wrong assumption and is logical from that point on, he will never get back on the road to truth.*"[3]

The writings of Marx, Lenin and Stalin used the philosophy that stated simply, "man has been alienated from his true nature in two ways, by religion and by private property." They contended that since man was alienated from himself by *religion* because it made him subservient to *God*; and man was alienated from himself by *private property* in that it made him subservient to an *employer*, the only way man could ever be restored to his true nature is to *destroy* religion and private property.

After World War II, because of his well-known stand on Communism, *he was canceled* as speaker in many of our cities. Angry words came from as high in our secular world, as an American can go, from the President of the United States, *Franklin D. Roosevelt.* It descended upon Sheen from high in our *religious* world, from within the Church itself, from an eminent prelate. Bishop Sheen was staying in *his* rectory when he asked him on what subject he would be lecturing, that night. When Bishop Sheen replied, Russia

---

[3]quoting Cajetan Esser, who was commenting on a text of Aquinas

and Eastern Europe and how Russia will take over all of Eastern Europe, Poland and Lithuania, Albania, Czechoslovakia and others, the prelate angrily burst out, "You're crazy. Russia is no longer communist; it is a democracy." As Bishop Sheen descended the stairs of the rectory, the prelate's words stormed after him, "Sheen, you're wrong." Bishop Sheen could only sadly reply (and prophesy), "*Someday you will discover that Eastern Europe will belong to the Communists.*"

Bishop Sheen's radio talks were carefully monitored because of his stand on Russia, with someone there ready to cut him off if he inferred in any way that Russia was not a democracy.

Just before World War II, when Russia and Germany were still enemies, Bishop Sheen prophesied on radio that, as "*Pilate and Herod were enemies and became friends over the bleeding Body of Christ, so one day Communism and Nazism, which are now enemies, will become friends over the bleeding body of Poland.*" The prophecy was fulfilled as the Nazis and Soviets became united (if only for a time).

Although he was passionately opposed to communism, Bishop Sheen *loved* Russia and the "*Russian soul.*" To understand how such a deeply religious people could have been suckered into accepting communism, he explained,

> "*Deeply imbedded in the Russian soul were passionate religious convictions; the universal vocation of Russia to call all men to brotherhood; the need of sacrifice and pain to accomplish this mission; and the supreme need of resigning oneself to God's Will. Communism in the face of a declining Church promised the people the realization of these three ideals, but without clearly telling them that they would be emptied of God!*"

As brotherhood *promised* became proletariat[4], and sacrifice was replaced by *violence*, the Will of *God* became the will of the *dictator*. Is this *past* history or is this *future* history? Is it *merely* affirmation that Bishop Sheen was a Prophet or is this *timely* for us, for *now*, for the salvation of our souls and our beloved country? In our country founded under God, by men who sought *religious* freedom, students are not free to *pray* in our schools. What (or Who) are we trading in (or *traitoring*), for what (and who) we are receiving?

Bishop Sheen and the Missions

"Evangelization is inseparable from professional teaching ever since the Word became Flesh." Evangelization, which started for Bishop Sheen, from East to West and North to South, within the borders of the United States, spread to the four corners of the World, when the Bishops of the United States invited him to become the National Director of the *Society for the Propagation of the Faith.*

Bishop Sheen said he came into the Society at just the moment in time when *"the Church was beginning to sense a conflict between divine salvation and human liberation, between working for personal salvation of those in a parish or in a community and having a concern about their social welfare. God never intended that individual and social justice should be separated, though they very often were divorced."*

In the Roman Catholic Church, we have the Complete Cross of Jesus, the Positive, the Plus-Sign, the Redemption, the Victory over death and sin. This Cross is composed of a *vertical* beam, an *arrow* of Faith, Hope and Charity which soars from the Archer to us, piercing our hearts, minds and souls. And because of this overflowing, burning love from

---

[4]proletariat-1. the class of the lowest status in ancient Roman society. 2.(Rare) the class of the lowest status in any society 3. the working class.

Left:
***Archbishop Sheen
speaking to his
"Pretty Lady
dressed in blue,"
at one of his
30 pilgrimages
to Lourdes.***

Above: ***Bishop Sheen and the Society for the Propagation of the Faith
supported the Mission Church in Africa,
Asia and other parts of the world.***

the Father, we cannot contain it and we are poured out as Christ was for our brothers and sisters. We call this the *horizontal* love of the Cross through which we recognize our brother in need. Without the vertical, we have a minus-sign, a negative because without God, even good intentions and good people become a playground for pride and power.

Bishop Sheen never took his eyes off the *Source* of his life, Who commissioned him to serve, and empowered him to love. But if we only connect Bishop Sheen with the *vertical*, that is this Divine inspiration to Whom, he always gave credit, we very often miss and never know the immense *horizontal* concern he had for the Universal Parish God gave him, through the missions.

Jesus, Who overcame the Cross as He became the Cross, was sent by the Father to *Israel*. He had come to be a *"ransom for all the sins"* of *all* men, but he left universal evangelization to His Apostles, saying, "Go out to all the world and make disciples." Bishop Sheen took up that Cross, in many forms, in many places, through many people; he carried it, like his Savior before him, to Calvary with his last breath giving up his spirit to the Father.

The missions, and the *martyrs* of the missions, were very precious to him. Because of the unequaled suffering of the missionaries under Communist rule, he wrote there should be a new type of Saint proclaimed in the Communion of Saints, *the Dry Martyrs*. Those who shed their blood for the Faith are called *"Wet Martyrs"*. Bishop Sheen wrote, *"since the enemies of Christ do not always kill, but instead torture, the dry martyrs suffered over a period of years pain that far exceeded that of the brief interval of the Wet Martyrs."* He cited that each day, hour, and minute of their lives was a Profession of Faith. He said the Church, in the last *seventy years* has had more martyrs, "Wet and dry" than in the first three hundred of her existence. In this Honor Roll of God's faithful, he included reverently the victims of Auschwitz, Dachau and other camps of cruelty, those Jews whose only crime was they believed they were the chosen people of God and were faithful to that belief.

There is not room here to speak of many of these *martyrs*, but there are a couple that we would like to share with you. Bishop Ford, when he was a boy, heard an Italian missionary speak at his church. On the last night of the mission, the missionary closed with, "Someday my *ambeesh* is to die a martyr." Little did the boy know *he* would be the one to fulfill the missionary's words.

When the communists took over China, Bishop Ford called in a nun and told her, he was worried they would confiscate his property. He said, "Here is the key to the Tabernacle. I want you to remove the Blessed Sacrament before It is desecrated." She took the key and a loaf of bread to the bishop's Chapel on the second floor of his home, removed the Blessed Sacrament and hid It in the loaf of bread. As she closed the Chapel door, a Communist Colonel, known all over China for his cruelty, said he was taking over possession of the Chapel. As he tried to unlock the door, it wouldn't open. He demanded the nun open the door. She replied, she could not as she had her hands filled with the loaf of bread. He demanded she give him the bread. She passed the bread to him and, she later recalled, he looked down at it as if it were an infant. The nun brought the Blessed Sacrament (hidden within the bread) to safety and was later imprisoned.

The bishop's Chinese cook who had served him many years, and whom, Bishop Ford regarded as a good friend and Christian, was the man who delivered him over to the Communist authorities and falsely accused him. This he did, knowing the tremendous love and compassion the bishop had for the people, always consoling the sick and burying the dead. And the reward he received for delivering his Bishop and friend over to the Communists? He was made chief of police of the village.

After weeks, days, hours and minutes of inconceivable suffering, the day finally arrived for Bishop Ford to process in the *death march.* The Communists would never kill anyone; they would just let him die. The Communist Colonel who had taken over the Chapel, tied a sack, weighing over twenty pounds, around the bishop's neck. The nun who had been with him at the Chapel, seeing what he had done to the Bishop, broke out of the death march; standing behind the bishop, she shouted at the colonel, "Look at the man." It was as if he could see the pain carved in the bishop's face for the *first* time. He soon recovered his Communist composure and ordered the nun back in line.

She watched, as the death march weaved in and out, her eyes never leaving the bishop. Barely able to walk, he was being supported by two Chinese men on either side of him, but *the sack was not around his neck*! Years later, when Bishop Sheen asked the nun why she believed the colonel removed the sack, she replied, "Because he once carried the Blessed Sacrament." The power of the Eucharist to change men's hearts! The colonel was placed into prison and the nun never heard of him again.

Bishop Ford died a "*dry martyr*" in February of 1952; the former cook went back to the Chapel, threw a rope over a rafter and committed suicide.

In another part of China, a priest had just begun celebrating Holy Mass when Communists burst in and arrested him. They made him a prisoner in the house next to the church. He could see the Tabernacle from his window. Shortly after his arrest, the Communists returned, took the Ciborium out of the Tabernacle and threw the Hosts on the floor, making off with the Sacred Vessels. Helpless to do much more, the priest kept watch from his window, day and night, adoring his Lord in The Fallen Hosts, keeping Him company. Shortly after the Hosts had been thrown on the floor, about three o'clock in the morning, a little girl, who had been present at Mass the day the priest had been arrested, climbed in an open window of the church, went over to the Sanctuary, knelt on both knees, pressed her tongue to a Host and gave herself Holy Communion. She did this each morning, at the same hour, until the thirty Hosts which had been in the Ciborium were consumed. The last morning, as she pressed the last Host to her tongue and consumed her Lord and Savior, a shot rang out. A soldier had seen her. It was to be her Viaticum.[5]

The next time, I receive my Lord and Savior, I want to praise Him, not only for His generous Gift of Himself, but for all the martyrs who lived and died, and *are* living and dying that I might have Eternal Life in His Holy Eucharist. As I meditate on those who have gone before us, the Altar becomes holy to me in a *new* dimension, a place before which all should take off their shoes not only because of the Savior's Blood that has been shed for us, but for that of the martyrs before us. As we approach this holy battleground let us not take for granted Him, for Whom our brothers and sisters died.

Bishop Sheen and the Church he loved

Bishop Sheen spoke *Christ*; he sought Christ in everything he read, everywhere he travelled. When speaking of his extensive travels, he said one of the teachings he received, as he journeyed to Greece in search of St. Paul, was that when St. Paul spoke in Athens (Acts:17), by all the rules of good speech-making, it was perfect. Yet, it was one of Paul's greatest failures. He left Athens, went to Corinth, never to return. Bishop Sheen sat evening after evening on

---

[5]Viaticum-Name of Holy Communion when it is given in a public or private manner to someone in danger of death, during an illness or to soldiers going into battle.

that same hillside where Paul had spoken. What had St. Paul done wrong? It finally dawned on him; he had not mentioned the Name of Christ and his *Crucifixion*. Bishop Sheen was convinced that as St. Paul walked to Corinth, the words he was to repeat, over and over again, came to life, "I am resolved among you to know nothing but Christ and Him Crucified."

Bishop Sheen wrote, "*Ephesus*" (through St. Paul) "*taught me the preaching of the Word will always provoke antagonisms.*" He said whether we speak out against abortion or divorce, communism or consumerism, there will always be not only the outcry of individuals, but wholesale organized mob-style persecution, as in the case of Calvary. Bishop Sheen, like his Savior before him, was and is not popular in many quarters. A priest once said that as Jesus spoke more and more the Father's Will, He became less and less popular. Bishop Sheen lived out Jesus' Words,

"*Before you, they persecuted Me.*"

Bishop Sheen, like St. Paul before him, would first approach someone, who was not of our Faith, by asking what and who they believed in. Then, respecting their culture and traditions, he would build a bridge upon which they, with dignity, could walk over to embrace the full Cross of Christ through the Church, He founded.

The more Bishop Sheen travelled to the far points of the world, to pain and helplessness, seeing with the eyes of the victimized and praying for the souls of the victimizers, he discovered Church to be as he perceived the Mother of God. She was a Lady of Many Faces, a Mother, a Sister, a Friend, a Lady of all colors, a Lady of no particular color, a Mother for all time and for all mankind. Bishop Sheen loved his Church as he loved the Mother of the Church, with a passion, not unlike the Passion of our Lord and Savior, when He opened His Arms and died for His Church. His Church, like his Heavenly Mother was best described by this poem...

I'm looking for an African painter
Who will make me a Black Virgin
A Virgin with a fine "Keowa"
Like our mothers wear.
Look, mother,
The yellow races have lent you
Their yellow tint.
The Redskins have made you
Like their own wives.
The Whites have pictured you
As a Western girl.
And would you refuse
To take our color?
Anyway since your Assumption,
Since the glorious day
When you were triumphantly
Carried away into Heaven
You no longer have any color.
You are yellow with the yellows
Like a mother who might have several children
of different shades
But who could be found in them all.
Isn't it true, Mother, that you
Are the Mother of the Blacks, too.
A Black Mother carrying the Infant Jesus
on her back.

Our Church was to Bishop Sheen, a bouquet of many flowers and of many shapes, each uniquely formed by its Founder Jesus, and precious in His Eyes and Sacred Heart.

Bishop Sheen and the Eucharist

On the day of his ordination, Bishop Sheen made a commitment to offer the Holy Eucharist, in honor of the *Mother of God*, and placed his *priesthood* in her holy hands.

He was faithful to his practice of spending an hour each day, with his Lord in the *Blessed Sacrament*. Begun one year *before* he was ordained, he continued until the day he gave his spirit up to the Lord to be in His Presence, accompanied by the heavenly hosts of Angels and his Lady for all eternity.

"Bishop Sheen tells us that priests go bad when they lose their faith in the Eucharist. "They may tell you," he says, "that they can't live without a woman, or that they can't take the rigidity of the priesthood, or that the religious life is just not for them, but what has happened is that they've lost their faith in the Eucharist." Bishop Sheen spent an hour before the Blessed Sacrament each day of his priesthood. When he prepared his very successful TV Show, "Life is Worth Living," he discussed his script ideas with our Lord in the Blessed Sacrament before he would finalize each program."[6]

Bishop Sheen spoke of the Holy Hour, not as a *"devotion,"* but as *a sharing* in the redemption of the world. He said when Jesus used the word *day*, He referred to it as belonging to God; whereas when He used the word *hour* in John's Gospel, He referred to the demonic. In His agony in the Garden, Jesus said to Judas "This is your hour"; and then from the Apostles, He asked for an hour to make up for that hour of *sin*. "Could you not watch (spend) an hour with Me?" Bishop Sheen said Jesus did not ask all the Apostles because He knew He couldn't *count* on all of them to give Him this *"hour of companionship."* If we reflect on Jesus' Words, then we know He *was* hurt, in that those He had trusted, could not be trusted. Then we know He *is* hurt with *us*, in that He has called us to be part of Him. By calling us to His Church and the Sacraments, He is *trusting* us with them. *Do we sleep?*

---

[6]excerpt from This is My Body...This is My Blood, Miracles of the Eucharist

Bishop Sheen said he kept up the Holy Hour because he wanted to be *transformed* into the Likeness of Jesus, becoming like Him, Whom he gazed upon, light from *Light.*

The Holy Hour's purpose, he said, is to encourage a deep personal encounter with Jesus. Neither knowledge of our Religion nor social action (that is the caring for our brothers and sisters) can *keep* us in love with Christ without this *personal encounter* with Him.

Just recently our Ministry went on a Retreat to St. Anthony's Seminary in Santa Barbara, California. Bob and I had gone there on our Marriage Encounter in 1975, so the *true* meaning of encounter is very much alive to me, as I write about Bishop Sheen's walk with and love of the Holy Eucharist. On our Marriage Encounter weekend, first we *learned about* one another; *then* we learned how very much we *loved* one another. We say we love Jesus but only through *knowledge* of Him in His Holy Eucharist, spending time with Him, can we get to know Him *personally.* On our Marriage Encounter week-end, we learned *communication* skills, how to share our feelings, how we could trust one another with our feelings, sad and glad. Is this not what Bishop Sheen was speaking of when he shared his relationship with the God Who is alive and in our midst in the Tabernacle?

If you have ever made a Holy Hour and fallen asleep, this happened to Bishop Sheen! One day, he knelt before the Blessed Sacrament, said his prayer of adoration and fell into a deep sleep. When he wakened *one hour* later, he asked the Lord: "*Have I made a Holy Hour?*" to which he believed the Angel of the Lord replied, "Well, that's the way the Apostles made their first Holy Hour in the Garden, but don't do it again."

Bishop Sheen and the Woman, he loved, Mary, his Mother

When Bishop Sheen wrote of the Mother of God, he wrote as a *boy-man*, very much like the boy-man in my life my Bob. His love for Mary was of a son, sometimes like a *little boy* sitting on her lap, learning from her. Other times, he was a young boy with his eyes fixed on his ideal woman. And at other times, Bishop Sheen, the *man* turned to her for wisdom companionship and consolation.

Defending Mary, Bishop Sheen said it was not the Church that made Mary important, but Christ Himself. The Church has *never* adored Mary because only *God* may be adored. But, after Jesus, *Mary* is the closest to God.

If we only trace the steps in the Redemption of the world where Mary was part of the Plan of the Holy Trinity, it is plain to see the relationship. In the Old Testament, in Genesis, as one woman is betraying God's Trust, He is promising *another*, with her "*yes*" to help with the redemption of that betrayal. And so, we see the loyal daughter Mary already in the Faithful Father's Plan.

At the Annunciation, she said "*yes*" to the Lord's messenger, and the Holy Spirit in cooperation with her "yes," brought forth The Word Incarnate, unto us a Savior would be born.

The last moments of His Precious Life, of all who had followed Him and swore loyalty to Him, our Lord chose His *Mother* to share His Cross for the salvation of the world. Yes, no one was closer, but no one paid a greater price for that closeness. Unlike the Apostles Jesus had chosen and trusted to spend that hour with Him in the garden, Mary could be trusted and she *paid* with her heart on the Cross with that of her Son.

This is the Mary, Bishop Sheen was in love with. This is the Mother, who brought him through all the valleys and high places of his priesthood. Just as she gave her "*yes*" to Jesus, and He continued His Way of the Cross, so those beautiful and yet sad eyes gave her son Sheen, the strength to carry *his* cross.

"*It is not good for a man to be alone.*" (Genesis 1:18) Bishop Sheen wrote that this verse applies to a *priest* as well as to the layman. Only with the priest, the woman in his life is Mary. Bishop Sheen said that although he was not *aware* when he, at Baptism, was consecrated to Mary by his earthly mother, nevertheless her (Mary's) mark was always there, on him. He spoke of Mary being the moon which reflects the Light of the Son, guiding us as we await *the Sonrise*. He said that he was confident that as he would someday appear before the "Judgment Seat of Christ," Jesus would say in His Mercy, "*I heard My Mother speak of you.*"

Bishop Sheen would never visit Europe, without making a Pilgrimage to Lourdes. During his lifetime, he made over thirty Pilgrimages to the Shrine of our Lady of Lourdes.

When he had open-heart surgery, he discovered "*the Blessed Mother not only gives gifts of sweets, but she also gives bitter medicine.*" Like St. Bernadette, before him, the Mother of God was telling him, he was called to "*eat bitter herbs and drink muddy water.*" It was on three of her feast days that he was to know his greatest (physical) suffering in the hospital. He said of that time,

"*If I had expressed a love for her as Mother of the priesthood, why could she not, in maternal love, make me more like her Son by forcing me to become a victim? If my own earthly mother laid me on her (Mary's) altar at birth, why should not my Heavenly Mother lay me at His Cross as I come to the end of my life?*"

"*After many years of courtship, the deep conviction pervades my soul; she really loves me - and if she can love me, then Christ is with me.*" Bishop Sheen's words echo the role Mother Mary played, in the days and nights of his walk as a priest. He spoke of his relationship with the Mother of God, as one would speak of the commitment a man makes to be faithful to that one woman, *"to the one I have been looking for,"* the one he is joined to in Holy Matrimony. He writes, as one makes a positive commitment to be faithful to that *one woman*, he makes a negative commitment by rejecting love of *other women*. This love and respect for the *ideal woman* becomes an armor for the man who loves her. He wrote, of our Blessed Mother, *"She protects her lovers - even when they fall."*

This towering man, priest and prophet, learned and inspired, was a little boy when it came to Blessed Mother. To quote from one of his favorite poems,

Lovely Lady dressed in blue
Teach me how to pray
God was just your little Boy
And you know the way!

And so, Bishop Sheen, till, we meet again, we love you

His life so full of conflicts, trials and crosses was lived like his name (in Gaelic), Fulton meaning *"war"* and Sheen meaning *"peace."* He was not a man who compromised His Lord and his call to That Lord for the *world's* peace; gladly doing battle; gratefully coming back for more when he suffered defeat and wounds, even from the brothers he loved so very much. As he fearlessly waged *"war"* on the enemies of Jesus, His Mother and His Church, he sought only the Peace His Savior could give him. Famous to some and infamous to others, he remained true to his destiny; born a priest, he died a priest.

When we began to write this book about *Saints and other Powerful Men in the Church*, we received a call from Sr. Briege, one of the *Powerful Women*, we wrote about in our book about *Saints and other Powerful Women in the Church*. She said she was reading our book[7] on her Retreat and the *thought* came to her, *Tell Bob and Penny to write a book*

---

[7]Saints and other Powerful Women in the Church

which will affirm the priesthood. As the words flowed, as we humbly attempted to share a glimpse of the life of this *faith-filled* and faithful son of the Church, what came popping out were his words, "*I can never remember a day I did not want to be a priest.*" And so, although this had not been our intention originally, Sr. Briege, we pray that this priest, who loved and lived his priesthood, will be *consolation* to his brother priests at times of hurts, *strength* at times of doubt, and *courage* to be who Jesus chose them to be, Him on earth.

Without the Eucharist, we have no Church. The Eucharist is the Heart that beats and pumps life into the mystical body of Christ. The priesthood is the means Jesus uses to bring us that *Life.* Beloved priests, we need you. Jesus needs you. Hands of Christ, we love you, Jesus loves you. This chapter is about you and for you. Thank you for your "*yes.*"

In the times of heresy and turmoil in the Church, the Lord raises up an Army of the Faithful with a standard-bearer. Bishop Sheen, you are still at the front, on the battlefield, only now your words are the swords our Lord will use to defend His Church against all the forces of hell.

As I say good-by, for now, there is the sadness of parting, like going to another state for awhile, the feeling I have when we are leaving a Shrine of Mary. I know Mary never leaves us, following us into our very homes, but I guess I am already grieving for this time we had just the two of us.

Adieu, good and loyal priest.

✝

Dear brothers and sisters in Christ, we pray we have been able to share a few moments in the life of this great and glorious man. Don't stop here. Bishop Sheen has left us a library of over sixty books about his Church. Read on and fall in love with your Church, your Mother Mary and your Heritage.

Bibliography

Auffray, A. - *Saint John Bosco* -
    Salesian Publications, Blaisdon, Longhope, Glos 1930
Bosco, St. John - *Memoirs of the Oratory*
    Don Bosco Publications, New Rochelle, NY 1984
Brighetti Amadio OSM *S. Pellegrino Laziosi*
    Servi di Maria, Forli Italy 1975
Brown, Eugene Fr. Editor -
    Dreams, Visions & Prophecies of Don Bosco
    Don Bosco Publications - New Rochelle, NY 1986
Butler, Thurston & Atwater *Lives of the Saints*
    (Complete Edition in Four Volumes)
    Christian Classics, Westminster Maryland 1980
Carretto, C, *I, Francis* Orbis Books, Maryknoll NY 1982
Cattozzo, G, Frasson, A. Gardin, G *St. Anthony Returns*
    Again Messagero di S. Antonio Padua, Italy 1981
Christiani L Msgr *The Village Priest who Fought God's Battles*
    Daughters of St. Paul, Boston 1977
Christiana L Msgr - *Monica and her Son Augustine*
    Daughters of St. Paul, Boston 1977
Clasen Sophronius OFM *St. Anthony, Doctor of the Church*
    Franciscan Herald Press, Chicago IL 1973
Fitzmeyer Jos. S.J. *A Life of Paul*
    Jerome Biblical Commentary
    Prentice Hall Englewood Cliffs NJ 1968
Gamboso, Vergilio OFM Conv *Life of St. Anthony*
    <*Assidua*> Messagero di S. Antonio Padua 1981
Gamboso, Vergilio OFM Conv *The Life of St. Anthony*
    Messagero di S. Antonio Padua, Italy 1965
Gibbons, S. OSM *St. Peregrine, the Cancer Saint*
    Servites of Mary, Western Province Portland, OR 1973

Hanley Boniface OFM *Ten Christians*
Ave Maria Press, Notre Dame, IL 1979
Lord, Bob & Penny *This Is My Body, This Is My Blood*
Journeys of Faith Westlake Village, CA 1986
Lord, Bob & Penny *Saints and Other Powerful Women in the
Church* Journeys of Faith Westlake Village, CA 1989
Norman, Mrs. G *God's Jester* - Benziger Bros. NY 1931
Omnibus of St. Francis of Assisi Franciscan Herald Press 1972
Padre Pio *Letters Vol. 1* Edited by Fr. G. Di Flumeri OFM
Editions Voce di Padre Pio
San Giovanni Rotondo, Italy 1980
Padre Pio of Pietrelcina, Spirituality Series 1 Edizioni Padre
Pio da Pietrelcina San Giovanni Rotondo Italy 1972
Ricciardi A. OFM
St. Maxmilian Kolbe, Apostle of our Difficult Age
Daughters of St. Paul Boston 1982
da Ripabotoni, Alessandro *Everybody's Cyrenean* Our Lady
of Grace Friary, San Giovanni Rotondo, Italy 1987
da Ripabotoni, Alessandro *Pio of Pietrelcina, Infancy and
Adolescence* Edizioni Padre Pio da Pietrelcina San
Giovanni Rotondo Italy 1969
Ryan J. Translated *Confessions of St. Augustine*
Doubleday & Co NY 1960
Sheen, Fulton J *Treasure in Clay* Doubleday & Co NY 1980
Stella, Pietro - *Don Bosco, Life and Work*
Don Bosco Publications, New Rochelle, NY 1985
Strode, Hudson *Timeless Mexico* - Harcourt Brace NY 1940
Sullivan James Fr *My Meditations on St. Paul*
Confraternity of the Precious Blood NY 1967
Trochu Abbe *The Curé d' Ars* Burns & Oates, London 1927
Voice of Padre Pio Vol XIX No. 7 1989 - Vol XX No 1 1990

Journeys of Faith

To Order: 1-800-633-2484 - 1-504-863-2546

Books

Bob and Penny Lord are authors of best sellers:

This Is My Body, This Is My Blood;
Miracles of the Eucharist Book I $8.95 Paperback only
The Many Faces Of Mary, A Love Story $8.95 Paperback $12.95 Hardcover
We Came Back To Jesus $8.95 Paperback $12.95 Hardcover
Saints and Other Powerful Women in the Church $12.95 Paperback only
Saints and Other Powerful Men in the Church $14.95 Paperback only
Heavenly Army of Angels $12.95 Paperback only
Scandal of the Cross and Its Triumph $12.95 Paperback only
The Rosary - The Life of Jesus and Mary $12.95 Hardcover only
Martyrs - They Died for Christ $12.95 Paperback only
This Is My Body, This Is My Blood;
Miracles of the Eucharist Book II $12.95 Paperback only

Please add $3.00 S&H for first book: $1.00 each add'l book - Louisiana. Res. add 8.25% Tax

Videos and On-site Documentaries

Bob and Penny's Video Series based on their books:
A 13 part series on the Miracles of the Eucharist - filmed on-site
A 9 part Eucharistic Retreat series with Father Harold Cohen
A 15 part series on The Many Faces of Mary - filmed on-site
A 12 part series on Martyrs - They Died for Christ - filmed on-site
A 10 part series on Saints and Other Powerful Women in the Church
A 12 part series on Saints and Other Powerful Men in the Church
Many other on-site Documentaries based on Miracles of the Eucharist, Mother
Mary's Apparitions, and the Heavenly Army of Angels. Request our list.

Our books and videos are available in Spanish also

Pilgrimages

Bob and Penny Lord's ministry take out Pilgrimages to the Shrines of Europe, the
Holy Land, and the Shrines of Mexico every year. Come and join them on one
of these special Retreat Pilgrimages. Call for more information, and ask for the
latest pilgrimage brochure.

Lecture Series

Bob and Penny travel to all parts of the world to spread the Good News. They
speak on what they have written about in their books. If you would like to have
them come to your area, call for information on a lecture series in your area.

Good Newsletter

We are publishers of the Good Newsletter, which is published four times a year.
This newsletter will provide timely articles on our Faith, plus keep you informed
with the activities of our community. Call 1-800-633-2484 for subscription
information.